PARADIGMS IN COMPUTING

MAKING, MACHINES, AND MODELS FOR DESIGN AGENCY IN ARCHITECTURE

DR. DAVID JASON GERBER

MARIANA IBAÑEZ

Published by
eVolo Press
6363 Wilshire Blvd. 311
Los Angeles, CA 90048

visit our website at www.evolo.us

Editor: Carlo Aiello
Designer: HI(NY), eVolo Press

Library of Congress Cataloging-in-Publication Data
Paradigms in Computing : Making, Machines, and Models for Design Agency in Architecture / Dr. David Jason Gerber and Mariana Ibañez, editors. – First Edition

ISBN 978-1-938740-09-1 (hardback)

PARADIGMS IN COMPUTING

MAKING, MACHINES, AND MODELS FOR DESIGN AGENCY IN ARCHITECTURE

DR. DAVID JASON GERBER

MARIANA IBAÑEZ

ACKNOWLEDGMENTS

This book was developed through the collaboration between two colleagues with adjacent domains of enquiry into new models of practice and research through the use of technology in design. The editors share a lineage of common mentors, institutions, and professional luminaries, from whom they have gained their critical project. Through a long-standing and close dialogue as to the notion of paradigms, the editors have concluded a venture for which they are thankful to many for their help, encouragement, patience, and contributions along the way.

We must first acknowledge the contributors to this volume for their generous production and for the help in building up the sample of work. The list of authors is comprised of leading figures and researchers including; Alisa Andrasek, Rachel Armstrong, Philip Beesly, Tom Bessai, Shajay Bhooshan, Brad Cantrel, Matias Del Campo, Pablo Eiroa, Marc Fornes, David Jason Gerber, Maria Paz Gutierrez, Alvin Huang, Jason Kelly Johnson, Simon Kim, Neil Leach, Greg Lynn, Elena and Ana Maria Manferdini, Alex McDowell, Phillippe Morel, Nick Puckett, Casey Reas, Alex Robinson, Jenny Sabin, Jose Sanchez, Patrick Schumacher, Kyle Steinfeld, Satoru Sugihara, Orkan Telhan, Kathy Velikov and Geoffrey Thun, Tom Verebes, Leire Asensio Villoria and David Mah, Jenny Wu, Eric Howeler and Meejin Yoon, and Zaha Hadid Architects.

We must also acknowledge and thank ACADIA conference chairs Jose Sanchez and Alvin Huang who have supported us in the development and launch of the book as well as with their own contributions.

We would also like to thank USC Viterbi Professor Burcin Becerik-Gerber and Simon Kim, Assistant Professor at the University of Pennsylvania, for their contributions to concept, structure and editing.

The editors would also like to thank the following people for their mentorship and support: Brett Steele, Patrik Schumacher, Tom Verebes, Hanif Kara, Mack Scogin, Preston Scott Cohen, Hernan Diaz Alonso, Jeffrey Huang, the late Daniel Schodek, the late William J Mitchell, Mohsen Mostafavi and Ms. Zaha Hadid. It must be acknowledged that through these mentors and progenitors we have come together to continue the investigation into our shared curiosity and lines of enquiry. We thank them all for the relationships that have greatly enabled this collection.

This book was developed from both coasts: at the University of Southern California and the Graduate School of Design at Harvard University. To our home institutions we express our thanks for providing an environment of continual development.

Finally, we would like to thank our editor Carlo Aiello and eVolo for his commissioning of the work and for taking it through to its final production. We thank those at ACTAR D for supporting the work and its distribution.

Dr. David Jason Gerber

Mariana Ibañez

CONTENTS

INTRODUCTION

DR. DAVID JASON GERBER   MARIANA IBAÑEZ

Paradigms in Computing: Making, Machines, and Models for Design Agency in Architecture sets out to investigate and collect critical, theoretical, and practical research and design that illustrates the plurality of computing approaches within the broad spectrum of design and mediated practices. It is an interrogation of our primary field that of architecture, through the lens of computing, and yet one that realizes a productive expanding of our métier's definition and boundaries. Whereas architecture is central to our enquiry, we purposefully promote its' disciplinary reach and incorporations beyond the design and construction of buildings and cities. The works collected here suggest possible paradigm shifts, schisms, amalgamations or categorizations for architecture. The book is a collaborative conjecture that intentionally expands the boundaries of our discipline given the prevalence and acceleration of computing in our field and allied fields, and frames this exponential curve as a paradigm in and of itself.

Included are a collection of essays and projects that enable a critical exploration of the contemporary paradigms where computation is central to the production of the work. In that regard, the book presents the 'digital' as a form and genotype of agency within architecture and the expanding design disciplines allied or akin to architecture. In doing so the collection questions our own evaluation and use of terminology such as the digital, parametricism, material ecology, agency, emergence, gaming, open source, heuristics, and numerous others. The book not only enables a critical evaluation of our terminology but also of their manifestations through positions, hypotheses and projects. Our strategy as editors was to collect a sample broad enough to identify both the ideas at the core and those at the frontier - the limits that designers and theorists are pushing and working through.

Our call for submissions expressly asked for positions from industry and academy thought leaders for their sensibility and production of computationally influenced practice and research. In essence, the provocation is in part a simple question - to which we received a rich and complex group of responses - if we are experiencing a singular or proliferation of paradigms brought about by the advancement of computing, and what those might be. Controversy and diversity were sought after through the variety of practice models, geography, experience and disciplinary type. Direct and indirect answers to the questions we posited of how and within which paradigm authors placed themselves and their work are found throughout. These answers and themes include forms of design and research that embody and address the notion of models, machines, and their production, in a way that might be suggestive of their own paradigm.

In each piece, the authors present their own fascination and focus on computing through lenses and concepts such as open source or proprietary, digital fabrication, robotics and artificial intelligence, the wisdom of the crowd, big data, the biological, the material, the analytical, the augmented and the interactive to call name but a few. The call's sub-topics themselves are expansive and perhaps dilutive, but in effect are descriptive and evidentiary of the original gene, that of computing. What is perhaps conclusive is this notion of the exponential curve understood through the plurality this compilation presents.

In pre-meditating the work, there was a sense of a parallel to the Precambrian explosion. For while it is true that we have been 'digital' architects and designers for over 40 years, if we trace back to Negroponte, Pask, Wiener, Sutherland and the like, we are at a point in time for design where the possibilities are becoming ever more expansive. As it was discovered in the Burgess Shale, a set of body plans and genotypes that are likely the origins for all of the present phenotypes and diversity of the five kingdoms, analogously we might argue that we should expect an equally productive explosion of design paradigms and possibilities. The compilation, we believe, lends itself to the continuing discourse and a development of a computational Linnaean nomenclature of sorts. One that emerges from the sampling, a phylogenesis in which one can position and reflect upon one's own work critically and productively in relation, opposition, or affinity to others' work.

The book's theme is inclusive of the notion of Design Agency, an instigation to those practices where computation is inextricably a part of the design process, but also considers work that privileges or acknowledges computation becoming more intrinsic to the methods, tools, and theories behind the informing of form and digital crafts. This collection of work, deciphers for us the convergence of the cyber, physical, and social as producing a potent set of possibilities that fosters an open polemical debate(s), inclusive of social, tectonic, formal, causal, economic, and pedagogical impact and values. Through our contributors from the fields of Design, Architecture, Media Arts, Science, Engineering, Landscape Architecture, Cinematic Arts and Architectural Theory, *Paradigms in Computing* has lent itself to furthering this discussion amongst practitioners, academics, and researchers.

The book does not provide a comprehensive nor historical account of computation and digital practices in the design disciplines, but offers a glimpse into the wide range of positions and experiences that are shaping practice and discourse today. As soon as the list is compiled, it may immediately be seen as reductive and counter to the point, as is the case with any exponential growth curve. Yet this collection of essays illustrates an array of computationally diverse approaches to design and architecture inclusive of trends such as complexity becoming cheaper, reality capture becoming accessible, interactivity becoming pervasive, multi-agent systems becoming deployable, data becoming drivers, and new forms of digitally enabled collaboration becoming agents of change and personalization. As with the Precambrian explosion, perhaps the collection posits the question whether we -as an allied set of design disciplines- are in fact experiencing a gradual expansion or a condition of punctuated equilibrium and cladogenesis. What for us appears to be a rapid diversification and an explosion of creative capability has yet to be seen in the digital-fossil record and maybe be a simple gradual growth pattern. In bringing this collection together, what is clear is that the works present for us a diversity of ingenuity and cultural production that is novel and astounding. In that regard computation, and the ubiquity of digital technology, has brought about a significant change in how architects and designers operate as well as how the work is conceptualized, framed, and discussed. Yet these principles are not a fixed condition, as computation and technology continue advancing, our means to produce, as well as our means to evaluate such production self critically, need to remain equally dynamic.

The compilation of new work, essays and projects included in *Paradigms in Computing* is evidence that *models* for enquiry are many and proliferating; that the *making* is ever more customizable, available, personal and social; that the machines with the now cyber-social-physical, human and non-human perspectives in which we experience design being developed are no longer controlled by the hegemony of engineers and computer scientists but have rapidly become the tools of the neophyte and expert alike within the design realm. We now imagine our own tools, with new curiosities and new sensibilities of authorship, signature, and with a new spectrum of artificial intelligence and autonomy for the advancement and renewed production of Architecture.

There is a purposeful reticence towards claiming the discovery of a paradigm without having any historical distance. As with any evolving model, there are trends to be observed, some of which may disappear or become peripheral to the discipline. Yet, as digitalization and computation continue to infuse our processes with new tools and new design environments, some of the trends collected in this book will continue to be central to the production and speculation of architecture, and others will, in retrospect, be recognized as the seeds of new, or perhaps multiple, paradigms.

SIMON KIM

DESIGN
METHODOLOGY
OR
MYTHOLOGY

M Méray wants to prove that a binomial equation always has a root, or, in ordinary words, that an angle may always be subdivided. If there is any truth that we think we know by direct intuition, it is this. Who could doubt that an angle may always be divided into any number of equal parts? M Méray does not look at it that way; in his eyes this proposition is not at all evident and to prove it he needs several pages. On the other hand, look at Professor Klein: he is studying one of the most abstract questions of the theory of functions to determine whether on a given Riemann surface there always exists a function admitting of given singularities. What does the celebrated German geometer do? He replaces his Riemann surface by a metallic surface whose electric conductivity varies according to certain laws... Doubtless Professor Klein well knows he has given here only a sketch: nevertheless he has not hesitated to publish it; and he would probably believe he finds in it, if not a rigorous demonstration, at least a kind of moral certainty. A logician would have rejected with horror such a conception, or rather he would not have had to reject it, because in his mind it would never have originated.

Henri Poincaré, *Intuition and Logic in Mathematics*

13|

In recent years the use of diagrams, and design procedures in general, have been examined anew in favor of an architectural presentation of an immediacy, or as an extant *a priori* condition. Process as an atlas of procedures has been preempted for a *force majeure* presentation of immersive environments given over to affect and percept. In some cases, plan and section drawings are also avoided for a totalizing visual and perspectival discourse.[1] This may be seen as a maneuver past a rational examination with critical distance, directly to the visceral nervous and corporeal senses. More cynically, it may be construed as a disavowal of form variation, or geometric variability vis–à–vis a constructed alibi of computational or digital procedures.

The harnessing of process as a metric or methodology of design production was valorized by the rapid deployment of rules augmented by consumer electronics at the end of the 20th century. Computer programming and its promise of machine intelligence – via neural networks, genetic algorithms, and multiagent systems – would find and assemble architectural scenarios otherwise unknown to a single human author. Diagramming and indexing were the control mechanism in the training of these processes for the discipline of architecture.[2] However, design methodology, as a practiced system of instructions and applications, was formalized in a small conference in London in 1962.

Three influential people came together at the Imperial College in London, in late September 1962 to present at the Conference on Systematic and Intuitive Methods in Engineering, Industrial Design, Architecture and Communication:[3] John Chris Jones, then lecturer of industrial design at Manchester College of Science and Technology as well as conference committee member, Christopher Alexander, a member of the Society of Fellows and recent PhD recipient from Harvard, and Gordon Pask, director of System Research Ltd and Cybernetic Developments Ltd.[4]

In 1962, the three individuals were at the beginning of their respective research and careers. The conference proceedings notes on each author revealed that Alexander was yet to publish his first book on pattern, structure, and physical organization, but was to spend 1963 to 1966 in Ahmedabad to produce a village for the Indian Government's National Design Institute. His paper is titled *Determination of the Components of an Indian Village*. Jones, a vocal proponent of Design Methods and co-organizer of the conference, would present *A Method of Systematic Design*, while Pask, listed as amateur painter and lyric writer, with a pointed exclusion of his 1961 publication *An Approach to Cybernetics*, has a lecture titled *The Conception of a Shape and the Evolution of a Design*. The following year Pask would start work with Cedric Price under a newly-formed Fun Palace Cybernetics Committee.

The conference centered on the development of Design Methodology, a tethering of systematic protocols and procedures to the design of physical objects and environments. The prevailing ascendance of intelligent machines,[5] as well as scientific rules applied to social phenomena, resulted in a cultural and industrial pursuit of scalable and well-tempered craft and design for human use. There was also a rise of consumer activity at an unprecedented scale for which all prior design practice could not cope. The resultant set of working guidelines, or an *ethos*, had wide-ranging effect on focusing design away from idiosyncratic prototyping, testing, and traditional project management, towards a goal-oriented satisfaction of criteria. Design methodology was to be the advancement of calibrated and scientific design for a post-industrial society ready to produce and consume products and goods beyond any previous measure. John Chris Jones' 1970 book *Design Methods* would become the centralizing publication on its implementation.

To achieve this, systems and controls were critical in the production of design, and in its management in order to ensure consensus, satisfaction of criteria, as well as profitability. From small groups to complex organizations, design methodology required scalability and transparent prediction of all input and outputs. Whatever impeded this flow and cause irregularity, organic or synthetic, was provided the new term black box. In human pursuits, it would be a more pejorative label of intuition, or worse, aesthetics. This black box is an ineffable component in a system where incoming data would undergo unknown procedures to yield non-predictive outcomes. Its suggestive title, implying mystery or chaos, would bring black box into popular culture as analogies and references. In architectural writing it is briefly referenced by Robin Evans[6] and used to construct an argument of distinction between architecture and building for Reyner Banham.[7]

Herbert Simon would address intuition as a systems component in 1968 in *Sciences of the Artificial*[8] where the bounded rationality of a closed set of factors, or design criteria, would produce a set of all possible outcomes. Upon this table matrix all decisions were to be made on a threshold of acceptability per the initial constraints, or what he would call satisficing. The limits of what is considered for satisficing from even a small set of bounded starting conditions would lead to a very large tree of possibilities. This growth of data would stagger human capability for optimizing difficult and often non-ideal conditions, let alone apply an intuitive decision-making tactic. Intuition and emotion runs counter to logic-based systems but Simon does not discount them. Instead he places intuition as an accumulative repository of experience and response "frozen into habit"[9] that helps to govern choices, from his standpoint of a system that learns. For a self-aware machine, building designs become a pattern or set of routines to establish actions within a specifically posed problem. As an ultimate device of design methodology, single values and subsets of elements are combined into a synthetic whole as determined from a number of possibilities from which choices were deduced.

As a design method, what Jones clarifies in his presentation at the conference is first an external system in which the creative mind is allowed freedom to produce "ideas, solutions, hunches, and guesswork". The second directive is the formation of a "system of notation to record every item of design information outside the memory". He then elucidates a number or steps in how best to organize the second while providing activity for the first. The best example of this is to provide "a free atmosphere in which any idea, however crude or naïve, can be expressed at any time without regard to its applicability."[10] The precision in the methods, still allows for any number of potentially non-linear thinking to be introduced at any time in the process. Jones' design method demonstrated a robustness of an autonomous system, with the inclusion of any amount of creative freedom, to such a high degree that his book of the same name would serve as a standard for decades.[11]

Another case for innovation or invention can be supplied by Nicholas Negroponte on the formation of the Architecture Machine Group at MIT in 1967, with the oversight of Marvin Minsky and Gordon Pask:

> 'We didn't completely know what we were doing, we just had gall. And enough gall in the department of architecture where people didn't bother us. We would never have gotten away with this in the school of engineering, the department of computer science.'[12]

Gordon Pask, in a similar role which he would hold at the Architectural Association in London, was an *éminence grise* who visited MIT several times to apply his comments and critiques. In the conference at Imperial College, he proposes a cybernetic treatment of the design process that would be congruent with Jones: that A as a designer – human or mechanism – produces a design R from which all decisions may be identified as a trace upon a malleable environment.[13] A similar description is found in Pask's introduction to the book of the Architecture Machine Group, *Soft Architecture Machines* – namely, that the designer need not necessarily be human, and that the interaction of conversation and even boredom would remain. Pask also distinguishes among the realm of design: extrapolative, interpolative, translational, and optimizing before positing the machine version of perception as a filtering device or as feedback. He concludes with a brief description of his project Musicolour as an example where perception of a stable state between a performer and machine is continually tested – by both agents equally and not in service to the other - to become an ideal design tool.

Against the more general approach of the conference, a direct application of a system is seen in the design of an Indian Village presented by Christopher Alexander. Following his recent doctoral dissertation, Alexander was in a rare situation of compiling a publication as well as implementing its contents in a built work. His paper holds closer to a type of prescriptive map that takes on complete organization in inflexible detail: from the orientation of buildings to animal husbandry.[14] This particular work that would later become an appendix in his *Notes on a Synthesis of Form* would forego the abstract or the symbolic in favor of a singular instance of the village. An underlying or operative method as agreed in Jones and Pask is noticeably missing here for its inevitability and certainty. Where Pask and Jones places a underlying premise with multimodal flexibility, Alexander uses a formulaic approach where objects of the village are substituted into predisposed nodes. His later work would revisit the continually bifurcating whole-to-part sequestering of finite and discrete data into a more flexible lattice.[15]

For architects in the wake of this conference, the use of methodology and the exercise of process – especially as a discursive presentation – would require an internal body of research, and its external references. Architectural design processes would also veer from the abstract diagram as fluid interface, to the diagram as a crystalline, plug-in map.[16] Without the reference to the larger field of precedents both disciplinary and analogical, the variety produced in the research becomes untethered in its large number of charts and tables. The risk of not producing this compendium of procedures, and presenting only what appears to be an intuitively designed project, is to warrant a binary reaction of acceptance or rejection. Without a procedural map, there is no point to show a decisive or staged hypothesis that determines the outcome of the building.

There are few other disciplines in science that would not avoid the former, and few areas in the arts that veer from the second. A painting from the renaissance may hold, within the layers of paint, various hand gestures and positions that were studied, but then would be covered by the ultimate depiction. A dancer would not perform every option tested in rehearsal during the final performance. Neither of these domains would require the developmental notation and process to determine the worth of the work. The disciplinary requisite of architecture – in the occupation of space and manifest in tectonic materials – to share the methodology for its appreciation and discourse is a reversal of motive from the advent of design methods as proscribed by this conference.

The following novel may represent the inversion: of the work of literature with an explication of its workings within its body. In the 1976 novel *Kiss of the Spider Woman* by

Argentine writer Manuel Puig[17], the main story between two protagonists are suspended above a running, second narrative. Staged within a Buenos Aires prison, Valentin is held and tortured for rebellion and plotting against the government. Molina is held for corruption of a minor. The exchange between them is heated, combative, and conciliatory. Puig also makes extensive use of footnotes quoting psychoanalytic and scientific sources to define and explain the nature of Molina, the homosexual character. It would appear that two biases are being established: firstly, that all of the dispositions of Molina are superseded by an external psychological review, and therefore made necessary for a presumed heterosexual audience, and secondly, a more subversive storytelling is happening in the footnotes. This second line of narrative – the prodigious footnoting - is where the author places his opinions and even wit as he often expands upon and clarifies the sources, going so far as to fabricate one of them. The graphic design of the novel would reinforce this as the footnotes sometimes take the majority of the page, leaving the reader racing through dual expositions to assemble a synthetic whole.

Puig's experimental narrative also expands outwards through the use of stories within the story of the two men in a prison cell. Using dialogue almost primarily – hurried first-person sentences floating above a compact and dense theory of homosexual behavior to underpin why Molina would use a certain turn of phrase, or act in a particular manner – the author also folds direct references to other fictional works. Molina's storytelling of plots from movies such as the 1942 film *Cat People* and 1943's *I Walked with Zombies* serve as portents as well as proxy desires for oncoming events between the principal characters.

If not obvious to the architectural designer, the formatting of this work contains the same method where all elements and organizations are consistently underpinned by a design methodology, and the links to other works as canon. The logics of the particular building and its conditions of spatial allocation, occupancy, and perceptive reading, are underscored by a phalanx of studies, diagrams, and combinatoric tables to suggest not a rightness, but a mediated outcome from a large field of possible outcomes. Whether done by hand (Eisenman's Biozentrum) or by computer cycles (Spuybroek's Off the Road: 5-speed), the swapping or transition of variable nodes within a set of functions or algorithms produces a wide catalog that confirms an identification of values. For example, *this* warping surface produces *these* social conditions, or this *gradient* of scalar spaces best fit these programmatic *types*. These identified values suggest a legitimacy or even an alibi, although what they best identify is the representation of an organized scientific method, without the actual verifiable proof outside of its productive machinations. The double-bind of course is that all building is largely bound to its site and context, reducing the possibility of a neutral and fixed absolute solution to be further removed from process. Even modular or prefabricated building units must touch ground and connect to prosaic requirements such as water and power, let alone fit within site constraints and local cultural values beyond its capacity as a patterned, premade global system.

17|

In the following decades, ersatz rationalist architects such as John Andrews, as trained by Sert, would produce clear maps of operations governed by necessity and clearly defined conformance to type and programme. So clearly does he conform to the prevailing attitudes set forth in this article regarding method, that in an article for The Harvard Crimson when he is named as architect for the new school of design, Andrews states an abhorrence of the artistic and the intuitive in favor of a cohesive design strategy with:

> "sociologists, economists, and other specialists. System programming, according to Andrews, is the critical factor in reaching his goals of movement and communication. A typical application is to the circulation plan of people. With system programming, he says, the designer reaches a rational decision on the number of elevators or the width of corridors for a building. "The role of the architect," Andrews says, "is to synthesize all recommendations and studies of the specialists." After digesting all (this), Andrews designs and whatever happens with the outside "happens", according to Andrews."[18]

Andrews' diagrams for Scarborough College which had just been completed, show a swelling and shifting of floor plates, repeated in his design for Harvard's Gund Hall a decade later. While Gund Hall is a compact array of trays around which an administrative and classroom bar is bent, the off-center stacking and setting back of the slab from the envelope at Scarborough produces an indistinct, open, vertical space to provide an environment given over to multi-channel observation and learning. These staggered carriage-and-shed sectional treatments are episodic throughout the masterplan, as the campus is made of attenuated wings of circulation and classroom/labs/offices stretched among pivotal lecture halls and auditoria. In his review of the campus as part of a global project on megastructure, Banham[19] writes of this Canadian predilection for protected walkways as a reflex to environment and climate. Andrews' sectional schemas reinforce this assumption. Depicted as a bunkering of concrete plateaux to provide sheltered promenades against the cold, these drawings certainly show a design responding to split-level terrain, solar orientation, and prevailing winds.

However, the composition of spaces displays a lyricism that cannot be ascribed to a dutiful answer of an assigned design brief. Given the same materiality as its contemporary Barbican in London, Scarborough College offers a nuanced interior with multiple vantages and tableaux to draw academic culture across and transversally from station to station. Its exterior is not a simple incidental resultant of technical happenstance but a modulated collection of otherwise monolithic concrete mass to a cascade of earthbound elements lightly perforated for direct and indirect lighting. The overall affect is one of a geo-spontaneous choreography that is wholly new and unformed without reference to other traditions. The Barbican, on the other hand, is a collision of low-level and vertical housing blocks that are inseparable and subservient to their two referents of hamlet-scaled row housing and high-rise towers. These horizontal bars serve as quadrangle-forming set pieces in the interstitial spaces among the serrated-edge towers and Barbican Centre. While the campus is unbound from a historical pretext, the latter serves as a context-savvy upgrading of a chronicled housing typology reconciled with the technological advancement of the tower, all within a precisely calibrated array of indirectly connected terraces, raised walkways, and promontories.

An analysis of the work of REX provides an interesting continuation of Andrew's problem-solving. The insistence on the hyper-rational serves as an armature for team-based innovations. Prince-Ramus has provided numerous interviews and presentations on the idea and while it disallows a singular, virtuoso vision - embodied in his former employer Rem Koolhaas and OMA - it is also not a relegation to off-the-shelf components and assemblies:

> Our observation is that if you do this hyper-rational, almost dumb process of taking everything back to first principles… you start to construct something that has never been done before -- something that transcends convention.[20]

This approach distinguishes itself from what Andrews calls his systems programming by replacing predefined collaborative approaches to design with an ad hoc super-assembly of consultants and fabricators to adroitly deliver bespoke solutions to existing problems. The example Prince-Ramus provides is the Wyly Theatre project and its acoustic enclosure and fly loft. The reconfiguration of these elements produced a machine for reconfigurable seating arrangement within an open and extendable space on all sides. This mechanical device with its sub- and supra- services negated any proscenium or traditional stage and legitimized the hyper-rational approach. Given the privilege of the machine over the building, much of the enclosure is minimally thin, with materials approaching the non-existent and inconspicuous. The disappearing material substantiates the performativity of the building over its corporeality.

Diagrams by OMA, and their derivations REX and BIG, operate as a production of conclusions. Clearly shown black and white abstractions or proxies of the building are distorted under pressures exerted by forces (market, views, vehicular access) to produce a building *res ipsa loquitur*. In the case of the second-generation OMA offices, these diagrams work as a *bande*-dessinée, not for the designer to work through a map of possibilities, but as a post-rationalized device of communication. Each successive step extinguishes a phylum of emergent options for a single pre-cast definition without peer. The consequences of what are considered logical impositions to found conditions, such as placing all book stacks within a consolidated circuit in the Seattle Library, are inherently startling and innovative, but presented without a danger of failure vis-à-vis other procedures of compound aggregation. There is a straight-line inevitability in this method that works in favor of public promotion. The hyper-rational must be either a predefined model that is worked through in prior projects – the lineage of a breakaway theater may be found in the 1993 OMA entry for the Cardiff Opera House – or it cannot abdicate a leadership role in order to promote one idea over others. A team of hyper-rational designers and consultants seeking first principles must be given a common goal, or have a single author to identify what is of value from the undifferentiated body of the search.

Information-rich environments presents an altogether different argument to a method of rationality.[21] Rather than an exegesis of a linear sequence of steps, Patrik Schumacher embeds both data and its communication in an ever-present mechanism; this parametric engine contains both questions and answers within its structure. He also takes pains to place it in the realm of diagramming that is semiological, and not based in the problem-solving method. In his recent design studios, an underlying relationship of formal variables occupies the center of a system for which his present experiment of vaults and shells are the recipient. A structural logic is immured within a flexing armature of ever ready syntactic inputs. The resultant of these mathematic devices present an expanding repertoire of digital and physical techniques from which a final building becomes incidental to its fecundity. If the external referent are the structural engineering works of Candela or Otto, the internal logics are completely architectural systems producing openings, passage, mass, scalar shifts, and adjacencies. The potency of this parametric approach is in pairing or sometimes forcing allegiances among disparate sets of objects or values – as mentioned in Pask – to produce fields of information. These fields – the combination of values from the product of source A and source B, where the sources may even be other fields of data - are the primary goal of producing intelligence or knowledge beyond the actual source themselves. The conditions of thickness and twist are secondary to the constructed possibilities of the super-deep twisting along a Fibonacci sequence, for example.

What is never hidden is the sovereignty of the author in choosing among the repertoire, and also of the expert. There is no mention of what Prince-Ramus calls "dumb process" as the means to communicate the nuanced articulation that is invented in the design method. From the previous example, innovation is positioned where the results of twist and mass may produce a curling of such magnitude that it is no longer a braided surface affect – as expected - but an unpredicted new volumetric function. Strings of investigation follow. The designer is the necessary driver of this machine who recognizes the unusual from what is anticipated. What follows is the presentation of the system as it becomes placed in a particular site. The communication and critical reception of this is in the fullness of the exploration and the resplendent skill in its application to site and programme within a rapidly evolving technological society. The context to which they are designing would be one that is approaching with new social and technological paradigms.

Another strain, and the method for which this article is an advocate, is the shift to machine agency as a design partner and occupant. This skipping of the ideas presented by Pask across decades presents great opportunities with the arrival of the electromechanical components and processors that are now widely available. Schumacher has reservations on the motivations and expertise of what is nonhuman, and there are many practices and labs who maintain the classical hierarchy of the robot as serf or laborer in service to humans. While the craft tolerance and accuracy of robots are not necessarily more precise than human endeavor, they are faster and, at a certain scale, more cost efficient. However, this ideology would never yield more than an inundation of buildings as human-centric enterprise.

For a full embodiment of architecture that is augmented, and not anti-human but pro-other, these agents (or actors as Pask defined them) must be unimpeded and also held responsible for their larger output. Architecture that self-assembles – and for whom – presents a dynamic that is not only found in formal parametric engines but are always present and self-regulating. What the Architectural Association started with the Design Research Laboratory in only digital simulation of augmented and actuated architecture is now present and available for application. Widely accessible sensors and programmable controllers are sufficiently easy to program and implement, but are not accounted in the core of the discipline. What future devices and controls that Jones, Pask, and Alexander anticipated in their time have come to pass without a full acceptance of their capacities. For this reason, the meaningfulness of these transactions must be installed. Rather than a continuous insistence on fetishizing the technology, the new design methods must be one of a new semiology written by both human and nonhuman.

A presentation at the 2014 Conference on Working Models at McGill University with Graham Harmon[22] prompted a discussion pairing Object-Oriented Ontology with behavioral machines. What was promoted yielded a realm of possible correlations. What is untested is the reception of electromechanical or nonhuman work in an institution that actively ignores its players and theorists as they have no 'medium of process' (as Harman may claim from Greenberg). In Harman's article on Greenberg and Duchamp, Greenberg frames a concern that:

> "Art should not be academic, meaning that it should not take its medium for granted. This final principle entails that art reflects a constant struggle to reinvent its form.... art avoids academicism when its content manages to reflect or embody the possibilities of its medium, rather than presenting content as an isolated figure whose ground or medium can be taken for granted." [23]

The implications across boundaries suggest that our medium, which by necessity should be separated from the material of the building – its boundaries and lineaments – and its design platforms, where methodology is empowered and ready. The medium, for which Harman now gives way to McLuhan, cannot be changed except by one of two methods of reversal or retrieval.

21|

In the reversal, the medium through a cosmetic or secondary feature breaks its meaning to its fundamental core: the medium itself has not changed but its delivery has been stemmed. For example, the resiliency of facade as an architectural element of identity is undone when buildings grow deeper to the point that only interior and roof remains (for Greenberg, the reversal in painting was from banality of perspective to the limits of flatness). The break of façade as a building tradition and as cultural signifier is too much to lose to what can be construed as a technical outcome. But with retrieval, the discipline's history as a repository provides a renewed source of active engagement and reference. What is antiquated or cast off is now open for transformation and to become a new medium. There cannot be a clean break from history for the sake of the medium's content, therefore, but a struggle to rediscover and remake the unfinished values created in the traditional. What is safe to claim is that the attempts at computation and dynamic environments in architecture did not start at the turn of the century, *sui generis* and ahistorical, but had its genesis in preceding epochs. The process or method equally needed to creating advances in architecture that is completely unknown, is to retrieve or find "what is most valuable in the past that this period has sacrificed and left behind"[24], and let it emerge as new media.

FOOTNOTES

1. Gage, M., and Pita, F., eds., LOG 17, Anyone Corp, (November 2009). The role of affective representation, and the efficacy of drawing, have also been discussed at depth at the Yale University symposium Is Drawing Dead?, February 2012.

2. Bos, C., and van Berkel, B., eds., ANY 23, Diagram Work: Data Mechanics for a Topological Age, Anyone Corp, (June 1998).

3. Jones, J. C., and Thornley, D., eds, Proceedings of Conference on Design Methods, London: Pergamon Press, 1963.

4. The missing figure in this seminal conference would be Horst Rittel, and the work that he pioneered at the Ulm School of Design. Jones and Thornley, co-editor and presenter, would certainly be familiar with Rittel as they were both involved with the Hochschule. Thornley would only make an oblique reference to his experience teaching at an institution in 'West Germany'.

5. There are several references to the sciences and computers within the papers of the Conference on Design Methods. See the papers of D. G. Thornley, "Design Method in Architectural Education", p 43, Jones, p 53, and Pask as he notes Marvin Minsky and Wiener at MIT, p 155. They reinforce the shift from what Thornley describes as an aesthetic and inspirational approach to architectural design, to one engaged with science and logic. Thornley is the only presenter who touches upon the apparent divide of logic and intuition by referencing – albeit by footnote - the mathematician Poincaré. In fact, the article of Poincaré, Intuition and Logic in Mathematics, is the exact location where Pask, Jones, and Alexander struggle to define the non-rational or intuitive, and that this paper attempts to address.

6. Evans, R., "Architectural Projection," in Architecture and its Image: Four Centuries of Architectural Representation: Works from the Canadian Centre for Architecture, Blau, E., Kaufman, E., eds., (Cambridge: MIT Press, 1989), 19.

7. Banham, R., "Black Box: The Secret Profession of Architecture," New Statesman, 12, (October 1990), 22-25.

8. Simon, H., Sciences of the Artificial, 3rd ed., (Cambridge: MIT Press, 1996), 89. The closest he comes to dealing with intuition is to describe it as a pattern recognition, and architecture as a process within a "semantically-rich task domain".

9. Simon. H., Ibid., 139.

10. Jones, J. C., "A Method of Systematic Design", in Conference on Design Methods, (London: Pergamon Press, 1963), 53-73.

11. Jones, J. C., Design Methods, London: Wiley, 1970.

12. Negroponte, N., discussing the formation of the Architecture Machine Group, at the Futures Past Conference, MIT, 2013. Rather than apply a centralized method, the early work of the Architecture Machine Group would be an ad hoc

series of largely interface-heavy projects that were free from an overarching agenda such as those in the AI Lab or Project MAC.

13. Pask, G., "The Conception of a Shape and the Evolution of a Design" in Conference on Design Methods, (London: Pergamon Press, 1963), 153-167.

14. Alexander, C., "Determination of the Components of an Indian Village", in Conference on Design Methods, (London: Pergamon Press, 1963), 153-167. In fact, the manner with which an object-oriented computer programmer could call a constructor to instantiate for a class may be founded here; such is the pattern to object transition so fully demonstrated.

15. Alexander, C., "A City is Not a Tree (Part 1)" Architectural Forum, Vol 122, No 1 (April 1965), 58-62.

16. Eisenman, P., "Diagram: An Original Scene of Writing", in Diagram Diaries, (New York: Universe Publishing, 1999), 26-43. Adjacency matrices, charts, tables, and diagrams originally found in science and engineering would be ascribed to Gropius' Harvard polemic, although it was widespread from Fuller to Price. The other diagrammatic strategy would be one of semiology centralized around Wittkower's nine-square exercise.

17. Puig, M., Kiss of the Spider Woman, trans. Colchie, T., NY: Random House, 1980. The author would also transcribe the novel into a screenplay in 1983. The 1985 film would suffer from the missing dimension of the psychoanalytic sources on which Puig would go to great lengths to base every nuance of Molina's dialogue.

18. Krim, R., "Andrews – Genius of Scarborough Coming to Harvard", The Harvard Crimson, December 1, 1967.

19. Banham, R., Megastructure: Urban Futures of the Recent Past, London: Thames and Hudson, 1976.

20. Blum, A., "The Koolhaas Kids Come of Age", Bloomberg Business Week, February 22, 2006.

21. Schumacher, P., "The Design of Information Rich Environments", Architecture In Formation – On the Nature of Information in Digital Architecture, Lorenzo-Eiroa, P., Sprecher, A., eds., NY: Routledge, 2013. The author of this paper has also taught with Schumacher in 2007 and 2013 at Yale University, and worked at Zaha Hadid Architects from 2003 to 2006 where Schumacher is partner.

22. Harman, G., "Overcoming Flatness in Architecture and the Arts." Working Models Forum, Jemtrud, M., ed., McGill University, May 2014.

23. Harman, G., "Greenberg, Duchamp, and the Next Avant-Garde" Speculations: A Journal of Speculative Realism V (2014), 251-277. The parallels between the academies of art and the counterpart in architecture are supported by the discussion of medium via McLuhan and Heidegger.

24. Harman, G., Ibid., 274.

23|

SIMON KIM is an Assistant Professor at the University of Pennsylvania School of Design where he directs the Immersive Kinematics Research Group. He is also an architect with professional registration in California, and is a founding principal of Ibañez Kim Studio. Simon has graduate degrees from the Architectural Association in London and at MIT where he was a research associate at the Design Lab. His academic papers and research in robotics in architecture and design has been presented in international conferences such as IEEE, ACADIA, and AAMAS. His work has also been exhibited at the ICA in Philadelphia, Storefront for Art and Architecture in NY, the Venice Biennale, and the MoMA.

Concurrent to his projects on augmented architecture at the Immersive Kinematics Group and Ibañez Kim Studio, Simon has expanded his research at Smart Geometry, Yale University, and Harvard Graduate School of Design. He has also produced performances on cybernetics with Carbon Dance Theatre, Pig Iron Theatre Company, jazz musician Grace Kelly, and the exhibitions Nervous Matter with the Dufala Brothers, and Unethical Machines.

PHILIP   BEESLEY

HYLOZOIC GROUND COLLABORATION, WATERLOO ARCHITECTURE

DISSIPATIVE MODELS

—

NOTES   TOWARD A DESIGN METHOD

I want to describe a particular kind of form language rooted intimately within our bodies. I argue for the use of diffusive and dissipative forms in architectural design. This morphology stands distinctly against Modern preference for stripped, minimal stages devoted to autonomous freedom. The language I argue for instead pursues culpable involvement. In this discussion I will make comments about emplacement in pursuit of a relationship with the environment affording subtle phenomena and expanded physiologies, embodying the forms of diffusion and dissipation. Building from this form-language, projects will be described that approach living qualities.[1]

An undulating, quasiperiodic metabolism is evoked by this series of projects. Rather than polarized working methods that follow only centrally controlled or opposing emergent, incremental models of organization, the fields of this working method oscillate. Deliberate ambivalence is inherent to the approach, yielding qualities where things convulse and stutter in emerging vitality. I will try to articulate traces of subtle phenomena seeking emplacement, measured by intense mutual relationships of exchange with surrounding environments. The qualities that I will describe are characterized by punctuated oscillation. They use paradigms of dissipative structures and diffusion as guides for their design and their forms. This form language will be used to describe architectural projects that I will claim have living qualities. This personal involvement results in shifting boundaries that fluctuate between hard facts and hopeful fictions for exploring the future.

25|

The sphere of a raindrop can be considered a kind of machine for resisting interaction. The surface tension of the meniscus encircling a drop of rain pulls inward, and the result is a kind of optimum where the least possible exposing surface encloses the greatest possible mass within. The potency of that equation can hardly be overestimated- it guides the design of a fort that protects, a bullet that pierces, a bathysphere that can fight the radical forces of the deep. As if guided by a moral compass founded in equations of distillation and purity, western traditions of architecture have tended to value these kinds of pure forms. The resulting architecture tends to seek strength and stability, resisting disruption. Yet, thinking of the elemental forms of rain and snow, need I assume that the perfectly balanced optimum of a spherical drop of rain is obviously better than the delicate outward-reaching branching spines that radiate from a frozen snowflake? Why, when I think of the myriad of forms that the natural world has offered, should we prefer closed, pure, gloss-faced cubes and spheres to tangled, dissipating masses of fertile soil? Ilya Prigogine, the great 20th century physicist, proposed **diffusion** and **dissipation** as key terms for understanding how materials could interact in a dynamic, constantly evolving and self-organizing world. In this study, I explore a renewed architecture following the dynamic form-languages implied by Prigogine's theories[2a]. This architecture pursues diffusive qualities, the opposite of reductive spheres and crystals. Following Prigogine, the design languages guiding this work evoke qualities found in veils of smoke billowing at the outer reaches of a fire, the barred, braided fields of clouds; torrents of spiraling liquids; mineral felts efflorescing within an osmotic cell reaction. Such sources are characterized by resonance and flux.

For twenty-five hundred years, Western artists and designers have been writing about emulating life[2b]. The imagery and forms from this tradition show potent hope for inanimate forms of craft and art coming alive. Yet the speech and evocations of visual art and architecture have often treated 'life' as a kind of boundary, defined by separation and distance from human craft. The symbolism that evokes life has been maintained by distinguishing human artifice from the viable organisms of nature[3]. The discipline of architecture seems to have been especially emphatic in maintaining this divide. Architecture seems a counterform to nature[4], staying deliberately distinct from the living world, preferring instead the role of a stripped stage that supports the living world by means of clear restraint. Perhaps that kind of separation has a moral kind of imperative, avoiding trespass. Indeed, if we think about atrocities this past century, then there would be a very good reason to make a clean, empty place where we could be free, where a clear sanctuary could support nuanced interactions that rebuild humanity.

Yet the distinct progress of science and technology in recent decades invites a change to this strategy of restraint. The achievement of comprehensive information within the human genome project[6], the accomplishment of potent learning functions in computational controls[7], and the increasing fluency in programming physical materials and projecting complex-system ecological modeling can conspire to demonstrate that living systems no longer need be maintained as a sacrament separate from human intervention[8]. The ability to see our traces and to understand dimensions of the impact with which we thread forms an ethical key to this change. With that sensitivity it becomes possible to speak about full-blooded fertile involvement for designers. The shift offers resistance to the kind of deliberately empty, existentialist freedom that has tended to define recent generations of architecture[9]. Emerging from the distancing functions of reverence into a new phase of highly involved stewardship, living systems can now occupy the space of architectural design.

The entire world is never stable. In poignant contrast to the architectural tradition framed by 'firmitas', today's environment seems distant from the stable hold of natural cycles. Instead of the eternity of nature, we are surrounded by turbulence. What kind of design methods might contribute to such instability? It would be tempting to follow optimums within natural form finding that they are exemplified by the space of a rain drop. If Plato were teaching today's designers he might say that the elegant reductions of primary geometry provide keys to architecture[10] by using the minimum possible envelope and the maximum possible territory enclosing interior territory. Yet the reductive form language that guides such efficiency is a kind of machine for resisting interaction as well. There can be no less surface for interaction than that of a sphere. The reductive form-languages of spheres and crystals achieve maximum possible territory and maximum possible inertia by minimizing their exposure to their surroundings[11]. Such a form can be effective in a cold climate that requires retention of energy. It can also be effective if you want to destroy as much as possible with embodied energy of ballistics. However, cooling requires the opposite. The opposite of a spherical raindrop appears in the form of snowflakes. Snowflakes epitomize dissipation; the operation harvests the internal heat by optimizing release through an efflorescence of exchange. Such a form offers a strategy for a diffusive architecture in which surfaces are devoted to the maximum possible intensity and resonance with their surroundings[12].

The form-languages pursued in this discussion can contribute to a lexicon, a system for design. This search for fertile, generative language can be informed by theories of growth in the parallel discipline of human psychology. A brief comparison of two theories of growth offered by mid-20th century American psychologists reveals quite striking differences. On one hand, a traditional sequence of growing from infancy might follow the mid-20th century American psychologist Abraham Maslow's ladder of self-actualization[13]. Maslow's series of developmental stages follows a sequence of growth. As a very young person you lose things, get hurt and take responsibility. You move into agency and increasing freedom, able to handle separation and opposition. In such a sequence a goal is set up that moves distinctly from a diffuse, turbulent beginning into the destination of a clear, isolated and bounded whole. Artists might use similar terms to Maslow, I think, when they speak about relationships in their visual compositions as 'figures' and 'grounds'. It seems to me that clear, bounded figures are almost always pursued as goals, emerging out of dark and uncertain grounds.

Donald W. Winnicott theorized the emergence of the infant psyche at the same time as Maslow, but his way of seeing our environment seems distinct from Maslow's prevailing views of growth and development. Similar to Maslow, Winnicott looked closely at the states that came before a person knows they are a person and before they know their name. However, instead of valuing separation and autonomy,

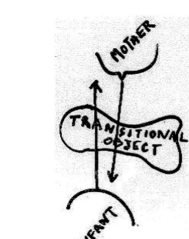

Figure 1: Donald Winnicott's hand drawings illustrate the mediating role that transitional objects can play for the emerging consciousness of an infant.

Winnicott talks about objects and physical things as having a key relationship with living bodies and with emerging consciousness[14]. He describes Transitional Objects – blankets, stuffed animals, favourite objects that as a child you would carry as a constant. In those early times such things can be said to be coterminous with your body and with your mind. I do, dimly, remember my own 'blanky'. Perhaps I was almost fused with it when I was a tiny boy. Winnicott's descriptions argue for deliberately extending and delaying the growth out of such an ambiguous state[15].

Rather than something being bounded by clearly marked territory, the developing form language implied by Winnicott encourages slow and gentle condensation, allowing self-determined forms to crystallize out of a continuum. His vision could be conceived in spatial terms, evoking an extended field that, far from wilful use of tools and manipulation of objects, evokes a continuum defined by complex interrelationships. The organizations imply a range of forms defined by infolding and connection- reticulated manifolds, entangled matrices. His spatial conceptions seem to include disorientation and even delirium as productive qualities, enabling integrated growth while avoiding premature polarization of relationships. Redefined models of individual identity can result from such sensitive conceptions.

From objects, Winnicott goes on to conceive of Transitional Fields, suggesting that cultural expressions could function in similar ways to objects handled by a pre-conscious infant, and implying in turn that public identity can emerge in ways analogous to the emergence of individual consciousness. Winnicott says "The transitional objects and transitional phenomena belong to the realm of illusion which is at the basis of initiation of experience… the task of reality-acceptance is never completed, that no human being is free from the strain of relating inner and outer reality, and that relief from this strain is provided by an intermediate area of experience which is not challenged (arts, religion, etc.). This intermediate area is in direct continuity with the play area of the small child who is 'lost' in play." [16] Illusions become prima materiae in such an exchange. To me, Winnicott gives confidence in the continuity of the world.

Figure 2: Cyclical exchanges of heat between a human figure and a Hylozoic series polymer frond are recorded through thermal imaging (image: Philip Beesley and Philippe Baylaucq, with thanks to IR Camera)

He offers a potent response to the lingering question of how the organization of individuals might contribute to the generation of collective experience.

We can look carefully and see the traces that we make. In my own work, I have started examining thermodynamics to seek a tangible exchange for the reality of an expanded physiology. Layers of exchange wrap around each of us. You can see the translucency of the heat as it propagates out through the polymer tines of the digitally fabricated frond in the image presented within this essay[17]. Asking as the subject being photographed in that image, I ask if I am pushing that heat-energy outward or whether the surrounding milieu of vapours is pulling energy out of me. Perhaps both of those states intermingle. If we look at the cycle, heat exchanges reveal themselves at first as obvious: I emit heat; the world receives my energy. The imagery presented here is aided by increased precision in which notch filters are tuned in order to reveal a flux of carbon dioxide in the air as it carries a thermal plume into this frond. We can see it propagate and then bleed into the mass and be pulled into the middle. However, certainty in a one-way flow fades when the later stages of this sequence of images appear[18]. In the final images of the cycle, we can see that the temperature of the tines of the frond nearest my face recorded in dark tones show levels that are distinctly lower that when the cycle began. The ambient environment is not only receiving my action, but is also actively pulling heat from me. The surrounding air has pulled that energy outward, perhaps literally ingesting part of me.

29|

I believe that the hardened boundaries exemplified by Plato's world of spheres and reductive forms might be opened and renewed by form-languages that pursue intense involvement and exchange[19]. I make footprints in the world, but not as an individual figure leaving things about for them to dissolve into nothing. Rather, there's an active sense of the environment recoiling in multiple cycles. This implies a mutual kind of relationship. In turn, it suggests a craft of designing with materials conceived as filters that can expand our influence and expand the influence of the world on us, in an oscillating register: catching, harvesting, pulling and pushing. While personal boundaries can readily be found as functions of central systems--brain, and spine, and hearts define cores that we know well- parallel to those cores lie bundles of ganglia in our elbows or in our sternum and pineal[20]. Neural matter is riddled throughout our bodies, making a great shambling series of overlapping networks. Much of our consciousness is bound up in loops and reflexes that happen at the outer edges of cognition. Such a model working internally could be expanded outward. In such a layered space, we could build up a deeply layered, deeply fissure set of relationships in which there are multiple sensitive boundaries. We might be able to build up in a sense of fertility reconstructing a kind of a soil and ground. We could measure values within that constructed ground by measuring resonance.

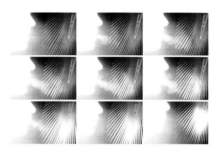

Figure 3: Revealing subtle dynamics within an ambient environment, an 'ingestion' of heat-energy occurs as temperatures within Hylozoic series polymer tine details travel inward, implied by the darker tones of outer tines. (image: Philip Beesley and Philippe Baylaucq, with thanks to IR Camera)

The projects that my collaborators and I have been making pursue the construction of a synthetic new kind of soil. The projects have moved through several stages of focus from scaffolding and structure, through integration of mechanisms and interactive controls, to chemical metabolisms. Structures tend to be lightweight and ephemeral. One stage has concentrated on geometry and on periodic structures, looking at the kind of resilience that comes from textile matrices, in turn moving toward quasiperiodic systems in which things shift and multiply and effloresce, producing conditions for active resonance.

A further stage of development has involved construction of diffusive metabolisms in which protocell chemistries show material flux, raising the possibility of construction of renewing skins of material.

Hylozoic Ground, installed within the Canadian pavilion at the 2010 Venice Biennale for Architecture, was organized by a hyperbolic waffle structure that could be pulled and pushed into continuous doubly-curved shell surfaces. The structural scaffold was clothed with layers of mechanisms. Kinetic components were grouped together, making tribal organizations of multiple clusters that would speak to each other and listen. In turn, these clusters would be

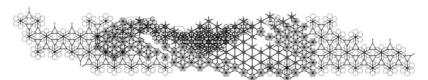

Figure 4: Epiphyte Veil, Hylozoic Series at Hangzhou Triennale, 2013: Hexagonal arrays related to Epiphyte Chamber include large-scale feathered triangular array, vertical expanded-mesh thermoformed diagrid spars, actuated filters and organic power cells (image: PBAI)

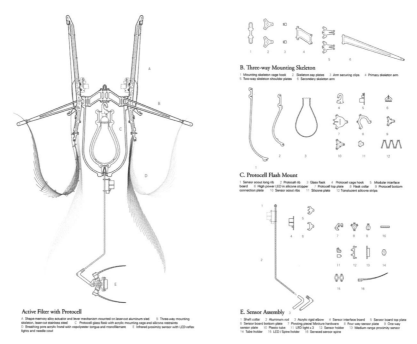

Figure 5: Active Filter Module, Hylozoic Series 2013: assembly drawing and patterns for hexagonal-array tiling unit with shape memory alloy actuated breathing pores, Traube protocell flask with LED stimulus, and proximity sensor with LED reflex functions (image: PBAI)

organized in larger familial groups that spoke in quasi localized ways. Ripples of reaction and counter-reaction flow in this exchange. The behaviour is only partially predictable, but it is by no means random. It is the result of a tissue like aggregation of multiple gestures.

The hyperbolic scaffold is a resilient network made of tetrahedral structures, clothed with hanging filters which pass gentle convective plumes of ear and filter the environment. Electro-acoustic 'cricket' fields of polymer are shown in an image accompanying this writing[22]. Each one of the elements is powered by a miniature shape memory alloy actuator. In concert, the mechanisms ripple out and resonate. They chirp as you come close, stimulated by touch. Protocell fields of glass flasks cycle water from the Venice canal and contribute cleaning and

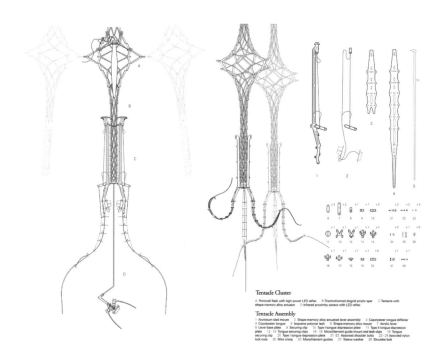

Figure 6: Tentacle Cluster, Hylozoic Series 2013: assembly drawing and patterns for modular unit with expanded thermoformed diagrid spar scaffold, protocell flask, shape memory alloy actuated tentacles, and proximity sensor

refreshment. These do not achieve high, efficient functions. Instead they offer a sketch of possibility.

Recent work expands into larger fields in which plumes of breathing vessels hover above and vibrations ripple through the entire field[22]. Multiple vibrations shiver through it, activated by direct-current miniature motors fitted with offset weights that create oscillating motion. Communications move out into rippling fields. Protocell environments start to work as a kind of a soil. Inside the flasks are slowly evolving reactions. Saturation is built up in layers using custom glass work that create suspended fluid reticulums. A copper compound blooms out under osmotic 'pumping' through an aqueous solution of potassium ferric cyanide, making walnut-like reticulated structures. Intensely multiplied small elements work together chained through vessels, imparting a blooming fertility. Humidity and scent are exuded. Small glands are wrapped around with traps. The elements with their humidity and with their scent gather, trap and start to harvest themselves. The sensation is on one hand, of being bathed but on the other of being eaten.

Our work pursues the beginnings for public emplacement. Large membranes made tangible rooms for gathering in a recent installation for Toronto's Luminato festival at Brookfield Place Galleria in 2012. The hanging layers of the Brookfield Place sculpture were programmed

Figure 7: Detail of suspended membrane from Hylozoic Ground, Venice Biennale for Architecture, 2009: shape memory alloy-actuated cricket resonators and capacitance touch sensors are arrayed in hexagonally oriented stratified membranes (image: Pierre Charron)

Figure 8: Upward view of Epiphyte Chamber, MMCA, Seoul, 2013: organic power cells, helical chains of glass flask liquid manifolds, and stratified tentacle clusters within thermoformed acrylic diagrid spars create an immersive chamber (image: Philip Beesley)

for slightly convulsive breathing motions, working to amplify the large flows of public movement that occurred each day. A whispering field of stories overhead were cued by arrays of proximity sensors. A breathing field employed approximately one hundred bladders, breathing and harvesting in response to people standing below. Such installations tend to be organized along two axes that work in parallel. Working laterally, the spaces are framed to support collective experience; the realm of the public common. Along with the mediation of who we are together, a vertical axes is used that frames personal physiology, encouraging perception of a fundament below and aerial dimensions reaching far above. This expanded emplacement reaches beyond social boundaries toward multiple dimensions.

Changing scale in recent work is a collaboration in fashion, starting to contribute to the sense of an expanded physiology in literal ways. Iris Van Herpen's studio offers a radical intimacy where the skin is only one boundary amongst many. Recent collaboration with Van Herpen includes three dimensional lace made of silicon and impact resistant acrylic[23], and fabrics that integrate fissured forms configured like leaky heart valves, hovering leaf-like layers that very slightly push and pump in the gentlest of ways. They encourage plumes of air to rise. They make a live performance as they harvest your own energy and ripple around you. Layers lying immediately outside human bodies are organized in octaves of potential exploration, moving into turbulence. Musculature could be considered a mask, and an active fire-like metabolism can be sensed radiating through human skin. A corollary can be seen in a building composed of multiple layers. Traces are pulling at you. You become aware of the impact of your own tread in the world.

In summary, this work has been guided by opposing Plato's idea of a sphere, of the kind of skin that might claim to be efficient, that might claim to be responsible by reducing consumption and yet, somehow, which speaks much more potently of mortality than of a kind of a fertility. Spheres can speak of a violence and of a claim. Instead of the optimal, reductive forms of raindrops, I have suggested that snowflakes offer potent form-language that could guide emerging architecture. New projects from my studio are deeply layered

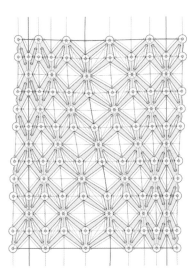 

Figure 9: Parametrically generated cutting pattern for silicone meshwork, Iris van Herpen/PBAI couture collaboration in progress 2014. Meshwork receives acrylic chevron inclusions arranged in progressively opposing arrays, creating a corrugated diagrid fabric. Free-form gradients control spacing of voids and attachment points in order to provide variable density for this hybrid. (image: PBAI)(image: Pierre Charron)

Figure 10: Voltage series, detail of Frond Dress, Couture 2013: Iris van Herpen with Philip Beesley. Mylar fronds originally developed by studio member Eric Bury are adapted in composite moulage (image: PBAI)

33|

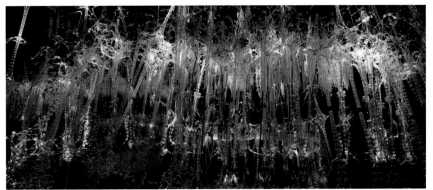

Figure 11: Epiphyte Chamber: detail view of core structure showing stratified expanded-mesh scaffold, organic power cells, interactive tentacles and glasswork manifolds, Epiphyte Chamber, Philip Beesley/Hylozoic Ground Collaboration, Museum of Modern and Contemporary Art, Seoul, 2013-4 (Image: Philip Beesley)

and are founded in intimacy and touch. These works invite practice where we can see our traces. We can start to design in a way that can pull and harvest and resonate. In the footsteps of Prigogine, the diffusive, dissipative form-language described here offers a strategy for constructing fertile new architecture.

FOOTNOTES

1. An earlier version of this essay was presented at Alive International Symposium on Adaptive Architecture, Computer Aided Architectural Design, ETH Zurich, March 2013.

2a. For Prigogine's conceptions with emphasis on spatial qualities, see Exploring Complexity: An Introduction, Gregoire Nicolis and Ilya Prigogine, Freeman (New York), 1989.

2b. Youngs, A. M. (2000). The fine art of creating life. Leonardo, 33(5), 377-380.

3. Crist, C. P., & Roundtree, K. (2006). Humanity in the web of life. Environmental Ethics, 28(2), 185-200.

4. Hagan, S. (2001). Taking shape: a new contract between architecture and nature. Routledge.

5. Plan of Organic Battery cluster

6. Collins, F. S., Morgan, M., & Patrinos, A. (2003). The Human Genome Project: lessons from large-scale biology. Science, 300(5617), 286-290.

7. Eliasmith, C., & Anderson, C. H. (2004). Neural engineering: Computation, representation, and dynamics in neurobiological systems. MIT Press.

8. Grimm, V., Revilla, E., Berger, U., Jeltsch, F., Mooij, W. M., Railsback, S. F., ... & DeAngelis, D. L. (2005). Pattern-oriented modeling of agent-based complex systems: lessons from ecology. Science, 310(5750), 987-991.

9. Markus, T. A. (2013). Buildings and power: Freedom and control in the origin of modern building types. Routledge.

10. Skinner, S. (2009). Sacred geometry: deciphering the code. Sterling Publishing Company, Inc..

11. Chernov, A. A. (2001). Crystal growth science between the centuries. Journal of Materials Science: Materials in Electronics, 12(8), 437-449.

12. Wallisser, T. (2009). Other geometries in architecture: bubbles, knots and minimal surfaces. In Mathknow (pp. 91-111). Springer Milan.

13. Maslow, A. H., Frager, R., & Cox, R. (1970). Motivation and personality (Vol. 2). J. Fadiman, & C. McReynolds (Eds.). New York: Harper & Row.

14. Winnicott, D. W. (2012). The family and individual development. Routledge.

15. Donald Winnicott's hand drawings illustrate the mediating role that transitional objects can play for the emerging consciousness of an infant.

16. Winnicott, D. W. (1953). (1953). International Journal of Psycho-Analysis, 34: 89-97 Transitional Objects and Transitional Phenomena—A Study of the First Not-Me Possession. International Journal of Psycho-Analysis, 34, 89-97.

17. Cyclical exchanges of heat between a human figure and a polymer frond are recorded through thermal imaging.

18. Revealing subtle dynamics within an ambient environment, an 'ingestion' of heat-energy occurs as temperatures within polymer tine details travel inward, implied by the darker tones of its outer edges.

34

PHILIP BEESLEY is a professor in the School of Architecture at the University of Waterloo who leads the Hylozoic Ground series, currently working with collaborators including Rachel Armstrong, Salvador Breed, Rob Gorbet, Dana Kulic, and Iris van Herpen. A practitioner of architecture and digital media art, he was educated in visual art at Queen's University, in technology at Humber College, and in architecture at the University of Toronto. At Waterloo he serves as Director for the Integrated Group for Visualization, Design and Manufacturing, and as Director for Riverside Architectural Press. His Toronto-based practice PBAI is an interdisciplinary design firm that combines public buildings with sculpture, stage and lighting projects. The studio's methods incorporate industrial design, digital prototyping, and mechatronics engineering.

Philip Beesley's work is widely cited in the rapidly expanding technology of responsive architecture. He has authored and edited eleven books, and appeared on the cover of Artificial Life (MIT), LEONARDO and AD journals. Features include national CBC news, Casa Vogue, WIRED, A Magazine, and a series of TED talks. His work was selected to represent Canada at the 2010 Venice Biennale for Architecture and the Biennale of Sydney. He has been recognized by the Prix de Rome in Architecture, VIDA 11.0, FEIDAD, Ars Electronica, two Governor General's Awards and the 2014 Architizer A+ Award. Beesley's funding includes core CFI, SSHRC, NSERC and Canada Council for the Arts grants.

SITUATING ARCHITECTURAL COMPUTING WITHIN DESIGN AND RESEARCH

MANNER, MEDIUM AND FUNCTION

SHAJAY BHOOSHAN   ZHA-CODE

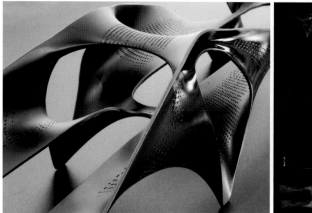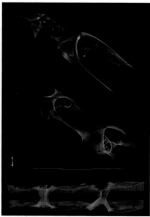

(Left)(Figure 1)
Hyper-Threads_
Autodesk_IDEA
Studio. 2011
(Right) (Figure 2)
Hyper-Threads_
Autodesk_IDEA
Studio 2011

In giving perspective to the experience and efforts of the group (Zaha Hadid Architects Computation and design group – ZHA_CODE) in its 7 year existence, it would be useful to borrow the terms - Manner and Medium of architecture, as described by Patrik Schumacher in his book Autopoesis of Architecture. Schumacher defines Medium as the design environment and its technical delimitation that enables and defines the scope and nature of exploration of design ideas. In our case the Medium is the digital 'universe of possibilities'. Further, Manners are the institutionalised axioms and protocol that are resultant of systematic exploration and allow for a straight-forward interpretation and execution of design ideas. Thus the work of ZHACODE could be viewed as articulating and expanding our design Medium to match design intent and evolution of the Manner of our practise.

To articulate further, it would be useful to introduce the concept of Function. If we view Function from its usage in biology and mathematics, it would include both notions of chains of causation from object to goal and the procedure of relating inputs to one or more results. Such a definition can be applied to both aspects of Manner as well as Medium and various theoreticians and practitioners have done so : Schumacher (the ordinary parametric diagram in Autopoesis of Architecture), Farshid Mossavi (proto-geometry in the Function of Form), Toni Kotnik (Computable functions in his article - Digital Architectural Design as Exploration of Computable Functions.)etc. It would suffice in the current context however to state that our work as a design-research group has been related to bringing Manner-Functions (design methods) closer to the Medium-Functions (computational procedures).

Functions in Manner

Manner or institutionalised axioms have been evolving since the inception of the office and encapsulates the stance of the office in regard to the 'weathered' concerns mentioned previously. In turn there exists established protocol and methods of articulating geometry, program, drawings etc. In other words there are known Manner-Functions that link inputs of design briefs, building types, program requirements, etc. to their architectural solutions

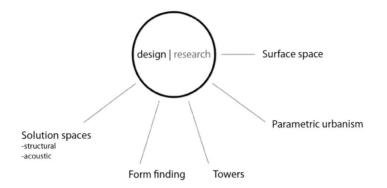

(Figure 3) ZHA-CODE Manner

/ results. On the one hand, the task and work of the research group has been to mine this vast legacy of design experimentation, built results and the design talent-pool to develop digital tool-sets to action these established Functions. For instance, seminal projects such as One North master-plan established some clear Functions related to urban design ideas and tasks. As a result, the earliest work of the research group was to decompose various ideas and protocols of such projects into constituent blocks / tasks and develop tool-sets for each of those tasks. These tool-sets were subsequently re-applied to produce the proposal for our first project as a research group. On the other hand, the work has also included in equal measure, continuing design experimentation and contributing to the establishment newer Functions.

Medium Functions: Complexity and 'Parametric' design

Architects are constantly evolving more refined understanding of computational geometry and' parametric' design systems, attempting newer forms computer programming, striving for greater understanding of complex, non-linear phenomena etc. In could be safely argued, that professional and academic discourse is moving past the nascent stages of 'happy discovery'

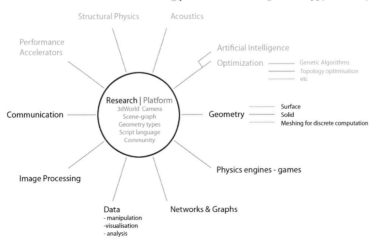

(Figure 4) ZHA-CODE Medium

37 |

towards a sophisticated understanding and use of computation within design. Various academic and professional architectural discourses now argue for the need for architectural design to embrace, manage and articulate complexity, differentiation and emergent behaviour. Further, it is now conceivable that these 'features' can emerge from systems based on an intelligent choreography of iterative, rule-based substrates. This aspect becomes crucial in designing computational procedures (Medium-Functions) towards generating design affect and solutions to given inputs and constraints. This because, computational methods are inherently dependent of iterative sub-tasks in that any problem is decomposed into smaller, constituent blocks that can be solved by repeating a simple set of operations. These subsets are usually, previously known solutions. Thus, Medium Functions can be seen as syntactic concatenations of previously known problems and their solutions.

In this concatenate nature also lies an essential conflict : as designers we wish a complex affect, whilst expending minimal resource – time and effort. Thus it is useful to know the relation between complexity and simplicity – Simplexity

"There are a lot of ways the push-pull between simplicity and complexity is being explored and explained. Consider how babies learn to speak—a job so complicated that by some measures they shouldn't be able to do it at all. .. What's more, since babies can't know where they'll be born, they must start life able to learn any of the world's nearly 7,000 tongues. It's processing speed that makes all this possible." (emphasis added) http://www.simplexitybook. com/SimplexityExcerpt.html

Similarly, architectural design process in all its complexity is iterative and reliant on speed of each of the iterations. This then points towards the need for Medium Functions to incorporate 'rules-of thumb' – approximate and simplified algorithms with real-time feed-back for the designer. Further, these 'rules' need to abstract, encapsulate and allow for the potential to integrate with more downstream computing logics of engineering and construction. This would allow for an informed-yet-fluent design process whilst remaining within realms of physical feasibility.

Our work on the technical side of expanding our Medium has been driven by need to take on various kinds of sub-tasks – geometry production, data manipulation, qualitative performance feed-back etc , endeavouring to develop real-time tools, and to interface reasonably with down-stream production processes such Building Information Modelling, fabrication information etc. Equally, various design-research agendas and projects have contributed tangibly and specifically to the growth of our Medium. This is because we aim to expand the technical limits of our Medium to match those design intentions – decomposing the emerging Manners into constituent tasks, development of tool-sets to automate / hasten each of those, devising algorithms that combine tool-sets to produce design affect etc.

In essence, we endeavour to bring computational procedures (Medium Functions) closer to the protocols that bind design ideas to design solutions (Manner Functions) and one serves to motivate the other.

Conclusion

Architectural computing could benefit significantly from incorporating technical advances from the sciences. Such efforts seem to come increasingly naturally to architects and they could be augmented by mining the long legacy of built and discursive history from within architecture. Also, juxtaposing these against explicit goals to retain the craft nature - iteration, expedience, exploration - of the design process can aid in collectively charting a unique disciplinary path in applied art and science.

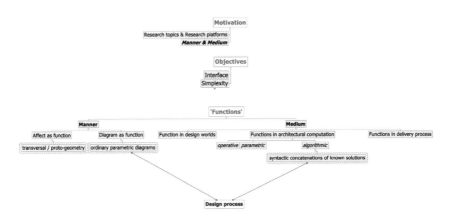

(Figure 5) ZHA-CODE

Overall structure

Architectural computing might not have quite reached levels of technical sophistication as other natural sciences or applied sciences. However, it is not mere utility and is indeed a manner of design 'thinking', requiring clear protocol of operation, modes of understanding constraints and means of manipulating information. It could provide the necessary means to bridge the ambitions of contemporary design of dealing with the complexities of the built economies and equally compelling technological advances. It simultaneously opens doors to design possibility and to enabling a truer manifestation of the imagined world.

ZHA_CODE is:

Shajay Bhooshan, lead Reseracher; Mostafa El Sayed, Senior designer; Suryansh Chnadra, Senior designer; Vishu Bhooshan, David Reeves, and Henry Louth, architectural assistants; Previously, Danilo Arsic, lead designer.

ACKNOWLEDGEMENTS:

ZHACODE was conceived as design-research group, as opposed to a specialist skills group, to incorporate emerging design and manufacturing technologies within a design ideology and method.

We would like to acknowledge the vision and guidance of Zaha Hadid and Patrik Schumacher in setting up a design-research group at a time of nascent interest. They have also continually nurtured ideas, talent and contextually situating architectural-computing and research.

We would also like to acknowledge the contributors of our various collaborators in the development of ideas as also the development and production of architectural prototypes, mentioned in the article:

AADRL, Architectural Association, London; Block research group, ETH Zurich; Kreysler Associates, San Francisco; Buro Happold Engineers, London; AKT Engineers, London; Chikara Inamura, Matsuro Sasaki Engineers and MIT Media Lab; John Klein, MIT Media Lab; Alicia Nahmad, Populous London; Asbjorn Sondergaard, ODICO.

REFERENCES
"Simplexity is an emerging theory that proposes a possible complementary relationship between complexity and simplicity. The term draws from General Systems Theory, Dialectics (philosophy) and Design."
http://en.wikipedia.org/wiki/Simplexity#cite_note-Wipperman-2

IMAGE CREDITS
All images courtesy Zaha hadid architects.

(Left and Center) (Figure 6,7) ZHA-CODE Bangalore Pavilion 2013 (Right) (Figure 8) ZHA Venice Biennale 2012

(Figure 9) ZHA China International Architectural Biennale Beijing 2013

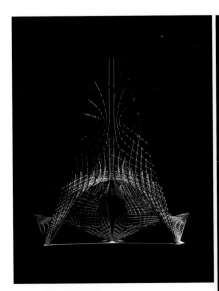

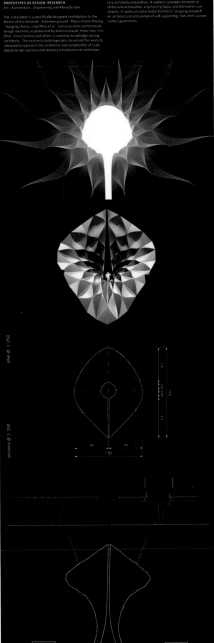

PROTOTYPES AS DESIGN ·RESEARCH
Art , Architecture , Engineering and Manufacture

The installation is a specifically designed contribution to the theme of the biennale - *Common ground*. Physical form-finding hanging chains, soap films et al   and associated architectural design methods as pioneered by Antonio Gaudi ,Heinz Isler, Frei Otto , Felix Candela and others is common knowledge among architects. This research prototype aims to extend this work to adequately represent the ambitions and complexities of scale digital design systems and delivery mechanisms of contemporary architectural practises. It explores synergies between architectural articulation, engineering logics and fabrication constraints. It continues Zaha Hadid Architects' on-going research on architectural articulation of self-supporting, thin shell ,curved surface geometries.

plan @ 1 :250

sections @ 1 :150

(Left)(Figure 9) ZHA China International Architectural Biennale Beijing 2013
(Right)(Figure 10) ZHA Venice Biennale 2012 Exhibition Board

SHAJAY BHOOSHAN is a MPhil candidate at the University of Bath, UK and a Research Fellow at Institute of Technology in Architecture, ETH , Zurich where he is a research assistant in Block Research Group. He also, heads the research activities of the Computation and Design (co|de) group at Zaha Hadid Architects, London and works as a studio master at the AA DRL Master's program. Previously he worked at Populous, London and completed his Master's Degree AA School of Architecture, London in 2006. His current interests & responsibilities include developing design research and maintaining computational platforms for the same at ZHA. He has taught and presented work at various events and institutions including simAud '14 ,Ingenio '13, Tensinet Istanbul '13, ICFF Bath '12 , Designers Gallery AU '11, Design computation symposium AU '10 , simAUD '10 , Siggraph '08, Yale University and University of Applied Arts , Vienna.

PROCESS COMPENDIUM 2004-2010

CASEY REAS
(A K A CASEY EDWIN BARKER REAS, C. E. B. REAS)

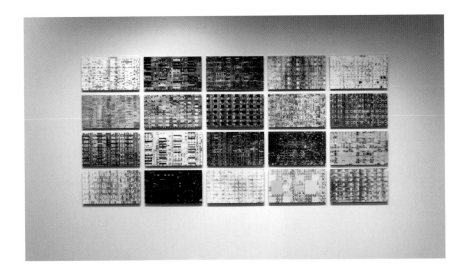

Control Room,
2013, Casey REAS

- This presentation summarizes seven years of following a line. The phenomenon of emergence is the core of the exploration. The system is idiosyncratic and pseudo-scientific, containing references ranging from the history of mathematics to the generation of artificial life.

- We start at the beginning.

// ELEMENTS

- This is Form 1.

- This is Behavior 1.

PROCESS COMPENDIUM 2004--2010 / CASEY REAS (A K A CASEY EDWIN BARKER REAS, C. E. B. REAS)

Constrain to surface

- ...Behavior 2.

Change direction while touching
another Element

- ...Behavior 3.

Move away from an overlapping Element

- ...Behavior 4.

Element 1:
Form 1 + Behavior 1 + Behavior 2 +
Behavior 3 + Behavior 4

- This is Element 1. An Element is a simple machine that is comprised of a Form and one or more Behaviors.

Element 1:
Form 1 + Behavior 1 + Behavior 2 +
Behavior 3 + Behavior 4

- This definition can be written more concisely.

- This diagram shows Element 1 in action: [PAUSE]

- The behavior is easier to see when we add notation.

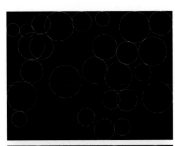

- These arrows show Behavior 1

- These arrows show Behavior 2.

- These arrows show Behavior 3.

- Observe what happens when we restart the system and modify parameters.

PROCESS COMPENDIUM 2004--2010 / CASEY REAS (A K A CASEY EDWIN BARKER REAS, C. E. B. REAS)

- Again, we restart the system and modify parameters.

Element 1

F1: Circle
B1: Move in a straight line
B2: Constrain to surface
B3: Change direction while touching
    another Element
B4: Move away from an overlapping Element

- For review, this is the full definition for Element 1.

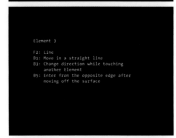

Element 3

F2: Line
B1: Move in a straight line
B3: Change direction while touching
    another Element
B5: Enter from the opposite edge after
    moving off the surface

- Now, we jump to Element 3...

- Note the omission of Behavior 2 and addition of Behavior 5.

- This diagram shows Element 3 in action.

- Observe what happens when we restart the system and modify parameters.

- Again, we restart the system and modify parameters.

- The last Element we'll scrutinize is Element 5.

- Note the addition of Behaviors 6 and 7.

- This diagram shows Element 5 in action...

- Unlike Element 3, notice that the elements form groups as the diagrams runs. They flock together as they search for a common heading.

- In the Library, there are three are currently 2 Forms, 7 Behaviors, and 5 Elements.

// PROCESSES

- Let's push forward.
We're now looking at a software interpretation of Process 4. A Process defines an environment for Elements and determines how the relationships between the Elements are seen.
- Process 4 fills a surface with Element 1 and draws a line between elements while they overlap. When it starts, the Elements have a random distribution, but structure emerges as they execute their behaviors.

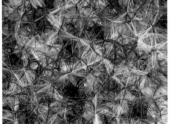

- This is Process 4. The text defines the Process through a description in English; it's written with the intent to interpret its content into software or some other form of dynamic media.
- Like a score, the text defines the work, but it needs to be enacted to be experienced

- This is an alternate interpretation of Process 4. Different decisions were made about how to define the text as code.

- From Process 4, I derived a series of additional work.

- This is a documentation image from Process 4 (Installation 1). It's is a two-channel software projection.

- This is Process 4 (Installation 4) a k a Network A. It's also a projected work. It combines the behavior of Element 1 with recorded drawings to choreograph the Elements. After each Elements has been instantiated, it follows its behaviors.

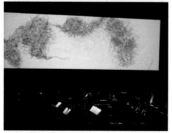

- This is a documentation images of Process 4 (Performance 1), a live visual performance for Music for 18 Musicians, composed by Steve Reich.

- Each Phase of the the music was interpreted visually in a different manner. I was performing the piece by drawing on a tablet from the stage.

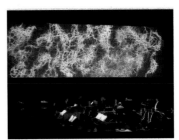

- Here, we have Clad, a series glass fiber reinforced concrete objects; the lines are determined by Process 4.

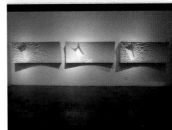

- These are 1:1 architectural prototypes for the Lunar House, a collaboration with the architecture studio davidclovers.

- Moving on, this is a software interpretation of Process 10.

  Like Process 4, Element 1 is the basis of Process 10. But this

  Process exerts more control.

  The Elements can only emerge from the center of the surface.

- This is Process 10

Process 10

Position a circle at the center of a rectangular surface. Set the center of the circle as the origin for a large group of Element 1. When an Element moves beyond the edge of its circle, return to the origin. Draw a line from the centers of Elements that are touching. Set the value of the shortest possible line to black and the longest to white, with varying grays representing values in between.

- Like Process 4, a number of works were derived from Process 10. This is 1 print from a series of 12 images.

- This is another print from the same series

- This detail better shows the resolution and texture of the image

- Process 10 (Installation 1) is a sofware installation derived from Process 10. Each of these disks contains its own system.

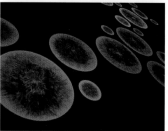

- This image is a more comprehensive view of the installation.

- Moving on, this is a software interpretation of Process 18. It utilizes Element 5.

- When two lines overlap, a shape is drawn from the endspoints of each line to form a quadrilateral. The structure emerges as the Elements find groups.

- This is Process 18.

- The Process works are typically exhibited as a projected diptych, flanked by the instructions. Here we see the Element and the definition on the right, and the Process text and software interpretation on the left.

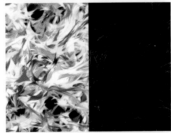

- The right side of the diptych shows the instantaneous interactions between the Elements and the left shows the aggregate surface that records the history of the interactions as an image.

- These are two parallel views of the same system.

- Each Process is exhibited as sofware and with its derived artifacts.

PROCESS COMPENDIUM 2004--2010 / CASEY REAS (A K A CASEY EDWIN BARKER REAS, C. E. B. REAS)

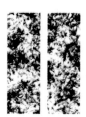

- This is a diptych of c prints from Process 18. Free from the constraints of realtime generative software, the prints evolve within the context of the new medium.

- This is a detail of one print.

- A detail from another print in the series.

- Process 18 was also used to derive a pair of reliefs, milled from a dense fiber composite material.

- This is a detail.

// PROCESS 18 COLOR

- A more recent interpretation of Process 18 shows how the software can be interpreted in a manner that breaks the constraints of the text. In this case, color was introduced to evoke a different quality.

- This sofware variation was used to derive a new series of Process 18 prints. Again, the software evolved within the context of the new medium.

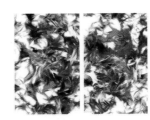

- This is a diptych from a similar series of 5.

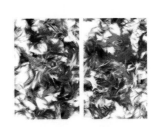

- X

- I recently completed the Process Compendium 2004-2010, a set of fifteen c prints that are the definitive archive of the Process work over the last 7 years. The final moments of this presentation review the fifteen image that comprise Compendium A from Process 18 to Process 4.

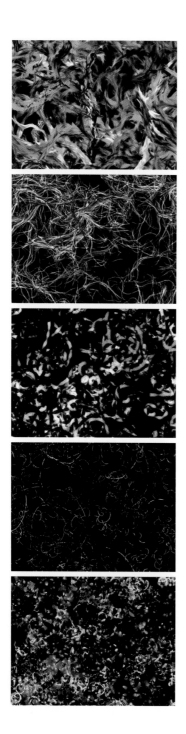

- Process 18

- ...17

- ...16

- ...15

- ...14

PROCESS COMPENDIUM 2004--2010 / CASEY REAS (A K A CASEY EDWIN BARKER REAS, C. E. B. REAS)

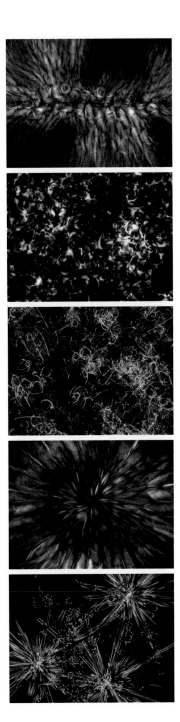

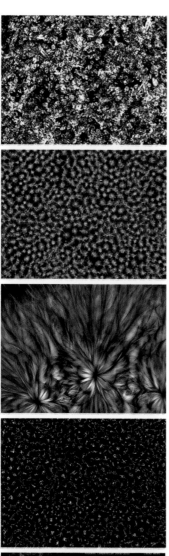

- ...08

- ...07

- ...06

- ...05

- We've now arrived back at Process 4. This is where
we began and it's also the end.

- Thank you.

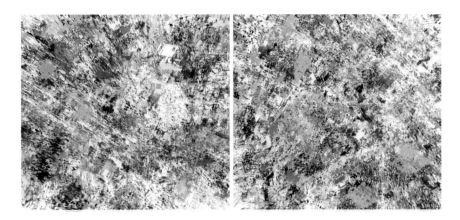

University Texas,
Austin 2014, Casey
REAS

CASEY REAS (a k a Casey Edwin Barker Reas, C. E. B. Reas) Born 1972 in Troy, Ohio. Lives and works in Los Angeles. Casey Reas writes software to explore conditional systems as art. Through defining emergent networks and layered instructions, he has defined a unique area of visual experience that builds upon concrete art, conceptual art, experimental animation, and drawing. While dynamic, generative software remains his core medium, work in variable media including prints, objects, installations, and performances materialize from his visual systems.

Reas' software, prints, and installations have been featured in over one hundred solo and group exhibitions at museums and galleries in the United States, Europe, and Asia. Recent venues include the San Francisco Museum of Modern Art and the Art Institute of Chicago, and recent commissions have been awarded by the Whitney Museum of American Art and the New World Symphony in Miami. Reas' work is in a range of private and public collections, including the Centre Georges Pompidou and the Victoria and Albert Museum.

Reas is a professor at the University of California, Los Angeles. He holds a masters degree from theMassachusetts Institute of Technology in Media Arts and Sciences as well as a bachelors degree from the School of Design, Architecture, Art, and Planning at the University of Cincinnati. With Ben Fry, Reas initiated Processing in 2001. Processing is an open source programming language and environment for the visual arts.

Reas recently co-wrote and designed the book 10 PRINT CHR$(205.5+RND(1)); : GOTO 10 (MIT Press, 2013). Reas and Fry published Processing: A Programming Handbook for Visual Designers and Artists, a comprehensive introduction to programming within the context of visual media (MIT Press, 2007). With Chandler McWilliams and Lust, Reas published Form+Code in Design, Art, and Architecture (Princeton Architectural Press, 2010), a non-technical introduction to the history, theory, and practice of software in the visual arts. Reas' Process Compendium 2004—2010 documents six years of his work exploring the phenomena of emergence through software.

GF42
TRIMARAN

GREG LYNN

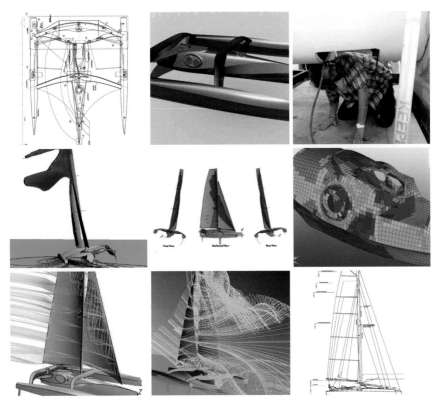

The design, engineering and construction of the GF42 Trimaran was informed by two specific events that occurred in 1999:

The first was the use of the example of a boat hull as a dynamic surface that did not change shape but instead changed orientation relative to movement and force. At the time I was working with animation software, primarily "Wavefront" and "Alias" both of which had simulated physics and particle animations. I was arguing for a use of dynamics for all design and not just the design of mechanical moving structures. Without knowing it I was aligning myself more with a Computational Fluid Dynamics (CFD) approach to design where a flow of particles is used to shape a surface rather than using the particle clouds to define surfaces themselves. As I wrote in the book Animate FORM[1] a decade-and-a-half ago: "Traditionally, in architecture, the abstract space of design is conceived as an ideal neutral space of Cartesian coordinates. In other design fields, however, design space is conceived as an environment of force and motion rather than as a neutral vacuum. In naval design, for example, the abstract space of design is imbued with the properties of flow, turbulence, viscosity, and drag so that the form of a hull can be conceived in motion through water. Although the form of a boat hull is designed to anticipate motion, there

is no expectation that its shape will change. An ethics of motion neither implies nor precludes literal motion. Form can be shaped by the collaboration between an envelope and the active context in which it is situated. While physical form can be defined in terms of static coordinates, the virtual force of the environment in which it is designed contributes to its shape. The particular form of a hull stores multiple vectors of motion and flow from the space in which it was designed. A sailboat hull, for example, is designed to perform under multiple points of sail. For sailing downwind, the hull is designed as a planing surface. For sailing into the wind, the hull is designed to heel, presenting a greater surface area to the water. A boat hull does not change its shape when it changes its direction, obviously, but variable points of sail are incorporated into its surface. In this way, topology allows for not just the incorporation of a single moment but rather a multiplicity of vectors, and therefore, a multiplicity of times, in a single continuous surface. Likewise, the forms of a dynamically conceived architecture may be shaped in association with virtual motion and force, but again, this does not mandate that the architecture change its shape."

During that same year, Prada was using detailed images of the load path oriented laminated fiber sails in their fashion advertisements related to the 2000 Americas Cup campaign they were sponsoring. The image of a wire frame like geometry of superimposed curved fibers immediately caught my attention as well as the attention of other architects from Renzo Piano who designed their training facility ion Valencia years later with used sails as an envelope to Johan Bettum who made several trips to North Sails in Minden Nevada to visit the manufacturing facility and their head of technology Bill Pearson. It became clear to me that sailboat racing was becoming not only a more innovative field than aerospace regarding design but also that it was fabricating at 1/10th the cost of aerospace with similar technology.

|60

These two events drew my attention to boat design and construction along with both Paola Antonelli's "Mutant Materials in Contemporary Design" exhibition at MoMA in 1995 that included many examples of composites including Eric Goetz's carbon laminates for race boats and later Matilda McQuaid's "Extreme Textiles: Designing for High Performance" exhibition in 2005 at the Cooper Hewitt that included North Sails 3DL laminated load path sails. I began working with Bill Pearson at North sails to develop building scale applications of his material and manufacturing on enormous flexible molds and this resulted in the Swarovski Carbon Crystal Sails at Design Miami in 2009 and the Carbon Tape Chair Prototypes for the Art Institute of Chicago in 2010.

The fact that every Sunday that Frank Gehry and I are home we have been sailing together on his boat for the last decade also reinforces the connection between sailboats and design for me. In addition, for six years I sailed and raced my own Beneteau First 36.7 monohull sailboat, complete with North Sails, which is designated as a cruiser/racer and the confluence of professional interests in digital design methods, material interests in construction using composites and a passion for sailing and racing using only the force of the wind and the dynamics of curved surfaces through the ocean instigated my foray into designing a boat.

Working in collaboration with Fred Courouble, a naval and aerospace designer and engineer, we began with the ambition to design a high performance boat that also pushed the field of boat design away from the classic hull plus deck plus cabin paradigm into something with more innovative aesthetics linked to performance. This involved some unprecedented surfaces that combined common sense experience with tested hydrodynamic shapes combined and modified in ways that were unique. The design of a

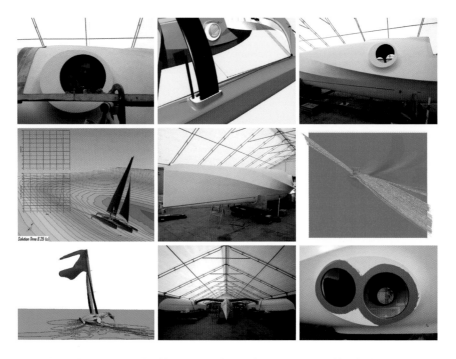

projectile rather than a static object was a rebuke of my own proposition in the 1999 book Animate FORM. It involved the use of software tools that I was familiar with for decades but with a requirement for both high performance as well as the aesthetics of a projectile rather than a mass.

These designs were all tested in a CFD software environment[2] where for six months we were moving between surface models and coupled aerodynamic and hydrodynamic software analysis of those surfaces. The extra volume or reserve buoyancy at the upper surfaces of the forward sections of all three hulls, the flared chines to deflect spray from waves and the volume of the interiors at the back section of the main hull are all examples of surfaces and volumes that were tempered and refined in their shape and magnitude during CFD analysis of the boat's dynamic motion through air and water. In addition, more refined aerodynamic analysis showed areas where flow detached from the surfaces generating drag. Minimizing these red areas of detached flow was used to refine the cockpit, cabin top and platforms for hardware.

Once the surfaces were defined the boat was engineered by Courouble along with Herve Devaux Structures who used Finite Element Analysis (FEA) to define structural loads. Based on the engineering a general omni-directional structural shell of one inner and one outer layer each of 0/90 and +/-45 carbon cloth was woven specifically for the boat. Additional structure was located in shape as well as fiber orientation using primarily

uni-directional carbon as well as some +/-45 carbon cloth in custom shapes; whether stringers, patches or regions. The particular shape and orientation of these reinforcing layers was defined by FEA and the fibers are placed and tapered along FEA determined load paths. This ability to place structure at the scale of fibers in custom orientations runs against the architectural practice of simplifying structural loads to vertical and horizontal paths defined by columns and beams. The experience gained in both the design, engineering and construction of high performance shells using load path oriented fiber and cloth foam sandwich construction has already been informative and provocative with applications to buildings[3].

Finally, every surface and structure was designed in collaboration with designers, engineers and software but in addition much of the construction was done in collaboration with the builders and mold makers. In many cases, including: all of the detail elements to support hardware, winches and electronics; the entire steering system including tillers; and the complete interior including kitchen, bathroom, shelving, couches, seats and beds (excuse my use of furniture and not nautical terminology for these elements); was built using CNC cut molds and laminated using vacuum bagged carbon epoxy laminate of foam cores by Greg Lynn FORM in the office. Small scale molds used by the boat builder Westerly Marine were also fabricated in the office. The 45' long foam tooling for the hulls, arms, floats and cockpit was fabricated by Kreysler Associates on their CNC mill and trucked to Westerly Marine. What would conventionally be metal components such as the rudder arms and steering quadrants were instead 3D printed in fiber reinforced nylon; a first for the use of 3D printing in the marine industry. The intimacy of modeling as well as shaping, smoothing, polishing, laminating and assembling many of the parts myself makes for an intimacy with not only the high-performance object but also the principles and methods of its design and construction. From this design of a projectile much has been discovered that is yet to applied and unfolded back into buildings.

FOOTNOTES

1. Greg Lynn. Animate FORM (New York: Princeton Architectural Press, 1999) p.10.
2. Naimish Barpal of CFD Max, Inc. using STAR CCM+ software.
3. For example in Greg Lynn & Mark Gage (Editors), Composites, Surfaces, and Software: High Performance Architecture (Yale School of Architecture Books), 2011; Michael Bell (Editor), Permanent Change: Plastics in Architecture and Engineering (GSAPP Books, Columbia University), 2014; as well as the design of the INDEX Pavilions in carbon reinforced plastics, the Bloom House ceiling and the Carbon Pavilion for the 2014 AIA Pavilion, both manufactured by Kreysler & Associates.

CREDITS

- DESIGN TEAM: DESIGN & NAVAL ARCHITECTURE: COUROUBLE DESIGN & ENGINEERING, VENICE, CA
- CONCEPT DESIGN: GREG LYNN FORM, VENICE, CA
- STRUCTURAL ENGINEERING: HDS, BREST, FRANCE
- COMPUTATIONAL FLUID DYNAMIC ANALYSIS OF BOAT: CFD MAX, NAIMISH BARPAL, CA
- COMPUTATIONAL FLUID DYNAMIC ANALYSIS OF FOILS: DR. BENJAMIN HERRY, CA
- RIG DESIGN: TORBJÖRN LINDERSON, SWEDEN
- CONSTRUCTION TEAM: BUILDER: WESTERLY MARINE, SANTA ANA, CA
- CNC FEMALE TOOLING HULLS AND ARMS: KRYSLER & ASSOCIATES, AMERICAN CANYON, CA
- ALL OTHER CNC FEMALE TOOLING: GREG LYNN YACHT, VENICE, CA
- INTERIORS & DAGGERBOARDS / FOILS: GREG LYNN YACHT, VENICE, CA
- CARBON SUPPLIER: METYX COMPOSITES, ISTANBUL, TURKEY
- STANDING RIGGING: MARSTROM COMPOSITE AB, VÄSTERVIK, SWEDEN
- RUNNING RIGGING: MARLOW
- HARDWARE: ANTAL

IMAGE CREDITS

All images courtesy of the Author

GREG LYNN was born in 1964. He won a Golden Lion at the Venice Biennale of Architecture, received the American Academy of Arts & Letters Architecture Award and was awarded a fellowship from United States Artists. Time Magazine named him one of 100 of the most innovative people in the world for the 21st century and Forbes Magazine named him one of the ten most influential living architects. He graduated from Miami University of Ohio with Bachelor of Environmental Design and Bachelor of Philosophy degrees and from Princeton University with a Master of Architecture degree. He is the author of seven books.

http://www.glyacht.com/
http://glform.com/

KYLE STEINFELD, LEVON FOXALEX, ALEX SPATZIER

THE DATA MADE ME DO IT,

DIRECT, DEFERRED AND DISSOLVED AUTHORSHIP AND THE ARCHITECTURE OF THE CROWD

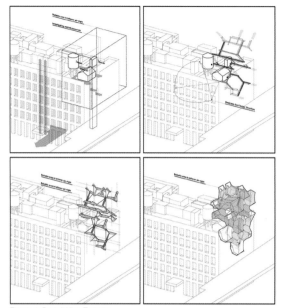

Figure 1: Dongil Kim, Tetrago

Figure 2: Dongil Kim, Tetrago

The balance of agency in architectural design culture is in a constant state of renegotiation. New technologies of design do not directly determine social relationships, but are one actor in the complex social network that link designers to specialists, professionals to clients, software to users, and data to drawings. Competition amongst these forces shapes the diffusion of design authorship and the social distribution of design work. This reality has become especially apparent in recent years, as many cultures of design have embraced new and ever more sophisticated data-driven techniques of automation - including parametric design generation, analysis, and optimization - while simultaneously experiencing major territorial shifts and challenges to their domains of practice.

In today's highly interconnected design practice, the many tasks required to realize a work of architecture are managed by individuals and groups through a varied set of software and digital file formats. While we often pretend that buildings were "designed by" a single architect, in reality we know that actual design most often occurs through a slow accretion of multiple agencies[1]. The myth of designer as sole author is disrupted by the parallel tales of the designer as conduit for client desires, and as mediator of environmental, social, regulatory and economic demands. Despite this reality, the status of expertise in the profession appears to be moved to crisis[2] by recently adopted technologies that emphasize collaboration, and the fact that design agency is increasingly located in neither human subjects nor non-human objects alone, but in the composite associations between them[3]. As computational tools have gained new prominence, so have the voices of those that bemoan the diffuseness of architectural authorship, lament the influence of non-human actors in the design studio[4], and question the role that generative algorithms rightfully play in the design process.

While contemporary discourse in design culture has been focused on the shift from a nostalgic notion of ***direct authorship***, a compositional relationship between a designer and the product of her work, to a multiplicity of ***deferred authorships***, wherein the stakeholders in the production of a design are mediated by systems of collaboration. Procedural design, parametric design, and BIM-enabled collaboration may each be understood as contemporary design systems that mediate the relationship between multiple authors. For the most part, these systems follow in the positivist tradition of applying scientific planning principles to the process of design, and are restricted to accounting only for the empirical and the easily quantifiable. Parametricism, for example, readily integrates structural, environmental, and energetic data, while conveniently and conspicuously leaving intact the subjectivity of the author, merely shifting her locus of authorship from a single design iteration series to that of a system capable of responding to a range of quantifiable variables, thereby producing many possible designs in parallel.

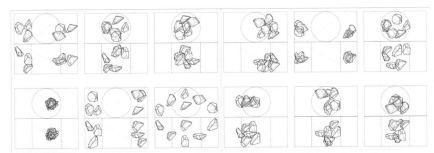

Figure 3: Alan DeMarche, software design by Erica Brett, Collection and Computation of Turker Compositions
Twelve compositions of faceted objects created by Turkers seen in plan and section. Turkers were given instructions to place the objects in some relationship or organization to each other and the boundary given in each view.

Figure 4: Alan DeMarche, Balayan Bay

In our view, current approaches such as these tap only a fraction of the potential latent in the broad category of generative design, and leaves the project of permanently banishing the myth of the designer as sole-author only half-finished. But what would it mean to see such a project through? In this essay, we explore the potentials and problematics of recently emerging technologies that suggest more radical alternative models of agency in generative architectural design. By applying techniques derived from machine learning, recent advances in crowdsourcing have demonstrated that it is now possible to extend the reach of generative design to account for architectural qualities currently left to the intuition of the designer.

However, the new territory opened up by reimagining crowdsourcing as a creative practice is both charged with the potential to invigorate generative design, and fraught with questions that its practitioners are not necessarily best equipped to address. To that end, we begin with a brief accounting of the shared histories of participatory design and computational design – two related narratives that converge in recent attempts to crowdsource architecture. Both finding renewed relevance today while experimenting with alternative modes of design agency.

From Communities to Crowds

The state of design and computation in the mid-twentieth century is no doubt familiar to our reader, as are the ways in which computing contributed to the reconfiguration of a range of disciplines at that time. Two historical forces briefly converged at this moment – participatory design and computational design. Each of which presented their own challenge to the prevailing model of direct authorship in architectural design.

Participatory Design

Throughout its more than sixty year history, proponents of participatory design[5] have sought to bring together stakeholders as equal partners in the realization of a design. Deeply rooted in an understanding of design as a social and political process, participatory design has come to be seen as a powerful agent for the democratization of design by some, and as a way of nullifying design responsibility by others. Contemporary technologies of crowdsourcing and microworking often adopt the rhetoric of this movement, typically in the course of promoting the legitimacy of a public project or the efficacy of a service, but how much do these two non-traditional models of agency in architectural design truly have in common?

Participatory design took root as an idea in the 1960s, disrupting the sole-author model of the architecture and planning process that had found heroic expression in the decade prior. Sherry Arnstein's canonical essay[6] was the first to outline a hierarchy of degrees of participation in the design and planning process in environmental design. In the lower rungs of participation, which Arnstein terms "non-participation" holders of power in the design process seek, at best, to "educate" the participants, at worst aiming to manipulate them into accepting pre-determined solutions. At the apex of Arnstein's ladder is "Citizen Control", wherein participants or residents are in direct control of the governing authority or institution. The central insight of Arnstein's work, one that will be useful in our examination of crowdsourcing in architectural design, was that simple 'participation' does little to bring about a reassignment of power. At both extremes of her spectrum, participants are assumed to hold a vested 'stake' in the design, 'stakeholders' in contemporary parlance. Holding status as a stakeholder, which is to say, any party that may be affected by the results of a design decision[7], is an essential prerequisite for participation under this model.

Design Methods

In a largely separate yet parallel trajectory to participatory design, a confluence of computer-related technologies was actively reconfiguring authorship in architectural design in quite a different way. Many of the designers and technologists driving the changes formed what they termed the Design Methods movement, and while these figures are not often cited in contemporary discussions of generative design, their legacy has had profound influence on our conception of computing in design. A short time after its initiation, the movement suffered a crisis catalyzed by a disagreement over the importance of problem formulation in the process of design. This crisis prompts us to discern two 'generations' of proponents of Design Methods, each envisioning a very different relationship between computing and the social construction of design.

To those belonging to the first generation of the Design Methods movement, including Herbert Simon, Christopher Alexander, and John Christopher Jones[8], there existed no inherent boundary between well-structured and ill-structured problems. A problem only seemed ill-structured until the proper formulation had been discovered[9], a characterization that remains with us to this day, providing the rationale for restricting generative design algorithms to account only for the empirical and the easily quantifiable. Working under this assumption, the most valued contributors to a design are domain experts, and those experienced in problem formulation. The lay public may be invited to participate in an advisory role, as they may possess certain contextual knowledge that would prove valuable, but their contribution would be negligible in comparison to the systemic knowledge of experts. Contemporary approaches to generative architectural design may be seen as the inheritor of those who held fast to this view of problem formation.

In contrast, to the proponents of the later stage of this movement, some problems were inherently and intractably ill-structured. From this point of view, public participation was seen as means not only to improve the quality of design outcomes, but essential to solving the most pressing problems faced by architecture and urbanism. The very definition of social problems are those that resist concrete formulation[10] - so-called "wicked problems". While insights from this period have often been overlooked by mainstream architectural design, they have found relevance in theories of management and computer science, and have formed the basis of an active and on-going line of research in these disciplines termed 'design thinking'[11]. Among the most influential ideas introduced[12] at this time:

The definition of a problem is subjective, such that when defining problems all stakeholders (experts, designers and the public) are equally knowledgeable.

Because one person cannot keep track of the full range of interdependent variables, taming wicked problems requires the cooperation of many people.

Stakeholders must communicate in the process of finding consensus in a problem definition: they must deliberate, persuade, and argue.

In a similar fashion as participatory design, the legacy of both strains of the Design Methods movement has proved disruptive to the sole-author model of design. Leaving aside the concept of 'wicked problems', which quickly converges with a participatory model, even the well-structured problems to which our generative algorithms are so well suited problematize authorship in a similar fashion through mechanisms of encapsulation[13].

Crowds

Figure 5: Alan DeMarche, FairBanks

The methodological and theoretical split between the early and late incarnations of the Design Methods, and the relationship of this movement to participatory design is helpful as we seek to better understand the dynamics of multiple agencies at work in contemporary generative design. While the ill-defined / well-defined schism appears to remain unresolved, an alternative approach to artificial intelligence has been developed that stretches the limits of computability through enlisting the assistance of the public in both problem definition and in the analysis of difficult-to-quantify attributes. Combining traditional artificial intelligence (specifically machine-learning techniques) with user-solicited contributions, an approach that has come to be termed "crowdsourcing" was developed in the early years of the twenty-first century.

In the section to follow, we detail the diverse incarnations of creative work that combines

KYLE STEINFELD, LEVON FOX, ALEX SPATZIER

machine-learning with contributions from an undefined public, all of which may be understood as 'crowdsourced'. Moving through this survey, it will be helpful to keep in mind the related history of participatory design and generative design. The contemporary notion of the crowd differs substantially from that of the participant, and, despite the rhetoric of participation that often surrounds crowdsourcing projects, it would be inappropriate to attempt to position this practice on Arnstein's ladder of participation. Arnstein's participants, for example, are presumed to be stakeholders in the design at hand - a condition which is very rarely true in crowdsourcing. Furthermore, according to Rittel, participation requires argumentation and engagement - a depth of interaction rarely provided by crowdsourced projects. As we shall see in our survey, crowds are necessarily anonymous, and are better understood through the instruments of markets rather than the devices of rhetoric.

We may also find that crowdsourcing confounds both the participatory and generative models: While participatory design remains a viable and active mode of production at urban scales, its ideals are simply not applicable to the anonymity of the crowd. Similarly, the so-called wisdom of crowds has been shown to be superior in certain cases than the domain experts upon which so much of generative design is based. Indeed, the very term was coined in an attempt to capture a disruption of expertise, and how "the internet was helping businesses use amateurs to replace professionals"[14]. Beyond the shift from direct to deferred authorship, the incorporation of this new kind of public in the production of creative work suggests that an entirely new conception of expertise and a new model of authorship will be required.

An Overview of Crowdsourcing as Creative Practice

First emerging in 2005 as a portmanteau of 'crowd' and 'outsourcing', ***crowdsourcing*** was originally understood simply as an "online, distributed problem-solving and production model"[15]. Since then, however, as the practice has been adopted by a variety of discipline, and the meaning of the term has loosened significantly, it has come to more broadly refer to any of a diverse set of practices for obtaining ideas, services, or content through a large group of anonymized individuals. Our survey here addresses these

Figure 6: Alan DeMarche, Delft

practices in rough categories: ***crowdfunding***, ***macrotasking***, and ***microtasking***, with considerably more attention given to the latter, as it suggests the most radical departure from current models of design. As our focus is on crowdsourcing as applied to creative production, we may omit prominent applications of the technique in astronomy[16], genealogy[17], and security[18].

Crowdfunding

Crowdfunding is the practice of soliciting funds for a project by raising small amounts of money from a large number of people. While there are a variety of types of crowdfunding, two have found the widest applicability in creative production: reward/donation-based and equity-based. The former is best recognized in the popular website Kickstarter, while the latter has recently been applied as a model for more traditional investment products, including real estate development.

The reward/donation model of crowdfunding largely functions as unregulated charity rather than investment: backers may give as much as they like in support of a project, and do not receive any security or equity in the project in return, but are sometimes offered a "reward" should the project succeed. Typical rewards include an early release the product under development and/or some form of recognition for having contributed. Only very rarely do they include any sort of participation in the design of the work itself. Mediating this transaction is the Kickstarter website, which takes 5% of any donation, not including another 3%-5% cut for Amazon, who provides a payment system for US donations to the crowdfunding website.

It is difficult to imagine that those who donate to a kickstarter campaign would qualify as stakeholders - although some campaigns do offer early versions of the proposed product in exchange for investment, thereby qualifying backers to be 'users' of the resulting product at best. While the application of this particular crowdfunding model to small to medium-scale design objects has proven successful and quite popular, the suggestion that it might similarly be applied to architectural or urban scales has been met with skepticism at best. Citing the explicit curation of fundable projects performed by Kickstarter employees, Alexandra Lange notes that the site "is not a popularity contest, or a democracy… a suitable funding platform for a watch is not a suitable funding platform for a city. The expectations, the timeline, the relevant community are all wildly different."[19] This skepticism, while common amongst architects, is not to imply a lack of precedent for crowdfunded projects in architectural design.

Crowdfunding in Architecture

Since the success of Kickstarter, the crowdfunding model has been widely popularized in design, embraced for its utility in generating public attention and hype, and, despite skepticism, some attempts have been made at applying the model to architectural design. An emblematic example is the Plus Pool[20], crowd-funded both through Kickstarter and a stand-alone website developed expressly for the purpose. Much like the 'donor brick'

73|

model of fundraising, donations to the project are rewarded with an inscribed pool tile "reserving a spot at the pool"[21].

Other examples of crowdfunded architecture are more ambitions, and present more of a challenge to the dominant model of the social production of architecture. Taking advantage of Title three of the JOBS act[22] of 2012, which included a crowdfunding clause whereby an exemption was created from the requirement to register public offerings with the SEC, developers have expressed an

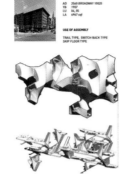

Figure 7: Dongil Kim, Lot 1, Lot2
Interventions generated from a spatial tiling overlaid upon a network generated by a diffusion limited aggregation (DLA) simulation. Growth is modeled as to optimize available light for plant growth and daylighting, lending each resulting volume a variety of potential program configurations.

interest in applying the crowdfunding model to real estate development. A case in point are the BD Bacata and 17 John projects, both ventures by developer Rodrigo Nino[23]. The funding model for both of these projects is a slight modification on the traditional investment model, with stakes in the project priced in units of approximately $20,000 - significantly smaller than the typical stake in such a project, but much larger than the average Kickstarter donation. Speaking of a related crowdsourced design for a larger redevelopment in Bogota, Nino states[24]:

Taking advantage of technology, through social media and the Internet, we invite all the people to participate with different themes that we will raise. Doing that, we will have a clear vision of how the ideal city will be. The Bogota of tomorrow.

Arguably, this model simply reproduces existing structures of design agency, with some of its negative aspects perhaps amplified as investors are even further removed from the process of design and from the longer-term implications of the quality of the design product. In both cases, the developer alone has initiated the crowdsourcing at the service of financing his venture, or in simultaneously publicizing and outsourcing the work of producing a design. Seen in the light of Arnstein's characterization of participation, Nino's claims of empowerment through participation are must be approached with a significant dose of skepticism.

Macrotasking

In contrast to the microtasking model presented below, wherein a large project is broken down and distributed amongst workers, macrotasking presents a project in its entirety to the crowd, who then compete in some way to participate in its realization. A host of web services have sprouted that, like an auction house, enable these market connections[25]. With its emphasis on expanding the scale of markets, Macrotasking seeks to realize a model of perfect competition, wherein a large number of consumers and producers seamlessly interact in a market with low barriers to entry, and all entities have perfect knowledge of prices and processes.

If macrotasking sounds familiar, it may be because it bears a striking resemblance to the social structure of architecture competitions, or the competitive bidding process common in construction, simply transferred to the context of the internet and increased in the scale of participation. While in macrotasking we see crowdsourcing (as the etymology might suggest) enacted almost purely as a form of outsourcing, the rhetoric surrounding this approach is couched in claims of empowerment and the democratization of design: "the power of macrotasking comes from empowering workers to help make decisions"[26]

Macrotasking in Architecture

In addition to being crowdfunded, the two projects developed by Rodrigo Nico are also macrotasked, with designers encouraged to apply to compete to contribute concepts for the new building's "collaborative public spaces," guest suites and digital services. Branded as a 'cotel', Nico's characterization of the role of professional designers in the project reveal the implications of the crowdfunding model for the profession, which threaten to supplant the expensive, high-quality expertise of a professional with an aggregate of cheap, low-quality contributions of amateurs[27]:

We are still working with architects on the project, but now they have taken on a role as judges of the crowdsourcing competition and therefore 'curators' of the project.

A similar suggestion for the transfer of agency from the expert to the amateur may be found in macrotasked marketplace websites, such as Arcbazar. Hewing closely to the architectural competition model, Arcbazar[28] offers a mediated[29] interface between people in the market for design services and those who are presumed to hold the requisite skills

75|

to provide a design solution. The creator of Arcbazar, Imdat As, describes his aim in founding the company as to "expand the architectural design market and offer an alternative path to clients who are not able to access exclusive design services..."[30], thus positioning the service as opening up markets for design that are currently inaccessible to architects. The response to the web service among established architectural designers has been largely negative, a reaction that no doubt confirms the 'disruptive' nature of the service in the eyes of its creator. Dwell

Figure 8: Dongil Kim, Lot 8, Lot 12
Interventions generated from a spatial tiling overlaid upon a network generated by a diffusion limited aggregation (DLA) simulation. Growth is modeled as to optimize available light for plant growth and daylighting, lending each resulting volume a variety of potential program configurations.

magazine called the site the "worst thing to happen to architecture since the internet started"[31]. Less hyperbolic criticisms ranged from expressing labor market concerns (e.g. the site will drive down fees for architecture services and devalue design), design quality concerns (e.g. the site will limit contact between client and designer and result in designs not well calibrated to their environment), and legal concerns (e.g. the credentials of designers are unregulated, therefore the site is aiding and abetting the illegal practice of architecture).

[32] Proponents respond to these criticisms not by extolling the virtues of this 'disruptive' new model of design, but rather by detailing the ways in which crowdsourced design competitions resemble traditional design competitions, and thereby offer the same

mix of challenges and opportunities: the opportunity for notoriety and some modest compensation most appropriate for giving a talented young architect his 'big break'.

Microtasking

In contrast with macrotasking, under the microtasking (or microworking) model, a large project is broken down into a series of small tasks, termed "Human Intelligence Tasks" that are distributed over the internet. Platforms that have developed successful platforms for microwork include MTurk, Crowdflower, LiveOps, and Samasource. Far more than crowdfunding and macrotasking, this model has proven to be transformative in its impact in the field of data science, and suggests a far more profound set of challenges and opportunities in architectural design. As such, we will explore microtasking at some length here, with an emphasis on the most popular platform, Amazon's Mechanical Turk, before discussing some of its potential applications to design.

Originally developed for in-house use, and eventually opened up to the larger world, Mechanical Turk (MTurk) is the world's most active marketplace of micro-work, presenting itself as a platform that connects those that have a discrete computational task (who are known as requesters) to individual human workers willing to accept them (who are known as turkers). Although referred to as Human Intelligence Tasks (HITs), as a way of distinguishing them from Artificial Intelligence tasks (AITs), the nature of the HIT is anything but intelligent. Typical tasks include[33] transcription of small pieces of scanned documents, translation to/from English, classification and 'tagging' of online content, moderating flagged images for offensive content, and, to some degree, content creation in the form of writing short summaries of existing blog posts or articles. The turker's view is that of a cog in the machinery that drives the internet, their labor exponentially divided to the point of dissolution into actions that often require less than a minute to complete, rarely pay more than a few cents per HIT, and, even if completed in rapid succession, result in an hourly rate of less than $5 per hour[34]. Understood through the lens of labor dynamics, the Mechanical Turk marketplace exhibits many of the qualities of a post-fordist neoliberal framework, wherein market fluidity is leveraged in the favor the job-creators and has rendered labor dispensable, disposable, and replaceable[35].

The ethics of Microworking model are contested. Some platforms, such as MTurk, remain conspicuously silent regarding the social dynamics at work, while other platforms adopt the explicit aim of improving the conditions of microworkers, and adhere to defined social impact guidelines[36] that seek to offer workers a way to "overcome poverty and participate in the global tech economy"[37]

Despite the contested ethics of this practice, much of the sophisticated "intelligence" of our web 2.0 experience is not purely algorithmic, but, in fact, relies upon these sort of human-intelligence interventions for calibration and validation. For example, the system that drives matching twitter posts with relevant advertisements is contextually calibrated by a MTurk HIT that displays a tweet, and asks the turker to 'tag' this content

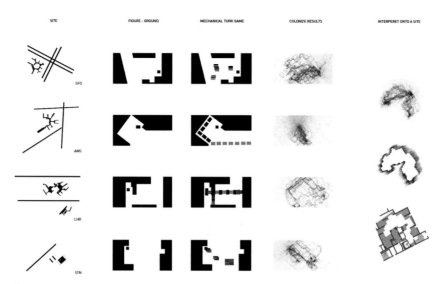

Figure 9: Kelsey Brennan, Figure, Ground
Four international airports are shown through three processes of translation via single, multiple, and algorithmic authors. Operating upon a base interior figure ground, Turkers were asked to compositionally place figure ground blocks. Overlapping block regions are shown in pink. The resulting human translated figure ground is used to run an ANT colony simulation, and are subsequently combined to formulate a site strategy.

with relevant cultural associations[38]. Branded as "artificial artificial intelligence", the system is in this way true to its namesake, an 18th century hoax involving a chess-playing automaton[39].

Building upon the success of MTurk, a range of online services have increasingly adopted a human-computer hybrid model for identifying and managing consumer desire. For example, Netflix's subgenre algorithm, which suggests movies based on a recombination of genre characteristics present in movies the consumer has viewed recently or rated highly, is based on a massive dataset[40] created by paid viewers who are compensated for watching selections from Netflix's archive and classifying them according to weighted tags about as many aspects of the film as possible[41], thus dissolving the high-level functions of a film critic into thousands of micro-tasks that require only low levels of expertise, and are subsequently reconstituted by an algorithm. This model, where human intelligence is 'sampled' to create a basis by which to 'train' a machine-learning algorithm is a common pattern in the development of contemporary AI systems. Taking this system to the next logical step, and moving from data analysis to the generation of new instances, Netflix has since built on this early success in the development of original content precisely targeted and calibrated by trends of micro-genres discovered among its viewers.

While the instrumentation of this practice has taken place in the context of applications that run behind the scenes, the foregrounding of microwork set in the service of creative practice is not without precedent. Most notable is the work of Aaron Koblin, who has produced a range of visual and interactive works using variants of microwork procedures. Among these are The Sheep Market, Bicycle Built for Two Thousand, and Ten Thousand Cents, all of which explicitly address the labor dynamics of microwork, along with two music video collaborations that have been nominated for Grammy awards. In an environmental design context, the range of microwork-driven projects is less extensive. In 2013, cartographer Joseph K. Lee and interaction designer Benedikt Gross used microtasking to map the outlines of 43,123 of L.A.'s pools, and produced a 74-volume set of the results. This absence of work addressing this technique in Environmental Design suggests that foregrounded microwork offers a fertile ground for experimentation in creative architectural practice, especially given the contested ethics of labor at play.

Microtasking in Architecture

The hoax of the Mechanical Turk makes a compelling metaphor for the model of authorship dominant in the architectural profession today: a studio of apprentices executes and actualizes the vision of the master, who, while retaining all the public rights of authorship, is simultaneously divested of certain types of direct agency in the process. Loyal to its namesake, the Mechanical Turk Marketplace offers us a means to intervene into this situation, and to conduct experiments on the diffusion of the design process into human tasks.

Applying the innovations of Amazon and Netflix, architects might supplement the current deficiencies of our own artificial intelligence systems, which we may understand as the ad-hoc synthesis of generative design, parametric design, performance analysis, and optimization. Supplementing these systems of *artificial architectural intelligence* with human intelligence suggests a significant extension of the functionality of existing design tools to move beyond the easily quantified performance metrics, such as the structural and energetic, and to address a host of aesthetic and subjective performances in a generative fashion. Much like the anticipation of structural performances, the projection of an aesthetic spatial experience (arguably the only domain of action that remains solely within the purview of the architect) also requires a predictive capacity for how other human actors will perceive a construction. While we currently rely on the carefully-honed intuition of expert designers, why does aesthetic performance not deserve its own form of numeric simulation? Given technologies that have recently become available, why wouldn't we seek to verify the intuition of designers by drawing upon the aesthetic wisdom of the crowd?

MTurk offers an ideal instrument to do just this. It has been well-studied[42] as an instrument in the social sciences, but more importantly it is a product of new market forces often seen as by-products of the shift to digital culture via ubiquitous computing. How can we begin to integrate these social and economic realities into architectural design? Whether we choose to see them as bugs or features; through Mechanical Turk we now have the socioeconomic structure and technology to manage the integration

78

of diffused human intelligence and micro-preferences into the design process. We are now able to dissolve the compound task of design and distribute the haptic, visual, and experiential analyses of forms, spaces, and materials. We are now able to think as the crowd thinks, operate as it operates, and move as it moves. With MTurk and other crowdsourcing technologies, we can leverage the crowd to lend a sorely needed depth to generative design tools.

We stand on the cusp of a new epoch of generative architectural design, rooted in machine learning, which radically supplants traditional models of direct-authorship in design, suggests new models of deferred-authorship, and

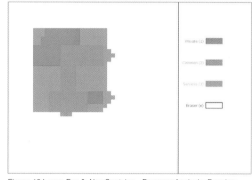

Figure 10:Levon Fox & Alex Spatzier, , Program Analysis: Drawing Interface
The turkers were supplied with an an ultra low resolution version of the ground floor plan of OMA's CCTV tower. Some respondents complained about the image quality, while most were unconcerned.

79|

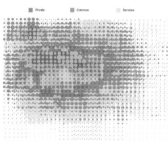

Figure 11: Levon Fox & Alex Spatzier, Composite Drawing of Living Space Results
A halftone overlay of thirty turker-produced house designs. Dots are sized according to frequency of occurrence.

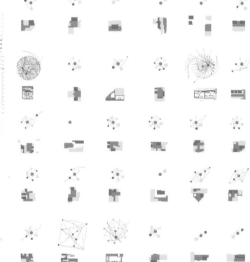

Figure 13: Levon Fox & Alex Spatzier, Sample Graphs
Turker layouts with adjacency calculations and generated graphs.

Figure 12: Levon Fox & Alex Spatzier, Graph Space
Adjacency graphs calculated from a set of thirty turker drawings. In examining the set, we can begin to see when the algorithm accurately summarizes the turkers's intentions, and when ambiguous readings are being created.

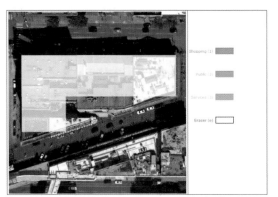

Figure 14: Levon Fox & Alex Spatzier, Pike Place Drawing Interface
The mechanical turk drawing interface, with an edited and rotated image of Pike's Place market in Seattle.

threatens to fully dissolve the solute notion of architect as sole author into the solvent of the crowd.

Direct, Deferred, Dissolved

In contrast with the emphasis on composition required by a direct- and (to a lesser extent) deferred-authorship models, crowdsourced models of design rely on mechanisms of statistics and search. In recognition of the shift to a digital mode of production, this new approach to architectural design integrates automated analyses and consumer participation: a crowd-sourced regionalism that is more demographic than geographical. The move toward dissolved authorship reflects the integration of the user into the process of production. Just as human analysis of data is used to train artificial intelligence routines, which are then used to create new sets of data; the cycle between architectural consumer and producer suggests an open endlessly repeating loop. Through feedback, changes may be made and users may become integrated into the process of production and reproduction. Over time, the roles of individual authors in this collective endeavor inevitably shift - some authors become obsolete, others alter their scope of operation, and new authors will assert themselves. Here we begin to understand the full implications of authorship dissolved, that collective authors can only be understood and defined relative to temporal cycles of use and production.

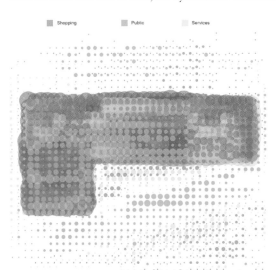

Figure 15: Levon Fox & Alex Spatzier, Composite drawing of Market Place Site Results
A halftone overlay of the turker submitted program zoning schemes for this shopping district.

Figure 16(left): Levon Fox & Alex Spatzier, Turker Response: Market Place Site
Different drawings implied a range of understandings of scale, as well as varying degrees of complexity.
Figure 17(center)): Levon Fox & Alex Spatzier, Turker Response: Market Place Site
Figure 18(right): Levon Fox & Alex Spatzier, Turker Response: Market Place Site
Some turkers seemed set on subverting the task at hand.

The integration of the turker and the dissolution of the design process raises unique questions about the nature of authorship, and consequently the role of the designer in the production of architecture and architectural space. As we examine these projects which integrate Human Intelligence Tasks with well understood computational methodologies, we might find it productive to ask:

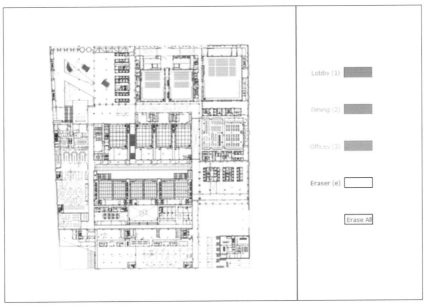

Figure 19: Levon Fox & Alex Spatzier, Program Analysis: Drawing Interface
The turkers were supplied with an an ultra low resolution version of the ground floor plan of OMA's CCTV tower. Some respondents complained about the image quality, while most were unconcerned.

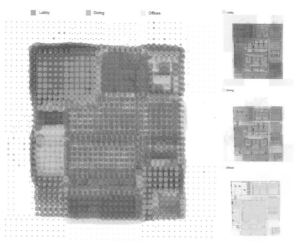

Lobby   Dining   Offices

Figure 20: Levon Fox & Alex Spatzier, Program Analysis: Composite Image
A halftone overlay of the turker submitted program analyses of an existing floorplan.
The shapes from the original floorplan begin to become legible again.
Figure 21: Levon Fox & Alex Spatzier, Program Analysis: By Program Type
The site colored as to how frequently the various types of program were assigned to
different areas.

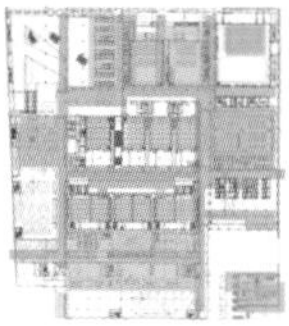

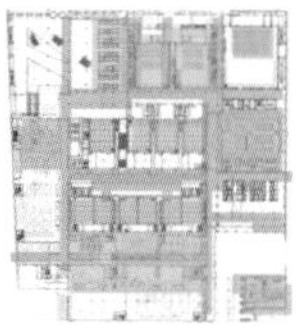

Figure 22: Levon Fox & Alex Spatzier, Turker Response: Program Analysis
Some of the turkers filled out the entire floor plan.
Figure 23: Levon Fox & Alex Spatzier, Turker Response: Program Analysis
Some chose to diagram the "lobby" space as a set of circulation paths, as opposed to
the large rooms shown above.
Figure 24: Levon Fox & Alex Spatzier, Turker Response: Program Analysis
Others intentionally left large areas and connecting pathways blank; maybe to account
for other types of program, circulation, or perhaps the poche of architectural space.

What does architecture know about the crowd, and what does the crowd know about us?

Should the fiction of the author be maintained, despite its increasing inaccuracies, or can it be productively modified to include our current social realities and our hopes for the future?

How are HITs best structured or designed to further understanding and produce generative results?

What are the diverse implications of the dominant modes of crowdsourcing practice, and how is agency distributed when applied to design?

|82

Towards an Architecture of the Crowd

We present below a number of experiments on how microwork and human intelligence can be integrated into existing computational and generative design practices, seeking to uncover arenas in which this integration is productive as well as those that it is not. There are many potential pitfalls, and one of the reasons we have focused on Mechanical Turk at this stage is its explicit, direct, and visible relationship to many of the problems, ambiguities, and inequities of the global labor force enabled by these new technologies.

The work depicted here is not necessarily positioned as models of design worth emulating, or even as likely future models of design, but rather endeavor to make explicit the relationship between the algorithmic and the subjective, and to reveal the potential subjectivity of both non-experts and non-human agents in the process of architectural design.

A Crowd of Principals

The esquisse, the initial sketch in the hand of the architect, can be seen as one of the last bulwarks of heroic authorship in the increasingly diffuse, collaborative, and cyclical contemporary design process. The esquisse was taken as a parti, a diagrammatic drawing which captures the essence of a design. All the work that takes place from here forward is presented as a linear progression, a faithful translation of the ideas in the sketch into their logical, buildable conclusions.

But this is largely a fiction, and a significant portion of the labor of design actually occur after the sketch. Furthermore, the idea of the napkin sketch is often apocryphal, and may actually be a reaction to, or critique of, many designs produced during a charrette, and many sketches are made throughout the process by many actors, and serve as, clarifying, communicative, or speculative gestures. Somehow, though, the myth of the initial sketch stubbornly persists as one locus of authorship and design authority.

What if the sketch were, in the parlance of our times, disrupted, and this locus of inspiration were passed off to the crowd? If a sketch were algorithmically composited from the aggregated whims and impressions of the crowd, then this 'gestural will', which might otherwise be

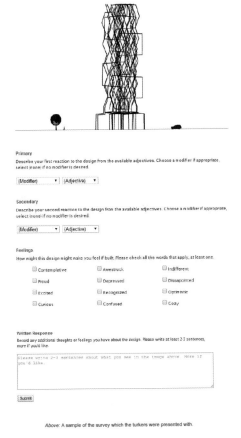

Above: A sample of the survey which the turkers were presented with.

Figure 25: Levon Fox & Alex Spatzier, Survey Example
A sample of the web survey viewed by the turkers

KYLE STEINFELD, LEVON FOX, ALEX SPATZIER

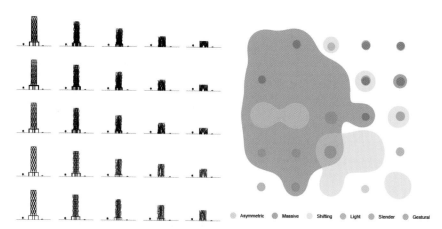

Figure 28: Levon Fox & Alex Spatzier, Hearst Tower Manhattan to TOD's Omotesando, Parameter Space
Turkers were shown a single design from the design space grid and asked a series of questions.
Figure 29: Levon Fox & Alex Spatzier, Hearst Tower Manhattan to TOD's Omotesando, Adjective Islands
Turkers were provided with six adjectives, of which only one could be chosen to describe the design. These "adjective islands" show the entire survey's responses. A small dot represents at least two responses.

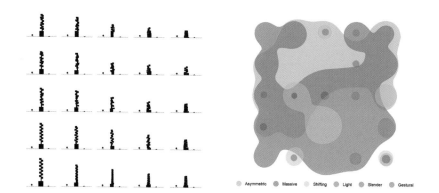

Figure 26: Levon Fox & Alex Spatzier, 80 South Street To New Museum, Parameter Space
Turkers were shown a single design from the design space grid and asked a series of questions.
Figure 27: Levon Fox & Alex Spatzier, 80 South Street To New Museum, Adjective Islands
Turkers were provided with six adjectives, of which only one could be chosen to describe the design. These "adjective islands" show the entire survey's responses. A small dot represents at least two responses.

misconstrued for true authorship, could be removed almost entirely from the equation. In this scenario, the role of the architect would mostly remain, as would the majority of the process and labor of architecture: staying true to design intent while realizing a built work which satisfies the numerous constraints and demands of the project.

While there are a number of genres of sketch that could be used as a generative source and could be implemented by the crowd (including formal gestures, expressions of site

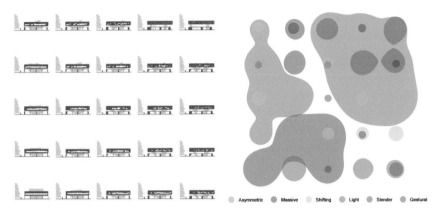

Figure 30: Levon Fox & Alex Spatzier, Villa Savoye à Poissy to Maison à Bordeaux, Parameter Space
Turkers were shown a single design from the design space grid and asked a series of questions.
Figure 31: Levon Fox & Alex Spatzier, Villa Savoye à Poissy to Maison à Bordeaux, Adjective Islands
Turkers were provided with six adjectives, of which only one could be chosen to describe the design. These "adjective islands" show the entire survey's responses. A small dot represents at least two responses.

85|

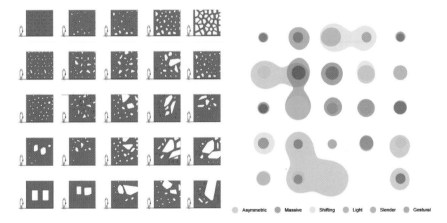

Figure 30: Levon Fox & Alex Spatzier, Villa Savoye à Poissy to Maison à Bordeaux, Parameter Space
Turkers were shown a single design from the design space grid and asked a series of questions.
Figure 31: Levon Fox & Alex Spatzier, Villa Savoye à Poissy to Maison à Bordeaux, Adjective Islands
Turkers were provided with six adjectives, of which only one could be chosen to describe the design. These "adjective islands" show the entire survey's responses. A small dot represents at least two responses.

conditions, and environmental response), here, as a proof of concept, we have chosen to explore the production of programmatic zoning diagrams through MTurk using two discrete HITs. We can use the data generated by these HITs to test methodologies for representing the work of a composited author. The image presented here is proto-architectural, and may eventually engage the architectural through the addition of information. To create sketches from a composited author requires techniques that result in a drawing which is simple and diagrammatic, yet either implies a set of relationships, or is annotated in such a way that expands or specifies the meaning already present in the drawing.

The first HIT offered to the microworker is to design the layout of a space for people to live, using three colors designated as common areas, private areas, and service areas. An open field was presented to the turker, but the amount of each color they could use was constrained. People came up with a variety of responses: the majority colored in at least some of the regions completely, some outlined regions, some people created exploding pixelated canvases, causing us to wonder whether these few drawings were very deliberate or the result of scribbling across the canvas. Of the people who created regions, some of them diagrammed continuous spaces, but many also included some white space within their composition, which in some cases appears very deliberate, and in others may just be a result of running out of "ink" before they could finish.

To begin to understand and describe these drawings as a set, the drawings were converted into graph representations that describe the adjacencies between program areas. These serve as a quick visual summary, and can also be compared statistically. More importantly for our purposes, when applied to some of the more complicated turker responses - those that don't fit the general pattern or those that lie on the border between legible types - they begin to produce results that are interesting, complex, and suggestive.

For our second experiment, we showed the turkers an aerial grayscale image of Pike's Place market in Seattle with an L-shaped area highlighted, and asked them to code areas to describe a shopping area on the site. They were again given a limited amount of three colors, representing shopping areas, public spaces, and private service areas.

The majority of turkers "colored within the lines", siting the majority of their programmatic spaces within the highlighted L-shape.
A significant subset chose to site a large portion of their program activities outside of the highlighted area, effectively expanding out onto the site. As above, this example also resulted in a small subset of deliberately off-topic and clearly representational drawings.

Finally, for a third experiment, we asked the turkers to use a similar applet to analyze and zone a low-resolution image of an existing floor plan as an 'orthographic Rorschach test'. We again gave the turkers a choice of three colors, one for lobby spaces, one for dining spaces, and one for office space. This time, however, we let them use as much of each color as they wanted. In light of our other results, these results are predictable, and it was easily the most well understood and earnestly attended to of the three tasks, with one turker contacting us about their confusion and even making an offer of further services:

"The plan wasn't clear to read even when I enlarged the screen, but I did the best I could. It would help to know the function of the building...is it educational, or corporate office, or museum, or hotel, etc.... Not all

the areas could be color coded (not enough color). PS. I have an office space planning background (more than three years actual experience in this field) if you really need help in this."

- Worker A3056EIAMR68GJ

We were not actually seeking a determination, or verdict, from the crowd as to how this building should be used. Instead, we sought to develop a set of techniques for composite reading and analysis that is simultaneously suggestive and directive, yet lacks any explicit specificity - much like the esquisse. The resulting documents do not explain, but are charged documents for discussion. This process does not directly uncover a mode of understanding crowdsourced representational thinking, but rather initiates a guided, productive, search for it.

A Crowd of Critics

The process of critique - through pin-ups, group meetings, juries, and journalistic criticism - is deeply embedded in the production of architecture. Despite the prominent role that critique plays, we lack in existing generative and computational design processes a method for the integration of explicit subjective analyses of design based upon the aesthetic, phenomenological, psychological, and a whole family of other qualities that are difficult to quantify and objectify. There are, as of yet, no plugins to ask whether a design is 'cute', or how it might make one feel. Still, subjective aesthetic judgments clearly drive designs that are self-consciously generative, and lie latent in contemporary cultures of generative design, which tend to adhere to specific aesthetic dictates that have no explicit technological correlation. With this experiment, we ask the ***crowd*** to become the ***critic***, and in doing so, seek to make explicit the role that subjective emotive analysis might play in the generative process.

The experiment is structured to highlight the role of machine-human learning, and how one might use the crowd to calibrate an aesthetic fitness function in a design optimization process. To integrate human analysis we generated four simple parameterizations - design spaces in hypothetical 'tweens' between iconic designs, as seen the in two dimensional matrices nearby. Each turker was shown one design from each of the four design spaces:

Santiago Calatrava's (unbuilt) 80 South Street residential skyscraper in the bottom-left corner to SANNA's New Museum of Contemporary Art in the top-right corner.

Foster + Partners' Hearst Tower in Manhattan (lower-left) tangles into Toyo Ito's TOD's Omotesando building in Tokyo (upper-right).

Le Corbusier's Villa Savoye à Poissy transmutes into OMA's Maison à Bordeaux.

A canonical set of rectangular windows fractures into a Voronoi window.

The turker was asked to describe each design using the grammar listed below, the contents for which were sourced from architectural criticism in popular media:

87|

- A single choice from 6 primary descriptors: *Slender, Massive, Shifting, Light, Gestural, Asymmetric.*

- A single choice from 12 secondary descriptors: *Soaring, Precious, Clear, Sexy, Organic, Cartoonish, Rugged, Bold, Monumental, Civic, Complex, Generic.*

- A set of descriptor modifiers allowed further specification of their primary and secondary choices: *Generously, Radically, Strikingly, Not-at-all, Contrastingly, Less-than, Disappointingly, Exceptionally, Fantastically, Somewhat, Broodingly, Poetically, Rebelliously, (none).*

- One or more choices from the following 12 feelings: *Contemplative, Awestruck, Indifferent, Proud, Depressed, Disappointed, Excited, Recognized, Optimistic, Curious, Confused, Cozy.*

Finally, a short 2-3 sentence written response was solicited, with a minimum requirement of 5 words be they English or gibberish.

We present the condensed result of the survey in form of a graphic overlay upon the two dimensional design space for each of the four parameterizations. The purposeful ambiguity of these island drawings highlights our desire to heighten the reader's awareness of the imprecise nature of the survey. In this graphic, the larger the adjective's region the more prominent it manifested in the survey. Below these colorful figures, one can see the design spaces themselves with each design's elevation shown on the parameter space.

While some matter of consensus is interesting and present in our results, we did not seek statistical averages or significance. Rather, the many diverging opinions and readings can are useful for their own merits, each suggesting a possible new direction for design. The individual and open-ended comments provided by each turker provide a sense of their analytic depth and, in some cases, reveal a technical, social, and/or cultural sophistication. Take the following responses for the first design space, *80 South Street to New Museum*:

"Confusion may result from a relatively sudden brain dysfunction. Acute confusion is often called delirium (also called acute confusional state),[5] although delirium also includes a much broader array of disorders than confusion (e.g. inability to focus attention; and various impairments in awareness, or temporal and spatial orientation). Confusion may also result from chronic organic brain pathologies such as dementia."

- A Critic's written response, this text was most likely sourced by the Turker from the English Wikipedia page on Mental Confusion.[43]

This subversion of our survey raises questions concerning the time-money economics of crowd-sourced labor, and the imperative to quicken the pace of work. Has the critic chosen to express their confusion about the survey through this uncited quotation or was this merely the fastest way to earn their reward?

A large segment of Critics interpreted the instructions as meaning they should describe the image:

"A car and a man going in opposite direction..a lone tree is standing on the left side of the high tower building"

"Man standing in the side of the well designed building"

"One lady is walking. Beside her, there is a board."

"Well looks like a child's drawing rather than a designed object."

One Critic (now a Theorist), perhaps unknowingly, wrote a brief manifesto. The first *Crowded* Manifesto:

"all designs should be unique and should be formal"

A few went beyond their call and critiqued our representation, bringing up an important issue concerning the public reception of representational techniques considered to be conventional in environmental design:

"Well looks like a child's drawing rather than a designed object."

A few personalized their response, revealing their mask of the crowd:

"Sorry, this looks like a concrete bunker built by the Germans to defend the Atlantic coast during World War 2. The roof is reminiscent of the camouflaged reinforced concrete bomb-and-artillery protective cover over an artillery emplacement. Not the most positive association."

"It reminds me of the winter time in Michigan. We had a very bad winter this year. Looks like snow."

Some incorporated their personal preferences into their response, also revealing of their identities and personal biases:

"I think this design has too many lines. I prefer more solid structures, and ones that are more practical."

The meta description, an understanding of our intentions and representation and critiques of our representational choices:

"It shows an innovative modern building. To describe the size of the building a human being, a tree and a car is shown"

"The building shape looks nonfunctional and just for design sake. Its unnatural design does not express itself well in black and white. I feel nervous and uneasy pondering its stability."

The comparison to previously encountered or widely known designs:

"I like the design. It feels a little uneasy at first glance, but then gives a feeling of comfort, as it is reminiscent of some Japanese architecture that I admire."

The Comedian in the Crowd

"The design is looking very strange and funny. its look like an old man laughing. Thank You."

The Critical Philosopher:

"This design feels busy to me. It feels like it represents city life. There's the traffic, the skycrapers, the occasional greenery, and the people, who are very small in the grand scheme of it all."

The Structural Critic and formal analysis:

This Building is very asymmetric in shape and structure. Engineers should do their part of load bearing calculations because this whole asymmetric building is build on pillar foundation.

"my first reaction is how does it stay up? The spine of the building appears thin and fragile. However the blocks give it a more robust sturdy impression."

Socialist:

"BUILDING STRUCTURE SHOULD BE STRAIGHT AND VERTICAL. IT SHOULD BE BUILT FOR THE POOR PEOPLE TOO. IT SHOULD BE BUILT USING A GOOD QUALITY MATERIAL."

FOOTNOTES

1. Yanni Alexander Loukissas. Co-Designers: Cultures of Computer Simulation in Architecture. Routledge, 2012.
2. Anders Hermund. "Building Information Modeling in the Architectural Design Phases: And Why Compulsory BIM Can Provoke Distress among Architects." In Computation: The New Realm of Architectural Design, 75–82. Istanbul, 2009.
3. "Algorithm Given Seat on Board." BBC News, May 16, 2014. Accessed Jun 24, 2014. http://www.bbc.com/news/technology-27426942.
4. Michael Graves. "Architecture and the Lost Art of Drawing." The New York Times, September 1, 2012, sec. Opinion / Sunday Review. Accessed Jun 24, 2014. http://www.nytimes.com/2012/09/02/opinion/sunday/architecture-and-the-lost-art-of-drawing.html.
5. Also termed cooperative design, community-based design, and user-centered design in the engineering disciplines
6. Sherry R. Arnstein, "A Ladder Of Citizen Participation." Journal of the American Institute of Planners 35 (1969, 4): 216–24. doi:10.1080/01944366908977225.
7. R. Edward. Freeman, Strategic Management: A Stakeholder Approach. (Boston: Pitman, 1984).
8. John Christopher Jones ed., Conference on Design Methods: Papers. (London: Pergamon Press, 1963).
9. Herbert Simon, "The Structure of Ill Structured Problems." Artificial Intelligence 4 (1973, 3-4): 181–201.
10. Horst Rittel and Melvin Webber, "Dilemmas in a General Theory of Planning." Policy Sciences 4 (1973, 2): 155–69.
11. The Institute of Design at Stanford largely follows in this tradition.
12. The list shown here was adapted from Chanpory Rith and Hugh Dubberly "Why Horst W. J. Rittel Matters." Design Issues 23 (2007, 1): 72–74.
13. Kyle Steinfeld, "Public, Private, Protected: Encapsulation and the Disempowerment of the Digital Architect." Room One Thousand 1 (2013, Spring / Fall). Accessed July 4th, 2014 http://www.roomonethousand.com/index/#/public-private-protected/
14. William Safire, "FatTail." The New York Times, February 8, sec. Magazine (2009). Accessed July 4th, 2014. http://www.nytimes.com/2009/02/08/magazine/08wwln-safire-t.html.
15. Daren C. Brabham, "Crowdsourcing as a Model for Problem Solving: An Introduction and Cases." Convergence: The International Journal of Research into New Media Technologies 14 (2008, 1): 75–90. doi:10.1177/1354856507084420.
16. Zooniverse – About https://www.zooniverse.org/about Accessed Jun 25th, 2014.
17. Family Search Indexing: Home. https://indexing.familysearch.org/newuser/nuhome.jsf?3.24.1 Accessed Jun 24th, 2014.
18. recaptcha. http://www.google.com/recaptcha/intro/index.html Accessed Jun 25th, 2014
19. Alexandra Lange, "Against Kickstarter Urbanism." Design Observer (May 5th, 2012). Accessed July 4th, 2014. http://observatory.designobserver.com/feature/against-kickstarter-urbanism/34008/.
20. The Plus Pool was designed by Dong-Ping Wong, Archie Lee Coates IV and Jeffrey Franklin, see Billy Gray, "PlayLab and Family Design Team Makes a Splash With Floating + POOL." Commercial Observer. September 24, 2013. Accessed June 24, 2014. http://commercialobserver.com/2013/09/playlab-and-family-design-team-makes-a-splash-with-floating-pool-project/.
21. "+ POOL." Buy a Tile, Build a POOL. Accessed June 24, 2014. http://www.pluspool.org/tilebytile.
22. Jumpstart Our Business Startups (JOBS) Act. 2012. http://www.gpo.gov/fdsys/pkg/BILLS-112hr3606enr/pdf/BILLS-112hr3606enr.pdf.
23. Eduadro Said. 2012. "BD Bacatá: The World's First Crowdfunded Skyscraper." ArchDaily. http://www.archdaily.com/276433/bd-bacata-the-worlds-first-crowdfunded-skyscraper/.
24. "Colombia's Tallest Skyscraper Inspires Crowdsourced City Design." Prodigy Network. Accessed June 25, 2014. http://en.prodigynetwork.com/bd-bacata/colombias-tallest-skyscraper-inspires-crowdsourced-city-design/.
25. Prominent examples include Elance, oDesk, Fiverr.com, 99designs.com

26. "Crowdsourcing: A Breakdown.", Crowdsourcing.org. Accessed June 24, 2014. http://www.crowdsourcing.org/document/crowdsourcing-a-breakdown/15930.

27. Rory Stott. "Rodrigo Nino: In Defense of Crowdsourcing and Crowdfunding." ArchDaily, April 24, 2014. Accessed June 24, 2014. http://www.archdaily.com/499150/rodrigo-nino-in-defense-of-crowdsourcing-and-crowdfunding/.

28. Imdat As, "Arcbazar." http://www.arcbazar.com/. Accessed June 24, 2014

29. The overhead is roughly competitive with Kickstarter, as Arcbazar takes 15% of the total 'prize' amount.

30. Imdat As and Maria Angelico, "Crowdsourcing Architecture: A Disruptive Model in Architectural Practice." In Proceedings of the 32nd Annual Conference of the Association for Computer Aided Design in Architecture (ACADIA 2012.), 439–43. San Francisco.

31. dwell (@dwell), "This Is the Worst Thing to Happen to #architecture since the Internet Started: Http://www.arcbazar.com/ #designers #devalued #again". January 16th 2011. Accessed June 21st, 2014. https://twitter.com/dwell/status/26889122173947904.

32. Michael J. Crosbie, "Why Criticisms of Crowdsourcing Don't Add Up.", ArchDaily. Accessed June 21st, 2014. http://www.archdaily.com/497828/why-criticisms-of-crowdsourcing-don-t-add-up/

33. Panagiotis G. Ipeirotis, "Analyzing the Amazon Mechanical Turk Marketplace." XRDS 17, no. 2 (December 2010): 16–21. doi:10.1145/1869086.1869094.

34. Ipeirotis, "Analyzing the Amazon Mechanical Turk Marketplace." p20

35. James Ferguson, "Global Disconnect: Abjection and the Aftermath of Modernism." In The Anthropology of Globalization, edited by J.X. Inda and R. Rosaldo, 136–53. (Malden, MA: Blackwell Publishing, 2002)

36. "Samasource Social Impact Guidelines" Samasource. Accessed June 25, 2014. http://samasource.org/mission/how-we-work/.

37. TEDxSiliconValley - Leila Chirayath Janah. 2009. http://www.youtube.com/watch?v=1Ce9EfF2lHE&feature=youtube_gdata_player.

38. Eileen Brown, "Twitter Turns to Amazon's Mechanical Turk Judges to Deliver More Contextual Ads." ZDNet, January 10, 2013. Accessed Jun 25th, 2014. http://www.zdnet.com/twitter-turns-to-amazons-mechanical-turk-judges-to-deliver-more-contextual-ads-7000009649/

39. "Artificial Artificial Intelligence." The Economist (Technology Quarterly, Q2: June 8, 2006). Accessed June 25, 2014. http://www.economist.com/node/7001738

40. James Bennett and Stan Lanning, and Netflix Netflix. 2007. "The Netflix Prize." In In KDD Cup and Workshop in Conjunction with KDD.

41. In total, there exist 76,897 unique genre classifications on Netflix, see Alexis C Madrigal's attempt to reverse engineer the Netflix's algorithm and interview with VP of Product Todd Yellin: Madrigal, Alexis C. "How Netflix Reverse Engineered Hollywood." The Atlantic, January 2, 2014.

42. Gabriele Paolacci, Jesse Chandler, and Panagiotis G. Ipeirotis. Running Experiments on Amazon Mechanical Turk. SSRN Scholarly Paper. Rochester, NY: Social Science Research Network, June 24, 2010.

43. A google search using the response confirmed our suspicion that the response was copied from another source. http://en.wikipedia.org/wiki/Mental_confusion#Causes. Accessed 20:13 Wednesday June 24th, 2014.

KYLE STEINFELD, Assistant Professor specializing in digital design technologies in the Department of Architecture at UC Berkeley, is the author of the "Archtiect's Field Guide to Computation", in contract with Routledge to be published in 2015, and the creator of Decod.es, a platform-agnostic geometry library, and a collaborative community that promotes computational literacy in architectural design. He teaches undergraduate and graduate design studios, core courses in architectural representation, and advanced seminars in digital modeling and visualization. He has been the recipient of a number of fellowships for research in design technology, most recently serving as an IDEA fellow at Autodesk in 2014 and as a Hellman Fellow in 2012. Professionally, he has worked with and consulted for a number of design firms, including Skidmore Owings and Merrill, Acconci Studio, Kohn Petersen Fox Associates, Howler/Yoon, Diller Scofidio Renfro, and TEN Arquitectos. His research interests include collaborative design technology platforms, design computation pedagogy, and bioclimatic design visualization. He holds a Masters of Architecture from MIT and a Bachelor's Degree in Design from the University of Florida.

SATORU SUGIHARA

GUIDELINES FOR THE AGENT BASED DESIGN METHODOLOGY FOR STRUCTURAL INTEGRATION

—

INANIMATE MATERIAL PHYSICS SIMULATION AND ANIMATE GENERATIVE RULES

Abstract

The agent-based design methodology has been recognized as a powerful design methodology to generate emergent, self-organized, complex, and yet consistent architectural designs through the implementation of behavioral rules. However, the development of this methodology is still in the early phases; various designers are currently attempting to create effective behavioral rules for agents. One of the areas where this methodology provides an advantage is in structurally integrated architectural design, where structural materials and space-making materials are highly integrated. This methodology provides designers with a way to encode structural material behaviors in agent behaviors, facilitating structurally integrated architecture. This paper proposes guidelines for behavioral rule design in agent-based algorithms for structurally integrated architecture design. Two different types of agent rules will be articulated: material physics rules to simulate material behaviors and generative rules to generate and reconfigure
a material configuration. The paper seeks to examine the mechanism of these behavioral rules in nature, whether animate or inanimate. To demonstrate the agent-based design methodology using the proposed guideline, a case study of a lightweight, wire-hung gallery installation was designed and constructed. The results of the case study show the effectiveness of the guidelines in achieving efficiency of material integration and
a generative quality in the design outcome. It also demonstrates certain challenges with integrating material physics rules and generative rules to make them interact reciprocally.

Introduction

The bottom-up design approach is rapidly becoming one of the most important approaches in contemporary architectural design practice (Sugihara 2011a). Computation using agent-based algorithms is the major tool in this approach. However, the development of methodology for the design of agent-based algorithms in architecture is still in an early phase, and various designers are making attempts to create effective behavioral rules for agents (Baharou and Menges 2013; Parascho et al. 2013; Sugihara and Mayne 2013).

An agent-based algorithm, in the broad definition given in section 3, is abstract and flexible enough to contain a wide range of agent rules. In addition, it can perform various types of computations that are equivalent to some existing algorithms, including particle-based physics simulations, genetic algorithms, L-systems, and cellular automata. To establish an agent-based design methodology in architecture, it is necessary to explore various effective agent rules, acquire a systematic understanding of the algorithmic characteristics of agent rules, and establish guidelines for the design of architectural agent rules. To contribute to this establishment process, this paper proposes guidelines for the design of agent rules for structurally integrated architectural design, where structural materials and space-making materials are highly integrated.

Animate and Inanimate Behaviors in Material Computation

Material computation is a term to describe a design approach with an active use of material properties for form-finding, fabrication, and construction (Menges 2012a, 2012b).

93 |

Traditionally, this approach is executed via experiments with physical materials (Otto and Rasch 1995), but today it is often performed by conducting computer simulations of material behaviors (Fleischmann et al. 2012; Schwinn et al. 2012). A wide range of material properties can be considered in this approach, including thermal response, moisture response, light transmittance, and surface tactile properties, but the primary properties considered are typically structural properties, such as load-bearing capacity and elasticity in compression, tension, and bending.

In a form-finding process that considers material behaviors, material configurations, and an environmental setting, the material computation approach can yield generative design qualities that are beyond a designer's ability to predict or are too complex to be controlled by a designer via other methods. On the other hand, material behaviors sometimes merely execute a process of structural optimization, which implies that, in comparison to form-finding, the outcomes of this process are simply fine-tuned results without increasing generative design qualities. This happens when material behavior experiments or constructions are performed in a static material configuration and in an environment without physical energy inputs. In this case, the process is governed by the physical principle of minimum energy, and the material system tries to reach a minimum or local minimum energy state at equilibrium.

This difference between form-finding and structural optimization has an analogy in the comparison of animate and inanimate nature. Inanimate nature is governed by the principle of minimum energy, whereas animate nature is driven primarily by energy exchanges between living organisms. However, inanimate objects or systems can sometimes exhibit complex and consistent animate qualities through complex interactions of different types of matter and various processes of energy exchanges; examples include geographical features, such as river networks and coastlines. Thus, animate and inanimate nature can be seen as a continuum rather than two distinct states. This applies to form-finding and structure optimization reciprocally as well. Form-finding by material properties and structure optimization are two extreme states of a physical, force-driven process with a continuous range of generative qualities in their results.

The definition of a generative quality is vague; although, it is sometimes associated with non-linearity (Frazier 2002). To perform further analysis of design processes, this paper presents a tentative definition of the generativity of a design process based on material behaviors for structurally integrated design as follows:

A design process that processes design inputs to an outcome is more generative when (1) complexity in a topological relationship of formal components increases or (2) formal complexity is increased if the topological complexity remains the same. Figure 1 shows examples of changes in topological complexity and formal complexity. The second measurement of formal complexity can be seen when the change is not large enough to be perceived as topological change, which implies that changes in topology and form are continuous and equivalent to moves in a certain direction and magnitude in the same morphospace (Schwinn et al. 2012).

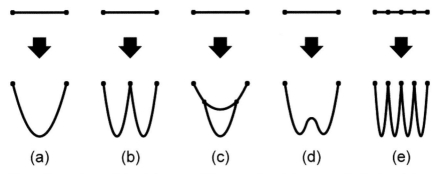

Figure 1: Diagram of generativity in a design process. (a) No topological complexity change and low formal complexity increase. (b) Topological complexity increase with emergence of a structural node. (c) Topological complexity increase with emergence of a structural link. (d) No topological complexity and high formal complexity increase. (e) No topological complexity change from the input configuration and low formal complexity.

Some examples of traditional design processes driven by material behaviors are more generative than others. Note that the design processes discussed here are only those parts driven by material behaviors and do not include designers' efforts to explore and set up material configurations before starting any experiments or construction. Frei Otto's soap film experiments (Figure 2) showed the process to create minimal surface area with equal tension distribution. When material configuration is set with a specific closed frame, the process of forming a surface with soap film does not change topological complexity and the formal complexity of the outcome is proportional to the complexity of the frame. The same applies to the example of a suspended chain (Figure 3). After a human-based design process to find a preferable material configuration with structural anchors and chain connections, the design process executed by material behaviors and gravity does not significantly change topological complexity nor increase formal complexity unless the configuration is complex. Antonio Gaudi's suspended model showed a certain complexity (Figure 4), but this complexity can be accounted for by the complexity of the architect's elaboration of the material configuration with highly topological connections and controlled weight distribution.

In contrast to those examples, other design process examples have shown an increase in topological complexity. The experiment of bubble clusters for pneumatic structure showed a

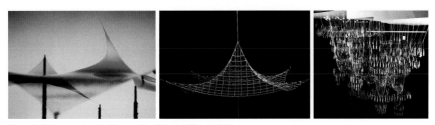

Figure 2: Otto's experiment with soap film (Otto and Rasch 1995).
Figure 3: Otto's experiment with suspended chain (Otto and Rasch 1995).
Figure 4: Gaudi's catenary model (Otto and Rasch 1995).

capacity to generate topological changes if the material process was controlled by pneumatic or thermal energy to create a dynamic reconfiguration of the structural connections of membranes (Figure 5). Experiments involving hydrated and dehydrated threads to create structural paths with branched construction increased topological complexity through bundling initially independent threads as a result of the energy of hydration and dehydration (Figure 6). The bifurcation points of bundled threads emerged dynamically, functioning as structural connection nodes (Figure 7). As result of this comparison, the bubble clustering process and the thread hydration and dehydration process showed higher generativity than other design processes.

In addition to generativity, another property was also evident in those design processes: behavioral similarity between materials in the experimental design processes and materials for the final target construction. If the material for the target construction was tensile membrane or wire, the experiments with suspended chain and soap-film surfaces would have

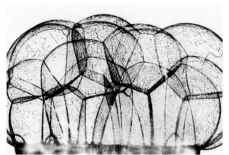

Figure 5: Otto's experiment of bubble clusters (Otto and Rasch 1995).

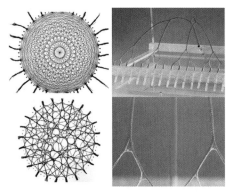

Figure 6: Otto's experiment with hydrated and dehydrated threads for creating a branching structure in two dimensions (Otto and Rasch 1995)
Figure 7: Otto's experiment with hydrated and dehydrated threads for creating a branching structure in suspension (Otto and Rasch 1995).

a greater similarity in tensile structural behavior to the target. The target construction of Gaudi's suspended model translated the model upside down and interpreted tensile behaviors as compression behaviors. Although the structural behaviors were opposites, this still lends support to the efficiency and rationality of the load paths. However, form-making behaviors imposed by gravity cannot be expected in the target construction. In the experiment involving hydrated and dehydrated threads, the network of bundled threads was likely to be replaced by segmented structural members and connection nodes; the target construction process would not have equivalent forces to the attraction forces that bundle threads in the experiment. This comparison of behavioral similarity suggests that if an extra energy exchange process like the hydration and dehydration process is the key to a higher generativity and the target construction processes tend to lack an equivalent process, any design method used needs to consider more than target material behaviors to achieve a higher generative quality in the outcome.

Computability of Agent-Based Algorithm and Guidelines for Agent Rules

In the broad definition of an agent-based algorithm, an agent is modeled as an entity with states and behaviors. Behaviors are rules meant to change an agent's own states, change the states of other agents, create new agents, or delete existing agents. An agent-based algorithm, then, is defined as an iteration of execution of all existing agent rules.

Different agent-based modeling tools use different techniques. Some agent-based modeling tools, such as NetLogo, distinguish subtypes of agents: agents with a location that can be changed by other agents (for example, particle, insect, and animal agents), agents with a location that cannot be changed (for example, cellular automaton, grid cell, environment, and attractor force agents), agents without location (for example, observer and gravity force agents), and agents with references to two other agents to represent a connection (for example, tension line agents) (Tisue and Wilensky 2004). Agentsheets restructure behaviors by using conditions to read agents' states and actions to change various agents' states (Repenning and Citrin 1993). iGeo restructures behaviors by using interaction behaviors to read or change other agents' states and update behaviors to change an agent's own state (Sugihara 2012b). Any of these models is capable of implementing physics simulations within the algorithmic frameworks because most physical laws are described as a set of differential equations, and these equations can be translated into agent rules to update their states as approximations in discrete time. Table 1 shows an example of this process in the translation of Newton's second law of motion into a pseudo-code for a particle-based physics simulation.

Table 1: Example of translation of physics rules to agent's rules.

The Second Law of Motion	Pseudo Code of Agent's Rule for Simulation of Motion
$F = ma$	agent.acceleration = Force/agent.mass
$= \dot{a}$	agent.velocity += agent.acceleration * timeIncrement
$= \dot{v}$	agent.position += agent.velocity * timeIncrement
F : external force vector	Force: force vector given by self or other
m : mass	agent.mass: agent's state of mass
a : acceleration vector	agent.acceleration: agent's state of acceleration vector
v : velocity vector	agent.velocity: agent's state of velocity vector
r : position vector	agent.position: agent's state of position
	timeIncrement: time interval of the algorithm iteration

In contrast to physics simulation rules, agent-based algorithms are abstract enough to describe rules that don't follow the laws of physics, such as creating agents, deleting agents, generating energy, and removing energy. When an agent-based algorithm simulates a biological phenomenon in animate nature, it contains those non-physics rules, such as growth and reproduction rules, without complying with the principle of minimum energy. These different types of rules can coexist in an agent algorithm because of the open-ended model of agent interactions. Multiple types of rules in an agent and multiple types of agents can exist together in the same simulation sharing the space and time.

As suggested in section 2, a generative design process for structurally integrated architectural design needs to have material behaviors that lead the design outcome to minimum energy at equilibrium but must also incorporate other behaviors that dynamically reconfigure the material configuration for higher generativity. An agent-based algorithm is capable of containing both behaviors simultaneously by performing a material physics simulation and a simulation of agents with nonphysics rules. Thus, I propose the following guidelines for the design of agent rules to achieve a high generative quality in design outcomes in the agent-based design methodology for structurally integrated architecture:

Agents should contain rules to simulate material behaviors to take advantage of the construction material's properties for structural integration (material physics rules).

Agents should contain rules to generate and dynamically reconfigure material configurations (generative rules).

Case Study of an Agent-Based Design Methodology

This case study was conducted to demonstrate the agent-based design methodology when following the proposed guidelines for structurally integrated architectural design and also to evaluate the validity and effectiveness of the proposed guidelines. The case study is a gallery installation entitled A(g)ntense, which was built and exhibited at the design exhibition "Blindspot Initiative Group Exhibition" in Los Angeles in 2014.

Design of Agent Rules

To follow the proposed guidelines, the agent-based algorithm should incorporate material physics rules to simulate the construction materials, along with generative rules to control material configurations. The target construction materials in the case study were high-strength fishing wires that provided high tensile capacity and acrylic sheet material used to provide rigid support to hold compression loads. The agent rules were, therefore, designed to simulate the tensile behavior of fishing wires and rigid support of acrylic sheets. To generate a network of tensile links and rigid links, the generative rules were added to the algorithm based on self-organizing swarm behaviors, along with force field rules to control the movement of the swarm agents.

The material physics rules were implemented in three agent classes: a structural node agent class, a rigid link agent class, and a tensile link agent class. The structural node agent simulated particle-based physics behaviors with properties of mass, position, velocity, force, and friction. It received forces from other agents and moved accordingly. It also connected multiple tensile links and rigid links. The rigid link agent connected two structural node agents and transferred compression loads to them; it also constrained the distance of two nodes to be a given length of the link. The tension link agent also connected two structural node agents and assigned tensile forces to them.

The generative rules were implemented into swarm agent classes, force field classes, and a force field controller agent class. The swarm agent class contained the swarm behaviors with rules for cohesion, separation, and alignment. The cohesion and alignment rules were implemented for consistency in the generated form of the swarm trajectories. The separation rule was for the construction constraint of minimum distance between two node joints. The swarm agent incorporated three behaviors to generate the configuration of the material simulation agents. First, it created the structural node agent in a certain time interval at the location of the swarm agent. Next, it created the tensile link agent to connect the structural node agent created at the current time frame and another structural node agent that was created in the recent past. Finally, it created the rigid link agent to connect the current structural node agents and other node agents that were created in the same time frame by other swarm agents and that existed within a certain proximity. The proximity rule corresponded to the maximum size constraint in the fabrication.

Three different classes of force field agents were used in the algorithm to control the movement of the swarm agents in a larger range than the local range that was controlled by the swarm behaviors. The first was an attractor force field agent used to generate an attraction force or repulsion force from its center point. The second was a spinning force field agent used to generate spinning force around its center point. The third was a force field operator agent that compounded multiple force fields by choosing only the closest field to be applied to the swarm agent, rather than the linear summation of all forces. Note that forces generated by these agents were applied only to the swarm agents, not to the material physics agents.

Another agent class implemented in the algorithm was a force field controller agent class, which contained multiple instances of force field agents; it changed their force intensities and moved their center point locations through time. So as to exhibit two different directionalities in the flow of swarm trajectories, two subclasses of the swarm class were created, and two groups of force field agents were used for each swarm subclass.

In addition to those behaviors implemented in different agent classes, several more rules were added to some of the agent classes to deal with certain design issues. One issue was that the material physics behaviors in the agent algorithm described above lacked rigid moment behaviors for the acrylic material. There should be a behavior to resist bending between two lines of the rigid link agents. However, to maximize the efficiency of the computation load and algorithm development workload, a simpler behavior was added to the structural node to stay on the same z coordinates all the time. The behavior of the tensile link agent was also modified. Instead of simulating a fixed-length string that caused zero tension if the distance between the two end nodes was smaller than the length and high tension with high elasticity if the distance was larger than the length, the behavior was simplified to generate tension proportional to the length at all times. In this behavior, the agent did not simply follow the material configuration with each member's length but actively self-optimized the wire length to generate a more optimal overall form under the topological relationship created by the generative rules.

Another rule that was originally implemented but later removed was a feedback rule linking the agents using material physics simulations to the agents using generative rules. More specifically, the swarm agent had a rule to connect the swarm agent itself with the structural node agent using a tensile link agent. It was meant to further integrate the material physics simulations and generative rules but because the result showed more limited behaviors of the swarm agent, decreasing generative quality in the outcome, this rule was omitted in the final application. The implication of this behavior is discussed more in section 5.

The agent-based algorithm in this case study was developed on Processing with the iGeo library (Sugihara 2012b). Most of the agent classes were not implemented from scratch because the library contains implementations of basic agent classes, including particle, swarm, tensile line, attractor, spinning force field, and compound force field agents. Furthermore, custom behaviors can be added and modified by class inheritance of the basic agents using the method overriding technique. Geometries created in the library were exported to a Rhinoceros file along with layer information and ID names for individual geometries for the purpose of fabrication management.

Fabrication and Construction

The geometry model generated in the agent-based algorithm was taken into another computational process to prepare for fabrication. The process for the laser-cutting fabrication of acrylic sheets involved a number of steps. The horizontal rigid link lines on each z level were reconnected with 2-D Delaunay algorithms to remove intersections and to create enclosed shapes. Next, outlines and triangle lines of the Delaunay patterns were converted into degree-2 NURBS curves for stylistic consistency with the smooth flow of swarm trajectories. Most of the triangular curves were kept to make holes, minimizing material weights; small triangles were removed to minimize laser cutting time. The structural nodes were converted into slotted holes on the acrylic sheets for the joints with labels of ID names of the wires scored into the sheets (Figure 8). To fabricate tensile wires, the generated 3-D polylines were unrolled for drawing sheets and marked with joint-tying locations. Unrolled wires contained extra length to account for what was consumed by tying ring joints (Figure 9).

The joint used to attach the fishing wire and acrylic sheets consisted of two interlocking metal rings: one was tied onto the wire, and another was loose on the wire. The acrylic sheets had slots that were small enough to put a ring through; once both rings went through, they interlocked, holding the acrylic sheet when the wire was pulled.

Based on the agent-based design process and the computational process for the fabrication, 31 layers of acrylic sheets and 153 tensile fishing wires were produced. The tensile wires were divided into four segments to make construction more manageable, and a total of 5,508 ring joints were tied onto the wires. Construction of the final installation involved first attaching the wires to the ceiling and then installing the acrylic layers from the top to the bottom. After installing the acrylic sheets and adding weights and tension to the wires, the sheets moved to their optimal location by

| 100

LAYER 11   LAYER 23

LAYER 19   LAYER 29

Figure 8: Examples of laser cutting paths for acrylic sheets.

themselves; the overall form was naturally created as modeled in the simulation (Figure 10).

Discussion

The case study of the installation A(g)ntense successfully demonstrates the agent-based design methodology using the proposed guidelines. The completed installation exhibits a close integration between form and structure, using acrylic sheets as a rigid support structure and fishing wires as a tensile structure. The material physics simulation leads the form to exhibit minimum energy at equilibrium; it's stable under the effect of gravity. The simulated behavior is precise and the assembled materials create the modeled form naturally, without using any jigs or temporary supports. The effect of gravity alone moves the materials into place, creating the desired final form. This proves the effectiveness of using material physics rules in the agent-based algorithm.

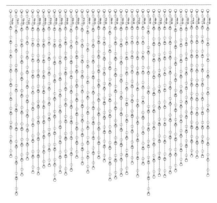

Figure 9: Examples of unrolled tensile wire drawings.

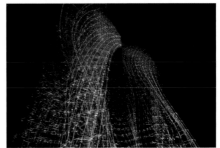

Figure 10: Completed installation (photo by Taiyo Watanabe).

The alternative to using generative rules is to use a manual design process to produce the desired material configurations, which are then used as an initial condition for the material physics simulation. When pursuing complex design outcomes, the initial material configuration is also complex, meaning that producing this configuration manually is very difficult. Applying generative rules overcomes this challenge, creating a complex and self-organized material configuration that also contributes to a complex and self-organized quality in the design outcome.

Because there are infinite possibilities for what agent behaviors can be used to create generative rules, the validity of using swarm behavior and force field agents in this case study is not obvious. However, the trajectories generated by swarm behaviors are suitable for tensile wire structures, and the proximity-based rigid link generation rule is suitable for material size constraints. For comparison purposes, Figure 11a shows the result of using a simpler material configuration in which the tensile lines are all straight lines proceeding in random directions, but the rigid link generation follows the same proximity-based rule as in the case study. In this example, many tensile lines fall down straight because many structural nodes on the random lines are placed farther than the proximity range of the horizontal rigid links. In contrast, the swarm behavior agents used in the case study include the cohesion rule, causing structural nodes to occur closer to connections by the rigid links. The result shows a greater degree of self-organization (Figure 11b). Figure 11c shows the case mentioned in section 4.1, in which the material physics rules contain a feedback rule that was later abandoned, connecting physically simulated and optimized structural nodes with the swarm agents by tensile links. The purpose of this feedback rule was to have more integration between generative behaviors and material physics behaviors. However, the result shows that the physics simulation constrains the movement of swarm agents and reduces the generative quality of complexity in the final design. To keep a higher complexity in the design outcome, this feedback rule was omitted in the algorithm of the final design scheme. Although this suggests that it is difficult to integrate feedback of material physics behaviors with generative behaviors, it is still desirable to develop a closer integration between the two, along with reciprocal interactions. This is especially true when we take inspiration from animate nature and how animate phenomena or living organisms interact and are integrated with inorganic matter.

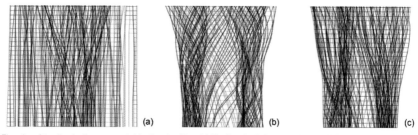

Elevation of tensile wire lines generated by the algorithm. (a) Physics simulation on random straight tensile lines. (b) The final scheme using the swarm agent rules. (c) The algorithm using the tensile feedback rule from the structural node to the swarm agent.

The case study uncovered one more feature of the generative rules that may be beneficial in the construction process. When some part of the generative rules creates a material configuration by adding new material components, this part of the rules seems to govern the growth of the material configuration. If these growth rules reflect construction constraints and sequences, the design outcome can satisfy the constraints; the growth process in the simulation would suggest the construction process and sequence for the real-world execution of the project. In the case study, the swarm agents start from the top and generate a network of material agents and rigid links gradually as they move toward the bottom of the structure. This setting of the swarm behavior made it easy to work with the construction constraint of structural anchor points located on the ceiling because those points can be fed to the algorithm as the initial locations for the swarm agents. This growth behavior can be observed in Martin Tamke's installation The Rise (Tamke et al. 2013), which used material physics rules and generative rules in its computation process. Its material configuration in branching network form was developed through branching and grafting behaviors executed from the ground upward. This growth process in the simulation can suggest an efficient and rational construction sequence for the final construction process.

A number of conclusions can be reached through observation and analysis of the case study. Simulation of material behaviors in a closed system using material physics rules can generate a static and stable outcome in equilibrium, driven by the principle of minimum energy. In contrast, applying generative rules configures and reconfigures material relationships and properties without complying with the principle of minimum energy. Whereas material physics rules correspond to examples seen within inanimate nature, generative rules correspond to animate nature. From the comparisons in Figure 1 and Figure 11, we can redefine a generative quality in design as a level of energy at equilibrium. A state of high-energy equilibrium means a high generative quality, whereas a state of low-energy equilibrium indicates a low generative quality (Figure 12). To have the optimal material integration for high efficiency, a design outcome should reach equilibrium—but to have a high generative quality, it needs to have a leap of energy. The generative rules can be viewed as a process that provides a surge of energy to cause that leap. In this case, highly generative design outcomes reside in local minima, not in the global minimum, on the energy landscape in morphospace. In terms of thermodynamic energy levels and states, we see a similar difference between low-energy equilibrium and high-energy equilibrium in inorganic matter and living organisms. Inorganic matter is governed by the principle of minimum energy and always lead to the low-energy equilibrium unless there is an external energy input. On the other hand, living organisms resist the principle of minimum energy by consuming extra energy, keeping their energy levels high but at equilibrium by using the constant flow of metabolism. If we further expand the nature analogy in architecture, architects' pursuit of truly generative and materially integrated design methodologies would go along with scientists' pursuit to understand emergence of living organisms out of inorganic matter. In other words, computational morphogenesis leads to computational abiogenesis.

Conclusion and Future Vision

This paper proposes guidelines for the design of agent rules in an agent-based methodology

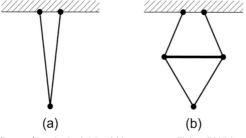

(a)   (b)

A diagram of two structural states. (a) Low-energy equilibrium. (b) High-energy equilibrium.

for structurally integrated architectural design. These guidelines consist of (1) material physics rules to simulate material behaviors, taking advantage of the properties of construction materials for structural integration; and (2) generative rules to generate and dynamically reconfigure a material configuration to create a generative quality in design outcomes. In addition, a component of the generative rules can be (3) growth rules to dynamically generate material components and connections for generativity and efficiency in the final construction sequence.

The case study project demonstrates the use of the agent-based design methodology following these proposed guidelines. The result shows the effectiveness of incorporating material physics rules and generative rules to simultaneously achieve efficiency and a generative quality. However, the result also shows the challenge of integrating material physics rules and generative rules and encouraging their reciprocal interaction without sacrificing the desired generative quality. By following the analogy of nature in architecture, it suggests that the key to overcoming this difficulty and to developing the agent-based design methodology further lies in the difference between inanimate and animate nature and in the mechanism of how living organisms emerge out of inorganic matter.

A(g)ntense: Installation of swarm formation and agent based self-optimization of tensile and compression structure Satoru Sugihara, The Blindspot Initiative, 2014.

REFERENCES

- Baharlou, E., and A. Menges. (2013). Generative Agent-Based Design Computation: Integrating Material Formation and Construction Constraints, In proceedings of the 31th eCAADe Conference, eds. R. Stoufffs, S. Sariyildiz, 165-174. Delft: eCAADe 2013.
- Fleischmann, M., J. Knippers, J. Lienhard, A. Menges, and S. Schleicher. (2012). Material Behaviour: Embedding Physical Properties in Computational Design Processes. In Architectural Design, vol. 82 no. 2, ed. A. Menges, 44-51, London: Wiley Academy.
- Frazer, J., J. Frazer, X. Liu, M. Tang, and P. Janssen. (2002). Generative and Evolutionary Techniques for Building Envelope Design. In 5th International Generative Art Conference. Milan: Generative Art 2002.
- Menges, A. (2013a). Material Computation: Higher Integration in Morphogenetic Design. In Architectural Design, vol. 82 no. 2, ed. A. Menges, 14-21, London: Wiley Academy.
- Menges, A. (2013b). Material Resourcefulness: Activating Material Information in Computational Design. In Architectural Design, vol. 82 no. 2, ed. A. Menges, 34-43, London: Wiley Academy.
- Otto, F. and B. Rasch. (1995) Finding Form: Towards an Architecture of the Minimal. Munich: Edition Axel Menges.
- Parascho, S., M. Baur, E. Baharlou, J. Knippers, and A. Menges. (2013). Agent-Based Model for the Development of Integrative Design Tools. In proceedings of the 33rd annual conference of the association for computer aided design in architecture, 429-430. Cambridge, Ontario: ACADIA 2013.
- Repenning, A., and W. Citrin. (1993). Agentsheets: Applying Grid-Based Spatial Reasoning to Human-Computer Interaction. In IEEE workshop on visual languages. 77-82 Bergen, Norway: IEEE Computer Society Press.
- Schwinn, T., O. Krieg, A. Menges, B. Mihaylov, and S. Reichert. (2012). Machinic Morphospaces: Biomimetic Design Strategies for the Computational Exploration of Robot Constraint Spaces for Wood Fabrication, In proceedings of the 32nd Annual Conference of the Association for Computer Aided Design in Architecture, 157-168. San Francisco: ACADIA 2012.
- Sugihara, S. (2011a). Comparison between Top-Down and Bottom-Up Algorithms in Computational Design Practice. In proceeding of the international symposium on Algorithmic Design for Architecture and Urban Design. Tokyo: ALGODE 2011.
- Sugihara, S. (2011b). iGeo: Computational Design Library. http://igeo.jp.
- Sugihara, S., and T. Mayne. (2013). Irregularity and Rationality Mediated by Agents: Modeling Process of Phare Tower. In Architecture in Formation, ed. P. Lorenzo-Eiroa and A. Sprecher, 254-257. New York: Routledge.
- Tamke, M., D. Stasiuk, and M. Ramsgard Thomsen (2013). The Rise—Material Behavior in Generative Design. In proceedings of the 33rd Annual Conference of the Association for Computer Aided Design in Architecture, 379-388. Cambridge, Ontario: ACADIA 2013.
- Tisue, S., and U. Wilensky. (2004). NetLogo: Design and Implementation of a Multi-Agent Modeling Environment. In proceedings of Agent 2004 Conference, Chicago: Agent 2004.

SATORU SUGIHARA is a principal and founder at the computational design firm ATLV founded in 2012. Prior to start his firm, he worked as a computational designer at Morphosis Architects for five years engaging in large scale construction projects, competition projects and research projects. He also worked at DR_D and Greg Lynn FORM as an architectural designer, and at International Media Research Foundation in Tokyo as a researcher in media art and interaction design. He is currently a faculty member at SCI-Arc teaching computational design seminars. He also taught computational design at the University of British Columbia, Ecole Nationale Superieure d'Architecture Paris-Malaquais, Woodbury University and Tokyo University of the Arts. He publishes open source computational design software iGeo to contribute to the computational design industry and education by sharing what he developed for his computational practice of complex geometry modeling, performance optimization and geometry rationalization and dynamic agent simulation.

Satoru Sugihara received his M.S. in computer science from Tokyo Institute of Technology in 2001 and his M.Arch. from the University of California, Los Angeles in 2006.

MATERIAL COMPUTATION: THE COLLIER MEMORIAL DESIGN USING ANALOG AND DIGITAL TOOLS

HÖWELER + YOON ARCHITECTURE
OCHSENDORF DEJONG & BLOCK

The contemporary enthusiasm for history as reservoir of technique, if not of form, is well documented in journals such as *Log 31*, The New Ancients, and the preservation journal *Future Anterior*. Whereas previous returns, such as the postmodernisms of the 1980's were marked by an interest in history as a source of form, image and language, the current returns seem to be marked by an interest in history as an instrument. The contemporary interest in plasticity, continuities, vaulted forms, and profile generation seem to be looking to historical techniques. This recovery of techniques is often coupled with new computational tools and specific commands: sweep, loft, split, etc. Another version of this contemporary is a new appreciation of pre-mechanical building systems: passive thermal strategies, use of mass and materials for thermodynamic purposes, as well as an interest in primitive forms and primitive techniques. Thermal mass is mobilized as an energy strategy. The use of large volume monolithic materials reduces joints and assembly time, while the deployment of massive stone blocks produces other material effects.

The Sean Collier Memorial at the Massachusetts Institute of Technology (MIT) falls within this category of contemporary historical instrumentality. Its design consists of a five-way flat stone vault buttressed by five slender radial walls. Situated where Officer Collier was shot and killed in April of 2013, the memorial marks the site with a contemporary masonry structure—translating the phrase "Collier Strong" into a structure that embodies both strength and unity.

The stone arch is among the most elemental of structural organizations, ordering materials in space and transferring loads in pure compression. The geometry of the arch visually indexes the flow of forces through a material, transferring loads from stone to stone, and translating *force* into *form*.

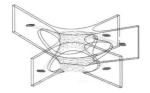 

The choice to use an un-reinforced masonry structure to memorialize Officer Collier is significant. The shallowness of the massive stone vault overhead creates an effect of suspension and weightlessness, while the tapered geometry of the individual stone blocks reveal the keystone geometry of the masonry arch. The design of un-reinforced masonry structures typically requires a form finding method, whereby all parts of the structure remain in compression during all loading scenarios. Funicular geometries explicitly follow the lines of force rendering visible the thrust lines within the masonry material. Analog techniques utilize the principle known as Hooke's Law which defines the correspondence between a hanging chain in pure tension and the inverted arch in pure compression for a given set of loads. Weighted physical models were famously used by Antoni Gaudí to form-find geometries in masonry and by Frei Otto to design the Olympic Stadium in Munich. These techniques use a physical model to "compute" the geometry of the arch or the membrane, and test the ability of the structure to support the range of applied loadings due to self-weight and live loading.

Building on the analog techniques of the past, the design of the Collier Memorial is representative of a synthetic approach to contemporary form-making, using a combination of tools, methods, models, and software platforms to arrive at an overall form. Central to the refinement and optimization of the design is the iterative analysis and modification of the force polygon, mapping and reconfiguring all the force vectors in each stone of the vault. This method, generated with computational graphic statics, is typically performed on simple arch configurations in two-dimensions. The 5-way vault arrangement required the graphic statics calculations to be performed in five individual segments, dividing the vault into radial pie-slices. Computational tools developed by ODB (Ochsendorf DeJong and Block) allowed the five-way vault geometry to be analyzed to ensure the global stability of the vault under gravity loads for conceptual design, allowing real-time feedback on static implications of any variation in the location and dimensions of the buttressing walls. The interactive thrust line analysis is implemented in Grasshopper and is pseudo-3D, with the thrusts from each of the five walls acting on a compressed plate at the center of the vault. To verify the solution and confirm reaction values, fully three-dimensional structural analysis is carried out via thrust network analysis, also implemented in the Rhinoceros environment. Finally, three-dimensional compressive solutions within

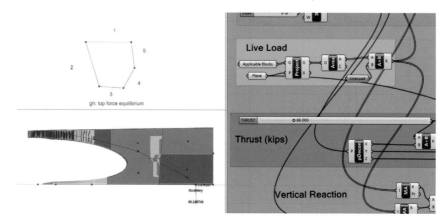

the stone were explored and computed using RhinoVAULT, a plug-in for Rhino which generates membrane solutions for shell structures.

The subdivision of the overall vaulted figure into *voussoir* blocks requires the design of a jointing pattern that contributes to the overall equilibrium of the memorial. The joint lines between stones are designed to be normal to force trajectories under self weight,

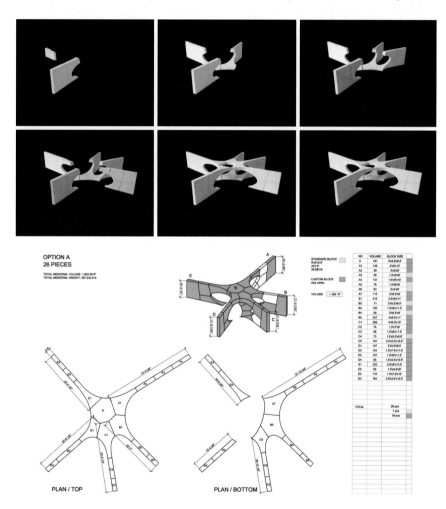

OPTION A
26 PIECES

TOTAL MEMORIAL VOLUME: 1,862.08 ft³
TOTAL MEMORIAL WEIGHT: 297,932.6 lb

STANDARD BLOCK
9'x6'x4.5'
242 ft³
28,560 lb

CUSTOM BLOCK
size varies

VOLUME > 300 ft³

NO.	VOLUME	BLOCK SIZE
K	191	3'x5.5'x6.5'
A1	146	2'x6'x12'
A2	38	2'x3'x6'
A3	56	1.5'x3'x8'
A4	131	1.5'x6'x10'
A5	76	1.5'x6'x8'
A6	63	2'x4'x8'
A7	115	2'x6.5'x9'
B1	212	3.5'x6'x11'
B2	71	2'x3.5'x6.3'
B3	100	1.5'x6'x11.5'
B4	99	2'x6.5'x9'
B5	347	4'x6.5'x11'
C1	305	4'x6.5'x12'
C2	76	1.5'x7'x8'
C3	96	1.5'x6'x11.5'
C4	73	1.5'x5.5'x8.5'
C5	181	3.5'x5.5'x10.5'
D1	147	3'x5.5'x9.5'
D2	124	1.5'x7.5'x11.5'
D3	101	1.5'x6'x11.5'
D4	66	1.5'x4.5'x10.5'
E1	333	5.5'x6'x10.5'
E2	65	1.5'x6.5'x9'
E3	110	1.5'x7.5'x10'
E4	164	3.5'x3.5'x13.5'
TOTAL		26 pcs
		7 pcs
		19 pcs

PLAN / TOP

PLAN / BOTTOM

while the pattern of notched connections minimizes the risk of sliding between stones and ensures that each stone is held securely by the resultant forces of the adjacent blocks. The last step in the process uses computational scripts to verify that the largest stones are within the bounding box limits of quarrying technology for a single block.

Methodologically, the design process for the Collier Memorial involved a back and forth process between the construction of physical models (foam, wood, stone and 3D printed powder), and simulations with digital tools. Physical models allowed the design to be tested mechanically and the erection sequence to be rehearsed. Rocking simulations and stability tests were performed with the physical model. Digital models allowed the design to be optimized and analyzed for material conservation and code compliance. The development of digital tools to produce contemporary forms with archaic building techniques highlights the methodological diversity that characterizes contemporary design

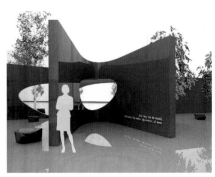 

which does not privilege any single design tool, but rather benefits from both digital and material computation techniques. The correspondence between the material properties and the designer's ability to manipulate them geometrically is highlighted by the methods of translating force into form with computational tools.

The explicit use of elemental and archaic material building technologies coupled with new computational techniques mobilizes history and its instrumentalities to produce a uniquely contemporary mode of practice.

IMAGE CREDITS
All Images Courtesy of the authors

Eric Höweler and J. Meejin Yoon

HÖWELER + YOON ARCHITECTURE LLP / MY STUDIO is an interdisciplinary design practice working across scales: from architecture and urban design to public space and media art structures. Their work focuses on the instrumentality of the built environment to engage audiences, create community, and encourage innovation. Their award winning projects include: Chengdu Skycourts Exhibition Hall, a 65,000 square foot exhibition and event venue and recipient of the Annual Design Review Awards 2012; BSA Space, the Boston Society of Architects headquarters in Boston; the Boswash:Shareway 2030, winner of the Audi Urban Future Award 2012; and White Noise White Light, internationally awarded for the Athens 2004 Olympics. Recipients of the Architecture Review Award in 2014, the Architecture League's Emerging Voices Award, and Architectural Record's Design Vanguard in 2007, HYA/MYS' projects have been exhibited at the Museum of Modern Art in New York, the Los Angeles

John Ochsendorf

Philippe Block

Matthew DeJong

Museum of Contemporary Art, the Institute of Contemporary Art in Boston, the Institut Valencia d'Art Modern, and the National Art Center in Tokyo, Japan. HYA's work was published in a monograph entitled: Expanded Practice, Höweler + Yoon Architecture / MY Studio, published by Princeton Architectural Press in 2009.

ERIC HÖWELER, AIA, LEED AP (b. Cali, Colombia) is an architect and educator, founding principal of Höweler + Yoon Architecure and a Assistant Professor in Architecture at the Harvard University Graduate School of Design. He received a Bachelor of Architecture and a Masters of Architecture from Cornell University and completed his high school education at the International School Bangkok.   Prior to forming Höweler + Yoon Architecture, Eric worked for two internationally recognized firms during his first ten years of practice. Höweler was a Senior Designer at Diller + Scofidio where he worked on the Institute of Contemporary Art in Boston and the Juilliard School/ Lincoln Center in New York. As an Associate Principal at Kohn Pedersen Fox Associates, he was the senior designer on the 118 story ICC Tower in Hong Kong. Höweler is LEED AP and a registered architect in states of New York, Massachusetts, Virginia, New Jersey, Rhode Island and the District of Columbia. He is the co-author of Expanded Practice, Höweler + Yoon Architecture / MY Studio (Princeton Architectural Press 2009) and author of Skyscraper: Vertical Now (Rizzoli/Universe Publishers in 2003). He received a Bachelor of Architecture and a Masters of Architecture from Cornell University.

J. MEEJIN YOON, AIA, FAAR (b. Seoul, Korea) is the Head of the Department of Architecture at the Massachusetts Institute of Technology where she has been teaching since 2001. Awarded the Irwin Sizer Award for most significant improvement to education at MIT in 2013, the United States Artist Award in Architecture and Design in 2008, the Athena RISD Emerging Designer Award in 2008, and the Rome Prize in Design in 2005, Yoon's work has been widely recognized for its innovative and interdisciplinary nature. She is the author of Expanded Practice: Projects by Höweler + Yoon and MY Studio (Princeton Architectural Press 2009), and Public Works: Unsolicited Small Projects for the Big Dig (MAP Book Publishers 2008). Yoon received a Bachelor of Architecture from Cornell University, a Masters of Architecture in Urban Design with Distinction from Harvard University in 1997. Yoon is a registered architect and founding Principal of Höweler + Yoon Architecture, LLP/ MY Studio.

OCHSENDORF DEJONG & BLOCK, LLC is a structural engineering consultancy with expertise in the assessment of (historic) masonry structures and the design of novel masonry structures. Our aim is twofold: to properly assess and preserve existing masonry structures, and to provide designs which reinvent masonry construction, making it economic, sustainable and relevant in current practice by developing exciting new forms from traditional materials.

JOHN OCHSENDORF is the Class of 1942 Professor of Architecture and Engineering at MIT, where he directs the Structural Design Lab and the Masonry Research Group. He is a founding partner of the structural engineering consultancy Ochsendorf DeJong and Block, together with Philippe Block and Matthew DeJong.

PHILIPPE BLOCK is Assistant Professor of Building Structure and head of the BLOCK Research Group at the Institute of Technology in Architecture at ETH Zurich, Switzerland. He is a structural engineer and architect, trained at the Vrije Universiteit Brussel (VUB) and MIT.

MATTHEW DEJONG is a Lecturer in Structural Engineering at the University of Cambridge, and a fellow of St. Catharine's College. He earned his PhD at the Massachusetts Institute of Technology.

JOSE SANCHEZ

POST-CAPITALIST

DESIGN

—

DESIGN

IN THE AGE

OF ACCESS

The coming together of the Communications Internet with the fledgling Energy Internet and the Logistics Internet in a seamless twenty-first-century intelligent infrastructure - the Internet of Things (IoT) - is giving rise to a Third Industrial Revolution. The Internet of Things is already boosting productivity to the point where the marginal cost of producing many goods and services is nearly zero, making them practically free. The result is corporate profits are beginning to dry up, property rights are weakening, and an economy based on scarcity is slowly giving away to an economy of abundance.' (Rifkin 2014)

Design in the Age of Authors

In the context of paradigms of computation, we inevitably need to pursue the path of how certain technologies can radically change the design landscape, as we know it today. This paper presents not only a computational design paradigm, but also the socio-economic implications of a disruptive shift that no longer focuses on 'what' to make but rather on 'who' is making.

The current paradigm of computational design can be described as an informative process one in which form, or the object to be designed, gradually absorbs the information required for it to exist beyond the computer screen in which it was conceived. This informative process is an analogy of the embryonic process in which a foetus gradually develops limbs and organs out of an undifferentiated intensive field. The architectural and design field certainly benefited from the philosophies of Gilles Deleuze and the further explanations of Manuel Delanda to co-relate skills of computation with the design process.

The process described above is certainly an analogy of nature, and with good reason, the recent 9th Archilab Exhibition in the Frac Center in Orleans, France was titled 'Naturalizing Architecture' (Various 2013). In this exhibition, the curators Frederic Migayrou and Marie-Ange Brayer contextualize the work of the current generation of designers as a process of learning from natural processes and applying such intelligence to the work of architectural design. My own work, Bloom The Game, made in collaboration with Alisa Andrasek, is featured in this exhibition, in which we can see a cross section of current design strategies and expertise in fabricating complex and performative geometries. From 3D printed objects to robotically manufactured panels, it is a display of the zeitgeist in the creation of form.

Figure 1: 9th ArchiLab, Naturalizing Architecture

However, one cannot but stop and wonder, how much further can we go?

One of the central pieces of this exhibition, the Digital Grotesque (Hansmeyer and

Dillenburger 2014) by Micheal Hansmeyer and Benjamin Dillenburger, is the largest 3D printed construction on display. It allows us to reflect on whether we have reached a terminal velocity in the field of digital manufacturing and the production of form. Hansmeyer uses a recursive subdivision algorithm that adds greater and greater detail to a piece of geometry, rendering its faces finer and finer. His algorithms control the way in which this happens, enabling the designer's agency in the process of formation. He also allows the computer to generate permutations and select from catalogues that have been automatically generated. The key aspect in this algorithm is its recursivity, meaning that it operates on its own output, generating a perpetual loop that is only stopped by the designer's intent or the computational capacity of the hardware. This process presents a truly poly-dimensional design strategy, one that could operate at the scale of the human eye or at the scale of the atom. The constraint of scale is imposed by the fabrication technology, and the 3D printers required to fabricate the Digital Grotesque are quickly becoming faster, cheaper and allowing for a higher resolution.

An important threshold is crossed once such printers allow us to generate detail beyond the perception of the human eye. This has already occurred through printers that create synthetic materials, which are only differentiated by their hardness or performance in light. These materials have different molecular arrangements that are imperceptible by humans, yet they carry out performative properties required by designers. It is the case that the level of detail in many of the architectural pieces in the Archilab exhibition is scaled precisely for the human eye.

I would argue that most Archilab pieces present a dual discourse; on the one hand the pieces are the result of research, displaying the capacity of materials and state of the art of techniques to manipulate matter and fabrication; on the other hand most pieces generate a gap between practice and research. They are obscurely described and often in terms far from what anyone else could implement. They represent encapsulations of knowledge, but a knowledge that is inaccessible to anyone else but the designer. Even the designers themselves are often constrained to develop this knowledge further by the urgency to develop new work.

Who benefits from such model?

Architects and designers from this exhibition do not operate under a model of proprietary products that will eventually hit the market, something that would justify such secrecy. On the contrary, exhibitions such as Archilab might be the apex of some designer's practices, which leaves behind a powerful set of tools and expertise that might never be evolved by anyone else.

I would like to argue that the current paradigm of the production of form goes hand in hand with the social dynamics of our discipline, and exposes a hierarchy of innovation over implementation. The preoccupation is to be the creator of the new, but there is little interest to follow up such discoveries and enable them to have impact. This creates a system where innovation's only purpose is for the self-promotion and preservation of the designer, generating an autopoietic system.

This model is in crisis and those who advocate such a paradigm risk the advent of a new value system; one in which collaboration and propagation of knowledge become a social currency and mode of recognition.

Design in the Age of Access

In his book, 'The Zero Marginal Cost Society' (Rifkin 2014), Jeremy Rifkin makes a brilliant attempt to forecast the end of capitalism by fleshing out the Collaborative Commons as an emergent economic system to replace the overarching hierarchy of capitalism. Rifkin's central argument revolves around 'near zero marginal cost'(Rifkin 2014), the idea that the costs of goods and services are reduced almost to zero after the initial costs of infrastructure are in place. This is possible by the development of technologies such as the Internet where the cost of distribution of, say, a music album becomes nearly zero. This concept has given rise to the idea of prosumers; consumers that have become a type of producer, and which share information between peer to peer networks.

For Rifkin, this idea is already happening in the field of information technology, however he takes it even further. The Internet of Things is allowing for such a paradigm to also be applied to physical goods. To explain this, he relies on the current development of an energy internet and technologies such as 3D printing. The energy internet is a project in development in Europe, which emphasizes the local production of energy, by either solar, wind or biofuels, and allows for users to share the surplus of such energy production through an intelligent network. By focusing on renewable energies with distributed propagation, the network can be resilient and allocate surplus in areas of shortage.

3D printing is also central to Rifkin's argument by nature of the accelerated development that the technology is currently experiencing. He suggests that 3D printing could effectively become the means to locally fabricate almost anything. When considering that digital files contain the full design specification of an object, and that the feed stock material for 3D printers could also become ubiquitous through their ability to use inexpensive and abundant materials such as sand, we can close the gap of a near zero marginal cost fabrication applied to the physical world, as well as the digital.

'The consumer is beginning to give way to the prosumer as increasing numbers of people become both producers and consumers of their own goods.

Three-dimensional printing differs from conventional centralized manufacturing in several important ways:

First, there is little human involvement aside from creating the software. The software does all the work, which is why it's more appropriate to think of the process as 'infofacture' rather than 'manufacture'.

Second, the early practitioners of 3D printing have made strides to ensure that software used to program and print physical products remains open-source, allowing prosumers to share new ideas with one another in a do-it-yourself (DIY) hobbyist networks. The open design concept conceives of the production of goods as a dynamic process in which thousands - even millions - of players learn from one another by making things together'. (Rifkin 2014)

While Rifkin positions 3D printing technology as a central argument, I would argue that there is a fundamental problem with current 3D printing technology, in that it operates under a system of waste. As Rifkin explains, the additive process of 3D printing considerably reduces waste over subtractive manufacturing processes, however 3D printing is currently not a reversible process, it does not consider the lifecycle of the product produced, allowing it to become a new stock material for a new product. In the Fabricate 2014 conference in Zurich, Neil Gershenfeld discussed this very point, suggesting an alternative path to the current development in 3D printing technology. He proposed
a concept of manufacture as 3D assemblers instead of 3D printers; machines that do not only arrange matter to become a new material but also do the opposite, disassemble products to become raw materials or discrete units that could be re-arranged in different ways. Gershenfeld's 3D assemblers operate over discrete materials that could allow for reversibility, making more accurate Rifkin's idea of near zero marginal cost.

The key issue here is to be able to think in parallel. While the form as nature paradigm, or world as organism concept that Neri Oxman describes ("Neri Oxman's Machines That Design Nature" 2012), focuses on a centralized idea of control, which advocates growing form and producing differentiation by a omnipresent designer, the democratization of tools and the collaborative commons searches for massive social recombination, allowing differentiation not to be designed but to emerge from the interplay of resources and social innovation.

Figure 2: OPEN SOURCE ECOLOGY

What is at stake here is what Rifkin calls a transformation 'from mass production to production by the masses'(Rifkin 2014). This idea suggests that the production of goods will be ever more in the hands of the end user, the new prosumer. We can already see projects within the architectural and design milieu that point to this shifting paradigm.

Open-Source Ecology (Jakubowski 2014) is a project initiated by Marcin Jakubowski with the ambition to generate an open source catalog of hardware that would enable anyone to generate the basic infrastructure for civilization. The catalog includes machines to create bricks, or trucks to cultivate the land, all of which have detailed blueprints to be assembled by a fraction of the cost of retail. The whole catalog can be found online and is open-source, enabling users to improve and upgrade current designs, keeping the technology up to date and tested.

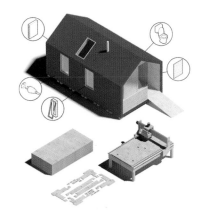

Figure 3: WIKIHOUSE

A similar model much closer to architecture can be found with the Wikihouse ("WikiHouse" 2014), designed by Alastair Parvin. The project consists of an open-source construction set for a modular house that can be constructed only in wood and with a CNC machine. By developing the core open-source principles, Parvin tackles the issue of access and distribution, whilst still allowing the community to alter and design updates to the current model. The constraints of the project act as guidelines to allow anyone to design systems that could operate in conjunction with the current Wikihouse kernel.

Both of these examples remove the hierarchy from form as envisioned by a brilliant designer, and instead place form into the hands of an empowered user.

Access to Tools

We cannot claim that these developments are something new, as many of these ideas are following in the footsteps of initiatives that paved the way for the propagation of knowledge that has established the current operating system of design. Between 1968 and 1972, Stewart Brand founded and published the Whole Earth Catalog (Brand 1968), an initiative to share and propagate information about a wide variety of tools and techniques. Buckminster Fuller is listed as a contributor and inspiration for the publication, a document, which even today seems progressive in its approach. Much of its content is dedicated to smart geometries that minimize the use of materials, or clever ways to harvest land in farming. Its subtitle Access to Tools points to the importance of the distribution of knowledge and access to performance and quality through the items presented. The legacy of the Whole Earth Catalog has been profound and far reaching, influencing a large number of other publications and business strategies, but is perhaps only now, on the back of a new and invigorated DIY, maker-movement, that one can refer back to the significance of this publication as seeding point.

The attitude of constant social iteration sits on the opposite side to the knowledge developed and research generated by centralized organizations. Here, crowd sourcing is not in the interests of a single entity harvesting ideas or labour from multiple users, but is a truly parallel network that gives rise to social capital and can gradually establish its own position, what Rifkin describes as the Collaborative Commons, in turn pushing back capitalism as the only possible recognizable economic model.

Towards Abundance

Figure 4: WHOLE EARTH CATALOG, 1968

The Whole Earth counter cultural movement, as argued by Fred Turner in 'From Counter Culture to Cyberculture' (Turner 2008) was one of the central influences of contemporary cyberculture. In its early stages of conception, a new field of computation was needed to define the ethics of production and reproduction of software. Out of this period we can identify the emergence of two opposing positions: the proprietary model led by Bill Gates who, in his 'Open Letter to Hobbysists' in 1976 (Gates 1976), accused the hobbyist community of infringing copyright of software; and the emergence of the Free Software Movement (Stallman 2014) led by Richard Stallman. For Stallman, the idea of 'free' software has nothing to do with its price, but rather with the social implications of how the community collaborates. In his 2001 speech at New York University Stallman states:

"What do you mean it's free software if it costs $150 dollars?' [Laughter] Well, the reason they asked this was that they were confused by the multiple meanings of the English word 'Free'. One meaning refers to price and another meaning refers to freedom. When I speak of free software I'm referring to freedom, not price. So think of free speech, not free beer. [Laughter].'

He goes on to describe what constitutes software freedom:

"The freedom to run a program for any purpose, any way you like. The freedom to study how the program works and change it so it does your computation as you wish… The freedom to redistribute copies so you can help your neighbour.

The freedom to distribute copies of your modified versions to others. By doing this you can give the whole community a chance to benefit from your changes." (Stallman 2001b)

Initiatives like the GNU operating system and GNU General Public License are a result of the paradigmatic manifesto of Stallman. The ultimate achievement of such initiatives is to give rise to twenty first century collaborationists, as described by Rifkin. Never before has it been possible

Figure 5: Linux Kernel.

|118

to coordinate and enable a global community to collaboratively develop one of the key ingredients of the communication infrastructure of today. The rise of a social agenda behind such enterprise and the democratization of tools defines an Age of Access'.

The Vector of Propagation

Unlike digital mediums, the ideas of Free Software or Open Source are more difficult to implement with physical products and hardware. The final form of an object, similarly to a closed software program, is a weak means to propagate the knowledge that it encapsulates. Code, alternatively, can represent both form and process, allowing for a strong vector of propagation. One could argue that blueprints are the base data for objects or products, and that if such documents are provided, that constitutes an open-source hardware. I would argue that this is not enough; the information required to make an object, let alone a building, is still encapsulated in the blueprint. This is one of the reasons why the popularity of DIY Instructibles has emerged. Social networks such as instructibles.com ('Instructables' 2014), recently acquired by Autodesk, crystallize the additional knowledge required to make something. The website celebrates the DIY movement allowing anyone to post an instructable, basically the algorithm for how to reproduce a product or technique by anyone else. This also enables the new user to tweak or alter any aspect of the process to improve or personalize the method. Form itself is in constant flux and quickly becomes obsolete by newer and newer versions. We see yet again a pattern of access over form.

Massive Recombination

While peer-to-peer communications and the idea of prosumers might start to become a stronger reality, we have to realize the important role that software plays in such a paradigm. Rifkin presents the importance of Massive Open Online Courses (MOOCS) in the role of a more dynamic education, one that no longer relies on degrees or disciplines, but rather allows the student to build their own curriculum, crossing between disciplines for a near zero marginal cost. Rifkin's argument in favour of open free online education is significant, especially when combined with the importance of software as a medium that can encapsulate knowledge and enable a non-expert user to achieve professional quality results in a limited time. The human brain can only absorb a limited amount of information in a given time limit, and properties of encapsulation of software, prevents people from having to reinvent the wheel each time. This is especially true if such software uses a free software ethics or is open-source, allowing access to the core of the encapsulated knowledge, enabling both higher and lower level access.

An industry that has developed fundamental skills in this regard is the video game industry. Today, video games are software intended for new and often young users, and they have to be able to quickly educate a player to perform complex tasks. On this learning curve, a player needs to understand the variables at play in a given system, and the power and resources required to alter the outcome of a given simulation. Due to their digital dynamic state, video games allows us, unlike other mediums, to engage thousands and sometimes millions of new users with complex simulations when playing a new game, and those users are able to quickly scan the possibility space of a given system, engage with it, and through their gameplay provide the best feedback any system designer could wish for.

Will Wright released SimCity in 1989, allowing any player, not only architects or urban designers, to design and manage a virtual city. To do so, Wright developed a system in the form of a game. A game in this context should be understood as software that encapsulates much of its behaviour and engages an audience with an interactive narrative, in this particular case, one of systemic relations and interdependence between variables. In his interview with the astrophysicist Jill Tarter for SEED Magazine in 2008 (Wright and Tarter 2008), Wright explains his personal view on how the accuracy of a computational model needs to be evaluated in contrast to the amount of people that can access such simulation. He refers to the power of games or software to be educational and rightly addresses the importance that access and implementation has in balance with the accuracy of the simulation.

'We make a lot of concession for gameplay, when I imagine if I want a game to have a certain amount of educational effect on the world, for me is a simple equation of what is the educational value times the number of players/hours spent. Ok, I can make something that is 5 times more educational and the other term of that equation will plummet down to nothing so you really need to multiply these 2 numbers to know what the ultimate effect is. On the other hand when you make the game more engaging, where you get to design the creature and you don't have to play a million generations we can make the number of player/hours skyrocket and what I'm really trying to do is maximize a product for those 2 numbers' (Wright and Tarter 2008)

Figure 6: SimCity 2000, by Will Wright, 1994

No other medium today has the power to design and teach systems thinking more than video games. Even a toy model, as Wright describes them, moves people closer to evaluating problems from a series of different perspectives, enabling a player to creatively find resources in what was considered waste in another process. The gamer community has also developed the skill of iteration, both individually and collectively, by accepting failure and challenge as key ingredients to video games. In this context failure is not a negative concept, it is more often a desired experience as it points out alternative paths and allows a player to visualize a learning curve. Collectively, failure represents a different kind of parallel processing, one in which a connected community can learn and succeed after many hours of trying to solve a particular problem.

As Jane McGonigal explains in 'Reality Is Broken' (McGonigal 2011) gamers are one of the most dedicated communities on the internet today, documenting and sharing progress and walkthroughs of videogames just hours after their release. Games are very much part of an instructable culture, sharing access and insights at all levels of a game experience. Players produce patterns, and a game or software defines a finite search space of possible combinations. What a player does is not to alter the system but to attempt to creatively exhaust the search space. This is carried out by thousands of players simultaneously.

Player patterns are one of the key ingredients to reach Rifkin's Collaborative Commons. For the world of design and making to move from mass production to production of the masses, perhaps the prosumers of tomorrow will look more like gamers, that are in direct feedback loops with the simulation and resources that they are using. This is what J.C.R Licklider would describe as 'Man-Computer Symbiosis' (Licklider 1960) in his book of the same name. Design will not end up automated and optimized by intelligent algorithms, but in the hands of many, mediated by layers of computational infrastructure that can facilitate and give evidence to expert knowledge. At the same time, such systems, if adopting a free software ethics, will have the possibility to be constantly modified and updated just like a Wiki.

Coda

The ultimate goal in pursuing the linkage of these technologies is precisely to put forward an idea to overcome the current economy of scarcity. With the advent of an intelligent infrastructure that has the potential to generate an age of abundance, where an energy internet could empower info-facturing in the hand of prosumers, we need to dedicate the time and effort to continue the democratization of tools and access, generating a computational literacy on the ethics, principles and ideas behind technological innovation. The narrative of struggle presented in the previous pages of this paper, can be synthesised by Stewart Brand in 1984 at the first Hackers conference:

'On the one hand information wants to be expensive, because it's so valuable. The right information in the right place just changes your life. On the other hand, information wants to be free because the cost of getting it out is getting lower and lower all the time.

So you have these two fighting against each other.'

He went on to say: 'That tension will not go away.' (Brand 1984)

The end of zero-sum games is not the obvious trajectory of current technology development but it should be acknowledged and defined as foundational literacy for a sustainable paradigm for the use of computation.

REFERENCES
- Brand, Stewart. 1968. Whole Earth Catalog. ———. 1984. "Information Is Free." Hackers Conference.
- Gates, Bill. 1976. "AN OPEN LETTER TO HOBBYISTS." Homebrew Computer Club Newsletter Volume 2, Issue 1. http://www.digibarn.com/collections/newsletters/homebrew/V2_01/gatesletter.html.
- Hansmeyer, Micheal, and Benjamin Dillenburger. 2014. "Digital Grotesque." Accessed June 16. http://www.digital-grotesque.com/#2.
- "Instructables." 2014. Accessed June 16. http://www.instructables.com/.
- Jakubowski, Marcin. 2014. "Open Source Ecology." Accessed June 16. http://opensourceecology.org/.
- Licklider, J.C.R. 1960. "Man-Computer Symbiosis." IRE Transactions on Human Factors in Electronics.
- McGonigal, Jane. 2011. Reality Is Broken: Why Games Make Us Better and How They Can Change the World. Penguin Books.
- "Neri Oxman's Machines That Design Nature." 2012. The Lavin Agency. http://www.thelavinagency.com/blog-cnns-next-big-thing-neri-oxmans-world-as-organism-design-model.html.
- Rifkin, Jeremy. 2014. The Zero Marginal Cost Society. Palgrave Macmillan.
- Stallman, Richard. 2001a. "What Is Free Software." https://gnu.org/philosophy/free-sw.html.———. 2001b. "Free Software, Freedom and Cooperation." http://www.gnu.org/events/rms-nyu-2001-transcript.txt.
- Turner, Fred. 2008. From Counterculture to Cyberculture: Stewart Brand, the Whole Earth Network, and the Rise of Digital Utopianism. University of Chicago Press.
- Various. 2013. Archilab 2013: Naturalizing Architecture. Edited by Marie Ange Brayer and Frederic Migayrou. Orleans, France: HYX.
- "WikiHouse." 2014. Accessed June 16. http://www.wikihouse.cc/.
- Wright, Will, and Jill Tarter. 2008. "Jill Tarter + Will Wright." http://salon.seedmagazine.com/salon_tarter_wright.html.

JOSE SANCHEZ is an Architect / Programmer / Game Designer based in Los Angeles, California. He is partner at Bloom Games, start-up built upon the BLOOM project, winner of the WONDER SERIES hosted by the City of London for the London 2012 Olympics. He is the director of the Plethora Project (www.plethora-project.com), a research and learning project investing in the future of on-line open-source knowledge. The project has over 150 videos and an open-source library of code with over 700.000 completed video session since 2011. His background in computational design and digital manufacturing is linked to Biothing with Alisa Andrasek, were he was one of the principal designers in numerous projects and exhibitions since 2009. Today, he is an Assistant Professor at USC School of Architecture in Los Angeles. His research 'Gamescapes', explores generative interfaces in the form of video games, speculating in modes of intelligence augmentation, combinatorics and open systems as a design medium.

PHILIPPE MOREL

A FEW REMARKS
ON THE POLITICS
OF
"RADICAL
COMPUTATION"

"…Is revolution still possible? The answer after the commercial break…"

(Frédéric Taddeï, TV presenter, announcing its TV show dedicated to Revolution with the participation of Antonio Negri)

"Saying that two and two makes four is close to becoming a revolutionary act"[1]

(Guy Debord)

"Each sentence in my books contains contempt of idealism. No more deadly fatality than this intellectual insalubriousness has ever threatened humanity since it began"[2]

Friedrich Nietzsche, Letter to Malwida von Meysenbug, Turin, October 20th, 1888.\

It must be acknowledged that there is little to distinguish between architecture and political vulgarity. Indeed, how could it be otherwise, since architecture includes common psychology? Ignorance, lazy ideology and the sum of personal interests take precedence over truth. Thus it comes as no surprise that the psychology that should in all reason interest the theorists of resistance, the subjectivists, the neo-Spinozist scholars, be they Deleuzian or otherwise, and most of those for whom original Marxist or positivist objectivity has not given sufficient thought to the individual, should be studied the least. This is because to deduce individual attitudes from the masses, or indeed the multitude, would show that the abstract theories so enjoyed by Western television shows have failed. That enjoyment and interest is actually shared by the philosophers they invite on their shows, which thus expose the vast distance between themselves and their models.[3]

|12

Re-birth of idealism

Figure 1: Approximative Man by Tristan Tzara.

Of the subjectivist theories, those linked to Operaismo are strongly favoured by architecture. Operaismo, simply put and in terms of theory of the multitude, appears to embody the rebirth of idealism, for several reasons. First, because of a lack of subjectivist radicalism - shared subjectivity is theorised in abstracto- which refers neither to the true power of the Ego nor to Wittgenstein's Solipsism, which "rigorously developed, coincides with pure realism"[4]. Then, because it is not avant-garde enough, insofar as "being avant-garde is being in tune with reality"[5]. The theory of the multitude seems to be yet another political ideal in the moralist tradition that our experience has shown to be an utter failure. Like every generalisation, it ignores, on behalf of the group or multitude of individuals, that "individuals are thus made that they show their lives. What they are, therefore, coincides with their production; just as much as it does with the way they produce it".[6] This omission is a problem, because behind the social abstraction termed "the creative and productive practices of the multitude"[7] lurks a huge number of productions of varying quality. One does not become an opponent merely by belonging to the cognitive multitudes, as it is shown by part-time advertising industry employees. The knowledge used or produced must be for another purpose than merely a reform of capitalism, where everyone claims his due in terms of money. The knowledge used or produced must be for another reason than just reforming a capitalist system in which everyone expects to be paid his due. As Wittgenstein perfectly expressed it

Figure 2: Tapes of Konstantinos Doxiadis' Fortran IV lecture series, given in 1969 at the University of California, Berkeley. Doxiadis, especially thanks to the Delos symposia, is one rare example of architect who went really deep into the understanding of technology. His writings are still providing highly valuable insights.

in "Tell me how you are searching and I will tell you what you are searching", you must make the "how" to produce more important than the product itself, thus developing a true "Critique of money" that goes much further than the criticism of commodity itself[8], by basing production on laws other than that of competition, while ensuring at the same time that there are indeed laws. Although many claim lofty anti-capitalist moral imperatives, the reality is much more mundane. So much so that most left-wing "resistant" theorists resemble Dühring or Rodbertus, who both forgot (as Engels and Marx pointed out in Anti-Dühring and in

the preface to the first German edition of The Poverty of Philosophy), that their Utopia either worked on capitalist laws or did not work at all. It is the same with the economic context in which the cognitive multitudes work, for it cannot escape the laws of capital gains or the value-enhancing

RATIONALISM ➡ **COMPUTATIONALISM**

Biology	Computational Biology
Chemistry	Computational Chemistry
Economics	Computational Complexity
Geometry	Computational Economics
Linguistics	Computational Geometry
Mechanics	Computational Linguistics
Politics	Computational Mechanics
Semiotics	Computational Neuroscience
Statistics…	Computational Politics
	Computational Semiotics
	Computational Statistics…

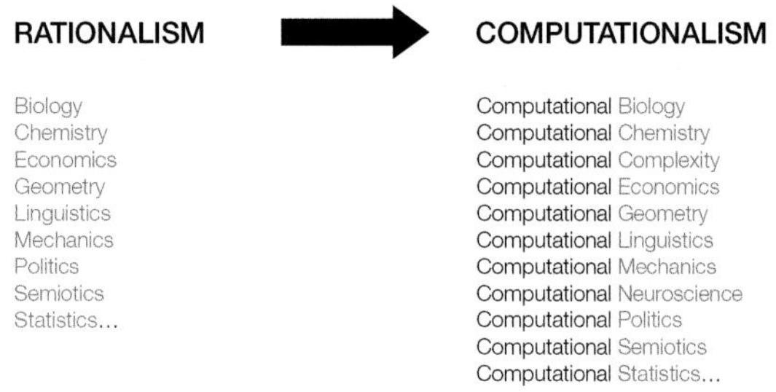

Figure 3: This diagram is part of the theory of Computationalism I started to establish in 2000 until today.

process just through abstract work. It is also the same for the collective intelligence, about which the only thing we can say is that it externalises production and (re-)training costs, since it is constantly being swallowed up by the market itself. Although the most optimistic hypotheses on the development of production argue that it is its scientific and social nature that brings richness for all while work as such is merely the accompaniment of automated production, in reality the work accomplished by all the multitudes is remunerated in traditional fashion and assessed in terms of its function in the capitalist system. The problem of the knowledge economy is not, therefore, that of the knowledge valorisation circuit, which would boil down simply to the opposition between good and

Figure 4: The book Men Minutes Money, published in 1934, presents a series of statements by Thomas. J. Watson, IBM Founder. Their main characteristics lie in an amazing anticipation of the importance of computational power (and therefore speed) in modern capitalism. An importance that one can acknowledge every day in the NTIC economy but also in every other domain, including the most traditional ones like finance, whose rules are fully redefined by the spectacular mathematization and computerization leading to high frequency trading.

bad capitalism, but the more classic one of how to use knowledge as a whole. This is a recurrent issue that has been widely explored, showing the boundary between revolutionary and reformist thought. The main line of exploration was to compare the respective roles of science, arts, the scientists and the intellectuals in society. This line can be traced from Alberti to Ray Kurzweil and includes Rousseau, Babbage, Russell, Oppenheimer and Wiener. Alberti's early work On the Advantages and Disadvantages of Letters – a book which revealed that he was much closer to Nietzsche than to a wise humanist – noted that "as of then (1430) all the sciences, all the liberal arts which had been the consecrated training of the soul, collapsed and became servile". Moreover, those whose job was animal husbandry and cleaning stables began to discuss human fate; those who were supposed to be lashing the backs of animals found themselves instead holding a sceptre and sitting among magistrates"[9]. Rousseau, although demanding in his most polemical early work "what would we think of scribblers who indiscreetly open the door to science and introduced an unworthy

populace into its sanctuary?[10], adding that «[…] Our souls have become corrupted while our arts and sciences have reached perfection" and "the same phenomenon has been observed at every time and in all places[11], considered that the encyclopaedists and the actual democratisation of knowledge were what should be combated because they had both taken Man from his natural state of innocence. Indeed Rousseau, unlike the neo-primitives that will be dealt with later, always presented this state as an analytical tool, a state that "perhaps never existed, which probably never will exist, and yet one that we need to understand in order to judge our current state properly".[12] Babbage, who opposed Rousseau's radicalism which petered out in England before merging into the Pre-Raphaelite reaction,[13] thought that it was not knowledge that threatened the social structure

Figure 5: Cover of the Automated Trader Quarterly, Fall 2011, dedicated to the Rise of the Robot Market: Machines on the Alpha Horizon.

but in fact its absence. He criticised first the lack of scientific knowledge among the aristocrats of the House of Lords, who "[…] hold high rank in a manufacturing country" and who "can scarcely be excused if they are entirely ignorant of principles, whose development has produced its greatness"[14], and secondly the economists themselves, for their poor understanding of the fundamental links between the economy and knowledge and between pure and applied sciences, understanding which should be based on new data such as the "division of intellectual work". For Russell and Oppenheimer, it was not so much the structure of industrial production itself that mattered as the relationship between this industry strongly reliant on science (and therefore rationalised) and ever-increasingly irrational and warmongering policy that was no less ignorant than that described by Alberti and Babbage. It was partly the same for Wiener who went into the relationships between science, technology, the civil society and structure of production and work. Wiener's advice to the American trade unions at the time, who were very involved in classical political contestation, passed unnoticed. Finally Ray Kurzweil decided that it was Singularity, based on a "law of accelerating returns" and described as "fundamentally an economic theory"[15], that enables analysis of economic structures, like that described by Babbage in The Economy of machines, but transposed to the age of computation.

If I refer to these authors who, apart from Rousseau, are not just philosophers and theorists but also scientists of uncontested merit, and although great scientific achievements do not confer moral authority, as Rousseau rightly observed when qualifying as "ridiculous" the philosophy of mathematical genius Leibnitz, they do give an idea of how to understand science: above all, it is that any political theory calling itself
  a revolutionary theory of resistance must first be completely based on fully-understood economic mechanisms. This is the understanding Marx acquired from his vast research, either original or borrowed from Babbage, for instance[16], into science and industrial production. The Neo-operaismo literature is far from being so well-informed. Marx said that such research would at the very least turn us from politics to political economy. Just as for Ruskin visiting the ruins of the Middle Ages and making their non-restoration his petit-bourgeois political

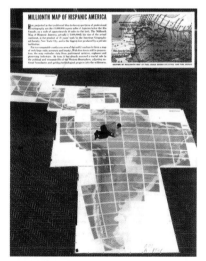

Figure 6: The first (and biggest) full map of South America at the scale 1:1 Millionth, opened the path towards large scale geomatics. In such maps, people could literally enter the space as one can do today on Google Map. Another common points is that this map was produced by a private institution, showing the shift from States owned maps towards corporations owned ones.

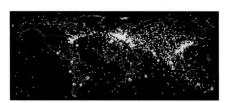

Figure 7: "Recent advances in high-frequency financial trading have made light propagation delays between geographically separated exchanges relevant. Here we (A.D. Wissner-Gross and C. E. Freer) show that there exist optimal locations from which to coordinate the statistical arbitrage of pairs of spacelike separated securities, and calculate a representative map of such locations on Earth. Furthermore, trading local securities along chains of such intermediate locations results in a novel econophysical effect, in which the relativistic propagation of tradable information is effectively slowed or stopped by arbitrage.) The map shows Optimal intermediate trading node locations (small circles) for all pairs of 52 major securities exchanges (large Circles)".

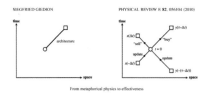

Figure 8: Juxtaposition of modernist belief in the power of scientific metaphors, expressed as diagram, and a 'Space-time diagram of relativistic arbitrage transaction. Security price updates from spacelike separated trading centers (squares) arrive with different light propagation delays at an intermediate node (circle) at time t=0, whereupon the node may issue a pair of "buy" and "sell" orders back to the centers' (A. D. Wissner-Gross and C. E. Freer)".

combat, while Babbage was visiting A. von Humboldt, Gauss or Berzelius and European factories, it is the very absence of explanation that gives charm to current political literature. As Anselm Jappe and Robert Kurz noted in what is currently the most acerbic criticism of Neo-operaismo and its most famous representatives Antonio Negri and Michael Hardt, "the authors of Empire do not wish to bore their readers with criticism of political economy. There are much more exciting topics. The only thing that interests them is whether PCs has given birth to a new revolutionary subjectivity, and thus whether there will be a new successor to the old working class as a subject ontologically opposed to capital"[17]. It is true that we are not bored by the critics of political economy, but on the other hand we are not convinced by the multitudes as a revolutionary subject or by the supposed separation of their production from capital, a fact that has still not been subjected to a theoretical demonstration. In fact, the problem with most of the current theories on political resistance is that on the basis of a partially accurate diagnosis – due for example to the highly integrated and computerised nature of the economy, the

profoundly reactionary and repressive warmongering policy of the western powers and the extraterritorial nature of some of them - both the prognosis and the cure appear to stem from the utopian pre- or post-Marxist socialism that we thought had disappeared. It is widely viewed that the idealism of the great majority of Neo-operaismo is identical, a century and a half later, to that of the Pre-Raphaelite Hunt, who "like most young people […] overcome by the sense of freedom pervading the revolutionary events that were taking place at that time" was ready to "call down the heavens to fight the tyranny over poor defenceless people […]". And precisely, what separates us from the heavens is that when it comes to new economic and social organisation, in fact including this new violence which requires each of us to be a little more than "overcome" in return (today's Greek anarchists rightly declare "we are not outraged, we are determined), it should not be a question of conviction nor of "belief, but of understanding".[18]

Abstract Criticism

Understanding the situation is not only a way to begin a theory of resistance or revolution. It is the sine qua non condition and the ultimate goal. "It is not enough that thought should seek reality, reality must seek thought"[19], such seeking being the way to avoid ideological and bureaucratic distortion and subjective and idealistic relapses. While idealism too often masks ignorance, and subjectivity, as in a love affair, is merely a vulgar reaction against technological means of action that have not been mastered properly, technological idolatry is not a solution either for understanding the mechanisms of contemporary civilisation. It must be admitted that these are increasingly complex, since each component depends on an infinite number of others around it, interacting with it. Cybernetic feedback has become the fundamental law of contemporary economy and knowledge, especially if it is amplified by the stock market. Faced with such intricacy it is not surprising that alternately, spontaneous reactions occur: 1) radical contestation of all technological civilisation, as in neo-primitivism; 2) more muted criticism of the movement and promotion of a sort of "amnesty on movement" or a return to various former positions, as if Windows Restore Point could be applied to civilisation; 3) taking refuge in an ideal imaginary world like John Ruskin; 4) a return to political and social progressivism. Although it must be admitted that all these positions alike are doomed to fail, the diagnoses and cures for each of them are far from being the same. The second and third positions are still, as commented in 1955, "[…] fighting on the same ground, with the same weapons, which are exactly those of petit-bourgeois idealism. They each proudly defend the rank and eternity of their standards".[20] They merely offer boring, erudite, or at best virtuoso variations on problems beyond their understanding, and make the mistake of treating history with a-historic methods at the very moment when, precisely because it is a historic mutation, the end of history requires a historic method. Conversely, despite the fact that its radicalism failed, anti-industrial anarchism (which we will come back to) at least had the merit of endowing today's events with the importance they deserve. Theodore Kaczynski, far more than his neo-primitive follower John Zerzan, is thus logical in his analysis of technology. He is well aware that a temporary halt or a return to a previous stage of technological development will change nothing. Although

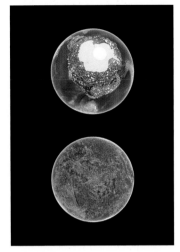

Figure 9: A speculation (2000-today) associated with my theory of Integral Capitalism and Computationalism, which acknowledge the end of the city. This might sound counter intuitive or counter factual as more and more people are living in cities, but in fact these cities are not cities anymore. They are floating and drifting post-urban magma, constantly moving according to the economics forces. This post-urban scenario refers to the last spatial organisation that our earth will see.

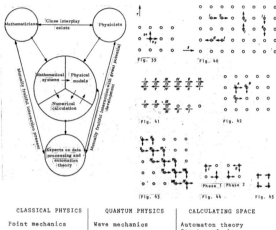

CLASSICAL PHYSICS	QUANTUM PHYSICS	CALCULATING SPACE
Point mechanics	Wave mechanics	Automaton theory Counter algebra
Particles	Wave-particle	Counter state, digital particle
Analog	Hybrid	Digital
Analysis	Differential equations	Difference equations and logical operations
All values continuous	A number of values quantized	All values have only discrete values
No limiting values	With the exception of the speed of light, no limiting values	Minimum and maximum values for every possible magnitude
Infinitely accurate	Probability relation	Limits on calculation accuracy
Causality in both time directions	Only static causality, division into probabilities	Causality only in the positive time direction, introduction of probability terms possible, but not necessary
	Classical mechanics is statistically approximated	Are the limits of probability of quantum physics explainable with determinate space structures?
	Based on formulas	Based on counters

Figure 10, 11, 12: Konrad Zuse, one of the fathers of programming languages and computing (including spatial computing) established a set of relationships between fundamental physics, mathematics and computation. At some point he really opened a new conceptual era in computer sciences, leading to the contemporary research in non standard computation, including quantum computing.

complete integration of technology dates only from the second half of the twentieth century, which precisely leads us to believe that an earlier, less radical stage of technical development could be returned to, it is clear that the new mentality emerging from the late twentieth and early twenty-first centuries will not be content with this. That would mean that humanity, after returning to the potential for technical evolution that it knew in the nineteenth and even eighteenth century, would busily try to reconstruct its lost world, at the same time blaming it! Spengler understood this: " […] unlike generic techniques, it is one of the essential characteristics of man's individual and modifiable technique that each discovery contains the potentiality and the NECESSITY to discover new things, that all satisfied wish wakes thousands of others […]"[21], and Kaczynski understood that too. He was not so naïve as to believe that if we abolish telescopes we will rediscover pre-Socratic mysticism in the stars, and that is why he theorises that the only solution is to destroy all technique and all the associated social and political structures. His understanding of the integrated nature of contemporary technology is lucid and that is why he should at least be read. Ray Kurzweil agreed, and so did Adorno when he drew attention to Spengler, who was also on the opposite side of the reader's intellectual spectre[22]. Understanding of this technological integration, the associated economy of which is by the way Integral capitalism and not Cognitive capitalism[23], is the only criterion for the radical branches of anarchist anti-industrialism – Neo-primitivist or not – and it is cruelly missing in the more modest forms of criticism described earlier. Even if, with all the historic significance of the term, a rationalistic Restoration or neo-Ruskinian idealism[24] is encouraged, a historical and therefore evolutionist assessment of today's developments cannot be arrived at: there is only confusion. By endowing the movement with an abstract character in the sequence of events and making it the sole cause of the progressive failure of western bourgeois democracy, we miss its "qualities", pure quantity and speed being intrinsic ones. We refuse to see the nature of technology as the effect AND cause of an economic and social organisation, and the complex structure of knowledge which today is itself highly dependent on technology with the IT revolution. Thus, not only is it impossible to extract only what suits us from technology[25], but even more, it is impossible to separate the knowledge acquired by our civilisation, from its technology. This includes the anti-industrial literature published on the Internet! It seemed possible enough, with a bit of simplification, to operate such a separation until the IT revolution (except that there would not have been any Pasteur without powerful microscopes, no more than contemporary genetic science without computers). But today it is clearly impossible, both in theory and in practice. As we can see, the return to a pre-technological era of society is clearly impossible because of the very nature of the technique, which leads inevitably to a thirst for new techniques. Nor is it possible to return to an ideal moment of rationalism that is still sufficiently Universalist and distinct from capitalism and technology – a sort of "Hegelian" stage – nor to a pre-rationalistic moment – incarnated in the Renaissance and Baroque periods – either. There are several reasons for this: the first, important but rarely discussed, is that we do not see what moral argument there is for saying that the 80% of humanity that did not have the luxury of knowing about the Age of Enlightenment should suddenly decide that it is the ultimate goal of their civilisation, on the say-so of a few blasé intellectuals. The second reason is that we have already gone beyond Rationalism. The interdependence of knowledge and technology, which I also refer to as "Computationalism", goes further than rationalism, while being based on the primacy of scientific knowledge that is inherent to rationalism itself. It is thus practically too late to take a step back, because the philosophical and cultural links between simple changes have been broken by jumping a ditch that is much too wide to cross back: the IT revolution. A revolution that has transformed the formal and political democratic process of the bourgeois revolution into an effective and social one. Thus what in time appears only a slight step backwards is, because of the true atomisation of contemporary society, a cultural gulf as difficult to cross as that separating us from the hunter-gatherers of the Neolithic age, which is where the Neo-primitives would like us to return. Indeed, if there are people tempted by Neo-primitivism, it is because the similarities between its hunter-gatherers and ourselves are just as seductive as the "absurd boundaries of race, nation and class"[26] of the Golden Age of pre- and post-revolutionary rationalism, the very boundaries that rationalism never crossed because it refused to draw lessons from the French

Figure 13: As traditional politics is failing, some researchers and theoreticians are trying to propose alternative models which would prevent the most obvious drawbacks of politics, for example massive corruption, thanks to stochastic models. As it is discussed in the present essay, no traditional political model, based on human representatives, can be saved. It should be replaced by computational substitutes, providing equal shares of the global wealth in a strictly socialist manner. Such a model, contrary to previous experiments in USSR, would still be based on the market, as market is not a problem in itself.

Revolution. Babeuf, to whom we will return when discussing his project of a "Perpetual Land Registry" and who, like the Jacobins, saw the revolution turn into just a formal reorganisation of civil society, already expressed doubts on this. Not only do "governments generally carry out revolutions just to govern"[27], but more specifically in law, he observed that "[…] the social laws have provided intrigue, trickery and dishonesty with the means of adroitly seizing common property"[28]. The first step out of line signals the failure of any politician wishing to convince the people that it "can do nothing alone and will always need a government". The second step out of line signals the failure of reason itself because, far from correcting the defects of natural laws, such as the randomness of births that justifies the Perpetual Land Registry, it helps to accentuate them. Falsely naïve, Babeuf addresses the bourgeois rationalists, asking "but if the social pact were really based on reason, should it not strive to abolish everything defective or unjust in the natural law"?[29]

Rationalism and Psychologism

Despite the three hundred years of politics that have proved Babeuf's scepticism, and have indeed fostered "intrigue, trickery and dishonesty", and "the means by which adroitly to seize common property", providing nothing to "limit the wealth that people are allowed to acquire", it can be wondered what still drives some people still to believe in politics. Believing that politics as a means of applying reason can be anything but the superstructure it has never ceased to be since Marx described it thus, is a strange behaviour on the part of those claiming to have read this greatest theorist of the nineteenth century. That people who have refused the status of concept to scientific thought itself, in the name of free choice, should view the concept of politics as a "good" one is nothing more than making politics essential and above all declare, incautiously, that "from this just knowledge just acts must come". "The greatest mistake", given that, according to psychology, the contrary is "[…] reality in all its nudity, demonstrated every day and every hour since time immemorial!"[30] This is a philosopher's, not a logician's mistake and it differs little from that committed by the philosophies of desire that perceive it as merely positivity and never envisage other kind of desires such as those of the opponents of the great realist Alberti, seen earlier. Nor does it envisage the "desires of

|132

the lowest, most abject individuals" or those "of people who can only be distinguished from animals by the image and place they claim and not at all by their behaviour". Today's politicians, TV show presenters and plagiarists of every kind are no better. While the aforementioned Neo-Ruskinian or Neo-rationalist idealism, steeped in history, is incapable of understanding phenomena in the light of history, the subjectivism of today's fashionable political renewal is steeped in psychologism yet bare of psychology. Thus what is presented as "renewal" is either 1) a reiteration of the refusal to "face up to the truth that all human form is in a continual state of transformation [...]"; yet this refusal led to the "failure of the rationalists" who "failed to understand that the only way to avoid the anarchy of change is to become aware of the laws under which change takes place, and use them [...] "[31], or 2) an anti-rationalism that does try to "arrive at a dynamic conception of form [32]. These renewals that are relying on politics miraculously impervious to economic trends or on old fashioned Vitalism end up merely to a new mysticism. That is precisely the subject of the recent criticism by Robert Kurz and Anselm Jappe against the Neo-operaismo representatives still believing in "primacy of 'politics' [...], where 'politics' are considered per se as the contrary of the market". Yet "despite their clear intention to implement a 'completely different' policy", these representatives of today's "left [...] continue to slide back into 'realism' and 'minor disorder', participate in elections, opine on referendums, discuss the possible evolution of the Socialist Party, and endeavour to make alliances and conclude a 'historic compromise' of some sort. For A. Jappe "confronted with this desire to 'join in the game' (and I would add, game including TV shows, in other words, all TV programmes) [...] we should recall the movements and moments of radical opposition that actually played anti-politics [...]" [33]. Some of the greatest expressions of anti-politics were Dadaism – Duchamp even clamoured for a time when, according to Nietzsche, "the concept of politics will be absorbed into a war of minds"[34] – and Octave Mirbeau's satirical pamphlet Electors on Strike (1902). Thus, the confidence in politics as a new fad was not the triumph of rationality in the world, but, in a civilisation that anyway had already gone beyond rationalism, yet another farce demonstrating the failure of reason, as noted already by Rousseau, Babeuf and the Jacobins. Indeed, in this farce on a giant stage, with "left wing" and "right wing" voters, it is not the left wing elector (who, according to A. Jappe, "has never [...] obtained what he voted for"), who takes the rationalist role, but "the right wing elector. He is not so stupid. He gets the little he expects from his candidates [...] for example tolerance of tax evasion and violations of labour law. His representatives do not betray him that much; and the elector who votes only for the candidate who will give his son a job or get a large subsidy for the farmers in his locality is in fact the most rational elector.[35]

Computationalism as a social theory

In 1969 M. McLuhan already noted that "in our rapidly changing environment, new technologies appear practically every month", and that "one of the effects of this huge acceleration of change in human organisation is very well expressed by the saying 'if it works, it is out of fashion', or that "When electronically controlled devices are perfected, it will be almost as simple and cheap to obtain a million different objects as to make a million identical ones".[36] He was observing empirical laws that have since been clarified and absorbed into common language under the names Moore law, Beta versions or non-standard production. McLuhan was not a precursor in this field – readings of My Discovery of America by Mayakovski[37] or Babbage, as mentioned earlier, will confirm this – but what is interesting is that he makes a number of hypotheses on the future solely for the purpose of describing the present more accurately. Not only does he avoid the trap of historical approximation common to the non-specialist trying to cover the entire past[38], his approach had the advantage of giving credit to all the avant-gardes of the twentieth century, starting with the biggest – Futurism. It has become commonplace in history and in theory in general, to consider the various avant-gardes as a linear succession and view the precious suffix as a seal of quality. Yet beyond the common suffix, not only are avant-gardes not equivalent, but some are even fundamentally reactionary such as the movements just after the war like Team X which was never anything but a "social reformist" version of Lettrism and Situationist movements. What is there in Computationalism, beyond the term whose suffix might cause confusion, that could give us clues? Neither an artistic nor an intellectual movement, nor modernism or postmodernism. It is merely a term linked to what lies beyond computerised rationalism as a concept having now acquired complete autonomy from human thought as the privileged framework of application. It refers to the old algebraic turn as well as to the present day computational turn[39] of all the fields of knowledge, and to a new relationship between physics, mathematics and money. This relationship was noted by Marx, who said "logic is the money of the mind"[40] and by Sohn-Rethel[41] – who, as noted A. Jappe, tried to draw up the philosophical genealogy of the links between geometry, philosophy and money in Ancient Greece, based on the hypotheses of George Thomson[42]. This relationship, which today concerns the parallel evolution of the infinite divisibility of electronic money and the ever more refined discretization power of computers – following the self-accelerating law described earlier – has developed so much that most of the earlier economic laws have become obsolete. It is this unprecedented transformation that is the main source of today's crisis. Virtual money, which must not be confused with value[43], is now regulated by knowledge and calculation power. Its growth is based on geometric progression laws while the growth of value is based on arithmetic progression ones. The gap is so great that it has become the San Andreas Fault of the economic and social world, an abyss in which economic and social theory got lost, due both to the intrinsic difficulty of the theoretical reconstruction and to out of date hypotheses and methods. The discrepancies between various social existences, life expectancies and many other parameters have reached cataclysmic proportions. When logic was "the money of the mind", counting was still the ascetic part of human activity, forming "the religion of this generation, its hope and its salvation".[44] The spirit of capitalism was the sum of the minds of the capitalists. In Integral Capitalism, on the other hand, computation – where the symbol includes the number - has replaced calculation and electronic money has replaced money: computation is the currency of the computer and since the computer becomes

ALL it is the identity of money. Computation is the new universal equivalent of which machine time is merely the most concrete side, the "post-historic" equivalent of Marx's work time. Computational finance and computational resources allocation platforms like Gridbus are constantly bringing new empirical proof. Computation that integrates physics, mathematics and money has replaced the Greek juxtaposition of geometry, philosophy and coinage. Physics, mathematics and money are a single thing, the new "(non) subject" of the "automated subject" the older of which was the folklore of finance. The traders in the old stockmarkets, shown occasionally on television, have become the new "savages", with their telephones cradled between ear and shoulder like so many feathered headdresses or belts decorated with bananas.

Confronted with this trend, which I named "Pangaea in the era of informed matter"[45] ten years ago without realising its full extent except intuitively, politics has as much effect as a group of hauliers and the "political theorists" the clairvoyance of foremen… We understand too much and too little of computationalism, just like for rationalism three centuries ago. Too much not to

35 |

see the dangerous pre-Marxist "explanation of religion by belief" in the ideological lies of the liberals. Too little to avoid seeing proliferation of illusionary replacement solutions labelled as "practical theories of resistance", and to avoid "the end of all understanding of the facts" being "peddled as a 'liberating fantasy', and perplexity being peddled as anti-dogmatic modesty"[46] Finally, computationalism as I understand it, this time not as a label for the present state of civilisation but as a theory, must be a social theory: a theory devoid of the technocratic nature of cybernetics, no less effective than the computer

```
------------------------------------------------------------------
Original Message-----
From: apXXX@thoughtsciences.com [mailto:apXXX@thoughtsciences.com]
Sent: vendredi 7 juin 2002 19:32
To: phillipe.morel@ezct.org
Subject: Neuromarketing

Dr. Morel,

My name is AlXX PXXX and I work for a company in Atlanta, GA called
ThoughtSciences. We are very interested in your article "The end of
communication, the end of products: from neuroscience to neuromarket-
ing". Our company has recently removed itself from the cover of secrecy
and is founded on the principles of neuromarketing. We are using fMRI tc
identify preference in the brain and use this information to create
better marketing campaigns.
Obviously, this is a very abbreviated statement of our company. On your
website, at ezct.org, your research has not been published yet, and I
was wondering if you could give me some insight as to what you are writ-
ing about. We are very interested to know about any others doing work in
this field, as we, to our knowledge, believe ourselves to be the first
company using neuromarketing. Thank you very much for your time. Sin-
cerely, AlXX PXXX

------------------------------------------------------------------
-----Original Message-----
From: Jim LXXXX <jlXXXX@bizjournals.com> [mailto:jlXXXX@bizjournals.com]
Sent: Tue, 11 Jun 2002 12:11:46
To: pr@ezct.org
Subject: Media assistance

My name is Jim LXXXX and I am a reporter at the Atlanta Business Chroni-
cle. I am working on a story about an Atlanta company that claims to
have pioneered neuromarketing. I noticed on your Web site that your
company also is exploring this field. I would very much like to discuss
this with someone there. Can you help me? My number is 404-249-XXXX. I
would appreciate anyhelp you can provide.
```

Figure 14: While working on my Master Thesis from 2000 to 2002, I coined the word Neuromarketing in order to define a new alliance between marketing and neuroscience, as well as the end of the efficiency of the traditional rational anticipation theory, due to the intrinsic noise of the market, in favour of a super-rational approach based on functional RMI. As I started to communicate on that matter, I then received messages from a company working on (real) neuromarketing tools… This was nothing else than a proof of the validity of this concept. As for today, such an idea is becoming mainstream.-

itself and no less concrete than Babeuf's Perpetual Land Registry project. This project, one of the only distant descendants of which was Broadacre City, can be seen as the most fantastic political theory produced in the form of an "urban" theory. Of all the

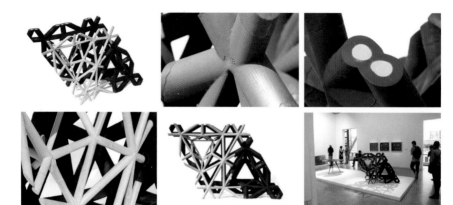

Figure 15, 16, 17, 18, 19, 20: STUDIES IN RECURSIVE LATTICES
©EZCT Architecture & Design Research, 2013
First prototype of a space frame entirely made of UHPFC (here DUCTAL), whose thin sections are inspired by steel construction rather than by the traditional concrete constructive models.
Project: EZCT Architecture & Design Research, 2013
Design Team: Tristan Gobin, Thibault Schwartz, Louise Deguine, Marie Lhuillier, Pierre Marquis, Mathieu Venot, Romain Duballet.
UHP Fiber Concrete: Lafarge Ductal®
Structural Engineering: Justin Dirrenberger (ENSAM Paris), RFR
3D Printed Fabrication of Sand Molds: Voxeljet Technology AG
Casting: Fehr Technologies
Materials: Ductal®, 3D printed sand
Prototypes realized with the support of Lafarge Ductal® and Fehr Technologies

projects up to the Situationist movement, the Perpetual Land Registry is the one that best addressed the social lie of all social lies, that of the rarity of land and its string of consequences. This lie has disseminated a kind of rough Malthusian ideology decidedly much too visible for current taste and politically correct thinking. Instead of saying that there are too many people on earth, Liberals and blind ecologists are now saying that there are too many animals and too much pollution, as well as too little space, arable land, water or energy. The problem is that while in Marx's time, and as he said, there was "only one individual too many on earth – Malthus himself", it is today very difficult to identify a single creator of the most harmful ideology produced since the end of the Second World War. All the more as it is a "pacifist" ideology. However, its unknown creator is less important than the known messengers, some of whom are architects or urban planners (although, as the Situationists say, there is no urban planning and therefore no planners either), but only this "group of techniques for integrating people (techniques that effectively resolve conflicts but create others, currently less well known but more serious). These techniques are innocently used by imbeciles, or deliberately by the police. All the speeches on urban planning are lies, just as obviously as the space organised by urban planners is the space of social lies"[47]. As a land registry employee, trying to "recover or draw up the list of seigniorial rights over the land to benefit the landowning aristocracy"[48], Babeuf was able to "discover in the dusty seigniorial archives the "mysteries of the nobility's usurpations"[49]. Noting the impossibility of a reformist approach of the "social institutions the universal principle [of which] was that, as long as a human being did not tear away by brute force the property his equal could possess, it was permissible, on the other hand, to use every ruse imaginable to take such property out of each others' hands", Babeuf projected a systematic re-distribution of lands to each generation, in accordance with strictly arithmetic laws, and obviously, independently of all previous ownership. Like Rousseau who preached that "fruits belong to all, and the earth belongs to no-one"[50]. Babeuf saw private property as the only basic problem to be dealt with. Reformism was not enough to counter property, because it did not attack the "differential" root of the problem, that is to say the mechanism which, over the generations, impoverishes those who cannot "invest", those, in fact, "who are superfluous and who were too poor to acquire" estates and who had "become poor without having lost anything, because everything had changed around them but they alone had not changed […]". The radical solution proposed by Babeuf was to divide all the land up to ensure a share to everyone that would be "made inalienable so that each citizen's property would always be guaranteed and un-losable". Since by sharing out the French territory there would have been around eleven acres per family of four at that time, Babeuf asks with false innocence "what charming manor would each family have enjoyed? A question that Wright and more modestly Melnikov would ask a century and a half later and that today's computational resources require us to ask again. In our profoundly algorithmic economy, where algorithms tame the turbulence of the markets, and the 700,000 billions' worth of financial products in circulation – derivatives, shares etc., every square meter of culture and cubic meter of natural resource, and ultimately, a mass of global information that is vastly more than the human mind can conceptualise, what is delaying the production of a social theory based on the knowledge and the means of our era? Here, positivism, stripped of all theoretical and scientific basis", "recycled in a new pragmatic realism and recognition of the market and the motor of profit, considered as the ultimate and indispensable", there, an "academic left […] as threadbare as the 'movementist' Marxists that play at politics" and which, depending on the public, drops titbits of historicism and abstract criticism of movement. The sole purposes of this text are to insist on the idealism of the second option and to show its counter-productive theoretical nature.

137|

FOOTNOTES

1. Guy Debord, Considérations sur l'assassinat de Gérard Lebovici, Editions Gérard Lebovici, Paris. The complete quote is: "But, like the proletariat, I am not supposed to be in the world. Thus Gérard Lebovici is immediately suspected of having dangerous commerce with ghosts. The defeat of rational thought, so obvious and so deliberately sought in the spectacle, causes any practice outside the official magic organised by the State or the omnipresent mirror of the world where everything is presented the wrong way round, to be vilified as black magic, or collaboration with the obscure forces of the gurus, the Voodoo and so on. Saying that two and two make four is becoming a revolutionary act. Dare we, in France, think outside the frame? NO – terrorism! The outside is wrong, and the frame – built by the government – is right".

2. F. Nietzsche, Last Letters, Winter 1887-Winter 1889, Editions Manucius. The complete passage of the letter is: "Dear

friend, forgive me for speaking again: this could be the last time. I have gradually eliminated all my human relationships, out of disgust for the fact that people take me for something other than who I am. Now, it is your turn. I have been sending you my books for years so that you will one day declare honestly and naïvely 'I abhor every word'. And you would have the right to, for you are idealistic, and I treat idealism as insincerity that has become instinct, like non-wishing to see the truth at all costs: each sentence in my books contains contempt for idealism. No fatality is more harmful than this intellectual unhealthiness that has hung over humanity as it has existed hitherto; we have devalued all reality so as to invent dishonestly an 'ideal world'

3. We should remember the refusals of Gilles Deleuze, Thomas Pynchon or Guy Debord to appear on TV, especially in political or cultural programmes.

4. "[…] Here we see that solipsism, rigorously developed, coincides with pure realism. The Ego of solipsism is reduced to a point without extension, and it remains the reality that coordinates with it". L. Wittgenstein, quoted by Ralph Rumney, in. Le Consul.

5. Mustapha Khayati, De la misère en milieu étudiant considérée sous ses aspects économique, politique, psychologique, sexuel et notamment intellectuel et de quelques moyens pour y remédier, by Members of the Situationist International Congress and the students of Strasbourg, 1967. § "Create at last the situation that makes any return to the past impossible".

6. Karl Marx, German Ideology.

7. In. Empire, quoted by A. Jappe and R. Kurz, Les habits neufs de l'Empire. Remarques sur Negri, Hardt et Rufin, Editions Léo Scheer, 2003.

8. In his preface to Alfred Sohn-Rethel : la pensée-marchandise, Editions du croquant, 2010, Anselm Jappe recalls that Sohn-Rethel, whose critical project paralleling that of Adorno was a "criticism of money", confronted the taboo represented by this criticism. Thus he writes that Sohn-Rethel, refusing the abstraction of the categories of understanding out of their context "brings us back to the blind action of what has governed societies over the past two thousand five hundred years: money. And this criticism of money is still as taboo today as it was in the German universities in the time of Husserl and Heidegger".

9. The complete quote is: "from now on, all the sciences, all the liberal arts, the sacred training of minds, have collapsed because they have become servile: law, the religious sciences, knowledge of nature, moral principles and the other remarkable fields where the thought of free men is bartered. Ah, what a terrible crime! We see pathetic creatures flocking to sell off literature, and men, what am I saying?- innumerable beasts- made for servile tasks, emerging from the countryside and the woods, even from the mud and filth, leaving their holes and rushing like a pack of dogs to sell and profane literature. What a disaster for culture! People who should have dug and raked have the incredible impudence to touch letters and books! And those whose job it was to guard over the livestock and clean the stables peremptorily discuss human fortune; those who should have whipped the flanks of the animals are now holding the sceptre and sitting among the magistrates; and finally, for people that differ from animals only by appearance and the place they claim, not by their attitudes, a thin icing of culture is enough for them to advance in the world with the audacity, as the poet says, of a pack of wolves […] is it thus that you, the nurse of letters, O philosophy, provide and submit to the desires of the lowest and most abject individuals?". L. B. Alberti, Avantages et inconvénients des lettres, trad. fr. Christophe Carraud, Rebecca Lenoir, Editions Jérôme Millon, 2004.

10. In. Discours sur les sciences and les arts, 1750.

11. Ibid.

12. In. Préface au discours sur l'origine et les fondements de l'inégalité parmi les hommes, 1755.

13. We know how much this movement influenced Arts & Crafts.

14. Charles Babbage, Preface to The Economy of Machinery and Manufactures, Charles Knight, 1832, p. V. "Those who possess rank in a manufacturing country, can scarcely be excused if they are entirely ignorant of principles, whose development has produced its greatness".

15. "The law of accelerating returns is fundamentally an economic theory. Contemporary economic theory and policy are based on outdated models that emphasize energy costs, commodity prices, and capital investment in plant and equipment as key driving factors, while largely overlooking computational capacity, memory, bandwidth, the size of technology, intellectual property, knowledge, and other increasingly (and increasingly increasing) constituents that are driving the economy", in. Ray Kurzweil, The Singularity is Near, Viking, NY, 2005.

16. Marie-José Durand-Richard notes that "the chapters on 'division of work and manufacture' and 'machinism and large scale industry' in Capital are based on Babbage's analysis" in. Marie-José Durand-Richard, « Le regard français de Charles Babbage (1791-1971) on the 'Decline of Science in England' », in Documents pour l'histoire et les techniques, n°

17. Anselm Jappe and Robert Kurz, Les habits neufs de l'Empire. Remarques sur Negri, Hardt et Rufin, Editions Léo Scheer, 2003.

18. "Singularity is not about faith, it is about understanding", Ray Kurzweil.

19. Mustapha khayati, De la misère en milieu étudiant, considérée sous ses aspects économiques, politique, psychologique, sexuel et notamment intellectuel et de quelque moyens d'y remédier, by Members of the Internationale Situationniste and students from Strasbourg, 1967. § "Finally create the situation that makes it impossible to return to the past".

20. Mohamed Dahou, Guy Ernest Debord, Potlatch n°21, 30 juin 1955.

21. O. Spengler, Man and Technique, 1933. French tr. by Editions Gallimard, Paris, 1958.

22. "The layman reading Spengler as he had done previously for Nietzsche and Schopenhauer, had become meanwhile a stranger to philosophy; the professional philosophers stuck to Heidegger, who gave a more successful, interesting expression to their depression. It ennobled the death decreed by Spengler with no consideration for the person, and promised to transform thought on death into a mystery that must be administered by the academic. Spengler was no longer a participant: his brochure on Man and Technique no longer competed with his day's cleverly expressed anthropology. His relations with the National Socialists, his quarrel with Hitler and his death all went unnoticed [...]". Theodor W. Adorno, in. Prismes, Payot, 1986. Here it should be noted that Adorno had enough intelligence to limit his own "cultural pessimism", something that Heidegger's philosophy preferred to forget. That defect is today a proudly exhibited certificate of authenticity brandished by all professional pessimists: "Cultural pessimism did not die with Fascism. On the contrary, it is only today that, in the form of ontologic fundamentalism and criticism of science and civilisation, that it has gained greater plausibility, given the undeniable importance of its old criticism of the destruction of life's natural foundations. It has always transformed this criticism into ontology, on the ground that 'a natural world order' had to be preserved, with all the reactionary features typical of this thought". Robert Kurz, in. L'honneur perdu du travail. Le socialisme des producteurs comme impossibilité logique.

23. Cf. Philippe Morel, The Integral Capitalism (from the Master's Thesis Living in the Ice Age, 2000-2002). English translation, with a new introduction, published by Haecceity, Quarterly Architecture Essay (QAE), Volume 2/Issue 2, Winter 2007. Available at www.haecceityinc.com. The concept of cognitive capitalism barely touches on the nature of today's capitalism and its dependence upon computing power and the global technological infrastructure. Thus it ignores "robot trading" or algorithmic trading against which it is theoretically powerless, and many other phenomena.

24. Many fashionable instances of this idealism may be found at http://thefunambulist.net/

25. "A further reason why industrial society cannot be reformed [...] is that modern technology is a unified system in which all parts are dependent on one another. You can't get rid of the 'bad' parts of technology and retain only the 'good' parts. Take modern medicine, for example. Progress in medical science depends on progress in chemistry, physics, biology, computer science and other fields". Theodore Kaczynski, The Unabomber's Manifesto, quoted by Ray Kurzweil.

26. F. Nietzsche, Rough copy of a Letter to Georg Brandes, December 1888, in. Last Letters, Winter 1887-Winter 1889, Editions Manucius, p. 192.

27. Gracchus Babeuf, Le tribun du peuple, n°40, février 1796, in. Babeuf, Textes choisis, Editions sociales.

28. Gracchus Babeuf, Le cadastre perpétuel, 1789, in. Babeuf, Textes choisis, Editions sociales, p. 97.

29. Ibid.

30. "Socrates and Plato, great doubters and admirable innovators were nevertheless incredibly naive in regard to that fatal prejudice, that profound error which maintains that 'the right knowledge must necessarily be followed by the right action'. In holding this principle they were still the heirs of the universal folly and presumption that knowledge exists concerning the essence of an action. "It would be dreadful if the comprehension of the essence of a right action were not followed by that right action itself" — this was the only outcome considered by these great men - the contrary seemed to them to be crazy and inconceivable - and yet the contrary position is in fact the naked reality which has been demonstrated daily and hourly from time immemorial."

31. Asger Jorn, Image et Forme, extract published in Potlatch n°15, 22 December 1954. The full quote is "We must arrive at a dynamic conception of forms; we must face up to the truth that all human form is in a state of continual transformation. We must not, like the rationalists, avoid this transformation; the failure of the rationalists is in not understanding that the only way to avoid the anarchy of change is to become aware of the laws by which this transformation is operated, and use them [...]."

32. Ibid.

33. Anselm Jappe, in. Politique sans politique.

34. F. Nietzsche, Rough draft of "Letter To the Emperor William II", December 1888. In. Last Letters, Winter 1887-Winter 1889, Editions Manucius.

35. Anselm Jappe, Ibid.

36. Marshall McLuhan, Mutations 1990, Tr. Fr. Editions Mame.

37. Vladimir Mayakovski published this work in 1926. The passages on the telephone that transforms the whole world into a village in which each person can, as if in the main square, talk about the weather although they are thousands of kilometres away from each other, is a forerunner of McLuhan's analyses.

38. McLuhan fell into this trap, but most of his speculative hypotheses remain valid. Cf. Sidney Finkelstein, Sense and

Nonsense of McLuhan, International Publishers Co., Inc., New York, 1968.

39. Cf. Ph. Morel, L'Architecture au-delà des formes : le tournant computationnel (Architecture beyond Form: The Computational Turn), exhibition, Marseille, 2007.

40. Karl Marx, Manuscripts from 1844, tr. Fr. Emile Bottigelli, Paris, Editions sociales, 1972, p. 4030. Quoted by par Anselm Jappe, in Alfred Sohn-Rethel : la pensée-marchandise, Editions du croquant, 2010.

4 Alfred Sohn-Rethel : la pensée-marchandise, Editions du croquant, 2010. Preface byAnselm Jappe.

42. Cf. George Thomson, The First Philosophers, Lawrence & Wishart, London, 1955.

43. Cf. the German school of "Criticism of Value" (Wertkritik) and Anselm Jappe, Les aventures de la marchandise. Pour une nouvelle critique de la valeur, Denoël, Paris, 2003.

44. Gertrude Stein, "Counting is the religion of our generation, its hope and salvation".

45. Pangaea in the era of informed matter ("Pangée à l'Ere de la matière informée") is the last sentence of an essay I submitted to Archilab2002/Earth Economics (Archilab2002/Economie de la Terre), with the title Matter matters – matter computes (original title: "La matière compte").

46. Robert Kurz, L'honneur perdu du travail. Le socialisme des producteurs comme impossibilité logique.

47. I. S. n°6, Août 1961, p. 11.

48. Claude Mazauric, introduction to Babeuf, Textes choisis, Editions sociales.

49. Gracchus Babeuf, quoted by Claude Mazauric, in. Babeuf, Textes choisis, Editions sociales.

50. Rousseau, In. Discours sur l'origine et les fondements de l'inégalité parmi les hommes, Part II, 1755.

PHILIPPE MOREL is an architect and theorist, cofounder of EZCT Architecture & Design Research (2000). He is Associate Professor at the ENSA Paris-Malaquais where he directs the Digital Knowledge program, as well as invited Research Cluster Master at the Bartlett. Prior to the Bartlett he has taught at the Berlage Institute (Seminar and Studio) and at the AA (HTS Seminar and AADRL Studio). His long lasting interest in the elaboration of a Theory of Computational Architecture is well expressed by some of his first published essays (including The Integral Capitalism, 2000-2002; Research On the Biocapitalist Landscape, 2002; Notes on Algorithmic Design, 2003; Notes on Computational Architecture, 2004; A Few Precisions on Architecture and Mathematics, Mathematica Day, Henri Poincare Institute, Paris, January 2004; or Forms of Formal Languages: Introduction to Algorithmics and Bezier Geometry with Mathematica, 2005). Philippe Morel lectured in various places (including MIT Department of Architecture, A Few Remarks on Epistemology and Computational Architecture, Lecture, March 2006; Architectural Association, Information Takes Command, 2007; The Laws of Thought, 2008; Pangaea Proxima, 2008; or recently What is computationalism?, 2012). In February 2007, he curated the exhibition Architecture beyond Forms: The Computational Turn of Architecture at the Maison de l'architecture et de la ville PACA in Marseille. Explicitly departing from Eisenman's dissertation The Formal Basis of Modern Architecture (1963) the exhibition addressed both historically and theoretically the linguistic and computational turns in architectural design. Philippe Morel book Empiricism & Objectivity: Architectural Investigations with Mathematica (2003-2004), subtitled A Coded Theory for Computational Architecture, exhibited at ScriptedByPurpose (Philadelphia, Sept. 2007), is to be considered the first architectural theory book entirely written in code. EZCT work, present in the FRAC Centre and Centre Pompidou permanent collections, as well as in private collections, has been presented recently in the exhibition Out of Hand: Materializing the Postdigital at the Museum of Arts and Design in NY.

THE EVOLUTION OF WORLD BUILDING AS A NEW DESIGN PRACTICE

ALEX MCDOWELL

(Figure 1) UCLA
IDEAS, Greg Lynn,
David Gerber,
Students and the
Robots

July 14, 2014, We are facing the most massive shift in history of our imagining of the capability of media, its place in the space of the world, and its role in the socio-politics of our everyday lives.

No longer constrained to entertainment and narrative media, this new media landscape nevertheless revolves around the stories we tell, and the worlds these stories inhabit.

From the days of tales told around the tribal fire, storytelling was always the way in which we contextualized ourselves, explained the unexplainable, and found the human place and scale in the dark, unknown and undiscovered world around us. This was a communal, collaborative weave of narratives that adapted and evolved in step with the knowledge we acquired while building a sophisticated system of metaphor, myth and poetic triggers to activate our own evolution.

In the new and largely unfamiliar landscape of our contemporary world, we find ourselves again in the darkness with a primal need to return to the power of story worlds to create navigational maps of multi-dimensional and extremely unfamiliar terrain.

MINORITY REPORT

In 2000, I had been designing worlds for movies and narrative media for 20 years, but they had followed traditional linear patterns, largely driven by the written script and the convention of the auteur director or dominant studio producers. When I was invited to join Steven Spielberg to design Minority Report, the project appeared to be radically different to those I had previously experienced. There was no script, the film was set in a grounded near future, and the director demanded a future reality rather than science fiction lens. And his name opened doors across multiple industries that made it possible to investigate far more deeply, and broadly, the ways in which one might use narrative to explore a plausible future. Without a script to drive us towards a linear set of solutions it seemed necessary to begin with framing the world within which this story might evolve.

In more recent world building terms we had to allow the world to build out horizontally,

| **142**

broadly, based on the absolutes of the world. We knew the time setting, the geographic setting, and a few basic interventions that would become the first points in a network of logic that would define the scaffolding of the world. Significantly, a fictional conceit is a central driver of the tendrils that form this structure.

So: in 2050 in Washington DC a disruption arises when a trial police program uses three precognitive beings to place a murder-free safe zone within a 50 mile radius of the center of the city. A rapid influx of population into the region causes a vast urban growth, mostly outside the zoning DC itself, but clustered around the city. This vertical development creates new social systems – a series of upper level city malls that connect different towers that in turn create large areas of shade in a lower city that serves to literally stratify the society. Targeted advertising becomes commonplace in the upper and wealthy areas of the city, and this in turn is commandeered by the security forces to track criminal activity and questionable citizens. Without the wealth of the consumer, the lower city is much less mediated, and consequently an easier place to hide.

Transportation changes radically as new vehicles are engineered to operate like a combination of elevator and driverless car, transporting the wealthy citizens to work from the comfort of their living spaces to their places of work.

All of this just scratches the surface of what became a compelling proof-of-concept of the power of world building to unpack design fictions from the fabric and logic of a world space, and the methodology that allows us to extrapolate forward to a fully integrated structure of narrative. If one were to use Google to make a search for 'how Minority Report prototypes the future' this week, one would find about 128m results. In the course of investigating the verticals that connect the horizontal logic of that world, we found that the world building process is also powerfully precognitive, revealing multiple real world innovations a decade after they were first prototyped for the film. In practical terms there is no magic, but rather good research driven by world building process.

THE EVOLUTION OF WORLD BUILDING

Design process itself was inverted as a new non-linear design emerged as a bottom-up/top-down, collaborative and constantly reevaluated methodology. This was not a familiar linear (cinema) process of pre-production, production and post-production, but a much more broadly applicable evolutionary system of inception, ideation, prototyping, capture (manufacturing), and finishing where all participants are collaborators who are connected though immersive and experiential design visualization.

Using a combination of visualization tools, mixed-reality lenses that allow the user to participate within the virtual space, driven by game engines, with procedural asset generation and crowd behaviors, the creators in any narrative design media platform are able to develop ideas and prototype them in real time and in a fluid and adaptive world space. Immersion in these methods radically alters the way in which we collaborate, and the freedom with which we imagine.

THE WORLD BUILDING MEDIA LAB AT USC

The applications of these methods are very broad and media and platform agnostic. Recent projects at the World Building Media Lab include research funded by Intel into the future of Storytelling, using a New York Times bestselling novel called Leviathan as the content driver. In this project we investigate multiple realities through augmented interactions by multiple users in the real world, virtual realities inside the full-scale world of a giant flying Whale, and multiple narrative strands experienced simultaneously in a braided narrative with multiple user viewpoints intersecting multiple fictional characters. Also work with Boeing into Experiential Design translations of Systems Engineering Language; with the Salk Institute and Greg Lynn's team at IDEAS at UCLA School of Architecture through a grant and investigating neuroscience and architecture; and a sustainable village in Saudi Arabia developed as an immersive portrayal of sustainability in ten years time – a true design fiction based entirely in the real world, and seen within the connective tissue of world building. And finally a project called Rilao designed to develop a fictional city as a vast world building collaboration between over 60 students at USC and now extending to students, faculty, and industry partners in 4 continents and a dozen schools.

All of these world building projects are focused on research though the intersection of storytelling and technology, stimulating a wide array of skills and disciplines to gather together and collaborate using whatever tools are to hand. Agnostic by design with regards to tools and platforms, these students learn to be massively adaptable, and to reimagine their roles in the future of design in the twenty-first century.

[END]

(Figure 2)
Worldbuild
Evolution

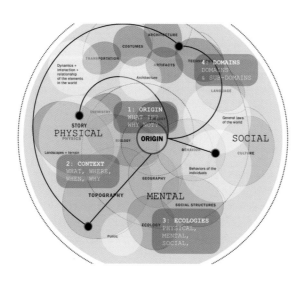

World Building

World building defines a philosophy and practice that exploits a rich collaboration of design and emergent technologies to create visceral narrative spaces - passive or interactive, virtual or real - through story logic, design process and user experience. These tools allow us to terraform new worlds.

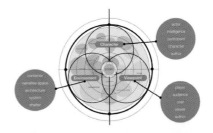

We are moving into a terrain in which the design of a world precedes the telling of a story; the richly detailed world becomes a container for narrative, producing stories that emerge logically and organically across media; and provokes emergent technologies that powerfully enable us to sculpt the imagination into existence.

(Figure 5) Boeing Experiment

Boeing

Boeing invited the World Building Media Lab to join forces with Vierbi School of Engineering, with co-PIs Alex McDowell and Professor Azad Madni, to investigate a new Experiential Design Language, connecting Systems Engineering Language to imagery and virtual environment that could be used to add visual depth and meaning to engineering concepts.

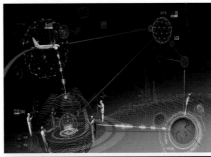

(Figure 6) Leviathan

Leviathan_Intel

The WbML has been working for over two years with Intel Labs to look at the future of storytelling through the lens of Scott Westerfeld's bestselling Leviathan series. Winding back two decades before the setting of the novels, the Leviathan Project imagines a parallel universe where a giant flying whale, the Leviathan, carries a payload of scientists and military crew and a vast number of fabricated animals,

(Figure 7) Leviathan Lab

(Figure 8) Leviathan Whalw

(Figure 9) Minority1

(Figure 10) Minority2

(Figutr 11) Minority Report

(Figure 12) New City

created like the whale herself by Darwinians who have discovered new ways to bio-engineer new species. This fictional world allows the WbML students and their counterparts at Intel Labs to immerse creators and audience alike in a new narrative space, through virtual and augmented realities, and using a combination of game and cinematic technologies. This world is a persistent discovery space, challenging the ways in which we negotiate time and space in future immersive stories. What is a camera, a viewpoint, how do we direct in a multi-braided narrative space, what does it mean to identify with character and emotion, or to edit the passage of time?

Minority Report

In Steven Spielberg's Minority Report, Alex McDowell and his team first explored the methodologies of world building, when they developed the world of the film prior to the script. Not only did unique story lines and opportunities for narrative unfold as the world developed, but the process encouraged a depth of research and extrapolation that even over a decade after release is still resulting in predictive (or precognitive) parallels in the real world.

The design team imagined a Washington DC in around 2050 which had undergone rapid vertical urban development die to the unique nature and tight radius of influence of the Precogs and their ability to predict murder and violent crime. As a result, the city has advanced socially and technologically in easy that not only predict the future but engender new ways of negotiating urban life: transportation, architecture, retail, communication, crime, and ecology.

New City

New City is a project that was developed by Greg Lynn, Peter Frankfurt and Alex

McDowell for the exhibition Design and the Elastic Mind, curated by Paola Antonelli for the MoMA, NY.

New City imagines a virtual world in motion, where radically different populations rub against each other, and engage in cultural interchange. It is conceived of as a seeded world at the scale of the sum total of the cities of Earth, a laboratory for experiments in visualization, architecture, design, information, simulation, and experience.

IMAGE CREDITS
All images courtesy of Alex McDowell

ALEX MCDOWELL, RDI, Professor of practice, USC Cinematic Arts, Media Arts + Practice division; director of USC World Building Media Lab and 5D Institute; creative director at 5D Global Studio.

Alex McDowell RDI is an award-winning designer and storyteller working at the intersection of emergent technologies and experiential media.

McDowell's career encompasses 30 years as production designer in video and feature films, working with directors David Fincher, Steven Spielberg, Terry Gilliam and Anthony Minghelia and others. He designed many films, amongst them Fear and Loathing in Las Vegas, Man of Steel, The Watchmen, Charlie and the Chocolate Factory, Fight Club and Minority Report. His production design work on Minority Report is considered seminal both for its vision of near future technology and its integration with the public imagination, and is believed to have resulted in nearly 100 patents for new technologies.

He is now a Professor of Practice in Media Arts + Practice at USC School of Cinematic Arts, where he teaches world building. He is director of the USC World Building Media Lab (WbML), where McDowell and his interdisciplinary students research and build immersive worlds for storytelling and narrative design practice across multiple platforms. The WbML was awarded the prestigious Future Voice Award at the 2014 Interaction Awards. He also leads the USC 5D Institute, renowned since 2007 as the preeminent narrative media knowledge space. He is recipient, from George Lucas, of the William Cameron Menzies endowed chair in Production Design.

McDowell's 5D Global Studio are high-end peddlers of modern-day magic; in a multi-platform, cross-discipline design studio practice he and his team combine emergent technologies with highly interactive storytelling to create deeply immersive experiences that surprise, provoke and delight.

As Visiting Artist to the MIT Media Lab (2005-2010) he designed the renowned robot opera "Death and the Powers" which premiered in 2010 at the Salle-Garnier in Monte Carlo. He is a Getty Research Institute scholar and an executive board member of the Academy of Motion Pictures Design Branch. In 2006, he was awarded Royal Designer for Industry by the UK's Royal Society of Arts and, in 2013, was given the UK Designers & Art Director's Presidents Award.

NEIL LEACH

THERE IS

NO SUCH

THING

AS

DIGITAL DESIGN

What can such a provocative title mean in an age seemingly dedicated to digital design? Is it a denial of the very basis of ACADIA and of the principles on which its members ground their research and practice?

This article is not intended as a dismissal of computer aided design. Rather it is intended as a means of reinforcing the potential use of computation in architecture, by offering a theoretical critique and questioning many of the received assumptions that still exist about it. As such, this article echoes the strategy of Jacques Derrida, who sees the role of theoretical critique not as a destructive gesture but as a supportive one, by problematizing and calling into question certain accepted beliefs: 'To go after it: not in order to attack, destroy or deroute it, to criticise or disqualify it. Rather, in order to think it in fact, to detach itself sufficiently to apprehend it in a thought which goes beyond the theorem - and becomes a work in its turn.'[1]

The article is structured around three provocations that are intended to challenge the reader into rethinking the very notion of 'digital design'.

We Will No Longer Refer to Digital Design

Back in 2002 I noted: 'Bill Gates has predicted that the present decade will be known as 'The Digital Decade' in that, by the time that it comes to an end, the impact of the digital realm will have been so far-reaching that there will scarcely be any facet of human existence which will remain untouched by it.'[2] If I were to make my own prediction about the end of this present decade I would perhaps claim that by 2020 there will scarcely be any facet of architectural production that will not use digital tools.[3] I therefore believe that we will no longer use the term 'digital'.

In the early days of cars, a carriage drawn by horses would simply be called 'a carriage', whereas it was necessary to specify a car – in other words, a carriage not drawn by horses – as a 'horseless carriage'.[4] Now it is automatically assumed that a car is the dominant form of transportation to the point that if we refer to a carriage drawn by horses we now need to specify 'a horse drawn carriage'. By extension, we might compare the way that we used to distinguish between hand drawings and digital drawings: initially – when most drawings were hand drawings, we would simply call hand drawings 'drawings', and would call computationally drawn drawings 'CAD drawings'. These days, however, the term 'drawing' more or less refers automatically to CAD drawings, to the point that if we wish to refer to drawings drawn by hand we need to specify them as 'hand drawings'.

By extension, I believe that we will not talk about 'digital design' by the end of the decade. This is not because we will not use computation, but rather for precisely the opposite reason. We will all be using computation. Computation will be everywhere. For this very reason the term itself will simply disappear. We will just assume that everything will be computational. We will therefore not refer to digital design. There will only be design.

There is No Such Thing as A Digital Design

For Patrik Schumacher there is a new global style of architecture – one that he calls 'parametricism'.

'There is a global convergence in recent avant-garde architecture that justifies its designation as a new style: parametricism. It is a style rooted in digital animation techniques, its latest refinements based on advanced parametric design systems and scripting methods. Developed over the past 15 years and now claiming hegemony within avant-garde architecture practice, it succeeds Modernism as the next long wave of systematic innovation. Parametricism finally brings to an end the transitional phase of uncertainty engendered by the crisis of Modernism and marked by a series of relatively short-lived architectural episodes that included Postmodernism, Deconstructivism and Minimalism. So pervasive is the application of its techniques that parametricism is now evidenced at all scales from architecture to interior design to large urban design. Indeed, the larger the project, the more pronounced is parametricism's superior capacity to articulate programmatic complexity.'[5]

Moreover, parametricism, is governed by its own distinctive aesthetic: 'Aesthetically, it is the elegance of ordered complexity and the sense of seamless fluidity, akin to natural systems that constitute the hallmark of parametricism.'[6]

For the moment, let us overlook the fact that Jean-Francois Lyotard proclaimed the end of Grand Narratives with the advent of postmodernity – implying that there can be no more universal style any more.[7] Equally let us overlook the fact that from a technical point of view we need to distinguish very precisely between 'advanced parametric design systems' (whose only genuinely parametric manifestations include Catia and Digital Project) and 'scripting techniques' (such as Grasshopper), and cannot simply lump them together under the banner of so-called 'parametricism'. [8] Let us also overlook the fact that most buildings are actually designed these days using explicit modeling techniques, rather than algorithmic generative techniques or parametric tools. Likewise let us overlook the fact that the notion of style itself seems to remain distinctly postmodern in the way that it privileges the scenographic and the visual.[9] Let us also overlook the fact that the example of Frei Otto, whom Schumacher cites in his article, would seem to suggest that we should be operating in a morphogenetic fashion and using digital tools to perhaps 'breed' buildings, rather than simply fashion them stylistically.[10] Finally, let us overlook the fact that much of the work produced under the banner of so-called 'parametricism' was already nascent in the pre-computational work coming out of certain offices, such as Gehry and Partners and Zaha Hadid Architects. Let us overlook all these issues – not because they are unimportant, but rather because the focus of this paper is somewhat different.

What I want to question here is not whether there is such style as 'parametricism' – whatever that term might mean – but rather whether there is any such thing as 'a digital design' or 'a digital building' that might be recognized in terms of its aesthetics or style.[11]

What is 'a digital design' exactly? Firstly, I wish to argue that the adjective, 'digital', refers primarily to a noun, 'tool', used in the process of design.[12] Secondly, we need to make a distinction between the noun, 'a design', and the verb, 'to design'. The noun, 'a design', refers to the end product of the design process, whereas the verb, 'to design', refers to the actual process of designing. It therefore follows that, if we agree that the term 'digital' relates primarily to tools, it is associated more with the process, 'designing', than with the end product, 'a design'. We might therefore refer to 'designing digitally' when describing the use of digital tools in the process of designing. However, we should be very cautious about referring to 'a digital design' as such. A building might therefore have been 'designed digitally', but – in and of itself – it cannot be described as being 'digital'. In other words, while there is clearly a practice of designing that involves the use of digital tools, there is no product as such that might be described as 'digital'. There is therefore no such thing as 'a digital design'. There is only a process of 'designing digitally'.

So what exactly do people mean when they refer to 'digital design' – or indeed 'parametric design' – as a style? Even if there were such a thing as 'digital design' as a recognizable product, what exactly would it look like? In short, is Patrik Schumacher correct in identifying a new aesthetic that owes its origin to the development of new digital tools?

The question is set in context by my own personal experience of working with these tools. For the 2006 Architecture Biennial Beijing Professor Xu Weiguo and I commissioned what we believed would be the first digitally fabricated building in China – a CNC milled and laser cut pavilion designed by Elena Manferdini as the West Coast Pavilion. It took us some time to find the right fabrication facilities in China, although we were informed that Yansong Ma, principal of MAD Architects, had in fact located a CNC machine in South China, being used to reproduce antique furniture.[13] We could surmise that this same CNC machine might have been used to also fabricate an entire Palladian villa, in which case our West Coast Pavilion might not have been the first digitally fabricated building in China. What then would a digitally fabricated design – Manferdini's West Coast Pavilion or a Palladian villa?

By extension, we might ask, whether there is anything that could be drawn using a computer that could not also be drawn using a pencil. The answer, surely, is 'no'. Equally we might ask whether there is anything that could be fabricated by a robot that could not also be fabricated by hand. The answer again, surely, is 'no'. There may be certain design outcomes that are facilitated by the use of certain tools, and that might take an impossibly long time to draft in an analogue fashion, but this does not make them digital designs.[14] Equally, there might be certain fabrication outcomes whose realization would benefit from robotic construction methods, but this does not preclude the possibility of actually fabricating them by hand, given a sufficiently high quality of workmanship.[15]

The history of architecture is, of course, full of examples of innovations in technology that have a direct impact on innovations in design. For example, the invention of the simple elevator made possible the high-rise buildings that we see in cities, such as New York, today, and it would be fair to say that whole history of architecture changed as a result of that straightforward invention. The same might be said of the air conditioning unit and many other technological innovations. Equally, the invention of certain software programs has afforded certain design procedures, such as duplicating, populating, subdividing and so on, that has influenced the development of design practices themselves, and – by extension – the invention of certain fabrication technologies has afforded certain construction methods. But neither of these developments actually caused these changes. This becomes abundantly clear when we compare a building, such as Gehry and Partners' Guggenheim Museum in Blbao, Spain, designed in a largely pre-computational era with one, such as their Disney Hall in Los Angeles, designed comprehensively using computational tools. The two buildings look remarkably similar in appearance.

Figure 1: Gehry and Partners, Guggenheim Museum, Bilbao

Figure 2: Gehry and Partners, Disney Hall, Los Angeles

If, however, we are to look for a theory that might explain the potentialities offered by digital tools, we might start by considering the 'theory of affordances'.[16] The theory of affordances suggests that there is a particular action or set of actions afforded by a tool or object. Thus a knob might afford pulling – or possibly pushing – while a cord might afford pulling. This is not to say that the tool or object has agency as such. In other words the tool or object does not have the capacity to actually 'invite' or 'prevent' certain actions. Rather it simply 'affords' certain operations that it is incumbent on the user to recognize, dependent in part on a set of pre-existing associations that have been made with that tool or object. Likewise that action or set of actions is also dependent upon the capacity of an individual to undertake those actions. Thus certain actions might not be afforded to small children or those without the strength or agility to perform them. Moreover, certain tools afford certain operations, but do not preclude other operations. For example, we might perhaps affix a nail with a screwdriver – albeit less efficiently – if we do not have a hammer at hand. We might also recognize that it is easier to cut wood with a saw than with a hammer, and that the technique of cutting with a saw affords a limited range of possible operations. Importantly also the theory of affordances has been applied to human computer interfaces to refer to the easy discoverability of certain actions. As such, we might be able to identify various operations afforded by digital tools that might thereby become hegemonic.

In this sense, computational tools might thereby be associated with a set of operations that are afforded by the accessibility and ease of use of such tools, so that 'searching' becomes increasingly popular in a culture colonized by the logic of search engines, such as Google. We might even recognize certain new patterns of behavior, such as the emerging tendency to embark on any research through the use of search engines, so that with time certain hegemonic practices begin to develop and the search engine becomes the de facto starting point for any academic research. Inevitably this will have an impact on the final form that the research will take.[17] By extension, we can observe various visual effects that are afforded by the accessibility and use of the computer in design, so that these visual effects will become hegemonic, thus engendering a certain recognizable aesthetic that we come to associate with designing digitally. Equally, there are certain visual effects that are not afforded by certain computational tools. It is, for example, very difficult to generate a straight line using Processing, just as it was relatively difficult to produce carefully controlled curved lines in the analog world of parallel motion drawing boards.

53

Figure 3: Elena Manferdini, West Coast Pavilion, Beijing, 2006

Figure 4: CNC Milled Organ Capital, Harvard University, Cambridge, MA.

So what, then, is 'a digital design'? Would we ever talk about 'a pencil design'? Presumably not. The term 'a digital design' is therefore seemingly absurd. In short, when we understand the term 'digital' in architecture we associate it with a series of techniques and technologies – a series of 'tools', in other words. These tools afford certain operations, and we thereby come to associate them with a certain hegemonic aesthetic that develops over time. But they do not enforce those operations. Thus, computational tools – in and of themselves – do not engender any particular 'style'.

Figure 5: Neil Leach, Kristina Shea, Spela Videcnik and Jeroen van Mechelen, eifFORM Installation, Academie van Bouwkunst, Amsterdam 2002.
\

'Design' Might Soon Become Obsolete

This provocation is set in perspective by my own personal experience of working with Kristina Shea, Spela Videcnik and Jeroen van Mechelen on the 'design' and fabrication of an installation for the Academie van Bouwkunst in Amsterdam, for which we used a software program, called 'eifFORM', developed by Shea.[18] This tool generates structurally efficient forms in a stochastic, non-monotonic method using a process of structural shape annealing.[19] The 'designer' merely establishes certain defining coordinates, and then unleashes the program which eventually 'crystallizes' and resolves itself into a certain configuration. Each configuration constitutes a structural solution which will support itself against gravity and other prescribed loadings, and yet each configuration is different. Such is the logic of a bottom-up, stochastic method. Moreover, the program can generate an outcome in around 20 minutes. It is therefore possible to generate an array of outcomes, and then select a preferred option on aesthetic or other grounds.

What has become clear is that with the introduction of certain generative programs, the whole nature of 'design' itself has been called into question. The architect/engineer no longer 'designs' the structure in the traditional way, but sets up a series of constraints and allows the program to search for possible solutions from which one is selected. Furthermore, at a most radical level, the introduction of these programs has redefined the role of the architect. No longer is the architect the demiurgic form-maker of the past. Rather the architect has been recast as the controller of processes, who oversees the 'formation' of architecture. With the development of new computational techniques, it would seem, we find ourselves on the threshold of a new paradigm for architectural design.

Of the many potentialities afforded by the computer, one of the most significant is its capacity to operate as a search engine. Not only does this reconfigure the entire domain of scholarship in that – once the project initiated by Google to scan all books in the world has been accomplished – it will soon be possible to scan through the entire body of published materials in a fraction of a second to search for all references to a particular term. As a result the logic of the search and of trawling for information will begin to exert itself as a hegemonic method of initiating research. But this also suggests that the entire domain of design, as we know it, might also be reconfigured. What might it be, for example, to 'search' for a range of possible building solutions?

If, then, we think through the logic of the search in the context of 'design', what such an approach suggests is that if all possible solutions already exist, it is simply a question of defining a set of constraints, conducting a search, and then selecting one of the many outcomes. The potential implications of this are far reaching. Not only does it challenge the traditional notion of the 'genius' of the architect/designer and the originality of the work of art, but it also suggests that if there is still any creativity in the 'design' process, it should lie, firstly, in defining the constraints that generate the range of possible solutions to a problem, and, secondly, in developing an effective method of filtering or evaluating them.[20] But can we still use the verb 'design' to refer to 'defining' constraints or 'developing' a method of filtering and evaluating the results? If not, then for many increasingly common computational operations, the term, 'design', will become obsolete.

Conclusion

Whether or not we accept that there can still be such a thing as 'a digital design', or 'a digital architecture', it is clear that with the introduction of an increasing array of computational tools, we need to rethink the role of design itself. Douglas Rushkoff refers to the current moment as a 'Renaissance moment', in that many of our accepted tenets – including the very nature of design itself - are being challenged: 'Renaissance moments happen when we experience a shift in perspective so that the stories, models, and languages that we have been using to understand our reality are suddenly up for grabs. But these renaissance moments are transitory, because almost as soon as our perspectives are shifted, we settle into new conventions'.[21] As such, at the very least we need to question whether the contribution of computation leads merely to a new style of architecture, as Patrik Schumacher argues, or whether it leads to an entirely different logic of not only generating or searching for new forms but also of understanding how the buildings and cities might operate.

At the launch of the recent 'Digital Design' stream within the European Graduate School in June 2014, an architect studying philosophy on the program commented that she was not interested in the Digital Design stream in that, as an architect, she already knew what 'digital design' is. As a Professor of Digital Design on that program I would have to say that I am no longer sure what 'digital design' is – and seriously doubt whether we can still use that term in any meaningful way. But what I do know for sure is that – if 'digital design' does exist – it is not what I used to think that it was. Moreover, it is also clear that a range of new digital tools and techniques is appearing that not only challenge our previous understanding of term 'design', but also hold out the promise of new, more efficient ways of generating or searching for possible solutions. So too digital tools are offering new, more effective ways of fabricating buildings and – through BIM – of controlling the logistics of construction itself. This can only be good for the discipline of architecture.

I am therefore tempted to add a subtitle: There's No Such Thing as Digital Design: And It's a Good Thing Too. [22]

REFERENCES

- Alberti, Leon Battista (1988). On the Art of Building in Ten Books, (Joseph Rykwert, Neil Leach and Robert Tavernor, trans.). Camb., MA: MIT Press.
- .Derrida, Jacques, 'Point de Folie – Maintenant L'Architecture', in Neil Leach (ed.) (1997). Rethinking Architecture: A Reader in Cultural Theory. London: Routledge
- Fish, Stanley (1994). There is No Such Thing as Free Speech, and It's a Good Thing, Too. Oxford: Oxford University Press.
- Gibson, James (1979).The Ecological Approach to Visual Perception. Hove: Psychology Press.
- Gibson, Eleanor, and Pick, Anne (2002). An Ecological Approach to Perceptual Learning and Development. New York: Oxford University Press.
- Leach, Neil (ed.), (1997). Rethinking Architecture: A Reader in Cultural Theory. London: Routledge.
- Leach, Neil (ed.) (2002). Designing for a Digital World. London: Wiley
- Leach, Neil, Xu, Weiguo (eds.) (2010). Design Intelligence: Advanced Computational Techniques for Architecture. Beijing: China Architecture and Building Press.
- Lyotard, Jean-Francois (1988). The Postmodern Condition, (Geoffrey Bennington and Brian Massumi eds.), Minneapolis: Minnesota University Press, 1988.
- Oosterhuis, Kas (ed.) (forthcoming). Next Generation Building. Delft: TU Delft
- 'Roundtable Discussion', Urbanism and Architecture, Harbin, China, September 2012, No. 96, p. 9.
- Rushkoff, Douglas (2002). 'The Digital Renaissance' in Leach (ed.), Designing for a Digital World, London: Wiley, 2002.
- Shaw, Robert and Bransford, John (eds.) (1977). Perceiving, Acting, and Knowing. London: Wiley.
- Shea, Kristina (2004).'Directed Randomness' in Neil Leach, David Turnbull and Chris Williams (eds.), Digital Tectonics, London: Wiley, 2004, pp.88-101.
- Shea, Kristina. 'Creating Synthesis Partners' in Architectural Design, no. 72, pp. 42-45.

|156

FOOTNOTES

1. Jacques Derrida, 'Point de Folie – Maintenant L'Architecture', in Neil Leach (ed.), Rethinking Architecture: A Reader in Cultural Theory, London: Routledge, 1997, p. 328. In poststructuralist terms, then, the article subscribes to the principle of 'problematization', where problematization is seen as a supportive gesture. For once one is aware of a problem as a problem, it becomes a different sort of problem – not a problem by which one is trapped, but rather a problem that one has identified and which one can potentially address.

2. Neil Leach, 'Introduction' in Leach (ed.), Designing for a Digital World, London: Wiley, 2003, p.6.

3. 'My own prediction is that by 2020 we won't even use the word 'computation' because it will be everywhere. In 50 years time the whole way in which we operate will be totally digitized. But I wouldn't want to predict exactly how, except to say that this is obvious in that even now we can't go back to using telegrams and writing letters once we have developed communication through emails. So it's moving forward irreversibly, but we have to understand the processes in order for them to work for the benefit of the society. One of the early predictions about computation was that it would automatically lead to a much better world. In fact what happened immediately was that we got spam in our email accounts, and so on - not at all what we expected. So it's important to understand what we can do with it and make it work for the benefit of humanity. It's up to us in the end.' On this see 'Interview' in Leach, Xu Weiguo (eds.), Design Intelligence: Advanced Computational Techniques for Architecture, Beijing: CABP, 2010, p. 8.

4. As Alvin Huang remarks about the relationship between the 'digital' and the 'non-digital': 'The closing slide of my

[lecture] is a photograph of a device which at the time was called the horseless carriage, which as we know now is called the car. It doesn't need to be identified by the fact that it doesn't have a horse, because it's actually a car. And that is kind of the direction we are going now with technology in architecture. We don't need to distinguish the "digital" from the "non-digital".' Alvin Huang in 'Roundtable Discussion', Urbanism and Architecture, Harbin, China, September 2012, No. 96, p. 9.

5. Patrik Schumacher, 'Parametricism: A New Global Style for Architecture and Urbanism' in Leach (ed.), Digital Cities AD, 2009, p. 15.

6. Schumacher, p. 16.

7. On this see Jean-Francois Lyotard, The Postmodern Condition, (Geoffrey Bennington and Brian Massumi eds.), Minneapolis: Minnesota University Press, 1988.

8. For a critique of Patrik Schumacher, and an attempt to define precisely the term 'parametric' for architectural design, see: Leach, Parametrics Explained, in Kas Oosterhuis (ed.), Next Generation Building (forthcoming)

9. This is not to deny that – as Gilles Deleuze would observe – every process is linked to representation through a process of reciprocal presupposition, and that every process produces a result that constitutes a form of representation.

10. The term 'style' implies a preconceived notion of what the end result might look like, as though it constitutes an aesthetic template that constrains and conditions the design process.

11. The term 'parametric' seems to cause considerable confusion. It would appear that for many people 'parametric design' implies adjusting the 'parameters' in the design process. But this makes little sense. From the very beginning of architectural history what building was ever designed without the parameters being adjusted during the design process?

12. Here we might further distinguish between software tools, and hardware tools. Although software tools are used primarily in the design process, they may also be used in the fabrication process as in programming robots and so on. By contrast, although hardware tools are used primarily in the fabrication process, they may also be used in the design process in terms of the computers themselves and 3-D printing and other technologies deployed in the refinement of a design.

13. See, for example, the website for alibaba.com: http://uk.alibaba.com/product/1777298937-Cnc-architecture.html, accessed 24/06/14

14. Let us take the example of a Google 'search'. We could spend many years searching through all the books in a library to find a particular quote, which we could find in a fraction of a second using Google.

15. This is not to deny that the accuracy afforded by robotic fabrication technologies offers certain advantages over manual construction.

16. The theory of affordances was introduced initially by James Gibson in an article, James Gibson, 'The Theory of Affordances', in Robert Shaw and John Bransford (eds.), Perceiving, Acting, and Knowing, London: Wiley, 1977. Gibson later elaborated on this theory in his book, James Gibson, The Ecological Approach to Visual Perception, Hove: Psychology Press, 1979. It was also developed by Gibson's wife, Eleanor Gibson together with Anne Pick: Eleanor Gibson, Eleanor, Anne Pick, An Ecological Approach to Perceptual Learning and Development. New York: Oxford University Press, 2000.

17. By way of example, the translation of Leon Battista Alberti's treatise on architecture was influenced significantly by the then recent introduction of the computer, in that the potential to revise the text again and again (which would not have been so viable in the old days of (re)typing on a typewriter) led to a pithy and precise use of language. Leon Battista Alberti, On the Art of Building in Ten Books, (Joseph Rykwert, Neil Leach and Robert Tavernor, trans.), Camb., MA: MIT Press, 1988.

18. On this see Kristina Shea, 'Directed Randomness' in Neil Leach, David Turnbull and Chris Williams (eds.), Digital Tectonics, London: Wiley, 2004, pp.88-101.

19. Annealing refers to the method of heating and cooling metals. The eifForm program simulates this process, so that the eventual form 'crystallises'. The process is stochastic because it contains a random element to the search process, which is controlled to allow for exploration of concepts that are initially worse than the current design. It is therefore also non-monotonic, in that it is constantly under revision, often negating previous developments. For a discussion of the eifForm program see Kristina Shea, 'Creating Synthesis Partners' in Architectural Design, no. 72, pp. 42-45.

20. This also begins to suggest that certain more conservative approaches to creativity, such as in the work of Martin Heidegger, need to be reconsidered. For example, Heidegger's notion of the work of art is somehow at odds with those who champion the genius of the designer, in that his understanding of art is linked to the Greek term 'aletheia', which mean 'not forgetting'. In other words, in producing the work of art the 'artist' merely uncovers – or 'remembers' – an already existing 'truth'. To those who believe in the creative genius of the artist and the originality of the work of art this might seem somewhat incongruous. After all, how can there be an original work of art when it has already been out there, and is just waiting to be uncovered or 'unforgotten'? With the introduction of the logic of the 'search', however, it might seem that Heidegger's position is not so questionable after all. On this see: Leach (ed.), Rethinking Architecture, London:

Routledge, 1997, pp. 98-99.

21. Douglas Rushkoff, 'The Digital Renaissance' in Leach (ed.), Designing for a Digital World, London: Wiley, 2002.
22. This contains an obvious allusion to the work of Stanley Fish, in which – somewhat controversially for an American academic operating in the country whose national anthem defines it as 'the land of the free' – Fish challenges this fundamental tenet of American believes: Stanley Fish, There is No Such Thing as Free Speech, and It's a Good Thing, Too, Oxford: Oxford University Press, 1994.

IMAGES CREDITS
Figure 1: http://commons.wikimedia.org/wiki/File:Guggenheim_Museum,_Bilbao,_July_2010_(06).JPG (image in public domain)
Figure 2: http://en.wikipedia.org/wiki/Walt_Disney_Concert_Hall (image in public domain)
Figure 3: Elena Manferdini
Figure 4: http://www.hfcustomcncmilling.com/white_oak_organ_capitals.html
Figure 5: Neil Leach, Kristina Shea, Spela Videcnik and Jeroen van Mechelen, eifFORM Installation, Academie van Bouwkunst, Amsterdam 2002.

NEIL LEACH is an architect and theorist. He is Professor at the European Graduate School, Adjunct Professor at the University of Southern California, Visiting Professor at Tongji University, and a NASA Innovative Advanced Concepts fellow. He has also taught at SCI-Arc, Architectural Association, Cornell University, Columbia GSAPP, Dessau Institute of Architecture, Royal Danish School of Fine Arts, IaaC, ESARQ, University of Bath, University of Brighton and University of Nottingham. He is the author of The Politics of Space (Routledge, forthcoming), Camouflage (MIT, 2006), Forget Heidegger (Paideia, 2006), China (Map Office, 2004), Millennium Culture (Ellipsis, 1999) and The Anaesthetics of Architecture (MIT, 1999); co-author of Mars Pants: Covert Histories, Temporal Distortions, Animated Lives (Architecture Foundation, 2000); editor of Digital Cities (Wiley, 2009), Designing for a Digital World (Wiley, 2002), The Hieroglyphics of Space: Reading and Experiencing the Modern Metropolis (Routledge, 2002), Architecture and Revolution: Contemporary Perspectives on Central and Eastern Europe (Routledge, 1999), and Rethinking Architecture: A Reader in Cultural Theory (Routledge, 1997); co-editor of Swarm Intelligence: Architectures of Multi-Agent Systems, (Tongji UP, forthcoming); Design Intelligence: Advanced Computational Research (CABP, 2013); Digital Workshop in China (Tongji UP, 2013) Scripting the Future (Tongji UP, 2012), Fabricating the Future (Tongji UP, 2012); Machinic Processes, 2 Vols. (CABP, 2010), (Im)material Processes: New Digital Techniques for Architecture, 2 Vols., (CABP, 2008), Emerging Talents, Emerging Technologies, 2 Vols., (CABP, 2006), Fast Forward>>, Hot Spots, Brain Cells (Map Office, 2004) and Digital Tectonics (Wiley, 2004); and co-translator of Leon Battista Alberti, On the Art of Building in Ten Books (MIT Press, 1988). He has also been co-curator (with Xu Weiguo) of a series of exhibitions at the Architecture Biennial Beijing: Fast Forward>> (2004), Emerging Talents, Emerging Technologies (2006), (Im) material Processes: New Digital Techniques for Architecture (2008), and Machinic Processes (2010). He also co-curated (with Roland Snooks) Swarm Intelligence: Architectures of Multi-Agent Systems in SH Gallery, Shanghai (2010), and (with Philip Yuan) DigitalFUTURE (2011) and Interactive Shanghai (2013) in Tongji University, Shanghai.

He is currently working on a research project sponsored by NASA to develop a robotic fabrication technology to print structures on the Moon and Mars.

OSAKA
A DISTINCTIVE
URBANISM

TOM VERBES, OCEAN CN

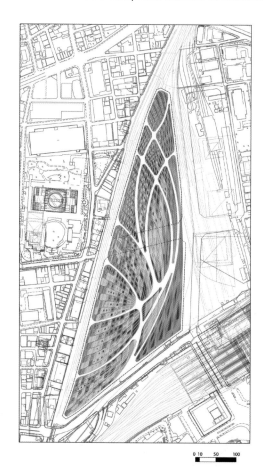

(Figure 1) Proposal for a single snapshot in time, as an instant in a process of formation and information, to be developed and adapted to future contingencies.

(Figure 2) Plan of building footprints and open spaces, describing patterns and textures of materials and planting for the six schemes

This essay, along with its featured project, the Umekita Second Development Area in Osaka, Japan, by OCEAN CN, articulates paradigms and methods, with which to heighten the distinctness of specific urban locales. In addition, the notion of an urban plan, and its guiding interactive model, is postulated as the outcome(s) of multiple influences and associations in time. The indeterminacies of the formative processes of urbanism require methods which specify its propositions provisionally. A masterplan, as a singular (tunnel) vision of a future which is ultimately knowable and determinable, lacks the intelligence to respond and process input in a feedback loop. What then is an intelligent urban model? Throughout the history of twentieth century masterplanning, the model, or two dimensional plan, was understood to be a static and final representation of the singular, and even ideal, outcome of a design process, most often obsolete before it is built. The early twenty-first century conception of the urban model is one of an interactive machine for issuing variance, through prototyping processes which aim for customised output, rather than uniform and repetitive production.

Until early in the twenty-first century, the city was understood ontologically as the center of economic, political, social and cultural activity, to and from which emanated all capital, authority, interaction, and meaning. A paradigm shift occurred, between the nineteenth and twenty-first centuries, which had challenged the conception of the city as the center of the nation state. Polycentrality, globalization, and unprecedented urbanization began to be facilitated by networks enabling flows of goods, capital, and people, with great speed and mobility. If the nineteenth century city emerged alongside new industrial models of standardized, repetitive production, consolidated by the evident causal relation of the ubiquity of generic architecture, and the further resulting monotony of twentieth century cities, what industrial paradigms will guide the expansive urbanity of the twenty-first century? Without much drama, the current unprecedented era of urbanisation is both a potential opportunity to articulate a new paradigm of urban heterogeneity, as well as teetering tenuously as a warning of the imminently regrettable perpetuation of the undifferentiated sameness of cities worldwide.

Kenneth Frampton's potent formulation of Critical Regionalism in the early 1980s, whose central argument was founded on a deep critique of the ubiquity, and the apparent inappropriateness, of modernism a global style. The disillusionment with universal civilization, led a series of 'post' modernisms and neo-traditionalisms, to pick up the fragments of modernism's failed unity. Critical Regionalism was rooted in the reassertion of national identities, and a call for the revival of their regional material traditions and a new valorization of the vernacular. Localised material techniques and systems served as meaningful vehicles with which to recapitulate regional architectural differences. However rear-garde and fuddy-duddy Critical Regionalism seems today, its formulation thirty-some years ago challenged the effects of universalisation to champion the survival of local culture. The aim of recalling Frampton's position some three decades ago, is to renovate how to conceive, articulate and produce specific and distinct attributes in the design and planning, in an era of unprecedented city building. It should be noted that a programmatic agenda of pursuing distinctness of cities lies in sharp contrast to the cult of the local. How can cities opportunise and innovate upon the constraints and practices of a locality? Far from a retreat to a reliance on historic traditional practices, the emphasis here is not on the perpetuation of traditional and vernacular material traditions, in the making of theme parks, to echo Frederick Jameson' critique of Critical Regionalism. In an era in which no greater extent of urbanisation has occurred, how can the qualities of cities be differentiated to be identifiable rather than indistinguishable?

As a contemporary alternative to neo-traditional culture, the information-based inputs of the new paradigm of the model as a prototype heighten capacities of these methods to tease out coherent local expressions. These inputs can include new planning policies, zoning, building codes, infrastructural flows, emerging industrial practices, local climates, ecosystems, and the specificities of demographics of a locale, amongst other data structures can serve as inputs to models. Given the ubiquity of software for design, analysis, simulation, and the management of large databases, information has, in the last thirty years, been universalised. The internet, big data, and the pervasive methods of urban planning, create cheap and cheerful facsimiles. Frampton's argument of the differentiation of regions based on their specific cultural practices, continues to be challenged by today's transnational cultures, in which the identity of cities is paramount over that of regions and nations states. What are the alternatives to the crisis of the masterplan within a world of vast data sets of information, much of which can be captured and processed?

The tools of non-standard production are well rehearsed in architectural design, building systems, interior design, industrial design, furniture, etc, yet the ambition of this essay, and its associated urban design proposal, charts the potential for the customisation of the city in the twenty-first century. Emerging out of the contemporary industrial paradigm of Personal Fabrication, is the possibility to characterise a new industrial culture, aiming towards the discovery of new social, political and material effects, as projective but not singular nor ideal. Speculating on new cultural practices which could emanate from industrial methods, the epistemological framework proposed is to look for formulations of future culture to be specified in a heterogeneous field of cities. An urban model is thus a vehicle for generating multiple options of possible future conditions, through the machining and prototyping of masterplans which are not images as representations, but provisional configurations of interactive models, shaped by a manifold of contingencies

The future vision of Umekita for the Second Development Zone in Umekita Area is driven by the objective of achieving a Distinctive Urbanism, predicated on the design of unique and memorable spatial experiences. OCEAN CN's proposal for the primary Gateway to Osaka aims to augment the diversity of built massing and open spaces. High density urbanism is mitigated with public green corridors and plazas, giving simultaneously a sense of openness within an intense metropolitan experience. The principle strategic objective of this proposal is to develop a manifold of possible future scenarios and configurations for the site, which can be adapted to diverging orientations of future investment models and planning considerations. Although one single design scheme is presented, this proposal is rather for an adaptive process of mediating towards

(Figure 3) Plan of land utilisation, programme areas and composition of six schemes, demonstrating the metrics of programme composition, ratios and mixes of six schemes, and relations of built and open space. 3D massing and open space diagrams of six differentiated schemes based on six programmatic scenarios

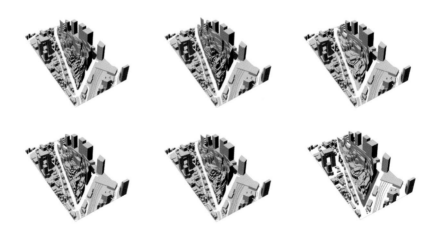

multiple possible futures, each contingent on how economic, political, social and environmental considerations play out in time.

Machining mixes of qualities and quantities of programs, typologies and densities, the principle strategic objective of this urban proposal is to develop a manifold of possible future scenarios and configurations for the site, which can be adapted to diverging orientations of future investment models and planning considerations. Although one single design scheme is presented, this proposal is rather for an adaptive process of mediating towards multiple possible futures, each contingent on how economic, political, social and environmental considerations play out in the future. Six zoning scenarios, each outlining a varied mix of programmatic ratios, are deployed as instruments to yield six different diagrams of massing and open green spaces. The resultant diverse urban morphologies demonstrate the openness of this methodology to the contingencies which will shape the development of the Umekita area.

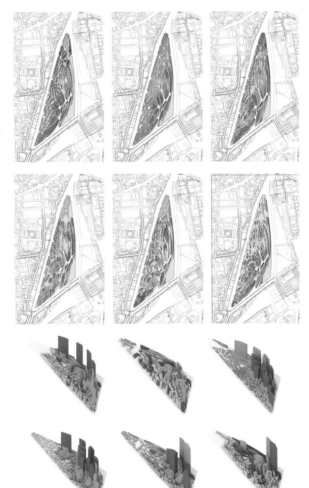

(Figure 4,5) Series of plans and massing diagrams indicating driving parameters such as point and field attractors, relations to roads and rail infrastructure, and their associated massing heights, footprints and setbacks.

A large part of the vast 7ha site of the Umekita Second Development Area is a top-side development above existing railway tracks. In OCEAN CN's proposal, the site is subdivided by three site influences: a principle north-south and east west array of intersecting grid lines, splaying off the traffic plaza in the West Exist of Osaka station above the proposed JR Tokaido Line; and a set of grid lines associating to the small scale urban morphology to the west of the site. In addition, the existing and proposed pedestrian flows on the site, between the stations and the existing streets and plazas, bring forth a fourth, more fluid grid of oriented pedestrian spaces. These flows, generated from minimal paths between the main channels of pedestrian movement, oscillate between efficiency and redundancy of an intensely connected urbanism. Subdivision patterns are formed from the amalgamation of the various grids, and together create Moiré patterns of a differentiated urban field. Varied scales and types of extruded pixelated massing are contrasted with diverse public open spaces with varied planting, material textures, and orientation. The traffic and infrastructural management of the site is embedded within a porous, pedestrian focused urbanism flowing around, under, and through fields of building mass.

The contemporary city can be projected as a pattern in time, shaped by the dynamic forces influencing it. The Umekita urban proposal recognises, and instrumentalises, the complexities of how cities are formed from a multitude of forces. Responding to the indeterminacy of these contingencies, the machining of various possible futures aims for a more customised, if not optimised urbanism, which, in turn, may also develop specific contextual identities to cities in the future.

FOOTNOTES
- Umekita Second Development Area, Osaka, Japan, 2013-2014
- Invited, Two Stage Competition: "Second Development Zone in Umekita Area, Osaka", City of Osaka
- Jurors: Tadao Ando, Kengo Kuma, Shigenori Kobayashi, Noboru Masuda, Yoshiteru Murosaki, Yuji Nemoto
- Team: Tom Verebes (design director) Mohamad Ghamloush (designer), Nathan Melenbrink (designer, scripting),
- Andrew Haas (post-production, scripting)
- Metrics:
- GFA: 290,000m2
- FAR: 2.0; Effective 2.8 FAR; Stipulated 60% Open Green Space

IMAGE CREDITS
All images courtesy of the Author

TOM VERBES is the Creative Director of OCEAN CN, a Hong Kong-based design consultancy network, and he co-founded the OCEAN design network in 1995, subsequently directing OCEAN UK within OCEAN D. Former Associate Dean (Teaching & Learning) (2011-2014) and currently Associate Professor of Architecture at the University of Hong Kong. Tom Verebes was co-Director of the post-professional masters' level Design Research Lab, at the Architectural Association in London, where he had taught from 1996 to 2009. He is the Director of the AA Shanghai Summer School (2007-2014); former Director and founder of the AA D_Lab (2006-2007), and former AA Diploma Unit Master. In 2004-2006, he was Guest/Visiting Professor at Akademie der Buildenden Künste ABK Stuttgart. Among over 140 publications of authored books, chapters, articles and features, his recent books include 'New Computational Paradigms in Architecture' (Tsinghua University Press, 2012) and 'Masterplanning the Adaptive City: Computational Urbanism in the Twenty-first Century' (Routledge, 2013). Verebes' work has been exhibited in over 50 venues worldwide, and he has lectured extensively in Asia, Europe, North America, and the Middle East.

CLOUD
OSAKA

ALISA ANDRASEK

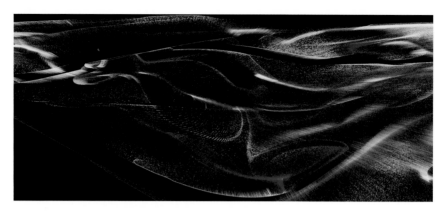

INCREASED RESOLUTION DESIGN SYNTHESIS

via Physics simulations and Multi Agent Systems

"Very little in nature is detectable by unaided human senses. Most of what happens is too fast or too slow, too big or too small, or too remote, or hidden behind opaque barriers, or operates on principles too different from anything that influenced our evolution. But in some cases we can arrange for such phenomena to become perceptible, via scientific instruments…" David Deutsch / Closer to Reality / The Beginning of Infinity

What Turing gave us for the first time (and without Turing you just couldn't do any of this) is a way of thinking about in a disciplined way and taking seriously phenomena that have () trillions of moving parts.

DANIEL C. DENNETT

With the recent increase in volumes of computing, architecture's "superpower" to synthesize the complexity of many negotiating agencies is radically accelerated. While data visualisation exposes the hidden beauty, intelligence, and complexity of observed systems, data materialisation can produce such beauty and complexity within new synthetic fields. In order to develop such data materialisation processes, it is necessary to descend to the finer grains of computational building blocks, where the design search is performed within constellations of billions of particles…

Biothing embraces the materialist tendencies of speculative thinking since it focuses on the materialities of anonymous elements (in biology, physics, chemistry), demonstrating transformations of their intrinsic properties via computational processing. Furthermore, this process of transformation is elucidated by the computational processing of varied and not equivalent elements.

Physics of matter are embedded in the design-search process, simultaneously incorporating the constraints and inputs of manufacturing and constructability. Thus the resolution of architectural fabrics is being gradually increased, where fabric refers to the

| 166

constellation of interlaced contingencies involved in the formation of architecture.

In the recent article for Artforum in which Biothing was referenced as one of the relevant examples, historian Mario Carpo follows the acute shift from "spline dominated" digital work towards upcoming data driven discretised models that are resonating "the inherent discreteness of nature (which, after all, is not made of dimensionless Euclidean points nor of continuous mathematical lines but of distinct chunks of matter, all the way down to molecules, atoms, electrons, etc.)."

In such context, Biothing is working with simulations via extreme volumes of parallel computing (GPU supercomputing), in which quantity of data opens the possibility for the explicit connection between material properties, constraints of production and computational physics applied to previously in architecture unimaginable discreteness of building blocks, as well as unimaginable extents of massive territories (with applications to urbanism and large scale territorial designs). For the first time, architects have the access to such massive span of different orders of scale, and ability to synthesise across _ from micro to macro.

By encoding algorithmic profiles of matter (a tendency widely practiced in the acute streams of science), we are now moving towards what could be understood as materialisation prior to materialisation, accelerating material processes and sometimes even bypassing them.

CLOUD OSAKA _ complex synthesis at the scale of a master plan

Cloud Osaka is a project developed for an invited competition for a new public space and adjacent 350 000 sqm development in the heart of Osaka. Addressing emerging forms of transient working culture, Cloud Osaka taps into potential of pervasive technologies and ubiquitous computing and its effects on networking, sharing and cooperation across fields. It offers a framework for transient programming targeted at increasing demand for plug-in work spaces for business travellers and convergence point for interdisciplinary and cross-industry innovation encounters. Through inclusive design synthesis it sets up a platform for creative potential of innovation to flourish in the heart of Osaka.

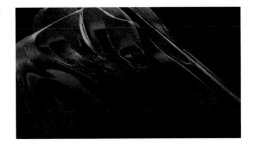

Envisioned as a new kind of nature in the city, it is conceived through

the dynamic blueprints of computational physics. Seeing highly dense urban node such as Osaka train station as an opportunity to embrace complexity, and understanding 2.5 million people per day passing through the site as a river of people, fluid dynamics distribute the flows with the primary fitness set to give the site its porous and connective nature. At a macro level urban massing of the Cloud resonates otherworldly beauty of Mars dunes (its inspiration), allowing city's specific pressures to inflect the flows of simulated natural fluids. Its intricate architectural fabric embraces fuzzy boundaries and ephemeral identities within acute cultures. It does this by the novel constructs of "resolution" cutting across range of scales and closing the gap between micro and macro.

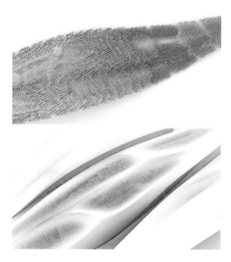

Highly adaptive structural field is proposed to address necessary heterogeneity of such a complex site.

Cloud structure is conceived through computational simulation of physics of fluids, like a river flowing through the complex landscape and finding paths of least resilience. It acts as an underlying dynamic blueprint, highly responsive to the complex organisation of flows of people, various forms of traffic and structural and programmatic forecasting. Intricate structural fabric distributes multitude of infrastructural systems, dense sensor fields and various systems for energy harnessing, all deployed through the Internet of Things. High numbers of people transversing the site results in a need for highly resilient dense structure in mostly frequented pedestrian zones.

Analysed by Multi-Agent systems applied to the crowd dynamics, zoning of the structure relative to the density and resilience is derived. Density of structure is in resonance with intensity of kinetic energy harnessing via distributing piezoelectric tilling in the pedestrian intensive zones. Furthermore such resilient thick structural cloud offers opportunities for a different architectural fabric, characterised by fuzzy edges. In spite of the volume of the structure deployed, because of its intricate and distributed nature, extreme porosity is achieved characterised by fine dispersal of light in such cloud spaces.

Cloud of data derived from the fluid dynamics simulation is subsequently mathematised into a Voxel cloud that can be programmed heterogeneously and adaptive to the local conditions across multiple orders of scale, bridging Macro organisation and Micro articulation. Same data is than applied at fine resolution to distribution of conditioning elements such as water, heat and light, as well as patterns for the planting and landscaping materials. Structural logic is than scripted that networks different nodes in adaptive

| 168

densities. Two states of the structural fields are proposed: Deep Cloud applied in zones with heavier weights, characterised by stronger concentration of pedestrians and fuzzy transient work related programming, and Tall Cloud for the large spanning structure.

Cloud's energy ecology evokes concepts of a Third industrial revolution, with distributed and localised energy production and accelerated communication fields of the Internet of Things. Such finer resolution conditioning opens potential for new kind of programming of architectural, urban and landscape fabrics.

At a finer scale the Cloud is highly conditioned through myriad of distributed infrastructural systems based on acute and the upcoming technological innovations for distributed and localised energy harvesting, lights and temperature conditioning, water, landscaping, communication, commerce and navigation amongst others. Public park and plazas could be re-conditioned to accommodate multitude of events. Project is inspired by the phenomena of Sakura that for a brief moment becomes a new form of weather in the fabric of Japanese city, an ubiquitous beautiful cloud attracting people to share, gather, celebrate...

IMAGE CREDITS
All images courtesy of Author

ALISA ANDRASEK is an architect, academic and curator. She is a founder of Biothing (biothing.org) operating at the intersection of design, material and computer science, and a partner of Bloom Games (bloom-thegame.com). Andrasek is directing Graduate Architectural Design at the UCL Bartlett School of Architecture and holding a Professorship at the European Graduate School (http://www.egs.edu/) and has taught at the DRL AA in London, Columbia University GSAPP, Pratt, UPenn, RMIT Melbourne, RPI Troy and UTS Sydney. She received Europe 40 under 40 Award, Metropolis Next Generation Award and FEIDAD Award. Biothing's work has been exhibited and is part of the permanent collections at the Centre Pompidou Paris, New Museum NY, Storefront NY, FRAC Collection Orleans, TB-A21 Vienna, Beijing and Sydney Bienale amongst others. She curated the US East Coast section for the "Emergent Talent Emergent Technologies" exhibition for the Beijing Biennial 2006 and for the "(Im)material Processes: New Digital Techniques for Architecture" for the Beijing Biennial 2008 and the UK section for "Machinic Processes" for the Beijing Biennial 2010. Andrasek is a co-curator of the PROTO/E/CO/LOCICS Symposium series in Rovinj Croatia (http://proto-e-co-logics.mlaus.net/).

OSAKA
A TOPOLOGICAL
GROUND-
SCRAPER
BECOMING A
GROUNDED
SKY-SCRAPER

E-ARCHITECTS | EIROA ARCHITECTS, NY-BA
PABLO LORENZO-EIROA

INTERIOR PERSPECTIVE.
-Coffee shops, retail spaces, event spaces
are integrated with the landscape, public green space

The poetics of the proposal:A grounded ground is an artificial ground. A green artificial topography. A grounded building weaving through a grounded ground becomes a ground-scraper. A topological groundscraper-building. It is not ground nor it is a building. It is not not ground, nor it is not not building. A park with buildings. A park and not building. A park not building. A park as a building-park and a building as a park. A park and an underground building. A not building-park. A street and a park. A street and a building. A street building becoming a park. A park-building with grounded-buildings. A park-building with topographical buildings. A park-building with grounded buildings. Grounded buildings that emerge from a building-park. Grounded buildings that emerge from a double grounded ground. A double ground weaving sequence: A ground surface and a building surface. An undulating ground surface and an undulated building surface. A park building surface weaving upon itself. A double park building surface. A park building double surface that becomes a grounded building. A grounded building surface that becomes a de-grounded building. A tall building that emancipates itself from the ground surface. An elegant non-grounded ground-like building. A non grounded ground skyscraper.

E-Architects | Eiroa Architects was invited by Kengo Kuma to a professional International Competition for the Umeda Umekita area in Osaka, Japan. E-Architects was pre-selected through a professional portfolio competition together with 20 international offices - only 5 from the USA / others local teams from Japan - to submit a proposal for urban redevelopment.

The landscape interventions propose a parametric topography displacing the natural grade reference level of the city of Osaka in Japan. The ground level is thickened and made inhabitable, providing different opportunities for diverse activities. The thickened parametric surface proposes topological continuous undulating spaces for public use.

Private buildings that allocate diverse urban functions emerge out of the displacement and splitting of the ground surface.

The project is developed with mathematical scripts to establish three sets of surface-relationships to produce different architectural conditions and emerging relationships.

The first set surface resolves through a topological continuity, the activation of an architectural canon: the thickening of the ground as inhabitable surface. Through this means, the typical ground surface that is usually the background of a figure-building splits in two and warps on itself. Therefore, the lower part of the underground surface and the upper part of the above ground surface become a unique topological surface. The parameters of the dimensions of the surface produce bridges that become topography. By this means, a poché space becomes activated and engaged within the thickened surface-space.

The second surface operates at a global scale integrating the entire urbanism of the site, parameterizing the previous topological relationships. The street level of the site is critiqued by the parametrics of the ground surface of the project, resolving a simple urban landscape in which every part of its surface can be used as a green park. This resolves the park as a horizontal building.

The third surface set resolves through a mathematical parametrics, the activation of another set of buildings. These buildings are sometimes part of the ground and sometimes emerge from the "ground" surface as figures, ranging from landscaped buildings to skyscraper buildings. The simple mathematics of these buildings motivate and unmotivate the surface, both as a mathematical computational sign and as architectural signification, exploring through parametric variations many sets of relationships.

The integration of these three surface levels produces a critique of the simple articulation among the different systems. Both the parametrics of each surface and the architectural parameters are displaced to enable architectural relationships. Each set critiques and displaces the signification of the other, producing a critical-parametric method. The mathematics, the parametrics and the parameters being displaced, fluctuate from each other resolving an emerging architectural landscape.

Land Usepark Area: 74.000 m2, Far 0.85, Coverage area 85%

Retail Area: 70.000m2, Far 0.8, Coverage area 23%

Public Circulation: 20.000m2, Far 0.23, Coverage area 23%

Exhibition Area / Event Spaces: 5.000m2, Far 0.0575, Coverage area 5.75%

Disaster Area Evacuation Center Bunker: 3.000 m2

New Technologies Information Center / Mediatheque: 30,000m2, FAR 0.34, Coverage area 2.3%

Cultural Area: 13.000m2, FAR 0.15, Coverage area 1.5%

Office / Residential Tower: 54.000m2, FAR 0.62, Coverage area 2.3%

Hotel Tower: 23.000m2, FAR 0.26, Coverage area 1.15%

Parking: 50.000m2 (2.000 cars), FAR 0.60, Coverage area 57% (below ground)

Total Park Open Green Area 74.000m2, Private Built Area 218.000m2 (including circulation), Parking 50.000m2 (below ground level -12m)

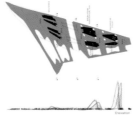

173 |

EIROA ARCHITECTS, P.C. | e-architects is a licensed architecture studio dually based in New York City and Buenos Aires design lead by Pablo Lorenzo-Eiroa. This studio has been integrating theoretical speculation and disciplinary expertise in different associations, with work ranging from academic research, through scholarships and publications, to architecture design in private and state commissions. This studio expertise is on architecture, design, the landscape of the city, and the architecture of the landscape. e-architect's design philosophy is to constantly question assumed cultural structures with conceptual designs that focus on recognizing, anddisplacing, the most stable spatial organizations through topology.

Operatively, this studio combines the qualities of a small focused team and a medium size office, as it is also out-sourced by an international network of recognized experts from architecture, ecology, digital architecture, digital fabrication, engineering, landscape, and multiple design fields. This studio offers cutting edge expertise in the design and fabrication of mind bending spaces. Parametric differentiation in topological spaces is developed by implementing unique advanced techniques and materials using digital fabrication provided by an associated company.

e-architects has been involved in the development projects, both real and actual, in South America, the U.S., Europe, and on the Internet. In New York and Buenos Aires this office has designed, built, published and exhibited many projects, including: an infrastructure project with the Department of Transportation in NYC, a Public Shore Park in Vicente Lopez-North Buenos Aires, and many residential buildings and houses.

e-architect's projects have been featured in different media, among others The New York Times. EA's principals have published widely on architecture and urban matters, organized conferences and won many competitions and prizes. e-architect's building proposal for the World Trade Center was part of the "Think Big: The Mater's Plan", a research group organized by the New York Times Magazine in 2002, which included world renowned architects and planners such as Peter Eisenman, Rem Koolhaas, Zaha Hadid, Richard Meier, Steven Holl and others, and this project was exhibited at the VIII Venice Architecture Biennale. e-architect's projects have been published in different media including: ARQ Clarin, La Nacion Newspaper, Architecture In Formation; and in lectures including: Princeton University, The Cooper Union, Columbia University, The University of Buenos Aires, Di Tella Institute, Biodigital Architecture Master Barcelona, etc. e-architect's practice Manifesto was part of FreshLatino at The Storefront for Art and Architecture; e-architect's environmental machine for soft landscapes was exhibited at the Disenny Hub Barcelona; and the studio's projects were presented at Pecha Kucha New York #11, as part of a series of events for the Festival of Ideas for the New City curated by the New Museum of New York City.

PATRIK SCHUMACHER, ZAHA HADID ARCHTIECTS

PARAMETRIC SEMIOLOGY

—

THE DESIGN OF INFORMATION RICH ENVIRONMENTS

All design is communication design. The built environment, with its complex matrix of territorial distinctions, is a giant, navigable, information-rich interface of communication. Each territory is a communication. It gives potential social actors information about the communicative interactions to be expected within its bounds. It communicates an invitation to participate in the framed social situation. Designed spaces are spatial communications that frame and order further communications. They place the participants into specific constellations that are pertinent with respect to the anticipated communication situations. Like any communication, a spatial communication can be accepted or rejected, i.e. – the space can be entered or exited. Entry implies accepting the communication as the premise for all further communication taking place within its boundaries. Crossing a territorial threshold makes a difference in terms of behavioural dispositions. Entry implies submission to the specific rules of conduct that the type of social situation inscribed within the territory prescribes. In this way, the designed-built environment orders social processes. This spells the unique, societal function of architecture: to order and frame communicative interaction.

The Built Environment as Societal Information Process

Society can only evolve with the simultaneous ordering of space. The elaboration of a built environment (however haphazard, precarious, and initially based on accident rather than purpose and intention) seems to be a necessary condition for the build-up of any stable social order. The gradual build-up of a social system must go hand in hand with the gradual build-up of an artificial spatial order; social order requires spatial order. The social process needs the built environment as a plane of inscription where it can leave traces that then serve to build-up and stabilize social structures, which in turn allow the further elaboration of more complex social processes. The evolution of society goes hand in hand with the evolution of its habitat – understood as an ordering frame. The spatial order of the human habitat is both an immediate physical organizing apparatus that separates and connects social actors and their activities, and a material substrate for the inscription of an external "societal memory." These "inscriptions" might at first be an unintended side effect of the various activities. Spatial arrangements are functionally adapted and elaborated. They are then marked and underlined by ornaments, which make them more conspicuous. The result is the gradual build-up of a spatio-morphological system of signification. Thus, a semantically charged built environment emerges that provides a differentiated system of settings to help social actors orient themselves with respect to the different communicative situations constituting the social life-process of society. The system of social settings, as a system of distinctions and relations, uses both the positional identification of places (spatial position) and the morphological identification of places (ornamental marking) as props for the societal information process. Compelling demonstrations for this formative nexus between social and spatial structure can be found within social anthropology, attesting to the crucial importance of cross-generationally stable spatio-morphological settings for the initial emergence and stabilization of all societies. Only on this basis, with this new material substrate upon which the evolutionary mechanisms of mutation, selection, and reproduction could operate, was the evolution of mankind out of the animal kingdom, and all further cultural evolution, possible. Thus, the built environment, as the cross-generationally stable, material substrate of the cultural evolution, acts functionally equivalent to the DNA as the material substrate of the biological evolution.

Increasing the information Richness of the Built Environment

The importance of the built environment for ordering and framing society remains undiminished. However, what, in former times, was left to the slow evolutionary process of trial and error has, since the Renaissance, become more and more the domain of competency and responsibility of the specialized discourse and profession of the discipline of architecture. Now, more than ever, the critical issue for an ambitious architecture wanting to contribute to the next stage of our civilization is how a designed territory operates as sophisticated framing communication that gathers and orders relevant (socialized) participants for specific communicative interactions. Accordingly, I have grounded my theory of architecture in communication theory, with particular reference to Niklas Luhmann's social systems theory and theory of society. Communication-theory does, indeed, provide a parsimonious, productive framework for architecture's reflective self-description. The implication of embedding architectural theory within communication theory is that all architectural spaces are conceived and designed as communications.

77|

A theory of society is a necessary framework for a comprehensive theory of architecture, starting with the explication of architecture's societal function. Luhmann, for instance, proposes to conceptualize the life process of society as a communication process rather than as a material reproduction process. This is, of course, a radical abstraction. However, I think this is a rather pertinent and powerful abstraction. All problems of society are problems of communication. Both the problems and the solutions of mankind have to do with society's self-generated complexity.

If all problems of society are problems of communication, then the focus on communication is a precondition for upgrading architecture's social efficacy. Especially within the Post-Fordist network society (information society, knowledge economy), total social productivity increases with the density of communication. The life process of society is a communication process structured by an ever more complex and richly diversified matrix of institutions and communicative situations. A Post-Fordist network society demands that we continuously browse and scan as much of the social world as possible, in order to remain continuously connected and informed. We cannot afford to withdraw and beaver away in isolation when innovation accelerates all around. We must continuously recalibrate what we are doing in line with what everybody else is doing. We must be networked all the time, so as to continuously ascertain the relevancy of our own efforts. Telecommunication only via mobile devices may help, but it does not suffice. Rapid and effective face-to-face communication remains a crucial component of our daily productivity. The whole built environment must become an interface of multi-modal communication, as the ability to navigate dense and complex urban environments has become a crucial aspect of today's overall productivity.

Information Density via Parametric Design

Everything must resonate with everything else. This should result in an overall intensification of relations, which gives the urban field a performative density, informational richness, and cognitive coherence that makes for quick navigation and effective participation in a complex social arena. Our increasing ability to scan an ever-increasing simultaneity of events, and to move through a rapid succession of communicative encounters, constitutes the essential, contemporary form of cultural advancement. Further advancement of this vital capacity requires a new built environment with an unprecedented level of complexity, a complexity that is organized and articulated into a complex, variegated order of the kind we admire in natural, self-organized systems.

The more free and the more complex a society, the more it must spatially order and orient its participants via perceived thresholds and semiotic clues – rather than via physical barriers and channels. The city is a complex text and a permanent broadcast. Therefore, our ambition as architects and urban designers must be to spatially unfold more simultaneous choices of communicative situations in dense, perceptually palpable, and legible arrangements. The visual field must be dense with offerings and information about what lies behind the immediate field of vision. The parametricist logics of rule-based variation, differentiation, and correlation establish order within the built environment, giving those who must navigate it the crucial possibility of making inferences. Employing associative logics correlates the different urban and architectural subsystems in ways that make them representations of each other. Everything communicates with everything. This is not a metaphysical assertion about the world, but a heuristic principle for parametric design under the auspices of parametricism. The rule-based design processes that inform all forms on the basis of informational transcoding imply the possibility of information retrieval through the user, as long as human cognitive capacities are reflected.

Organisation, Articulation, Signification

The three terms of this section title spell out how architecture's societal function – the framing of communicative interaction – can be broken down and concretized into three related subtasks. Organization is based on the distribution of positions for spatial elements and their pattern of linkages. Articulation is based upon the constitution of morphological identities, similitudes, and differences across the architectural elements to be organized. Organization is instituted via the physical means of distancing, barring, and connecting via circulatory channelling. These physical mechanisms can, in theory, operate independently of all nuanced perception and comprehension, and can thus, in principle, succeed without the efforts of articulation. However, the restriction to mere organization without articulation, and without facilitating the participants' active navigation, severely constrains the level of complexity possible in the pattern of social communication thus framed. Articulation presupposes cognition. It enlists the participant's perception and comprehension, and thereby facilitates the participants' active orientation. The distinction of organization versus articulation is then based on the difference between handling passive bodies and enlisting active, cognitive agents. These two registers relate in this way: articulation builds upon, and reveals, organization. It makes the organization of function[1] apparent. In so doing, it elevates organization into order.

The dimension of articulation includes two distinct sub-tasks: phenomenological and semiological articulation (signification). Their distinction is between the enlistment of behavioral responses from cognitive agents, on the one hand, and the communicative engagement of socialized actors, on the other. The phenomenological project enlists users as cognitive agents, perceiving and decomposing their environment along the lines of the principles of pattern-recognition or Gestalt-perception. It makes organizational

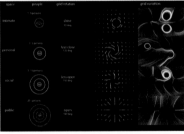

Figure1: Parametric Semiology: Semio-field, differentiation of public vs. private as parametric range.

Figure 2: Parametric Semiology: Semio-field, master-plan with program distribution.

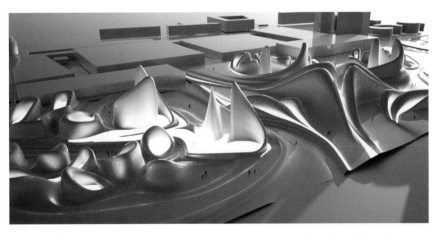

Figure 3:Vienna University of Applied Arts, Masterclass Hadid, Parametric Semiology: Semio-field. Project authors: Magda Smolinska, Marius Cernica, and Monir Karimi.

arrangements perceptually legible by making important points conspicuous, avoiding the visual overcrowding of the scene, and so on. This is a necessary precondition for all semiological encodings that can only attach to the visually discernible features of the environment. In other words, users can only read, interpret, or comprehend what they can discern. However, the comprehension of a social situation involves more than the distinction of conspicuous features. It is an act of interpretation that presupposes socialization. It is an act of reading a communication: namely, the reading of space as both framing communication and the premise for all further communications to be expected within its ambit. (These framing communications are attributed to the institutions hosting the respective communicative events, i.e. – they are attributed to the clients, rather than to the architects or designers.) Communication presupposes language, that is, a system of signification. The built environment spontaneously evolves into such a (more or less vague and unreliable) system of signification. The task of architectural semiology as design agenda, therefore, is to go beyond this spontaneous semiosis (that every talented designer navigates intuitively), and build up a more complex and precise system of signification.

The Refoundation of Architectural Semiology within Parametricism

After the failed attempts of the 1970s and 1980s, architectural semiology can now be effectively theorized and operationalized as parametric semiology. It is important to note that a semiotic system can neither be reduced to syntax nor to semantics. This was the mistake of the attempts in the 1970s. Eisenman's work had no sematic dimension, and Jencks had no syntax. The postmodern architects tried to build on the spontaneous semiosis of architectural history and were thus restricted to the recycling of clichés, and without the chance to build up a more complex syntax. Instead the refoundation of architectural semiology promoted here suggests a radical severance from all historical semiotic material, promoting the construction of a new, artificial spatio-visual language in analogy to the creation of artificial programming languages, taking full advantage of the radical arbitrariness of all languages. The construction of this language must proceed step by step, oscillating between syntactical and semantic advances. This is made possible via parametric agen-based modelling that realizes the signifying relations as associative functions that systematically make agent behaviours dependent on architectural features. At the same time the pragmatic layer is anticipated as the (never fully predictable) social appropriation process that commences when the design spaces are finally utilized and re-utilized.[2]

In the second volume of my treatise, The Autopoiesis of Architecture,[3] a set of axioms and heuristic principles are formulated that outline strategies for semiological projects conceived as complex architectural designs – for instance, the design of a university campus – as the design of a coherent visual language or system of signification. The first axiom restricts the domain of architecture's signified to the social events that are expected to happen within the respective buildings or spaces, defined along the three dimensions of function type, social type and location type. The second axiom states that the relevant

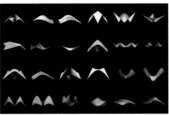

Figure 4: Dialectic Fields: Shell morphology as semiological system of distinctions: smooth vs creased vs faceted.

Figure 5:Dialectic Fields: Cluster of creased shells with semiologically distinctive surface articulation..

81|

Figure 6:AADRL 2012 Parametric Semiology: Dialectic Fields. University campus designed as a system of signification, by Ganesh Nimmala, Leonid Krykhtin, Kwanphil Cho, and Sharan Sundar.

unit of architectural communication, the architectural sign, is the designed/designated territory (just like the sentence is the minimal relevant unit of speech). Territorial thresholds mark differences that make a difference in terms of social situation. These differences in use constitute the meaning of architectural signs/communications.

My most recent academic design-research, at the AADRL and elsewhere, shows how architectural semiology can be operationalized via agent-based crowd modelling. The scripting of the agents' specific behavioural dispositions, in relation to specific spatial and/ or morphological features of the designed environment, allows designers to model and work on the signification relation. The domain of the signified – the patterns of social interaction expected within designed territories, can thus be brought into architecture's design medium as one more subsystem (the crucial subsystem) in the set of correlated subsystems constituting the parametric model.It therefore becomes possible, for the first time in the history of architecture, to model this life-process, thus incorporating it into design speculation. This was made possible by the use of computational crowd modelling techniques, via agent-based models. General tools like "Processing", or specific tools like "MiArmy" and "AI.implant" (available as plugins for Maya), and "Massive" now make behavioural modelling within designed environments accessible to architects. Agent modelling should not be limited to crowd circulation flows, but should encompass all patterns of occupation and social interaction in space. The agents' behaviour might be scripted so as to correlate with the configurational and morphological features of the designed environment, i.e. – programmed agents responding to environmental clues. Such clues or triggers might include furniture configurations, as well as other artefacts. The idea, then, is to build dynamic action-artefact networks.

Morphological features, as well as colours and textures that, together with ambient parameters (lighting conditions), constitute and characterize a certain territory can now influence the behavioural mode of the agent. Since the 'meaning' of an architectural space is the (nuanced) type of event or social interaction to be expected within its territory, these new tools allow for the re-foundation of architectural semiology as parametric semiology. The semiological project therefore implies that the design project systematizes all form-function correlations into a coherent system of signification. A system of signification, in turn, is a system of mappings (correlations) that map distinctions or manifolds, defined within the domain of the signified (here the domain of patterns of social interaction), onto the distinctions or manifolds, which are defined within the domain of the signifier (here, the domain of spatial positions and morphological features defining and characterizing a given territory) and vice-versa. This system of signification works if the programmed social agents consistently respond to the relevantly coded positional and morphological clues in such a way that expected behaviours can be read off the articulated environmental configuration. However, rather than modelling scenarios frame by frame, agent based modelling works by defining the agents' behavioural dispositions and biases relative to environmental features. The event itself then becomes an emergent global pattern resulting from the local interactions of agents with each other inside the environment. If this succeeds, architecture will have done its job of ordering the event scenario. That is, the meaning of architecture, the prospective life processes it frames and sustains, will have been modelled and assessed within the design process as an object of direct creative speculation and cumulative design elaboration. In this way, architectural semiology can finally be operationalized; in this way, it will have a real chance of succeeding as a promising, rigorous design-research project.

REFERENCES

- [1]Patrik Schumacher, The Autopoiesis of Architecture, Volume 1: A New Framework for Architecture. London: John Wiley & Sons Ltd., 2010. See Part 5:The Societal Function of Architecture. The same societal function applies to other design disciplines. All designed artefacts of everyday life (furniture, fashion) are involved in the structuration of communication/society.
- According to the functional heuristics of parametricism, the functions of spaces are conceived in terms of dynamic patterns of social interactions/communications, i.e.– as parametrically variable, dynamic event scenarios, rather

than static schedules of accommodation that list functional stereotypes. See: Patrik Schumacher, The Autopoiesis of Architecture, Volume 2: A New Agenda for Architecture. London: John Wiley & Sons Ltd., 2012. See Chapter 11.2.2:Operational Definition of Parametricism: The Defining Heuristics of Parametricism.

• The computational information processing thus simulates the final users' information processing that occurs when users read their environment as clues for their actions and communicative interactions. The agent based modelling also allows designers to anticipate how individual dispositions and reactions aggregate into emergent patterns of social interaction that are the final consciously recognized and expected signifieds that constitute the function designations of the respective designed spaces.

FOOTNOTES

Previously published in: Architecture In Formation – On the Nature of Information in Digital Architecture, edited by Pablo Lorenzo-Eiroa and Aaron Sprecher, Routledge, Taylor and Francis, New York, 2013

1. Patrik Schumacher, The Autopoiesis of Architecture, Volume 1: A New Framework for Architecture. London: John Wiley & Sons Ltd., 2010. See Part 5:The Societal Function of Architecture. The same societal function applies to other design disciplines. All designed artefacts of everyday life (furniture, fashion) are involved in the structuration of communication/society.

2. According to the functional heuristics of parametricism, the functions of spaces are conceived in terms of dynamic patterns of social interactions/communications, i.e.– as parametrically variable, dynamic event scenarios, rather than static schedules of accommodation that list functional stereotypes. See: Patrik Schumacher, The Autopoiesis of Architecture, Volume 2: A New Agenda for Architecture. London: John Wiley & Sons Ltd., 2012. See Chapter 11.2.2:Operational Definition of Parametricism: The Defining Heuristics of Parametricism.

3. The computational information processing thus simulates the final users' information processing that occurs when users read their environment as clues for their actions and communicative interactions. The agent based modelling also allows designers to anticipate how individual dispositions and reactions aggregate into emergent patterns of social interaction that are the final consciously recognized and expected signifieds that constitute the function designations of the respective designed spaces.

4. Patrik Schumacher, The Autopoiesis of Architecture, Volume 2: A New Agenda for Architecture. London: John Wiley & Sons Ltd., 2012.

IMAGES CREDITS

Figure 1, 2, 4, 5: courtesy of the author and Zaha Hadid Architects.

Figure 3: Vienna University of Applied Arts, Masterclass Hadid, Parametric Semiology: Semio-field. Project authors: Magda Smolinska, Marius Cernica, and Monir Karimi.

Figure 6: AADRL 2012 Parametric Semiology: Dialectic Fields. University campus designed as a system of signification, by Ganesh Nimmala, Leonid Krykhtin, Kwanphil Cho, and Sharan Sundar.

DR. PATRIK SCHUMACHER is partner at Zaha Hadid Architects and the co-author of most key projects. He joined Zaha Hadid in 1988 and has been seminal in developing Zaha Hadid Architects to become a 450 strong global architecture and design brand. In 1996 he founded the "Design Research Laboratory" at the Architectural Association in London and continues to teach in what has become one of the world's most prestigious architecture programs. He is lecturing worldwide and has been a guest professor in many prestigious schools of architecture, and recently held the John Portman Chair in Architecture at Harvard's Graduate School of Design. Over the years he has contributed over 80 articles to architectural journals and anthologies. In 2008 he coined the phrase Parametricism and has since published a series of manifestos promoting Parametricism as the new epochal style for the 21st century. In 2010/2012 he published his two-volume theoretical opus magnum "The Autopoiesis of Architecture". His writings are available on www.patrikschumacher.com.

NONLIN/LIN PAVILION FRAC CENTRE ORLEANS FRANCE

PRE-ASSEMBLY V1.0

MARC FORNES / THEVERYMANY™

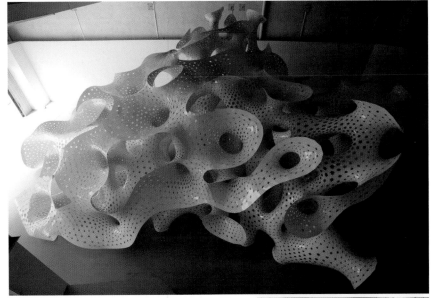

(Figure 1)
nonLin-Lin Overall
Dimensions: 10.1
m length, 7.15m
width, 3.9m height
(33'4"L * 23'6"W
*12'10"H)

nonLin/Lin Pavilion - is a prototype which engages in a series of architectural experiments referred to as *text based morphologies.* Beyond its visual perception of sculptural and formal qualities, the prototypes are built forms developed through custom computational protocols. The parameters of these protocols are based on form finding (surface relaxation), form description (composition of developable linear elements), information modeling (re-assembly data), generational hierarchy (distributed networks), and digital fabrication (logistic of production).

(Figure 2)
Spatial
configuration

Prototypical Scale

The Pavilion project refers to its own scale. It is not considered a model of a larger structure or a building, neither is it an art installation. It is not made out of cardboard, or connected through paper clips. Its structural integrity does not rely on any camouflaged cables and it can resist water. It is light yet very strong. One could sit on it, even hang or climb it. It is scalable to a degree. It is not produced through academic facilities. It is a *prototypical architecture.*

(Figure 3)
Components

Non-linear Structure

The cohesive morphology of the pavilion originates from a "Y" model referred to as the basic representation and lowest level of *multi-directionality*. Such a premise was established in order to challenge issues of morphology since tri-partite relational models can not be formalized and described through a single bi-directional surface (ie: Nurbs surfaces) - which is yet still one of the main medium of representation within the avant-garde architectural repertoire.

In order to resolve such an issue, it is required to address morphological models of change and introduce *split or recombination* – or in other words, how can one become two and two become one.

The paradigm shift from linear spaces (tube or donuts alike) is important, not necessarily on a formal level, but rather in order to engage a multiplicity of social situations – pushing further than "bi" or dual alike.

Dramatic Change of Morphology: From Network to Surface Condition.

This prototypical structure is an investigation into transformations from one state to the other. Members within the structural network are opening up and recombining themselves into larger apertures while their reverse side is creating a surface condition providing that as density increase eventually provides to the person evolving within a sensation of enclosure.

Local protocols of transformation are corrupted with overall hierarchies - such as varying radii for the members based on their position within the structural network. This orientation to the system results into a spatial environment with intrinsic and extrinsic moments.

From Descriptive Geometry to Parallel Search as a Model of Description

Custom computational protocols are describing the structure of the pavilion as a set of

186

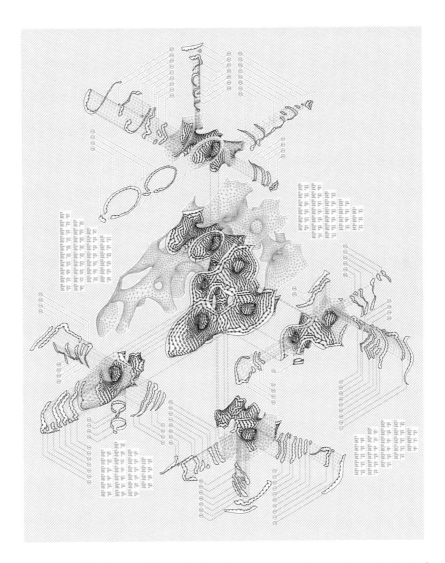

(Figure 4) -
269,991 square
inches (1875
square feet)
Surface Area
- 155 780 holes
(CNC drilled)
- 9 325 texts (CNC
engraved)
- 6 367 stripes
(CNC cut)
- 570 single
components (CNC
cut)
- 75 000 white
aluminum rivets
- 145 sheets
4*8 (2/2.5 hours
machining)
- 40 modules pre-
assembled
- 4 weeks pre-
assembly

linear developable elements. Those singular elements can then be unrolled and cut out of flat sheets of material.

Though due to the non-linear property of the model, this *discretization* process cannot be applied globally onto the morphology, but rather requires a search process.

A global application strategy would fail due to its nature of reoccurring shift of defects within the distributed network (nodes with differentiated numbers of branches, changing types of double curvature, varying radii, etc). A local application strategy would distribute

187 |

(Left)(Figure 5)
(Right)(Figure 6)
Interior space

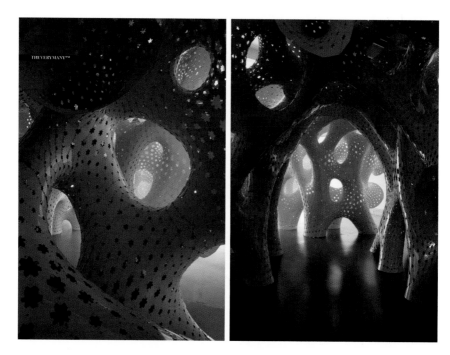

agents with local 'search behavior' tracing along the surface. These agents would provide immediate solutions based on local decision making, while in parallel, constantly communicating with their proximity based agents. This set of information can then be translated and materialized into a series of paths or stripes.

From Mass-Customization to Massive Customization and High Degree of Morphological Differentiation

The Pavilion is redirecting from a current avant-garde strategy of applications populating discreet components onto an overall surface or host. This strategy also includes introducing iteratively varying and blending proportions (with linear or non-linear acceleration) across a range of surface domain.

A precise description of such a prototypical structure requires massive number of elements, not only all unique but also morphologically extremely different. In order to describe and formalized all the different cases present (connection stripes to stripes, part to part, end rings, open edges, etc) -all requiring different properties (branches, holes, connection, grounded, etc)- one needs many types of agent behaviors, which generate forms of radically different morphologies.

From a Holistic Computational Code to Series of Protocols

This kind of prototype deviates from a strategy of singular protocols or codes. The emphasis is now focused on multiple ontologisms, which form a sum of many different steps, procedures, and codes, where each component focuses on its own specific fitness. Such dichotomy of individual per formative processes allows a parallel development of multiple codes. A serious advantage of this process is highlighted within any decision making, allowing additional testing, trails, errors and a series of variations. This overall strategy allows controllability on a specific local level, while identifying nodes of complexity within the structure. This comprehensive understanding supports a precise level of repercussion of any relationship or variable within each code.

From a Fiction of Precision back to a Fantasy of its Re-appropriation

The project is conceived as a resultant product of a very explicit research line, investigating the design and build component of a coherent environment. It is considered to be self-supporting and to affect its participants, while engaging basic notions of limitation, filtration, and spatial depth. The structure is forming a eccentric **universe** where familiar elements such as openings or dimensional measurements turn out of model or scale. This visual phenomenon is allowing spectators to suspend disbelief while assigning cultural references or analogies from nature (corals, flowers) – yet nonLin/ Lin Pavilion is only a very precise experiment toward constructability within a precise economical and cultural context.

IMAGE CREDITS
All images courtesy of Marc Fornes. Photos courtesy of Marc Fornes and Francois Lauginie

MARC FORNES is a registered Architect DPLG and founder of THEVERYMANY™, a New York based studio engaging Art and Architecture through the filter of systematic research and development into applied Computer Science and Digital Fabrication.

His prototypical structures and unique organic environments are included within the permanent collections of the Centre Pompidou, the FRAC Centre and the CNAP. He has been exhibited at institutions worldwide including the Guggenheim ("into the void") and sold work at Art Basel Miami/GGG, Art Paris, Phillips de Pury and Sotherby's.

Marc is a TED Fellow. He was artist in residence at the Atelier Alexander Calder (2012). His pop up store for Louis Vuitton & Yayoi Kusama is the very first carbon fiber self-supported shell structure applied to architecture and was awarded an A+ Jury Award as well as the 40th Annual Interior Design Award by the IIDA. His practice was also awarded New Practices New York by the AIA (2012), the Architectural League Prize (2013), Design Vanguard by Architectural Record (2013) and the WAN 21 for 21 Award.

Marc's on going involvement with academia includes co-starting with Francois Roche (n)Certainties, a graduate studio mixing custom computational protocols with open ended narratives, at Columbia University, the University of Southern California and Die Angewandte in Vienna. He is currently teaching at Princeton University and with Patrik Schumacher at Harvard GSD.

www.theverymany.com

DR. RACHEL ARMSTRONG

NATURAL COMPUTING

—

OPERATIONALIZING THE CREATIVITY OF THE NATURAL WORLD

91|

DR. RACHEL ARMSTRONG

Abstract

My work in synthetic biology and ecological systems proposes that – following 30 years of biotechnological advances – an alternative computational system than digital programming of machines exists. Natural computing, a term inspired by Alan Turing's interest in the computational properties of nature (Denning, 2007) could give rise to new forms of design practice based on completely different spatial tactics and design programs than are currently employed by architects as they are founded on an alternative paradigm to the current modern, industrial approaches. Such technological transformation is possible if the technical power of the natural world is appreciated and operationalized. Yet, a different material philosophy than that which underpins the modern age is required, which assumes that matter is brute, inert and awaiting human instruction or consumption by machines. This shift in organization is of great importance architecturally, as Brian Massumi observes that the material realm may be equated with the non-human and Nature. Indeed, in this millennium an appreciation of the liveliness of matter is necessary if we are to have a different engagement with Nature that regards the natural realm as being more than a 'standing reserve' for industry (Heidegger, 1993). The conceptual frameworks that underpin this vision of the natural realm do obey a Newtonian form of logic, which describes the modern world through the hierarchical organization of objects at equilibrium, when they possess the least possible amount of energy but are more consistent with 'general systems theory' (Von Bertalanffy, 1950) and the behaviour of matter at non-equilibrium. Indeed, these fundamental qualities characterize a unique image of 21st century, or 'Millennial' Nature, which is not obedient and bucolic, like Modern Nature, but restless, empowered and uniquely - possesses a technological character. Following 30 years of biotechnological advances we can now orchestrate natural processes through their metabolisms, which are networks of chemical interactions that shape relationships in their surroundings and set the stage for life's processes, such as growth, movement and sensitivity. Owing to its undeniable agency, Millennial Nature actively participates in socioeconomic and political systems, such as through natural disasters, crop productivity or biodiversity. This activity may be directly engaged by natural computing, which not only implies a new framework for considering the material realm as 'living architecture', which possesses some of the properties of living things, such as metabolism and environmental sensitivity, without being granted the full status of being truly 'alive'. Potentially natural computing techniques offer a range of opportunities for meeting human needs while simultaneously promoting the widespread recovery of our planetary ecosystems and potentially ending the irreconcilable conflict between humanism and environmentalism in architectural practice.

NATURAL COMPUTING: Operationalizing the creativity of the natural world

At the start of the 21st century the frameworks of classical architectural design such as, landscape/building, machine/biology, human/non-human have become conceptually blurred. Our capacity not only to share ideas but also to respond to their inevitable convergences and unstable trajectories have created new conditions for architectural design that go beyond postmodern deconstruction and enter into a new realm of proposition and synthesis. Critical to an emerging era of visionary architecture that proposes new, potentially environmentally positive relationships with the natural world, is the need for a new technical operating system that can deal with the complexity and dynamism of our millennial reality.

Millennial Nature as a creative agency

Indeed the character of our natural realm has radically altered in the last few decades. It is now clear that we have reached a tipping point in human development where the detrimental impacts of the Industrial Revolution are causing geological scale impacts. These are changing the biotic character of the planet and contributing to a sixth great extinction (Wilson, 2003; Doughty, Wolf and Field, 2010). The material relationships that constitute this new "Millennial Nature,"[1] appears to possess liveliness, creativity, strangeness and a corpulence that does not comply with the quaint aestheticisms of Modern Nature. It is not 'green, but forged through strange material relationships such as, continent sized plastic deposits that accrue in our ocean gyres. Yet, while we are aware of our planetary scale influence in this new era called the Anthropocene (Crutzen and Stormer, 2000), we have not yet managed to direct these anthropogenic activities into environmentally beneficial activities. Indeed, the unmediated effects of industrialization are reaching catastrophic environmental tipping points that are likely to bring about biospherical collapse. It would be tragic indeed, if the species that set out to control its environment through industrial systems actually precipitates its own demise through the production of uncontrollable hybrids that arise from the massive hemorrhaging of Millennial Nature into the modern world. These disruptive material qualities of Millennial Nature are radically different to an image of twentieth century nature, which is obedient, bucolic and functions as a "*standing reserve*" for human consumption (Heidegger, 1993). In fact, Millennial Nature is transgressive and not compatible with the established dichotomies of landscape/building, interior/exterior, or form/function that characterize modernity. Rather it is creative and generates new hybrids (Latour, 1993) and relationships that demand new approaches toward architectural design.

Millennial Nature as a technical platform

Millennial Nature demands a technological platform that does not spring from industrial origins but establishes a new relationship with Nature that can operationalize its material processes. The technical systems that enable us to do this, such as genetic engineering are still emerging and are at their earliest stages of development. Yet, they are already enabling us to harness metabolic systems to perform useful work where, for example, gene modification may enable organisms to make entirely novel substances – like the mass production of spider silk protein from goat's milk (Elices et al., 2011). While many of these developments in natural technologies have been understood within the context of industrial systems as 'soft' machines for economic reasons[2], their full portfolio of impacts is being explored in the emerging scientific fields of living technology (Bedau, 2009), synthetic biology (Armstrong, 2013), the origins of life sciences (Hanczyc et al., 2007) and natural computing (Denning, 2007).

Yet the impact of these emerging 'making' platforms are not simply limited to technical advances, but also have social impacts when considered in combination with cultural practices such as, Speculative Design (Dunne & Raby, 2014) and Bio Design (Myers and Antonelli, 2013). Such potential was observed in a report for the National Science Foundation, whereby the merging of up-and-coming technical platforms, namely nanotechnology, biotechnology, information technology and cognitive technologies, the so-called 'NBIC' convergence, would offer significant benefits to the economy and the wider public (Roco and Bainbridge, 2003). Engaging the unique qualities of material transformation as a technical system may result in novel impacts as the side effect of making and other forms of human development. Instead of reducing environmental fertility, such technologies have the potential to enhance biotic activity on which our survival depends by becoming an attractor for new metabolic networks, which may be gardened and shaped by human activity through natural computing techniques. However, such emerging practices do not propose to become a new totalizing system that render industrial systems obsolete, rather they aim to diversify our technical portfolio whereby existing 'making' practices may be regarded as incomplete - rather than obsolete. The enhanced deployment of natural technologies could therefore transform the impacts of current practices, such as industrialization that Michel Serres calls a 'war on matter' (Brown, 2002) and transform them into potent new landscapes of possibility.

Beyond sustainability

93|

Yet, while the political elite has gradually responded to the persistent concerns of environmentalists through their support for sustainable practices, in reality, solutions pander to the very institutions that have been responsible for anthropogenic environmental changes in the first place (Armstrong, 2011), where government and industry work in tightly coupled partnerships, clinging like the drowning to the float of the modern dream. Sustainability is now the buzzword of the new millennium and loosely refers to the aspiration for a 'better' kind of human development, inspired by the Brundtland Report (World Commission on Environment and Development, 1987), which strives to meet the needs of the present generation without compromising the ability of future populations to also satisfy their own requirements. It is now widely applied to describe a whole range of activities such as, business (Tomorrow's Company, No date), social networks (Imperial College London, 2013) and sustainable living (The Guardian, 2013), where environmental impacts of industrial processes are minimized and new forms of governance are implemented to maintain the basic principles of an industrialized society. Notions of sustainability are therefore not conscious efforts to create new paradigms for human development, but have been reactively shaped in response to industrial, technological and political parameters. Rather than embracing radically new process, sustainable solutions operate within a gradualist framework, applying the principles of austerity and material conservation to justify their improved environmental status. In other words, sustainable products consume less energy, use fewer resources and cause fewer carbon emissions, yet they are not sufficient to ensure future prosperity as they do nothing to enhance the productivity of the environment, on which all manufacturing processes depend. So, despite our investment in sustainable practices, in reality we continue to found the production of architecture on industrial processes (Swartz, 2010) that take the slow, rather than fast route towards environmental poverty (Armstrong, 2012).

Natural computing

Natural computing reclaims the material realm from its consumption by industrial paradigms, and situates productivity within an ecological framework that embraces the characteristics of Millennial Nature – namely, that it possesses agency, forges new interactions and undergoes spontaneous and unpredictable transformations. Natural computing constitutes a technical system that has the potential to create radical transformation within the material realm and therefore reach escape velocity from the gradualist approach of modern practices. However, natural computing operates according to a unique set of principles that embrace risk and always evade accurate prediction – sharing many of the phenomena that we recognize as 'life'. These not only possess a clear set of operations that suggest how material events may continually unfold, but also reveal how these structures maintain uncertainty as an ongoing and fundamental quality of creativity.

The technical systems that could transform modern systems into ecologically beneficial practices do not yet formally exist. While Gilbert Simondon proposed that two distinct forms of technical system exist – namely, machines that operate through totalizing programs and cybernetics, which are capable of adaptation (Massumi, 2012), natural computing represents a third kind of technology that is characterized by its transformational capacity. However, the term natural computing is currently very broad and relatively recently established, so its application has been developed and interpreted according to the aims of the various participating research groups from a range of overlapping scientific research practices that include artificial life, complexity chemistry, synthetic biology, biomimicry and genetic algorithms. Fundamentally, the field of natural computing is inspired by the capabilities of natural phenomena the operations of lifelike[3] systems. These exist at far from equilibrium states and therefore spontaneously possess abundant energy, which empowers them to act without human instruction to seek rich material connections that issue the substances of life and underpin the dynamic process of assemblage production. Researchers include Martin Hanczyc at the Southern University of Denmark (Hanczyc et al, 2007), Lee Cronin, at the University of Glasgow (Cronin at al, 2006), Klaus-Peter Zauner at the University of Southampton (Palmer, 2010), Gabriel Villar at the University of Oxford (Villar, Graham and Bayley, 2013), and Andy Adamatzky at the University of West England (Adamatzky et al, 2007). The main goal of natural computing is to develop programmable, lifelike systems using a spectrum of platforms to better understand and reflect the properties of living things such as, adaptation, learning, evolution and growth.

The language of physics and chemistry

The operations of lifelike systems require a new framework to observe, construct and describe them, so they do not become assimilated back into the language, ideas and possibilities that frame modern practices. Indeed, the programming language that instructs natural computing

Figure 1: Photographs by Rachel Armstrong, 2013. The matrix of jellyfish operates as a kind of natural computing, as the creatures are able to swim without the need for central control over this movement since the physical properties of their gel matrix enables their locomotion.

is based in physics and chemistry, which constitutes the material substrate and programming language that ultimately results in transformation of one kind of matter into another. In natural computing chemistry and physics can therefore be thought of as an integrated

195

software and hardware platform, which can process in parallel and generates physical outcomes that are woven into the substance of reality. Indeed, matter has been proved to be capable of classical kinds of computation (De Silva and Uchiyama, 2007; Adelman, 1994) and is faster than digital information at solving complex problems owing to its parallel processing capabilities. Bonnie Bassler and her colleagues have conducted research into bacterial languages, which they describe as being enabled by chemical 'words' (Bassler, 2012) that can influence non-bacterial agents (Hughes and Sperandio, 2008). Thomas

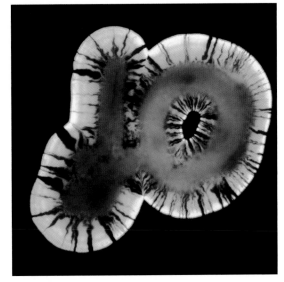

Figure 2: Photograph courtesy Simon Park, 2013.
This bioluminescent bacterial colony is changing its genetic expression according to environmental opportunities. 'Cheaters' within the community are benefiting from the community interaction by saving biological energy through not expressing the protein and are therefore creating dark patches.

Scott-Phillips and his team demonstrated that bacteria use 'combinatorial linguistics', which is a complex linguistic structure that can even evolve (Scott-Phillips et al, 2014). Such findings are preliminary but these sophisticated communication systems may not be exclusive to large, centrally organized brains. It therefore appears that molecular interactions are semiotic tools for bacteria. Yet the broader association between language, cognition and bacterial communication systems is in its earliest stages of development and much further work needs to be done to verify the importance of these discoveries in this controversial field. Yet the chemical operations of natural computing are ubiquitous and may occur at scales and over geological time periods that are difficult for humans to observe and appreciate - such as in the movement of Earth's tectonic plates, the self-assembly of replicating viral proteins, or even in the world's longest running Pitch Drop experiment where a vial of tar takes decades to produce a falling droplet (Johnston, 2014; Zhao, Simon and McKenna, 2013).

Holding a chemical conversation using natural computing techniques

The Bütschli dynamic droplet system offers an experimental model system that may conduct a conversation with the material realm an experimental model and is readily observable at the human scale. Zoologist Otto Bütschli first described it in 1892, when he added a drop of strongly alkaline potash to olive oil (Bütschli, 1892) and noted the spontaneous emergence of dynamic structures that he likened to a 'protist', which is a species of single celled animal, like an amoeba. Bütschli was interested in countering the claims of vitalists by demonstrating simply chemical principles could underpin complex biological phenomena and captured his observations as a series of drawings. Yet, the Bütschli system was a simple soap-making recipe that was not examined with modern laboratory equipment until the phenomenon was recreated using 3M sodium hydroxide and Monini Olive oil (Armstrong and Hanczyc, 2013). On addition to the olive oil, the strongly alkaline droplets quickly broke up into organizing fronts of activity and a collection of centrally placed droplets that were about a centimeter in diameter. The droplets were an ideal model system for observing complex material relations over short time scales that lasted up to an hour. They were inexpensive to produce, could be readily viewed at the human scale and demonstrated lifelike emergent properties. Using a modern light microscope, the droplets exhibited a range of phenomena such as, movement, group interactions, the production of structures and environmental sensitivity. Bütschli droplets possess a set of simple operations that originate from an internal force that is conferred by

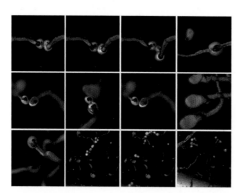

Figure 3: Photographs by Rachel Armstrong, Magnification x4, 2012. Bütschli droplets produce a range of environmentally sensitive forms and behaviours that may be influenced through natural computing techniques that alter these variables, or change the composition of the droplet body by, for example, grinding minerals into the oil – a technique that was used in Future Venice.

its metabolism, which provides the energy that the droplets use to exert effects on their surroundings. These interactions are performative and provide a set of testable proposals that can be observed as aesthetic experiences and relate to the spontaneous creativity in the system. Bütschli droplets can move around their environment, sense it, and even produce products in parallel forms of organization and without a hierarchy of order.

These spontaneous groupings form 'assemblages'[4] by making loose, reversible interactions between each other and generate the flexibility, robustness and environmental sensitivity of the system. Perhaps surprisingly, the behaviour of assemblages is rather conservative and predictable although these groupings operate within 'limits' of possibility. This can be likened to making a cake. When sugar, flour, butter and eggs are mixed together and put into an oven at a particular temperature a spectrum of outcomes is likely, ranging from a dirty black biscuit to a delicious cake. The same is true for the Bütschli system, which also has a predictable range of behaviours. The exception to this rule is when the assemblage reaches a tipping point, where group interactions also give rise to novel, emergent, complex events that are not characteristic behaviours of any of the participating agents but yet are striking and recognizable. Occasionally, a range of different phase change in the internal condition of active Bütschli droplets takes place that may occur at the level of individual droplets or within populations. An individual droplet phase change may be observed during the 'werewolf' moment. Although the exact events that bring about the transition have not been fully characterized it appears that when a droplet reaches a critical stage in the amount of surface area it presents for chemical reactions and the mass of the body, then crystalline deposits are rapidly deposited at the interface. At first, this increased precipitation occurs away from the direction of travel, which creates the illusion that the droplet is growing a furry tail. This precipitation alters the centre of gravity of the droplet, which begins to move erratically as the mass and drag of the crystals begins to alter its movement through the medium. This stage of agitation is quickly followed by complete occlusion of the droplet interface with crystalline deposits, so that it appears to be completely 'hairy' yet inert. The werewolf moment is therefore a pre-terminal event for the droplet, since it results in quiescence. In contrast, population scale changes in behaviour and morphology have also been observed where droplet assemblages suddenly change shape and move away from each other. How such tipping points works is not understood, but the transformation in the system is likely to be the result of multiple, synchronous 'werewolf' events that culminate in an irreversible state. As the droplets evolved over the course of many minutes within the oil field, they formed a microcosm of manifolds, whose undulating interfaces imply the possibility of countless worlds nested at many scales within each other. The droplets possess a unique set of aesthetics that are not fixed but are continually transforming themselves and their environment by creating the conditions in which further populations of droplets could act and be guided through the space. This system provided a unique environment where far from equilibrium systems could be observed, which relentlessly spin interfaces whose chemical interactions form networks that fabricate worlds – like tiny 3D printers. While the dynamic events can just be seen with the naked eye, through a low powered microscope observers are offered a new lens on reality - or a form of chemical visualization software - that reveals material events and relationships from previously unimaginable perspectives. Indeed, the lifelike patterns are quite unlike the inert matter of modern paradigms, that assume the material world is at equilibrium from which stable objects are forged such as, tabletops, buildings and machines.

Yet for an assemblage to be experimentally useful, it must be possible to shape its operations using chemical software. As technical systems, assemblages may be regarded as leaky groupings of materials that form the operating system of natural computers, which deal with the computational properties of matter. Natural computing techniques can shape the outputs of the droplet 'hardware' by adding new chemical 'software', by giving the droplets a metabolism. Natural computing does not use top-down instructive programming such as, genetic codes, but orchestrates the creative agency of matter through soft control systems that encourage horizontal coupling between unlike chemical bodies, to open up new design and engineering possibilities. This enables the internal and external conditions of the system to be altered through soft control strategies. For example, internal conditions can be manipulated by adding a soluble mineral to a droplet it may produce solid matter in the presence of carbon dioxide. Additionally, introducing organic solvents to the olive oil medium such as, alcohol, reduce surface tension and cause a rapid mass movement of droplets towards the source. Yet, for natural computing to have cultural relevance the systems must exist at a scale by which they can be observed, manipulated and inhabited. Although in the Bütschli system droplets usually self-assemble between the microscale to millimetre scale, by adding an inhibitor, which slows down their interactions, they can be increased up to several centimetres in diameter. These technologies can even be applied at an architectural scale in the most pragmatic sense, by entangling their interactions with other assemblages. In the 'Hylozoic Ground' cybernetic installation designed by architect Philip Beesley for the 2010 Venice Architecture Biennale, modified Bütschli droplets operated as a giant smell or taste system that responded to exhaled carbon dioxide from gallery visitors by changing colour.

Dynamic droplets achieve their striking outcomes by inserting time and space into matter, which enables the system to evade decay towards equilibrium. This is consistent with biological systems that are highly reticular and are spatially and temporally organized, such as the endoplasmic reticulum which catalyzes a host of metabolic processes and allows substances to be transformed so they may be the end produced of one reaction and the beginning of another. In this way living systems maintain their operational integrity as transformers, as not all their chemical relationships are simultaneously active or in the same place, which creates an opportunity for assemblage formation. Through its performativity, the Bütschli system provides a glimpse of a dynamic reality that infuses our material realm – not as an exclusive pocket of possibility – but as a pervasive, scalable model with definable limits of operation that offer a window to the actions of lifelike chemistries. These are not representation of relationships like those modeled by digital software but are direct encounters with real events. While no two systems are exactly alike, they display consistent patterns and behaviours, which provide opportunities to develop theoretical models of their interactions, so that their technical qualities may be developed further. Digital modeling of Bütschli droplets has been explored with Autodesk using principles of positive and negative feedback to shape droplet morphology. However, the range of types produced by an algorithm approach has so far been very limited in comparison with the diversity of forms produced by the actual system. An incidental observation, where homologies between populations of droplet interactions were noted with Stephan Rafler's Smooth Life (Doctorow, 2012), a version of John Conway's Game of Life (Gardner, 1970). Although the digital model exhibited many similarities in terms of pattern generation, it did not however, exhibit the striking phase changes noted in the chemical system.

The Bütschli system not only serves as a tool for natural computing that offers a lens on the capabilities of the material realm that is at far from equilibrium but also represents an active body that is not historically loaded in critique. Dissipative chemical bodies are malleable and shaped by their context but at the same time also possess distinctive material programs that confer them with recognizable characteristics and patterns of behaviour. However, these phenomena resist empirical definitions, as they are restless and therefore evade easy definition. Indeed, such agents seek pluralism and elude being reduced to the same sort of explanation – whether it is through morphological typologies, or actor-network-theories – and demand that their existence is supplemented by new theories of modes of existence and different forms of knowledge. It is important to note that these exchanges are literal. They not imagined, represented or translated in any way. They constitute a virtual field of

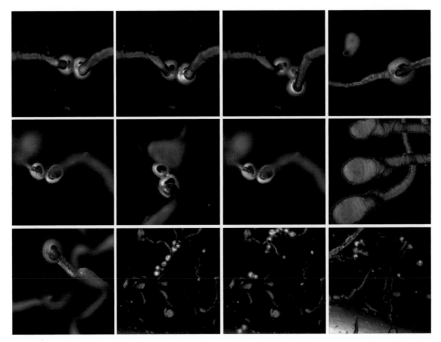

Figure 4: Diagram, designed by Rachel Armstrong and drawn by Simone Ferracina, 2013.This diagram depicts dynamic droplets as 'actors' that operate within the many variable influences encountered in their oil field as an ontolological 'map' of events. While the diagram is drawn as a 2D topology, the possible events within the field are manifold and open up multi dimensional spaces through their interactions with, continuous, multiple agents that shape the evolution of the system.

possibilities that manifest as evolving material expressions over time. Yet because they are ultimately real, they can only embody one potential virtual set of relationships from many possible outputs within the system. Indeed, such immanent bodies court post-epistemological status (Latour, 2003) and question existing categories and identities. To interrogate meaning in these transitional bodies, I recorded the structural and behavioural performance of over 300 Bütschli droplet experiments using a Nikon Eclipse TE2000-S inverted microscope with Photometrics Cascade II 512 camera and in-house software. I then used these findings to map their relationships according to Matt Lee's notion of oceanic ontologies, which produces maps rather than theories of concepts (Lee, 2011).

The diagram reflects the potential activity of Bütschli droplets on an oil field, which may be considered as a stage in which the interactions between droplets are 'actors' that generate events and leave physical traces on an ever-changing stage. A central cross represents the origin of the Bütschli system as a single droplet of alkali meets the olive oil field. From this point, concentric circles radiate outwards representing an exponentially increasing series of time intervals, where novelty and event frequency rapidly decrease. Complexity within the system is represented as a tightly curled spiral around the origin of the reaction and again is more intense around the origin, weakening as the system decays towards equilibrium (Schrodinger, 1944). This provides an instrument through which the relationships between the Bütschli forms and their progeny may be grouped according to design preferences.

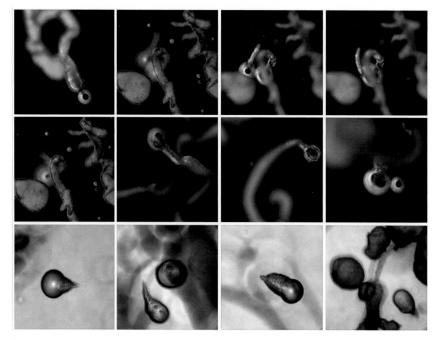

Figure 5: Photographs by Rachel Armstrong, 2012. Highly structured deposits produced by Bütschli droplets may be provoked within the system by raising the alkalinity of the environment.

Droplet phenomena were grouped according to design preferences within the topological chart and arranged according to their morphology and behaviour. For example, the assemblage termed 'complex oyster chains' are distinct in appearance but only differ by degree from the group called 'complex marine landscapes'. 'Oysters' produce a large mass of solid material and their soft bodies bulge from the material shell-like tethers that anchor them. 'Marine landscapes' on the other hand are almost entirely composed of a variety of inert forms that have been produced by oyster droplets that have reached escape velocity from their residues. Metaphor has also been used to convey a variety of striking qualities of the system to succinctly capture complex behaviour, morphological characteristics and even time-based events, which cannot alone be deduced from a graphic. For example, protocell 'snakes' emerge when the molarity of the alkali is extremely high at around 5M, indicated on the diagram by a broken yellow arrow. At these concentrations dense precipitate is formed which causes the droplet to travel more slowly in the oil field and also move from side to side, like a snake, as small inequalities in the distribution of the crystalline deposits are amplified by the droplet motion. The topological chart also documents external events, which are indicated by a curved trajectory that may cause agents within the system to reach tipping points.

The oceanic ontology of Bütschli droplets therefore embodies the transformation of objects, specifically dissipative structures, within a silent network of material systems, which are conjured when substances are mixed. The resultant bodies may be engaged in acts of design and engineering as a technology of assemblages that produce events that are so naturalized they have receded into the background of our daily lives and are now completely invisible to us. When viewed at the human scale, this technical system is of course, Nature – or as Latour prefers - OOWWAAB (Out Of Which We Are All Born) (Latour, 2013) and embodies a horizontal plane of making from which life on Earth has sprung.

Figure 6: Photograph by Rachel Armstrong, 2010. A modified preparation of Bütschli droplets, which slowed down their metabolism, persisted over the 3-month duration of the Venice 2010 Architectural Biennale, transforming dissolved carbon dioxide into sculptural forms which broke free of the droplet body and formed stalagmite like structures on the base of the container.

Working with natural computing

Yet, while proto-ecologies may be regarded as open fields of unevenly distributed assemblages, boundaries are continually forged between them. Haraway (Haraway, 1989) and Peter Sloterdijk (Sloterdijk and Hoban, 2011) suggest that such indeterminate fields are patrolled by immune systems. Yet in a nonhuman world, boundary interactions are not exclusive to the behaviour of populations such as, flocks of migrating birds, schools of dolphins, or dynamic droplet assemblages, but also exist as strong and weak forces between objects including gravity, electromagnetism, strong and weak nuclear forces. These generate a host of interactions including, attractions, repulsions, amplifications and extinctions that may be observed at the interface of trembling dynamic droplets. Matter has its own immunology and object-technics that exert their effects where assemblages overlap with and are infused by the medium in which they exist. Such intersections may be observed in the production of striking chemical phenomena that betray foundational dynamic exchanges, such as those curated for the Hylozoic Ground installation (Armstrong and Beesley, 2011), a cybernetic installation by Philip Beesley that incorporates a responsive chemical system into a mechanical framework, where brightly coloured carbonate precipitates are produced on exposure to carbon dioxide as a seamless element within the construction process of a 'living' architecture.

These 'matterings' (Barad, 2007) call upon nonhuman actors to exert effects on the ordering of material relationships and produces a synthetic system that builds new groupings, identities and forms of order that do not pander to existing structures but propose new networks of operations that are associated with alternative value systems such as, fertility. A technical relationship with Nature provides opportunities to harness metabolic systems to perform useful work, where substrates are not denatured and consumed, but transformed and even integrated into new networks. Such hybrids are creating the context for new forms of human development such as, Future Venice, is a project that hybridizes chemistry and architecture and imagines an alternative sustainable future for the city by growing a synthetic reef under its foundations. It is experimentally developed through the actions of programmable droplets, which act as an urban scale natural computer and form an accretion technology that spreads the point load of the city over a much broader base that attenuates its sinking into the soft delta soils on which it was founded (Myers and Antonelli, p72-73). Also Dune by Magnus Larssen, is a biological and architectural hybrid that proposes a giant bacterial biofilm printer could transform sand into sandstone in the Sahara and therefore combat desertification (Myers and Antonelli, p p63-65). By engaging material transformation as a property of lively matter as a technical strategy that enhances the biotic activity on which our survival depends, such emerging ideas are developing new design and engineering practices that render industrial systems incomplete rather than obsolete. For example, SymbioticA's Victimless Leather project exhibited at MOMA seeded the possibility of a time when meat products could exist without animal suffering through tissue culture (Myers and Antonelli, 2013, p131-132). Although this avant-garde art group did not technically create the technology to enable this, they inspired a range of meat products such as, tissue culture burgers (Jha, 2013) and synthetic leather (May, 2013), which do not involve the farming or slaughtering of animals. The enhanced deployment of natural technologies could therefore transform the current relationship between architecture and the material realm from one of consumption, into a potent revolution of alternative values and power structures that enhance the performativity of matter and enliven our ecosystems.

Natural computing and living architecture

The technical systems of the natural world are not yet culturally real, in that they have not yet been productized and are therefore not generally accessible. They currently take the form of a range of research practices that employ speculative and experimental techniques that iteratively re-inform each other to produce material tactics and spatial programs that give rise to architectures with lifelike properties, as in Future Venice. Yet, although the outputs of these emerging technologies are currently prototypes and ongoing experiments, it is nonetheless possible to use the lens of natural computing to propose alternative forms of architecture, in which matter and information are entangled as 'living architecture', with the potential to develop unique relationships with humans and Nature. Such approaches do not guarantee corrective measures in redirecting the performance of natural systems, for example, to 'fix' climate change - but instead offer alternative, habitable futures by engaging the technological potential of Millennial Nature.

Potentially such new approaches may produce a range of opportunities for meeting human needs concurrently with the widespread recovery of our planetary ecosystems, ending the irreconcilable conflict between humanism and environmentalism in architectural concerns.

REFERENCES

- Adamatzky, A. Bull, L. De Lacy Costello, B. Stepney, S. and Teuscher, C. eds. 2007. Unconventional computing. Beckington, UK: Luniver Press.
- Adelman, L.M. 1994. Molecular Computation of Solutions to Combinatorial Problems, Science 226, pp. 1021–1024.
- Armstrong, R. 2013. Coming to terms with synthetic biology, Everything under control, Volume Magazine, Archis Press, No.35, pp. 110-117.
- Armstrong, R. 5 December 2012. Lawless sustainability. [online] Available at: http://www. architecturenorway.no/questions/cities-sustainability/armstrong/. [Accessed 12 June 2014].
- Armstrong, R. (2011) Architectural Synthetic Ecologies, Kerb – 19- Journal of Landscape Architecture, Paradigms of Nature: Post Natural Futures, Editors Caitrin Daly, Sarah Hicks, Adrian Keene and Ricky Ray Ricardo, Melbourne Books, Melbourne, Australia, pp.92-98.
- Armstrong, R. and Beesley, P. 2011. Soil and protoplasm: The Hylozoic Ground project, Architectural Design, 81(2), pp. 78-89.
- Armstrong, R. and Hanczyc, M.M. 2013. Bütschli dynamic droplet system. Artificial Life Journal, 19(3–4), pp. 331–346.
- Bassler, B. February 2009. How bacteria 'talk', TED.com. [online] Available at: http://www.ted.com/talks/bonnie_bassler_on_how_bacteria_communicate.html. [Accessed 12 June 2014].
- Barad, K. 2007. Meeting the Universe halfway. Durham: Duke University Press.
- Bedau, M. 2009. Living Technology Today and Tomorrow. Technoetic Arts A Journal of Speculative Research, 7(2), pp.199-206.
- Bennett, J. 2010. Vibrant matter: A political ecology of things. Durham: Duke University Press.
- Brown, S.D. 2002. Michel Serres: Science, translation and the logic of the parasite. Theory, Culture & Society, 19(3), pp.1-27.
- Bütschli, O. 1892. Untersuchungen ueber microscopische Schaume und das Protoplasma, Leipzig.
- Cronin, L. Krasnogor, N. Davis, B.G. Alexander, C. Robertson, N. Steinke, J.H.G. Schroeder, S.L.M. Khlobystov, A.N. Cooper, G. Gardner, P.M. Siepmann, P. Whitaker, B.J. and Marsh, D. 2006. The imitation game—a computational chemical approach to recognizing life. Nature Biotechnology, 24, pp. 1203-1206.
- Crutzen, P. J. and Stoermer, E.F. 2000. The 'Anthropocene'. Global Change Newsletter, 41, pp. 17–18.
- Denning P. J. 2007. Computing is a natural science. Communications of the ACM, 50(7), pp. 13-18.
- De Silva, A. P. and Uchiyama, S. 2007. Molecular logic and computing. Nature Nanotechnology 2, pp. 399–410.
- Doctorow, C. 11 October 2012. Game of Life with floating point operations: beautiful SmoothLife. Boing Boing. [online] Available at: http://boingboing.net/2012/10/11/game-of-life-with-floating-poi.html [Accessed 12 June 2014].
- Doughty, C. E., A. Wolf, and C. B. Field. 2010. Biophysical feedbacks between the Pleistocene megafauna extinction

and climate: The first human-induced global warming? Geophys. Res. Lett., 37, L15703, doi:10.1029/2010GL043985.

- Dunne, T. and Raby, F. 2014. Speculative Everything: Design, Fiction, and Social Dreaming. Cambridge: MIT Press.
- Elices, M. Guinea, G. V. Plaza, G. R. Karatzas, C. Riekel, C. Agulló-Rueda, F. Daza, R. Pérez-Rigueiro, J. 2011. Bioinspired Fibers Follow the Track of Natural Spider Silk. Macromolecules, 44(5), pp. 1166–1176.
- Gardner, M. 1970. The fantastic combinations of John Conway's new solitaire game 'life'. Scientific American, 223, pp. 120-123.
- Hanczyc, M.M. Toyota, T. Ikegami, T. Packard, N.H. and Sugawara, T. 2007. Fatty acid chemistry at the oil-water interface: Self-propelled oil droplets. Journal of the American Chemical Society, 129(30), pp. 9386 – 9391.
- Haraway, Donna. 1989. The Biopolitics of Postmodern Bodies: Determinations of Self in Immune System Discourse. In: differences: A Journal of Feminist Cultural Studies, 1(1), pp. 3-43.
- Heidegger, M. 1993. The Question Concerning Technology. In: William Lovitt and David Farrell Krell (Eds.), Martin • Heidegger, Basic Writings. Revised and expanded edition, pp. 287-311.
- Hughes, D.T. and Sperandio, V. 2008. Inter-kingdom signaling: communication between bacteria and their hosts. Nature Reviews Microbiology, 2, pp. 111-120.
- Imperial College London, 2013. Sustainable society network +, Digital economy lab. [online] Available at: http://www3.imperial.ac.uk/digital-economy-lab/partnernetworks/sustaina- blesocietynetwork. [Accessed 25 April 2014].
- Jha, A. 5 August 2013. Synthetic meat: How the world's costliest burger made it on to the plate. Guardian. [online] Available at: w.theguardian.com/science/2013/aug/05/synthetic-meat-burger-stem-cells. [Accessed 12 June 2014].
- Johnston, R. 18 July 2013. World's slowest-moving drop caught on camera at last, Nature News. [online] Available at : http://www.nature.com/news/world-s-slowest-moving-drop-caught-on-camera-at-last-1.13418#/ref-link-1. [Accessed 12 June 2014].
- Latour, B. 2013. Once out of nature: Natural religion as a pleonasm. Gifford lecture series, University of Edinburgh. [online] Available at: http://www.youtube.com/ watch?v=MC3E6vdQEzk. [Accessed 12 June 2014].
- Latour, B. 1993. We have never been modern. Cambridge: Harvard University Press.
- Lee, M. 2011. Oceanic ontology and problematic thought, NOOK Book/Barnes and Noble. [online] Available at: http://www.barnesandnoble.com/w/oceanic-ontology-and-problemat-ic-thought-matt-lee/1105805765. [Accessed 12 June 2013].
- Massumi, B. 2012. 'Technical mentality' revisited: Brian Massumi on Gilbert Simondon. In: A. De Boever, A. Murray, J. Roffe and A. Woodward eds. Gilbert Simondon: Being and technology. Edinburgh: Edinburgh University Press, pp. 19-36.
- May, K.T. June 13 2013. How to print meat and leather: Andras Forgacs at TEDGlobal 2013. TED Blog. [online] Available at: http://blog.ted.com/2013/06/13/how-to-print-meat-and-leather-andras-forgacs-at-tedglobal-2013/. [Accessed 12 June 2014].
- Myers, W. and Antonelli, P. 2013. Bio Design: Nature, Science, Creativity. London: Thames & Hudson /New York: MOMA.
- Palmer, J. 11 January 2010. Chemical computer that mimics neurons to be created. BBC News. Available at: http://news.bbc.co.uk/1/hi/8452196.stm. [Accessed 12 June 2014].
- Roco, M.C. and Bainbridge, W.S. 2003. Converging Technologies for Improving Human Performance, Nanotechnology, Biotechnology, Information technology and Cognitive science. NSF/DOC-sponsored report. Dordrecht: Springer.
- Schrödinger, E. 1944. What is life? The physical aspect of the living cell. Based on lectures delivered under the auspices of the Dublin Institute for Advanced Studies at Trinity College, Dublin, in February 1943. [online] Available at: http://whatislife.stanford.edu/LoCo_files/ What-is-Life.pdf. [Accessed 12 June 2014].
- Scott-Phillips, T.C. Gurney, J. Ivens, A. Diggle, S.P. and Popat, R. April 23 2014. Combinatorial Communication in Bacteria: Implications for the Origins of Linguistic Generativity. PLOS One, DOI: 10.1371/journal.pone.0095929. [online] Available at: http://www.plosone.org/article/info%3Adoi%2F10.1371%2Fjournal.pone.0095929. [Accessed 12 June 2014].
- Sloterdijk, P and Hoban, W. 2011. Bubbles: Spheres I - Microspherology: 1 (Semiotext(e) / Foreign Agents). Cambridge: MIT Press.
- Swartz, J. 2 November 2010. Can profit and sustainability go together? Guardian sustainable business. The Guardian. [online] Available at: http://www.guardian.co.uk/sustainable-business/blog/jeff-swartz-timberland-sustainability-profit. [Accessed 12 June 2014].
- The Guardian. 2013. Sustainable living hub. Sustainable business. [online] Available at: http://www.guardian.co.uk/sustainable-business/sustainable-living. [Accessed 12 June 2014].
- Tomorrows Company. No date. Sustainability and models of business success. Tomorrows Company. [online] Available at: http://tomorrowscompany.com/sustainability-models-of-business-success. [Accessed 12 June 2014].

- Von Bertalanffy, L. 1950. An Outline for General Systems Theory. British Journal for the Philosophy of Science, 1(2), pp. 134-165.
- Villar, G. Graham, A.D. and Bayley, H. 2013. A tissue-like printed material. Science, 340(6128), pp. 48-52.
- Wilson, E.O. 2003. The Future of life. New York: Vintage Books.
- World Commission on Environment and Development.1987. Our common future. Report of the World Commission on environment and development. Published as Annex to General Assembly document A/42/427. Available at: http://www.un-documents.net/our-common- future.pdf. [Accessed 12 June 2014].
- Zhao, J. Simon, S.L. and McKenna, G.B. 2013. Using 20-million-year-old amber to test the super-Arrhenius behaviour of glass-forming systems. Nature Communications 4 (1783), doi:10.1038/ncomms2809

FOOTNOTES

1. Brian Massumi, "'Technical mentality' revisited: Brian Massumi on Gilbert Simondon." In: A. De Boever, A. Murray, J. Roffe and A. Woodward eds. Gilbert Simondon: Being and Technology. Edinburgh: Edinburgh University Press, pp. 19–36.

2. Industrialization is accompanied by a particular kind of economics that is based on the scarcity of resources and the profits gained by mass-producing commodities that are in short supply. This leads to a set of principles that underpin manufacturing processes that include, conservatism to protect fundamental infrastructures, gradualism in development of new products and very short time-scales (typically 3-5 years) to product development.

3. Lifelike systems exhibit many characteristics of living things, such as growth, sensitivity and metabolism but do not have the full status of being truly 'alive'. An example is the Bütschli droplet system, mentioned as an example of natural computing in this essay.

4. The concept of assemblage is from the French word 'agencement' used by Gilles Deleuze and Felix Guattari to denote specific connections between groupings of actants7 that form loose, reversible associations with each other, which produce complex agents composed of many different, interacting bodies such as, soil. Bennett notes, "Bodies enhance their power in or as a heterogeneous assemblage ... Assemblages are ad hoc groupings of diverse elements, of vibrant materials of all sorts." (Bennett, 2010, p23).

IMAGE CREDITS

All images courtesy of Rachel Armstrong

Figure 4: Drawing by Rachel Armstrong & Simone Ferracina 2013

RACHEL ARMSTRONG is a Co-Director of AVATAR (Advanced Virtual and Technological Architectural Research) specializing in Architecture & Synthetic Biology at The School of Architecture & Construction, University of Greenwich, London. She is also a 2010 Senior TED Fellow, and Visiting Research Assistant at the Center for Fundamental Living Technology, Department of Physics and Chemistry, University of Southern Denmark. Rachel is a sustainability innovator who investigates a new approach to building materials called 'living architecture,' which suggests it is possible for our buildings to share some of the properties of living systems. She collaboratively works across disciplines to build and develop prototypes that embody her approach.

Rachel has been frequently recognised as being a pioneer. She is listed on the Wired 2013 Smart List, is one of the 2013 ICON 50 and described as one of the ten people in the UK that may shape the UK's recovery by Director Magazine in 2012. In the same year she was nominated as one of the most inspiring top nine women by Chick Chip magazine and featured by BBC Focus Magazine's in 2011 in 'ideas that could change the world'.

Black Sky Thinking

www.blackskythinking.org

PABLO LORENZO-EIROA

FROM CODING TO REPRESENTATION, TO FORMAL AUTONOMY, TO MEDIA REPRODUCTION

—

FOUR LEVELS OF ARCHITECTURE AGENCY

The past Log 29 conference at the MOMA, "In Pursuit of Architecture," explored the changing constitution of architecture over the last ten years. As part of this conference, architectural critics were placed into conversation with architects who presented their buildings from the past decade. Despite the diversity of architectural discourses being presented, the façades of the buildings dominated the conversation. Silvia Lavin, in particular, noted that the relationship between the buildings' images and their reproduction was a recurring theme. For instance, multiple factors informed the design of the buildings' façades, including: computer algorithms that parameterized their forms; various subject-object relationships based on perception; and the influence of their iconicity by media reproduction. However, as Emmanuel Petit observed, none of these buildings seemed to address any longer the ground condition. He noted that in previous decades, this reference had actually been fundamental to the discipline, thereby implying that these newer buildings lacked disciplinary reference.

It is interesting to make sense of two seemingly unrelated issues: first, the earlier disciplinary reference to the ground condition, and second, the current appeal of the image of a building as it is activated by media reproduction. What determines the agency of contemporary architecture after decades of referencing the ground? How can one understand architecture agency through media motivation? In contemporary architecture, it can be argued that the envelope of a building, its façade, is what indexes multiple design agencies, from parametric codes to media reproduction. Considered as a thickened surface, the façade synthesizes the previous experience of grounded buildings by redefining the building's containment. Therefore, contemporary façades reference complex, parametric algorithms that not only index formal differentiation, but also engage the thicker, topological interior/exterior relationships of the spaces within. Through their intrinsic iconicity, then, the façades of buildings also index the signification forced upon them by media reproduction. These are the two aspects of signification in contemporary architecture, i.e. – the structuring of codes that organize differentiation and media reproduction, that are synthesized in the surface of a building.

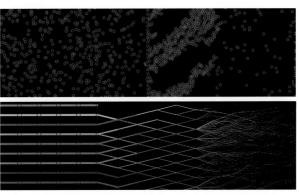

Figure 1a, 1b : Fig. 1a Algorithm based on increasing bifurcations from nodes. Fig.01b Dynamic simulation of sedimentation by depositing floating aggregates. The combination of these two algorithms is dynamically related to site-specific topographic data following flooding zones. Thus the resulting algorithm conforms three distinct modes of establishing a complex shifting structure. The agency of this shifting dynamic organization is activated once the growth of artificial landscapes is induced by promoting natural side effects which are latent in these environments. The School of Architecture of The Cooper Union, Professor Pablo Lorenzo-Eiroa computation design seminar, students: Katheryn Bajo and Gregory Schikhman; S2013.

Reference and Origin in Architecture

How can one identify agency in digital architecture? When does architecture agency originates? Where can we identify the conditions that prescribe architectural form relative to information processing and media communication? How can architecture put into question the set of conditions that prescribe both its own production and reproduction? These are the questions we must confront to understand how architecture is defined.

Modernist buildings tended to prescribe order through a generic, undifferentiated order. The modern grid embodied not only an ideal of infinite, predetermined order, but also a condition of origin. After the Second World War, post-structuralism emerged to oppose the determinism of the Modern Movement. Poststructuralist concepts, such as mapping, were driven by the emergent indeterminacy of topographies and heterotopias. As a consequence of this reading, the site, the ground became a reference for architecture as it was the originator of a different idea of order, an heterotopic open order informed by the intrinsic quality of a place. Because of the specificity of the congruence of multiple parameters that define a topo-logos, due to its entropy, the idea of a spatial specificity building up from particular circumstances could open up possibilities to emergent systems. If one could code the initial parameters that could generate an emergent system, one could strategize a first level of coding agency [Fig 1, 2, 3].

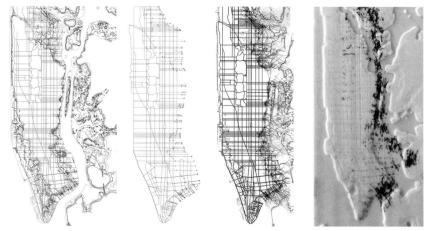

Figure 2 : Biodigital landscape urbanism. Working with biodigital concepts, these artificial landscapes are generated by activating natural feedback exchanging information and energy. Indeterminacy in architecture can be related to a topo-logos, or a logic of the place, a condition that cannot be designed but that it is emergent. This project places two conditions of indeterminacy relative to computer determination. First, satellite images of indeterminate topographies are processed using layering mapping techniques, proposing a transfiguration, but filtered through deterministic algorithms. Second, a bifurcating structure is designed to produce variations relating to indeterminate landscape conditions. Thus the form of the project is defined by its dynamic shifting agency, which emerges by combining deterministic algorithmic operations with non-deterministic topographies, informing the design through digital dynamic simulations and analog simulations (using digital fabrication). This project raises the question whether or not post-structuralism is possible through computation. The School of Architecture of The Cooper Union, Professor Pablo Lorenzo-Eiroa computation design seminar, students: Katheryn Bajo and Gregory Schikhman; S2013.

Figure 3a, 3b, 3c, 3d: Fig. 3a and 3b. Manhattan urban fabric typologies (or a new building code for NY) is informed topologically by processing topographical data and dynamic environmental data. Fig. 3c and 3d. Biodigital Manhattanism post Hurricane Sandy: displaced parametric urban typologies are designed to work with environmental forces, integrating landscape urbanism strategies that induce the growth of soft landscapes for coastal protection. The School of Architecture of The Cooper Union, Professor Pablo Lorenzo-Eiroa computation design seminar, students: JA Alonzo, Yoonah Choi, Febe Chong, Daniel Hall, Mabel Jiang, Anna Kramer, Sehee Lee, Binhan Li, Aisa Osako and Rosannah Sandoval, S2014.

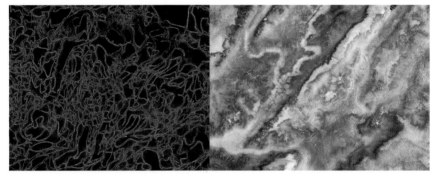

Figure 3e,3f: Fig. 3e. Landscape urbanism strategy by layering interrupting dissections to a dynamic delta using recovered large data from satellite image. Fig. 3f. This landscape urbanism project emerges both informed by external data and by affecting the same information that is indexing. The result is an emergent landscape that reacts simultaneously to dynamic natural forces proposing informed indeterminate topographies. Analog simulation using digital fabrication. The School of Architecture of The Cooper Union, Professor Pablo Lorenzo-Eiroa computation design seminar, students: Derrick Benson, William Hood and Jeremy Jacinth, S2013.

Architects sought to un-motivate the figure of the object-building and motivate the figuration of the existing ground surface, thereby critiquing the notion of a stable, deterministic origin. The resulting architectural projects indexed existing sites and activated a topo-logos, which motivated the figuration of the background. A logic of continuous formal differentiation then informed the architectural envelope and its relationship to the ground, so that a thickening of the ground as inhabitable surface disseminated the figure of the building relative to the site, as exemplified by grounded buildings and site specific interventions, such as Eisenman Architects' City of Culture in Galicia.

After decades of such disciplinary expansion, the surface of a building progressively acquired autonomy from the ground plane. FOA's Yokohama Port Terminal created an artificial topo-logos, which indexed its own interior-exterior continuous relationships, completely dissociated from any site condition. This project presented an autonomous artificial horizontal surface-building but conceptually detached from the ground plane, activating a process of figuration of the envelope and the architecture container.

During the last ten years buildings started enfolding the previous experience of expansion dealing with open landscapes to redefine rather the stability of the architectural container. This transformation replaced the horizontally grounded condition of a non-figural building with a vertically differentiated picture plane. Recently the O-14 building in Dubai by RUR, embodied a progressively differentiated envelope. This building, like many others of the last decade, enfolded the earlier expansion of site-specific architecture to project an artificially differentiated topo-logos to the architectural container. That is, the façade surface exchanged the indexing of undetermined conditions, which referenced a place, for the promotion of an undetermined, self-referential surface-object. Thus, the building façade became an artificial ground, an apparently non-deterministic differential "topographical" surface, which indexed its constitution through deterministic parametric algorithms. These algorithms have since become the struggle for the discipline, constituting a new frame of reference.

Computation as Origin: The Politics of Digital Representation

Besides the post-structuralist influence, the autonomy of the building-surface, relative to the ground, had also been prompted by the gradual shift to digital representation. Specifically, computers induce a groundless matrix, a vectorial isotropic space as the medium of representation for dynamic architectural objects, thereby negating gravity. As a result, the ground condition was progressively displaced and then ignored. Furthermore, NURBs-based geometry, mathematical plots, parametric relationships and algorithms enabled the manipulation of complex curvatures and surfaces, which resulted in dynamically differentiated, thickened architectural façades. By displacing interior/exterior relationships, the thickened digital envelope of parametric mathematical surface-models directly engaged the spaces within through topology. This thickened digital envelope actualized a contemporary poché.

Figure 4: World Trade Center NYTimes Think Big research group, curated by Herbert Muschamp, New York, 2002. Housing Prototype for WTC site, veiled façade by Pablo Lorenzo-Eiroa. Rather than indexing the ground, this project anticipated the shift towards indexing computer codes in the design of a differentiated facade, displacing the stability of the architecture container.

One may argue that the computer screen accelerated this transformation by provoking the transition from horizontal to vertical representation. Historically, the floor plan constituted the logos of space – an organizational matrix that is not visual. Meanwhile, the vertical picture plane activated subject-object relationships. The plan was related to the picture plane only by organizing the experiential aspects of a building through the activation of spatial, bodily affection. The computer screen shifted the horizontal surface of the drafting table, where space was defined by XY in plan and Z as an extrusion, to the vertical. Thus, the screen displaced the tectonics of the floor plan, and activated XY as a picture plane and Z as its depth, and assimilated architecture with media for which depth, not vertical extrusion, defines space. This shift replaced structural reasoning by a perceptive, visual, iconographic logic. As a result, the surface of a building envelope started indexing an iconic object, a development conditioned by media reproduction.

The notion of site specificity proposed a condition of reference, a non-deterministic origin for post-structuralist architecture. This condition of reference, of origin, has since shifted from the horizontal topo-logos to a predetermined, indexed vertical picture plane informing the building's envelope. As a result, the condition of origin has been displaced by the predetermination of digital, representational structures. Such a displacement is identifiable by the digital signifiers that index the constitution of form.

Digital Signifiers And The Politics Of Representation: New Emerging Disciplines as Agency

Stan Allen's "Mapping the Intangible"[1] in early 2000's referred to problems that emerge in mapping events, territories, heterotopias or conditions which are intangible by exploring the boundaries of representational techniques. In this sense, the content to be represented is extrinsic to the available mediums of representation. In this context it is interesting to raise the opposite problem: how mediums of representation produce signification and therefore induce content. Computation inversed Stan Allen's equation, proposing a structure to the world. Computation as an inductive structure produces signification even with simulation algorithms that are represent complex fluid systems. Computation replaced representation with performance. Computation shifted the mapping of extrinsic content to the coding of emergent content, or agency. By mapping indeterminate content, the medium was under question and new means of mapping would relate to new tools; on the opposite by focusing on the emergent quality of a code the medium became stronger. This problem can also be taken further since the medium of representation may also activate a content unique to its frame.

Software interfaces and codes constitute implicit frames were artistic expression is originated. If the mediums of representation have such a power to regulate the work, then interfaces are spaces of differentiation that can activate a performative aspect in the work, promoting agency by triggering a formal generative capacity of differentiation that originates a conceptual continuous loop of responsive and interactive feedback. Marshall McLuhan was one of the first ones to identify that the medium constitutes, in reality, the message[2]. Badiou critiqued the logic of systems addressing the impossibility of arriving to solutions outside of their structure. And part of this problem is how a project starts, as the first sign in a project may be already structured by systems of representation, cultural frames, visual judgment, etc. Late post-structuralism resolved this question by disregarding the departing structures, resolving within variations alternative solutions that place a problem in movement, focusing on the variation and not its relationship with the underlying dominant system.

Formal logic is an autonomous cognitive system that produces signification. The representation of data as an extrinsic reality through any medium or form (mapping, data mining, form making, etc) should be questioned since this process informs the same reality it is depicting. Representation implies an empowerment, the creating of a signifier which is independent from what it is representing, the emergence of an independent object. What is interesting is that there is no data without representation and any index will influence its represented data. Representation is usually thought of as fiction when the interesting aspect is that it is more powerful than reality: it defines an agency. In artistic disciplines it becomes problematic when there is no agency at a representational level, such as when the content represented is extrinsic to the performance of its medium._

Computer representation has induced a groundless matrix that originates all architecture, a process which, through computational codes, has resulted in a new structuralism[3]. The new structuralism, which defined its project in the late 2000's is manifested in the artificial man-made bit of information. Codes present an alternative to the mirroring of biomorphic tendencies in digital architecture of the 1990's. The concern for blob surfaces has been displaced by the coding of relationships, taking a step towards abstraction in coordination with the shift from drawing to encoding information. Information technologies enable the communication between computer interfaces. Architecture form, and as a consequence architectural space, is standardized, homogenized and parameterized through information processing. Language mediates reality and influences the way we think. In reference to the second digital revolution, information processing in digital architecture motivates the inevitable reduction of mathematical binary codes. That is, information processing necessarily standardize, homogenize, and parameterize form – and by extension, the representation of space. Since there can be no information without representation, the reduction of information to codes results in this new structuralism. Informational interfaces have been activating a new politics of representation since digital architecture has become self-referential due to computation. While interfaces process information they re-structure extrinsic content to fit its medium, activating a topological loop that ends up informing reality.

There is a consistently common ground in the exploration of the current emergence of new disciplinary boundaries, or even such expansion that breaks into multiple new disciplines, which is representation. It seems that the several expansions or new disciplinary investigations are driven by new strategies of representation. New technologies of representation, sometimes even informed by a cultural kunstwollen, enable the manipulation of data and visualization strategies that open up new possibilities and by doing so, inform new discourses. In this sense, the expansion of the discipline is often informed by new means of representation. Even if new discourses present cultural problems not addressed by the previous limits of the discipline, many times these discourses become enabled by technological possibilities. New technologies have historically enabled new ways to look at the world and therefore opening up new possibilities for representing it.

For instance, the ecological crisis has been questioning architecture from an efficiency point of view, a merely technological problem which did not influence the cultural project of the discipline. But more recently, the ecological discourse was able to enter the cultural project of architecture through representation. Novel dynamic energy modeling was able to consolidate a new aesthetic, a new vision, the possibility to manipulate energy, a new practice for the discourse on ecology relative to architecture shifting many of its ideas on spatial boundaries, and its tectonic. This agency through representation was instrumented into a new discipline, those which understand spatial boundaries as energy boundaries. This has been taken to the point that if these new means of representation may or may not be technically efficient at a certain point becomes irrelevant, since new cultural questions emerge.

Similar problems could be traced relative to social responsibility in architecture or more politically active positions in the practice of architecture. The interesting point is that after a first apparent rupture with formal discourses, alternative practices will be able to sustain their agendas insofar as they are able to break through representation in architecture, proposing new aesthetic agendas, new agency through new codes, not only for the architectural object but also for any abstract relational manifestation of architecture.

Representation is common to all new disciplinary expansions and new agendas. What is interesting is that any new disciplinary explorations, are based on the recognition of the potential of new ways of seeing. The problem is when new visualization ideas are based on similar representational strategies that are based on identical codes. In this sense, even if Stan Allen's argument has to be revisited relative to computation, it is interesting to think that the exploration of new spatial representational techniques, new computing algorithms that infer new formal logics and new information structures which may have the potential to become a language and affect architecture from within, would eventually, expand the boundaries of the discipline and even may initiate new disciplinary discourses. Architecture at this point would be the initiator of questions in the interdisciplinary discourse, rather than importing and translating content or knowledge extrinsic to its disciplinary boundary. In other words, this would imply an autonomous architectural agency.

Derrida's critique of Saussure's equation is that structuralism disseminates categorical thought. Derrida defined language as the creation of signifiers, meaning that each time we name something we are creating an independent entity, an artificial construction independent from what it is being named. A sign, such as a digital signifier, is an artificial construction independent from what it is representing. Conrad Fiedler opposed the Kantian idea that art was a lower form of cognition, since artistic form constitutes an autonomous logical system which its purpose is not to mean through linguistic translation or to represent extrinsic content. Consequently, digital architecture must acknowledge an autonomy and an agency implied within its digital signifiers, developing an expression with its own attributes, constraints and problems.

These are the reasons why the background that defines the set of conditions in an informational interface, that defines agency in contemporary architecture by prescribing computer space, must be questioned in relation to its generated content, which indexes into the form of a project the set of parameters that constitutes its very logic. This presents a second level, a representational agency, an agency that becomes active by promoting, critiquing or resisting the ideological implicit agendas of the medium of representation. Digital representation created a revolution in architecture, the structuralism of which has not yet been displaced. Moreover, this structuralism has not been questioned culturally from the set of constructions defining the boundaries of architecture as a discipline.

If one could question the background representational space relative to what's being generated in a single topology, one could place at the same level of signification, the project and the interface in which is projected. An interesting cultural aspect of Processing® is that the canvas or the space of representation is not given by the language, but it has to be coded. A processing exercise as a critical reading of the conditions of the software became the agency of a house project. This project dissipated its original determination by motivating the figuration of the background structure-space of the canvas [Fig. 5].

Another critical parametric misuse of computer space to reveal its projective logic and

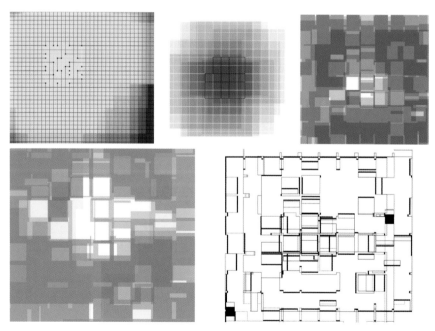

Figure 5: Processing exercise. The constitution of the space of representation in Processing® becomes motivated by generating the architecture of the project. The School of Architecture of The Cooper Union: Head Professor and Coordinator Pablo Lorenzo-Eiroa with instructors Matt Roman, Katerina Kourkoula and Will Shapiro, design II students: Piau Liu and Maya Krtic, F2013.

displace its structure can be related to a Cartopological diagram [Fig. 6]. This diagram integrates the background parametric computer space-plot that prescribes a surface as part of the topology of the project. Historically, the Möbius surface model was incorporated to the discipline and displaced the XY "ground plane" in architecture; later on, the Klein surface model displaced the XY-YZ planes, integrating the ground plane to the picture plane. A Cartopological diagram relates a three-fold surface model displacing the three XY-YZ-XZ Cartesian planes. The three coordinate axes and the planes' positive and negative sides are integrated into a three-fold continuity, presenting a multidimensional space. Therefore these series of diagrams work topological displacements of their own computer plot coordinate reference-space by self-intersection. In this way, this diagram critiques the determination of the systems of representation with the space represented displacing both frame and content._

Redefining the Relative in Parametric Variations: Big Data and Agency

Big Data[4] has intended to displace reference ignoring the structuralism imposed by computation, mathematics and any deterministic formulation of reality by contrasting large sources of data through statistic analysis. The contrasting position resides on the previous restriction of working with controllable amounts of data in the 1990's to the emergent possibilities to work with large sources of data in the 2000's. Mario Carpo understands the consequence of dealing with big data as architecture finally unrestricted from any culturally based structural or typological reference. Judgment, memory and the artificially constructed orders that our brain establishes as reference to anticipate control could be suspended if architecture is able to get rid of the heavy load of reference. Carpo places this process as the natural development of the last phase of a post-structuralism and the final deconstruction of all reference. But there are several questions that can be asked. Is it possible to develop a post-structuralist project through computation which is intrinsically deterministic? For instance, independently from its output, how is data gathered, managed, filtered, organized

Figure 6

and represented? How open, dynamic and emergent are the algorithms that manage big data?

Many are working to displace and eventually dissipate the heavy weight of reference as initially identified by structuralism, which usually implicates cognitive problems, such as the tendency of our brain to value certain decisions over others. Many are working in pushing the boundaries of computation with an experimental architecture which displaces reference with complex organizations that cannot be anticipated or even designed. But it seems problematic to understand such architecture differentiation free from the reference given by the initial parameters that process large sources of data. The issue is not in the flow of data that emerges as a result of computation, but rather the issue is which are the set of politically charged parameters that define its output. It is, of course, necessary to suspend cultural preference in the production of difference. When working with large quantities of data it seems that we could suspend personal judgment relative to a known factor by analyzing statistically objective information. We can hope to open the end result of a project to the emergent quality of the computed information. But the question is whether the processed data is only indexed by the initial parameters that computed its processing or if it is actually open to emergent relationships that go beyond the initial parameters. The relevant factor is not much the way computed data may look like as a differentiated result, but the way data it is processed, collected, layered, organized by several structuring algorithms and interfaces. For instance it may be a concern what was left out, what are the relationships of the data that emerges as a result and the form of the relationships that were computed and anticipated a priori.

The reading of the examples Carpo gives present artistic projects that aim for a certain excess which may be able to go beyond a complex order in which one may not be able to distinguish the set of parameters that constitute the object, tending to a certain informal dismembering of any idea of order or pre-conceived organization. But this may also be more of a visual effect than an actual intrinsic condition of emergence and agency of their architecture. Part of the problem is how to come up with a question not determined by the system within which it emerges, and this could be traced in architecture all the way back to how a project starts. The very first sign in a project may have already been structured by systems of representation, implying several cultural frames. Late post-structuralism attempted to solve this problem by disregarding the departing structure and finding alternative solutions within variations that placed the problem in movement. This approach focused on the variation of parametric solutions rather than relationships that would question the structure of the system.

In the last few years, it has become quite clear that if architects do not break or displace the source codes given by conventional algorithms and interfaces in order to create their own, their work will remain confined by the predetermined set of ideas, cultural projects, and aesthetic agendas of existing informational interfaces. Such a departure necessarily puts into question the notion of authorship[5] within the design process, i.e. – the process of creating structures that can organize and process information based on an architectural understanding.

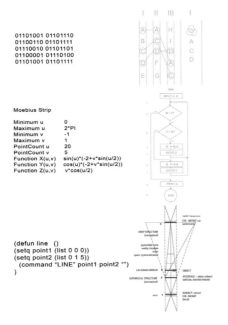

```
01101001 01101110
01100110 01101111
01110010 01101101
01100001 01110100
01101001 01101111
```

Moebius Strip

```
Minimum u        0
Maximum u        2*PI
Minimum v        -1
Maximum v        1
PointCount u     20
PointCount v     5
Function X(u,v)  sin(u)*(-2+v*sin(u/2))
Function Y(u,v)  cos(u)*(-2+v*sin(u/2))
Function Z(u,v)  v*cos(u/2)
```

```
(defun line  ()
(setq point1 (list 0 0 0))
(setq point2 (list 0 1 5))
  (command "LINE" point1 point2 "")
)
```

217|

There is a structuralism common to algorithms that organize information through typological structures, e.g. – binary bifurcations that structure form and relationships. Consequently, there is also a structuralism common to software interfaces that determine how they define space and, consequently, inform reality. Computer codes constitute the basis of architecture today, they compose its genetics. Computer codes became digital signifiers that by representing space, presenting the set of conditions that prescribe representation, these codes infer an artificial signification of the space they constitute.

In order for truly new models of architectural process to emerge, it is necessary to displace, and then transcend, the typological structures of the computer codes that process information.

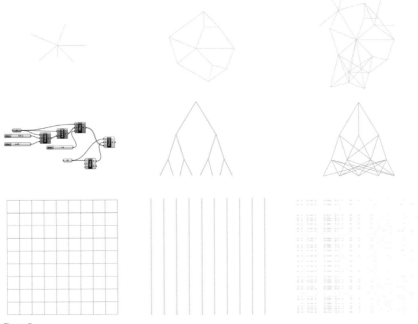

Figure 7

One can understand these issues comparing information representation, the way information is structured in interfaces, and the types of spatial organization [Fig 7 from left to right]. For instance, in the first row we can identify a binary code, a genetic diagram, a radial organization, but then a displaced bypassed radial organization and a decentralized network structure which critique the initial organization. In the second row: a mathematical scripting, a flow diagram-algorithm, a grasshopper visual algorithm, a bifurcating structure, and a displaced bifurcating structure result in a lattice structure. In the third row: a parametric script, a perspective-interface diagram, a grid, a striation, and a grid displaced logarithmically seeking for a new structuralist space.

Agency could be identified in the landscape projects introduced in Fig 1,2,3, in which two sets of algorithms are combined with emergent unforeseeable site conditions gathered by open data. The project activates its agency by promoting landscape opportunities actualizing form through big data and dynamic simulation algorithms. But the challenge today is to be able to design a polymorphic shifting organization that could define its agency from a topological algorithmic structure that could bypass simple hierarchical bifurcation. As each architect is on his or her way to define their own computing language to claim authorship over their design, architects must also identify the linearity of structure of the algorithms they work with, to bypass typification and be able to create differentiated non linear informational structures. We usually work following paradigms closer to the fourth column in Fig. 7, whereas we should be displacing processing information structures to be able to work closer to the paradigm of the fifth column.

Any architectural process must overcome the arbitrariness of the point of departure to be able to understand what is under question. Digital architects have already addressed the critique of utilizing generic, typological structures through their use of progressive, topological displacements. But, these displacements need to go further to define new agency at a structural coding level. Architects working through displacement must look for a break in their conceptual differentiation and aim to achieve a structural change, which is typologically significant enough to transcend simple variations of both the implicit or explicit, initial structures. This suggestion is therefore proposing a series of implied conclusions with a critical understanding of the relationship between typology and topology, and the possibility of a criticism, that can overcome their intrinsic predetermination.

Reversible logic is part of computation's deterministic project. However, architecture form acquires a relative autonomy once it is constituted, even as a end result of information processing. This autonomy goes against a linear information exchange. Once form is constituted new conditions emerge that may induce relationships further than those originally determined, in the case the result may acquire a set of relationships that may surpass the initial parameters. When such autonomy is not recognized in a formal configuration, form works merely indexing quantitative information without qualitative relevance, dismissing its potential to become self referential, which could be able to induce further relationships than the ones predicted. In this sense, there is a third level of formal agency that may become active once form is constituted, that is proportional to its capacity to induce further signification, dependent of course, of the potential socio-cultural readings, subject-object relationships, perception, affection and any other conditions that may emerge. These problems present aesthetic and logical questions, the consolidation of a formal logic intrinsic to the conformation of the architecture of the project as a whole.

To overcome the predetermination of information processing codes, a potential solution may be to overcome the initial determination that structure form. As a continuation of the previous series diagrams [in Fig. 6] and as an architectural means to explore these concepts, a synthetic Cartopological diagram for House IIb displaces different source codes through many interfaces [Fig. 8]. House IIb overcomes the initial, spatial structure comprising the referential frame from which the project originates. But topology as relative displacement is understood also as a means to transcend the initial, organizational spatial structure, in this case a centralized courtyard house. The resulting diagram transforms the center and corner conditions into a continuous, inside/outside relationship. The topological envelope of House IIb integrates the façade with the space contained in a thick continuous poché space. Generally speaking, spatial organization plays an essential role at the cognitive level by establishing limits on how we measure and understand different space-time paradigms, an understanding that challenges the many disciplines dealing with systems of representation and spatial definition. Some of these are manifested as progressive models that can fully displace the ultimate, the most stable of architectural references: the Cartesian coordinate system in which the project has been generated.

Parametric Mediums And Media Affection As Reference

We can question the intermediation of mediums and media by identifying how the determinate architecture, from origination to destination. Tension has emerged between the two sides of the picture plane materialized in the envelope of contemporary buildings. The two sides consist of the determination of codes that prescribe origin to architectural form and the media reproduction that defines architectural relevance through its destination to society. This tension derived from the false opposition produced when the discipline is artificially divided between those who were interested in the relational space and those who are interested in the immanence of the object-building. The tension devolved into a crisis when reactions to digitally-based formalisms progressively disregarded their relational logics in favor of relying solely upon the visual effect of an object. Late poststructuralist formalisms further ignored their relational logics by discounting their indexing of interfaces that structured form, thereby problematically ensuring their continuing stability even at deeper levels. In the meantime, the current transformation of the discipline has been driven by a growing awareness of the need to both revolutionize referential structures and build up a form of abstraction, which is motivated by relationships rather than by the design of saturated objects. As a result, algorithms are replacing the primarily visual logic of previous decades, and bringing back a mental pensiveness, based on structuring relationships, towards the parametric object.

We can ask, then, what are the ideologies that media motivates? What's its implied agency? Are we running other's agencies? We can further ask, what structures does media motivate, but continue to purposely hide? Media has certainly advanced both a sensibility and an education based upon the understanding of a visual logic, which have been highly beneficial to architecture. With its basis upon formal logic, architecture has been rendered more accessible through the optic and tactile senses by the field more commonly known as visual art. But, the visual has long exhausted its capacity to be critical, since media has been progressively inserting underlying, ever more rigid protocols in order to ensure mass control, to drive capitalistic, systemic crises, and to separate visual appeal and affection from the foundational political structures that were engineered to manipulate behavior. The likes of Facebook, Google, architectural magazines, blogs, and other forms of social media have motivated ever faster, shorter gazes that rely upon the impact of the image itself, resulting in more and more superficial readings. As part of this process, the interfaces for social media intentionally hide their informational processing codes, thereby restricting their means of communication only to those capable of controlling mass behavior. In this context, an interesting, critical form of media emerged. Several academically driven forms of media[6] emerged during the last decade, many which un-motivate the effect of images by specifically promoting the relationship between reading and writing as an integral part of architectural discussion, as a means of influencing architecture's productive and creative processes, and as a way of defining an intellectually and academically based architecture.

Media has motivated several disembodiments to architecture. By emphasizing visual affection through promoting images of buildings, for example, media has flattened

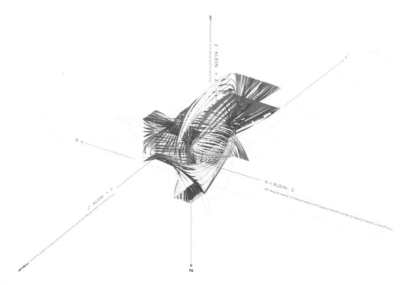

Figure 8: The previously mentioned synthetic diagram for House IIb [Fig. 8] enfolds the previous process of expansion of the discipline to redefine containment, or the envelope of a building. The diagrams presented in Fig. 6 activate a process in which House IIb critically engages with its origination by acknowledging its referential system of representation and by displacing the set of parameters that constitute its formal logic. House IIb critically engages also with the destination side of the discussed picture plane by relating spatial organization to spatial affection. House IIb. Eiroa Architects | E-Architects, NY 2012.

architecture to two dimensions; it has un-motivated the notion of space by numbing the body's capacity to be affected by three-dimensionality. In this sense, by projecting signification to architecture, media certainly hides its structuralism. This problem motivates another fourth level of agency: a media agency that becomes active in architecture reproduction through media.

Consequently, the necessary, critical attitude for us is that of: rethinking the relationship between structuralism and post-structuralism, bringing hidden structures to the foreground by addressing their roles in qualifying affection, and avoiding the favoritism of one structure over another. Therefore, we must critique the set of conditions that determine architecture as it transitions from origination to destination.

FOOTNOTES

1. Allen, Stan "II...Notations + Diagrams: Mapping the Intangible" in Practice: Architecture Technique + Representation, Routledge 2009 (orig. 2000).

2. McLuhan, Marshall The Medium is the Massage, Penguin books, London 1969

3. In ACADIA 2010 chaired by Pablo Lorenzo-Eiroa, Aaron Sprecher and Shai Yeshayahu with Chandler Ahrens, Axel Schmitzberger and Michael Wen Sen Su, the author defined computation as the motivator of a new structuralism.

4. Carpo, Mario "Breaking the Curve, On Big Data and Design" Art Forum, February 2014.

5. The notion of authorship in computation was one of the main issues raised at the ACADIA 2010 by this essay's author. The raised argument was whether or not contemporary digital architects are the authors of what they produce relative to the set of interfaces they work with. Mario Carpo's The Alphabet and the Algorithm published in 2011 refers to how computation has dissolved authorship in shared input, reproduction of information and collaborative environments.

6. Log Magazine was one of the first media to purposely motivate writing and intellectual discussions in architecture resisting the impact of the image.

PABLO LORENZO-EIROA is currently an Associate Professor Adjunct of Architecture at the School of Architecture of The Cooper Union, where he is the head professor and coordinator for the Master Program Fall Semester (2014), a digital representation and computation professor, and is also the Director of a Digital Representation and Fabrication Program. He is a Fulbright and National Endowment for the Arts scholar and holds an M.Arch II degree from Princeton University and a Diploma Architect from the University of Buenos Aires. He has edited and authored, among others, Architecture In Formation

with Aaron Sprecher, 2013. Pablo Lorenzo-Eiroa is the Design Principal of Eiroa Architects | E-Architects NY-BA. Through this architecture office he has been integrating theoretical speculation and disciplinary expertise in different associations, with work ranging from academic research, through scholarships and publications, to architecture design in private and state commissions.

www.eiroarchitects.com

SYNTHETIC LANDSCAPES

ELENA MANFERDINI, ANNA MARIA MANFERDINI

Abstract

In the field of visual arts, painted landscapes have always offered the opportunity for artists to prove their ability to faithfully portray natural scenes and vistas. In addition to that, this specific natural subject has often represented the manifestation of the level of cultural and technical knowledge of a society in its various historical moments.

Since contemporary digital technologies are now offering the possibility to directly derive spatial and matter characteristics of 3D objects and to interact with matter in digital environments, faithful depictions of Nature have become once again instrumental for investigations in representational tools. These kind of contemporary landscapes assume realism, familiarity, narrative, involvement of the audience as crucial ingredients, and re-open the debate about a new level of photorealism.

This paper collects the results of a three years research undertaken with the purpose of exploring how digital depictions obtained from high-definition reality-based acquisitions can contribute to widen the iconic visual repertoire of Nature and can be used as source of inspiration within the design process.

Introduction

Through the centuries, landscapes have always had the ability to portray not only natural scenes, but also to measure the level of cultural and technical knowledge of a society in its various historical moments. In western visual arts, artists have always proofed their ability in imitating reality by drawing case studies from Nature. Nevertheless, for a long time their capability was permeated and often limited by cultural beliefs that relegated landscapes representation to act as background for religious altarpieces, and at times charged them of symbolic, dramatic, moral and ideological meanings.

Landscapes became the subject of an independent pictorial genre only after the Flemish renewal of the Sixteenth century that was permeated by a novel sensibility towards light and nature. Some of the main reasons of this development can be found in the scientific research of that era and in the widening of knowledge that took place during the Renaissance. Within the visual arts, Renaissance scientific processes of 3-dimensional measurements determined the refinement of representation of nature into different sub genres ranging from botanic illustrations to cartography.

During the Nineteenth century, after almost five centuries of faithful natural representation, the depiction of landscapes was enriched by a new attention towards lighting effects and by a new visual sensibility. For impressionist painters the landscape genre was not intended any more as a realistic transcription of reality, but as a pictorial interpretation of optical phenomena perceived through human senses. On the other hand, for pointillists the attention towards details was a tool for the investigation of new chromatic effects rather than accurate descriptions of reality (Kenneth 1949).

All these attitudes were bred within different cultural contexts and were deeply influenced

223 |

by the scientific research achievements that contributed to enlarge the knowledge of the time. The advent of photography, for example, focused the attention of art towards light exposure techniques, as well as on the relationship between real movement and multiple picture frames. In visual art, landscape went through similar changes and was no longer contemplated in its unitary form, but became a way of seeing nature from a series of different points of view.

Similarly to the deep cultural renewal that gave life to new attitudes towards Nature, the recent widespread use of digital technologies that allow analyzing and restoring reality beyond human senses is offering new codes of visual communication to representational tools. Microscope and satellite images have widened our possibilities of vision; at the same time reality that we can experience through the senses has ceased to satisfy our imagination.

In addition, the extremely wider repertoire of images that are actually captured through digital technologies gives access to a new knowledge, were each observed element is constituted by smaller ones and where spatial complexity and intricacy is strictly related to the scale of observations. Digital technologies are the means through which we can actually experience the continuity of matter.

Methodology

In this context, the present project participates in the current debate on the state of contemporary digital technologies and their ability to widen the iconic visual repertoire of Nature. It investigates a new breed of landscapes, where photorealistic representations are synthetically modeled starting from high-definition reality-based acquisitions.

The actual possibility to interact with analog matter in digital environments allows using faithful depictions of nature to investigate new experiences that embrace realism, familiarity, narrative and involvement of the audience as crucial ingredients.

Within the present project, the original materials for each depiction are reality-based 3D information derived from natural elements such as flora and fauna (Figure 1). Surveyed

(Figure 1)
Examples of
3D analog data
acquisitions.

data consist in 3D point clouds and high resolution images that are digitally manipulated using the Pixologic® ZBrush® 3D modeling package. This technology is particularly useful for our purposes, since it allows interacting with digital matter using tools whose characteristics and functionalities remind the ones used in painting in fluently following the modeler's gesture. In this process, frozen photorealistic 3D geometry slowly melts under a series of digital brush strokes into liquid paint on a computer color palette.

Within the whole process, particular attention was paid towards small and hyper realistic details derived from Nature in order to allow the maximum freedom in the manipulation of digital matter and at using the out of scale expedient as an indispensible ingredient to break any pre-defined hierarchy and rule and experiment a new sense of order within the composition.

Familiarity of details confers resemblance to reality, but the whole composition is incongruous with respect to our cognitive rules and codes. Recognition attracts and leads to exploration, but the new sense of order disorients and brings the reading into fantastic realities. The role of imagination played between real and fake, is central in the relationship with the audience and lends an uncanny character to synthetic landscapes (Mori 1970).

These synthetic landscapes are fragments of wider environments in which the whole composition is the result of the mutual relationship between what is represented and the viewer. These landscapes are theoretical, since they lead to a new discovery and knowledge but meanwhile neglect any single perspective. They correlate with the eastern approach of landscape, were no hierarchy derived from pre-defined point of view is privileged.

Similarly to cartography that allow the comparison, the measurement and the scientific analysis of what is represented, the selection of a precise direction of gaze allows to analyze all single details of the composition, inquiring about the scale of representation and therefore what is familiar or unknown, real or synthetic.

Since vision is selective and depends on physiological and psychological factors, distance and focus determine the progressive perception of single details or their merging into a single texture, where the entire landscape is captured through one single glaze.

3 Results

These landscapes embody a new generation of synthetic environments in which special attention is paid to the literal reproduction of matter and its tactile effects, where familiarity is the result of multiple mutations from reality and becomes an indispensable ingredient to establish a connection with the audience. These landscapes are descriptions; they are the staging of single elements derived from Nature that are transformed and mixed together following different interactive forces. They act within novel and unexpected syntactic frameworks.

Realism and familiarity are therefore crucial ingredients of representations grounded in popular culture and in the relationship between artistic production and the viewers understanding.

The entire process takes place in a continuous contrast between what is considered ruled and disorder, between what is expected and what is novel. These landscapes establish a relationship between the building of new spatial connections and their perception, where complexity is strictly related to the balance between unpredictability and the ability of the audience to perceive subtended rules (Figures 2-8).

Conclusions

This paper collects the results of a three years research undertaken with the purpose of exploring how digital depictions obtained from high-definition reality-based acquisitions can be used as source of inspiration within the design process (Manferdini and Manferdini 2011; Manferdini and Manferdini 2013).

This project highlights on one side how figurative representation can play an emerging role within the actual visual culture. On the other side, it aims to show how the correlation between photorealistic representation and public reaction has become (once again) of interest to architects.

The motivation of this project came from the realization that the ongoing digitization of culture production is slowly reducing the varieties of textural qualities with which we interact. The work presented here outlines new workflows that attempt to find ways for architecture to transmit materiality in a creative way through contemporary representational tools. In a certain way this project represents a reaction to the actual use of renderings. It aspires to prove that photorealism, so dear to architects of this digital era, has the ability to move beyond commercial applications and become instead a powerful and evocative creative tool.

(Figure 2a, 2b) Examples of synthetic landscape

(Figure 3a, 3b) Examples of synthetic landscape

(Figure 4a, 4b) Examples of synthetic landscape

(Figure 5a, 5b) Examples of synthetic landscape

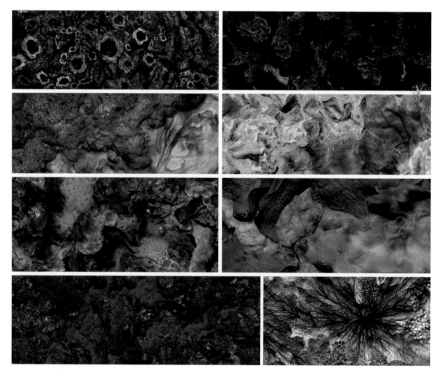

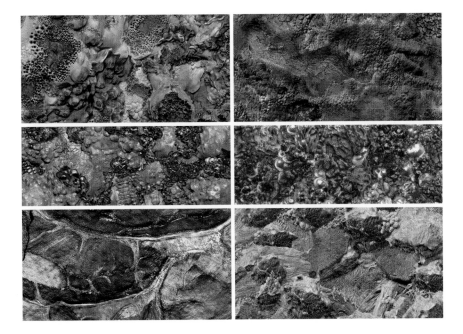

(Figure 6a, 6b) Examples of synthetic landscape

(Figure 7a, 7b) Examples of synthetic landscape

(Figure 8a, 8b) Examples of synthetic landscape

REFERENCES
- Gombrich E.H. (1979). The sense of Order. A Study in the Psychology Decorative Art. Phaidon Press Limited, London.
- Kenneth C. (1949). Landscape into Art. John Murray, London.
- Manferdini, E. and A.M. Manferdini (2011). Synthetic. Proceedings of the ACADIA Conference: 66-71.
- Manferdini, E. and A.M. Manferdini (2013). From Still Life to Living Picture. In Shijie Jianzhu, 09,ed. World Architecture, 124-126.
- Mori, M. (1970). Bukimi no tani - The uncanny valley (K. F. MacDorman & T. Minato, Trans.). In Energy, 7(4), 33-35.

FOOTNOTES

This research was undertaken in collaboration with several institutions. It presents some examples of a collection of landscapes created by students from various schools, the Southern California Institute of Architecture, the Cornell University, the Kyoto Seika University, Singapore, the Polytechnic of the Tshingua University in Beijing and the University of Pennsylvania. The equipment used for the initial 3D reality-based acquisitions were been provided by the Department of Architecture of the University of Bologna, Italy. The authors would like to reserve a special thank to all the students that have adhered to this project, in particular: Graella Bongo, Rebekah Bukhbinder, Qingyi Chen, Lung Chi, Jun Ding, Nicholas Earle, Alex Franco, Jeffery Halsted, Haibo He, Sierra Helvey, Gregory Ingalls, Patricia Joseph, Jill Koeingsknecht, Mustafa Kustur, Jaegun Lim, Bonnie Liu, Yu Liu, Ziye Liu, Smita Lukose, Shouquan Sun, Ursla Trost, Carlos Vargas, Hsing Chen Wu, Wehnshen Xie, Nan Yen.W

IMAGES CREDITS

Figure 1: Courtesy fo the Authors.
Figure 2: Examples of synthetic landscape (credits: Graella Bongo, Patricia Joseph and Rebekah Bukhbinder).
Figure 3: Examples of synthetic landscape (credits: Sierra Helvey, Nan Yen, Lung Chi).
Figure 4: Examples of synthetic landscape (credits: Hsing Chen Wu, Jun Ding, Yu Liu, Qingyi Chen).
Figure 5: Examples of synthetic landscape (credits: Alex Franco, Smita Lukose, Wehnshen Xie, Ziye Liu).
Figure 6: Examples of synthetic landscape (credits: Ursla Trost, Haibo He, Gregory Ingalls, Carlos Vargas).
Figure 7: Examples of synthetic landscape (credits: Mustafa Kustur, Jaegun Lim, Jeffery Halsted, Shouquan Sun).
Figure 8: Examples of synthetic landscape (credits: Bonnie Liu, Nicholas Earle, Jill Koeingsknecht).

ELENA MANFERDINI, principal and owner of Atelier Manferdini, has over fifteen years of professional experience in architecture, art, design, and education. She is a licensed engineer in Italy, and a licensed architect in Switzerland. She received a Professional Engineering Degree from the University of Civil Engineering (Bologna, Italy) and a Master of Architecture and Urban Design from the University of California in Los Angeles (UCLA).

In 2004 she founded Atelier Manferdini in Bologna, Italy and in 2009 she established her firm in Venice CA. The office has completed art and architectural projects in the US, Europe and Asia. Notable among the firm's projects are the Pavilion for the Museum of Contemporary Art in Los Angeles, Bianca, a three stories boat in Japan, and a series of interior design renovations in Los Angeles. Elena Manferdini work has appeared internationally in books, professional journals and reviews. She has been featured in several publications: Domus, New York Times, Elle, Vogue, ID, Icon, Form, Contemporary, Metropolis, and Architectural Design are selected examples. In 2013 a monograph on the firm's work "Elena Manferdini" was published by Equalbooks. Elena currently teaches at the Southern California Institute of Architecture (SCI-Arc) and is the coordinator of their Graduate Thesis program. She is also currently Howard Friedman Visiting Professor of Practice at the University of California Berkeley (UCB). She has also held Visiting Professor Positions at Cornell University, University of Pennsylvania and Seika University. She frequently lectures, and her work has been exhibited internationally in both architecture and art museums. Selected examples are LACMA and MOCA in Los Angeles, MAXXI in Rome, MAK center in Vienna. In 2006 Ms. Manferdini was invited to design the West Coast Pavilion representing the USA at the Beijing Biennale in the Chinese Millennium Museum. In 2008 and 2010, she curated the West Coast USA session of theBeijing Biennale exhibition. She has lectured widely, including at MIT, Princeton, GSD, UCLA, USC, UIC, UCB,Seika University, Tsinghua University and Bauhaus.

Elena Manferdini was recently awarded the 2013 COLA Fellowship given by City of Los Angeles Department of Cultural Affairs to support the production of original artwork. In 2013 she received a Graham Award for architecture, the 2013 ACADIA Innovative Research Award of Excellence, and she was selected as recipient for the Educator of the Year presidential award given by the AIA Los Angeles. In 2011 she was one of the recipients of the prestigious annual grants from the United States Artists (USA) in the category of architecture and design.

ANNA MARIA MANFERDINI, Building Engineer, PhD in Architecture and Urban Planning, Assistant Professor at the University of Bologna, Department of Architecture. She won a research grant at the Scuola Normale di Pisa, Italy, for the definition of standards for the building of digital models from real data of the archaeological site of Pompeii.

Her interests are focused on representation and on the use of multimedia technologies to communicate architecture and Cultural Heritage. She actually conducts researches on the digitization of Cultural Heritage, on relationship between pictorial art and digital modelling, on the influences of the use of digital technologies within the design process. She taught at the Design Faculty of the Politecnico di Milano and at the Faculty of Engineering of Bologna.

MARIA PAZ GUTIERREZ

L A B
IN THE BUILDING
/
BUILDING IN THE
L A B ?

PLURIPOTENT MATTER & BIOINSPIRATION

ABSTRACT:

The intelligibility of nature has been largely shaped by how science makes sense of the world. The tension between making and knowing in science has been jostled by numerous revolutions both explicit and latent teasing the reliability of a given view around nature. While affinities and discrepancies are inherent to this course, a radical shift took place in the last century regarding our ability to "see" nature. The advent of quantum mechanics has allowed us to question our previous conceptions of "how" nature is and how it "crafts" matter. Through this new frontier, science opens and cements unfathomable constructs around material theory and production leading us to reassess material invention. In architecture, we have related to the inorganic and organic world, as physical and socio-cultural intertwined factors that require the exercise of design inventiveness and resilience. Principles of economy of means and precision have been at the center of material invention. If material creation has proven pivotal to enable resilience in past design models, then which equations can be defined between craft, technology, information, and materials as our ability to shape matter transforms? Where are its boundaries in design and how can they be tested? What is the role of material invention in architecture in an era where science creates one atom thickness matter (graphene) and uses nanoscale self-assembly as a construction method? Inspired by nature's principles of efficiency and supported through pioneering collaborations with scientists architects are programming matter across unforeseen scales of investigation, shaping the frontier of multiscale design. BIOMS research centers in testing material invention in architecture. A quest for shaping *pluripotent matter* through programming functions. Matter becomes the system for sensing, actuating and regulating multiple functions. BIOMS' inquiries examines the association of organic and synthetic matter, methods to supplant mechatronics with programmed material sensing and actuation (chemo-opto and/or mechanic) and the integration of live matter as pivotal opportunities for multifunctional building systems. These material frontiers are pursued by integrative multi-optimization (simulation and characterization) models. Through interdisciplinary convergence, these design inquiries test the transformative potential of integrating nano and micro photonics and fluidics for resource efficiency in architecture. By interfacing the lab into the building and the building into the lab, we can shape a new culture of material invention in design. Beyond products and technologies a new ethos of material invention and design agency transforms our intelligibility of matter.

Keywords: multiscale, nano and micro science, design, matter, invention, multifunctional, programming.

1. Multiscale Design

What are the boundaries relating craft, technology, information and matter? How is material experimentation forged in construction today differently than before? Material invention faces critical interrogations in design. In era where scientific inquiry shapes one single atom thickness and tests the anti-correlation of materials in the unforeseen frontier of strange metals and establishes nano self-assembly what is the architect's role in material invention. Can architecture forge new opportunities for production and technologies through reinventing the invention of matter?

Material intelligibility shifts through time. Descartes offered in *The World* a wide perspective of the universe where all elements including living beings are explained through mechanisms of lifeless bits of matter pushing against one another (Descartes, 1998). His mechanical philosophy challenged the core of the Aristotelian vision of matter rooted on teleology (Meyer, 1992) Since that period, our intelligibility of matter and nature changed drastically pivoting from a mechanical view of the world to a quantum mechanical model (Dear, 2008). Previous to Einstein's Special Theory of Relativity (Galileo discovered what is recognized as the Original Theory of Relativity), physicists like Maxwell believed that a *material aether* carried the forces of light, electromagnetism and gravity shaping new thoughts around matter (Dear, 2008; Harman, 1985). While during a period Maxwell's work was to some extents overlooked, time has proven his thoughts and equations critical to science. Studies in linear conservation laws in geometrically complex domains and homogeneous and inhomogeneous problems from nonlinear magnetostatics and electrostatics to time dependent field problems are some of the areas where Maxwell's equations are fundamental (Hesthaven, 2002; Monk, 2003; Weiland, 1984). Likewise, entanglement, which so puzzled Einstein, Podolsky, and Rose, continues to be a prominent area of scientific inquiry and speculation in quantum mechanics whose research relies on highly abstract material theory constructs (Wiseman, 2007). So how do critical transformations in how science tries to make sense of matter affect our notions and making of material invention? If we understand science to be as much about deduction as about surveying possibilities how do shifts in the science of materials impact our understanding of matter-space in architecture? How do new habits of thinking and making around crafting matter and the very role of invention emerge?

In *Summa Theologica II*, Aquinas defined *scientia* as the state of mind in which one is engaged with the prelude or precondition of knowledge, the process itself. The shift from *scientia* as a state of mind or what he would term a virtue to solely a body of knowledge is what literature (e.g. Harrison, 2001; Gaukroger, 2006) has defined as the pivotal separation from Natural Philosophy shaping the emergence of the modern scientific culture. Yet, in essence science is still as much about surveying possibilities as it is about establishing deductions. From this framework, the convergence of design and science is less about taking science as the absolute truth and overriding answer to a question. Rather as a complimentary means to establish interrogations and survey possibilities around natural phenomena in design.

The ability to understand and see natural phenomena from the latter quarter of the last century has opened ground to unfathomable thresholds of material innovation. The capacity to create materials with tunable properties including controlled actuation, regeneration and growth has rendered visions of future spaces and performance that would have been otherwise classified science fiction. And while many of these applications in architecture still remain fiction they are less so, as we test the scalability of material systems innovation. In this task the very nature of innovation in architectural research is put to question. The potential paradigm shift in material systems derived from the emerging collaborations between scientists and architects venturing into unprecedented scales of inquiry and the shaping of new research methods shaping *multiscale design* (Gutierrez and Lee 2013). This new frontier aims to establish building enclosures through the programming of matter which performs as "living walls".

2. Nano and MicroScale Science and Engineering and Architecture

The scale and functions of matter-to-form have both unlocked and limited design choices. Cultural and aesthetic considerations have also been crucial in this process. For example, the swift development of the dome was only partially facilitated by advances in concrete (Mainstone, 1975). The desire to achieve larger spans was likely a reaction to cultural desires which drove this technological leap. Paradigm shifts in material invention are largely products of cultural considerations where technology is part of the equation not the standalone solution. The design agency and computation of recent transformations in material technologies is no exception. Explorations of new fabrication methods and programming of matter defy previous models of material production. While digital modeling and fabrication technologies were initially developed to facilitate the design and production of complex geometry, these technologies opened opportunities for experimentation with new materials. Withdrawing from fields such as mechanical engineering and material science research, architects and designers are printing new composites, including ceramics and metal, in order to develop new construction methods and materials (Bassoli et al., 2007). As a continuum, these explorations are coupled with evaluating geometries for structural optimization (Vaezi, 2013). In tandem, advances in various digital fabrication techniques, such as sectioning, casting, have been rapid and numerous (Iwamoto, 2013).

While prolific and fruitful, these explorations have up to date remained within the millimeter to centimeter scales. These past two years we have begun to also observe more concrete attempts in the engineering community to test for example large scale 3d printing technology leading to prototypes such as the 3d print house at USC (http://www.contourcrafting.org/). While architects have accomplished key advances in material technologies through digital fabrication and simulation only recently have designers begun exploring the potential of nano and microengineering fabrication processes

(Gutierrez, 2013(a)). The growing interest in nanotechnology in design is moving beyond the application of images and even visualization methods. For one part, architects are becoming aware that nanotechnology may altogether transform design and design processes (Schodek et al., 2009). Although, this implies that adopting nanomaterials in construction offers plural advantages, architects are venturing into the very role of material invention through nano and microscale searching new computational models and fabrication processes. And the recent collaborations between architects with disciplines such as biology, physics, and bioengineering pursuing material systems innovation are enabling this volition providing field for a potential paradigm shift. The transformative force of this frontier lies in the shifts in how a design problem is understood and tested across multiple scales in an integrative fashion. Furthermore, it provides distinctive opportunities for developing new research methodologies regarding how we articulate variables, system-wide correlations and address the complex parameters implicated in material systems in architecture (Gutierrez, forthcoming, 2014).

The emerging funding opportunities for collaborations between architects, scientists and engineers rising in recent years are playing a key role for shaping multiscale design. These interdisciplinary structures are atypical. Characterized by design shared goals around which rather than project driven are theme-oriented, these collaborations aim to advance design as well as basic science. Consequently, these interdisciplinary research models must encompass longer timeframes as required by investigations in basic science (Gutierrez, forthcoming, 2014). For instance, the NSF-EFRI SEED program in 2010, has provided support for a four year research in sustainable building technologies. Examples of multiscale design stemming from this program driven towards material systems includes the *Microvascular Networks Walls* (UC Colorado team) for optimized thermal and water regulation, *eSkin* (UPenn team) inspired by human smooth muscle cells for a microengineered façade that controls solar energy, light and humidity and the *SOAP* (UC Berkeley) which incorporates microphotonics and microfluidics for water and energy regeneration (Gutierrez and Lee 2013). However, multiscale design carries multiple challenges. Beyond the frequent disciplinary communication barriers this frontier faces the complex negotiation of varying value perspectives and research methods. Additionally, to establish robust multiscale design researchers face the challenge of limiting multi-objective computational platforms. Currently, multi-objective optimization platforms are not equipped to take into account the inherent need for scalar continuity and interdependence with other design criteria (e.g. socioeconomic, aesthetics, cultural, etc.) factors involved in building systems.

As a new frontier, multiscale design is bound to revolutionize collaboration structures, research methods including the generation of new computational models and multiscale fabrication towards creating potent material systems. With this aim, architects are intensively seeking how to program matter with multiple functions to work in synergy

233|

with nature and internal building demands. Lab fabrication is far from architectural digital fabrication. These arenas remain largely parallel and unreconciled. For one part, multistage processes that require separate preparations with varying degrees of material losses (i.e. supporting material in 3d printing) are typical. On the other part, nano and microscale fabrication is critical for programming materials with sensitive functions. Yet, the scalability of these manufacturing processes is far from being reached. Funding organizations are placing significant support towards research in areas of nano-scalable manufacturing (http://www.nsf.gov/pubs/2014/nsf14544/nsf14544.htm). Addressing the present fabrication gap between the lab and the building digital processes is to many extents the crucible for advancing material systems performance in architecture. Advancing this arena contributes to streamline multiscale fabrication of material systems where many functions are seamlessly integrated while optimizing manufacturing itself by eradicating unnecessary assemblies and joints (Gutierrez, 2011). Through this advances in areas such as multifunctional materials for construction can be accomplished in a much closer future. In essence it opens opportunities for architects to manipulate matter at quasi unfathomable scales. By defying scalar restrictions our preconceptions of material performance boundaries can transform design agency.

3. Pluripotent Matter and Bioinspiration

With the desire to capture nature's intelligence scientists pursue establishing multifunctional matter. This material classification refers to substrates whose advantages are greater than the sum of its parts characterized by multiple functions seamlessly integrated (Bar-Cohen, 2011; Vincent, 2012). The potential advantages of materials with programmed capabilities to generate energy, regenerate, respond and adapt to multiple external stimuli with sensitive sensing and actuation with structural efficiency is inspiring architects to study multifunctional matter. Its pluripotency offers a singular and quasi chimeric opportunity to reimagine the future role of building enclosures or the wall (Gutierrez, forthcoming, 2016). Sensing and mechanical responses to environmental inputs can support energy generation, structural resilience, waste regeneration, and self-repair without the need for electricity or robotics, met solely by intrinsic material reactivity. Literature in material science points to leaps in multifunctional matter particularly in the last five years (Haglund et al., 2009; Park et al., 2009; Corr et al., 2008; Yu et al., 2013; Yun et al., 2012; Liu, et al., 2010; Omenetto and Kaplan, 2010; Liu and Jiang 2011; Maspoch et al., 2007; Xie et al., 2012; Dong and Ha, 2012; Sanchez et al. 2013; Yao et al., 2012; Drisko and Sanchez, 2012; Perineau, et al., 2014; Fuentes-Alventosa et al., 2013). Nonetheless, this frontier still faces critical challenges ranging from multi-objective response calibration and costs, to manufacturing limitations (Nicole et al., 2010). The already puzzling development of multifunctional materials designed from nano scale upwards is aggravated by complex construction parameters challenges (Aizenberg and Fratzl, 2009; Meyers et al., 2008). If accomplishing multifunctional matter in science is challenging for construction even more. By definition any given architectural system must not only respond to multiple-objectives, but also comply with other conditions (e.g. aesthetic, cultural socioeconomic, etc.). Multi-objective performance criteria is inherent to advancing material technology in construction and overall design (Gerber and Lin, 2013). Although critically challenging, architects are taking the risk of pursuing multifunctional matter. Through it the very notion of the role of matter within enclosures is put to challenge. Not only can in principle such materials adapt and balance internal and external building flows they are meant to do it through multi-optimization through matter as the system programmed to make inert materials "alive". Chasing this pluripotency in materials, architects as scientists are turning to nature for principles of integrative efficiency.

Nature provides us with myriad models of efficient exchange between a given organism and its surrounding environment. It designs integrative structures across scales to optimize resilience and efficiency to maximize existence. Nature constructs complex systems with varied compositions, densities, morphologies, and internal and exchange functionalities are built seamlessly across scales. An abalone's shells' differentiated strands across scales of organic "beams" and mineral "pillars" provide compressive strength and elastic resilience just as the spider's web interchange of varying geometries to maximize tensile strength supported by highly efficient coating technologies (Espinosa et al., 2012). The capability to adapt and respond to internal and external stimuli through tailored biomechanical processes is carried through complex structural differentiations across scales.

Scientists and engineers embarked into studying nature for advancing science and technology over twenty years ago (Vincent, 2012). Over two decades of research has rendered major advances in structural efficiency of biomaterials, as well as, innumerous inventions in areas such as bioinspired micro and nano photonics, fluidics and robotics (Bar-Cohen, 2006). The progressive understanding of how natural processes occur and of the structural complexity of biomaterials and organisms has led to an exponential growth in bioinspired science and technology. The path of bioinspiration in architecture has been unsurprisingly less linear. Architects were drawn first to the geometric complexity of natural organisms for formal pursuits. More recently, design explorations have turned into structural optimization, environmental control systems seizing bioinspiration for problem construction and solving (Knippers and Speck, 2012; Kellert et al., 2011; Zari, 2010; Pawlyn, 2011; Vincent, 2009; Mazzoleni, 2013; Badarnah and Kadri, 2014). Yet, another research area in bioinspiration in architecture is surfacing focused on how materials programmed with multifunctional capabilities developed through multiscale design approaches can revolutionize environmental systems. Through integrated principles of architectural design, chemistry, biophysics, and engineering from the nano scale upwards research teams aim to establish multifunctional matter specifically tailored for building systems.

235|

Multifunctional materials are modelled as hybrid networks. The fulcrum of multifunctional matter is design and fabrication crafted seamlessly across scales so various functions are optimized in an integrative fashion. Four vital characteristics of these new materials are of particular relevance to architects: self-actuation, hybrid responsiveness, energy generation and waste regeneration, designed to perform through scale-specificity. Real-world conditions demand hybrid responses to environmental inputs such as light, temperature, and humidity in constructions. Hence, single-optimized performance is insufficient to meet practical demands. These materials offer the opportunity not only of single responsiveness, but the ability to synergistically generate energy and regenerate waste derived from hybridized material actuation. Material properties and functions depend on scale. The scale-based structural optimization follows the principles of efficiency founds in nature. The programmed hybrid networks endow multifunctional matter with distinctive performance means. It is in this capacity that lies the transformative force for revolutionizing future building enclosures. However, the fabrication of multifunctional materials which involves bottom-up strategies including self-assembly and intercalation chemistry is challenging (Nicole et al., 2010). These fabrication processes demand a synthesis of traditional nano and microengineering fabrication methods. The already complex demands of multiscale fabrication between the nano and micron spans becomes significantly more challenging as designers seek to develop these materials for construction applications. In response, robust interdisciplinary frameworks are critical. The challenges of fabrication depend heavily in computational innovation and inventiveness. Not only are the manufacturing processes digitally controlled and characterization carried through advanced computation, but multiscale simulation itself requires integrative computational platforms. Consequently, establishing bioinspired materials with programmed multifunctional capabilities designed through intersecting nano and microscale science and engineering and architecture demands transformations on multiple spheres of design and computation. It is within this challenging framework that BIOMS research operates seeking the potential of pluripotent matter for a new frontier in the exchange of the wall and the elements.

4. The Wall, the Elements & Scalability (BIOMS inquiry)

Structural advances and conceptual transformations of the building enclosure or the *wall* enabled early modern buildings to construct a continuum with their surrounding environments. This very same capacity eventually became affected by contradictions as a result of material technologies which culminated decades later in façades insensitive to orientation and climate (Leatherbarrow, 2009). As Le Corbusier freed the wall from load bearing constraints, he gave architects unprecedented opportunities to inquire relationships between internal and external conditions (Roth and Hildebrandt, 1927). Jean Prouvé's translation of the façade *libre* led to curtain wall studies that challenged previous notions of the wall through technology transfer and pivotal cultural and socioeconomic transformations carried with it. Manually controlled devices such as Prouvé's façade in Square Mozart in 1953 became the tangible expression of adaptability in environmental control systems (Pfammatter, 2008). Yet, as known contradictions and ironies is characteristic to the history of construction, which in this case led to neutral enclosures fundamentally indifferent to surrounding environments. The turn into transforming façades into intelligent enclosures carried from the latter quarter of the twentieth century up to date has been largely the result of transformations in our understanding of adaptability and resilience in the articulation of the wall and the elements. From Piano's early light-controlling terracotta tiles to current EFTE pillow systems during this period we broke into this century predisposed to seeking alternative building enclosures that could revolutionize the role of active/adaptable building enclosures. Advances in thin film technologies with capability to generate energy, control ventilation and thermal transmission and advances in simulation platforms and parametric optimization in architecture streamlined a new era of ultrathin functional substrates. This field provided the fertile ground necessary to explore multifunctional materials in architecture carrying with it the complex challenges previously discussed.

Scalability- One of the most critical challenges of bioinspiration in the development of material systems in architecture is systems scalability. The initial extraction of fundamental principles from nature largely discussed in literature is far from simple or easy (Vincent, 2009; Mazzoleni, 2013; Badarnah and Kadri 2014). Explorations in academia around this exercise are driving new pedagogic approaches in the studio setting (Fig.1). These entail not only establishing a design problem across multiple scales of investigation, but also exploring alternative modes of production and testing of material performance. Through it new interdisciplinary partnerships, informal and formal discussions are emerging where bioinspired systems in design are fueled by intersections of architecture, engineering and science. The *2014 Studio One Symposium* at UC Berkeley "The Nature of Programming Matter and Programming Matter and Nature" exemplifies this interest and efforts. Scholars from history, philosophy, design in academia and practice, bioengineering and material science where brought together to assess the role of material invention in architecture carried through multisale design approaches (http://ced.berkeley.edu/events-media/studio-one/previous-symposiums/2014-studio-one-symposium/speakers-respondents-x-2; http://bioms.info/studioone/speakers.html).

Discussions and interest in architecture, but also in the scientific community towards bioinspired material systems are leading to a series of new forums for exchange (e.g. 2015 MRS Symposium co-chaired by author and J. Sabin will include for first time architects). These instances are critical to strengthen and overcome the strong challenges implicated in the development of multifunctional material systems in architecture. To advance this frontier innovation in areas such as computational frameworks in programmable matter (multiscale/multiphysics analysis), 3d printing for reactive materials and

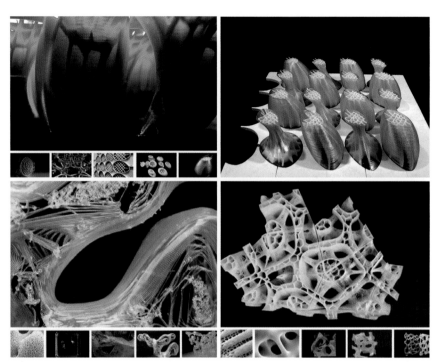

Figure 1: Studio One Work (M.P.Gutierrez Studio Director)- 2013-14 UC Berkeley; Top: A. Nasiri 3d prints (biopolymer) material probes bioinspiration (eupletcella aspergillum- fluid filtration/light concetration); Bottom left: S. Chai 3d prints (biopolymer) material probes bioinspiration (physarum polycephalum- delayed absorption); Bottom right: L. Yao 3d prints (biopolymer) material probes bioinspiration (clypeasteroida- fluid filtration)

simulation of nonlinear nano-to-micro material properties at the architectural scale such interdisciplinary forums and new funding is crucial. Advancing these areas is the fulcrum for overcoming the widely known scalability barriers in bioinspired material systems in architecture.

BIOMS- To develop fundamental research in material systems in what is traditionally deemed an applied discipline as architecture inevitably confronts multiple obstacles and challenges. Innovation requires a reassessment of research scales, methodologies and evaluation, cross-grained with design decisions across all its processes of inquiry. Paradigm shifts in building technology calls for problem formulation and solving where inventiveness is interlinked to concrete realizations. Through material invention BIOMS explores new modes of *investigation, collaboration, consolidation, and dissemination* in the field of building technology. The research carried at BIOMS (bioms.info) is to explore building technology and performance by understanding matter as the system to balance the dynamics between man-made and natural environments. In summary, this approach entails three fundamental shifts. First, synthetic/active, live, and biosynthetic matter function as the sensor and actuator of building systems similar to biological organisms. When matter has embedded intelligence, systems do not need complex mechatronics and display solid reversibility. Secondly, the development of these materials entails the seamless fabrication from laboratory to large scale productions. Nano and micro engineering and science are threaded to the architectural scale. Thirdly, active matter is designed to integrate and balance flows of energy and matter including waste. BIOMS research aims to establish means to resource resources through closed-loop material systems. Creating active matter that can improve the means by which we capture, concentrate and transfer energy, as well as, regenerate waste and water carries programming materials with multiple functions. Such inquiries involve opening new opportunities in multiscale fabrication processes and multi-objective optimization through integrative models from the nano to the architectural scale.

BIOMs material investigations research primarily biopolymers and biosynthetic polymer composites. In fact, biopolymers are the oldest building material. Animal hide, bones, and plants such as straw are known to have been some of men's first enclosures. Across time these early biopolymers where supplanted with the use of ceramics, metals, and composites such as concrete. Biopolymers became rather rare in the development of new building technologies. During the twentieth century polymers resurfaced in constructions but as synthetic matter. Although most constructions up to date use small amounts of polymers these materials are projected to have an exponential growth in construction (Fernandez, 2012.). Synthetic polymers derive primarily from crude oil and gas bearing strong detrimental environmental implications. Yet, they are proven excellent media for sensing and actuation capabilities due to the affordance to program such functions primarily in elastomers (Brochu and Pei, 2010; Wilson et al., 2007; Meng and Hu, 2010). Programming non mechanical sensing and responsiveness in thermoplastics and thermosets has also proven highly efficient in recent decades (Mallkpour and Zadehnazari 2011; Bauri et al., 2013; Fernández et al., 2011). Biopolymers while largely restrictive due to durability and weathering challenges in construction are very promising for environmentally sensitive strategies. Yet, with obvious exception of wood and wood composites biopolymers remain as one of the least investigated material families in construction. While largely present in new digital fabrication technologies (e.g. PLA additive manufacturing) the myriad inventions in material science in bio and synthetic polymers have not made way into real-world construction applications with few exceptions. BIOMs research explores new opportunities for biopolymers and biosynthetic integration as medium for programming multifunctional matter in architecture. The span of the research ranges from simple material mixtures where multiscale fabrication enables light and thermal control to photoactive microlenses for radical improvement of light capture and transmission for water recycling and thermal management.

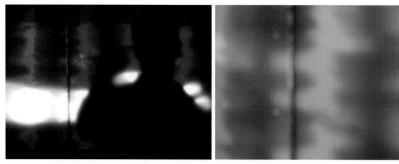

Figure 2: SucroseWall Phase 1 (M. P. Gutierrez & D. Gensler)- Installation at Project RowHouse, TX (2006) (Gutierrez, 2008)

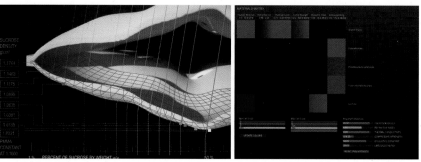

Figure 3: Left: Cross-sectional diagram of sucrose crystals concentration through multi-scale fabrication (Image by author). Right: Material selection criteria platform (Image by author and P. Suen).

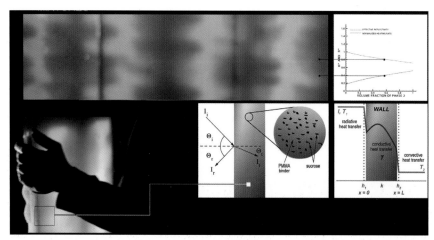

Figure 4: Top Right: Effective Reflectivity and Normalized Heating Rate based on volume fraction (Gutierrez, and Zohdi, 2013). Bottom Left: SucroseWall Prototype 2 Nature Toolbox by M. P. Gutierrez and D. Gensler (Field Museum Chicago, 2013, Leonardo Museum, Utah, 2014). Bottom Right: Diagram of PMMA Sucrose Mixture optical and heat transfer.

4.1. Organo-Synthetic Association

Case Study: SucroseWalls- Sucrose & PMMA mixtures for Effective reflectivity and Heat transfer (M.P. Gutierrez, T. Zohdi- UC Berkeley).

The progressive incorporation of PMMA into facades is largely a product of this material's singular optic and structural advantages over other thermoplastics (Schittich et al., 2007). Advances in PMMA's recyclability are under development, yet current processes present multiple challenges regarding maintenance of structural integrity and environmental efficiency (Achilias, 2007). The opportunity to create a mixture where PMMA's structural advantages are balanced with low carbon emission substrates, such as agricultural wastes offers distinctive potential. The production of sugar carries critical environmental and socioeconomic paradigms. It is a material that has strong environmental impact (water and energy) while market fluctuations in many developing nations are largely implicated in stimulating socioeconomic problems (Martinelli and Filoso, 2008). Yet, as debatable as its production is a large quantity of lower grade crystals are often lost. This research proposes to utilize this material as a potential mixture due to its unique optical and thermal properties (Yunus et al., 1988). SucroseWalls research consists of probing into agricultural waste and PMMA (polymethyl methacrylate) a synthetic polymer with strong structural potential for potential façade panels. Sucrose's unique optical properties are probed as a means for effective reflectivity and thermal control (Gutierrez, and Zohdi, 2013).

A major challenge of cladding pertains to how the façade material can improve energy efficiency, e.g. acting as thermal mass, while providing light transmission control avoiding conditions such as glare (Fig 2). The early research phase of this investigation involved a parallel testing of the stability of the mixture maximizing the percentage of the sucrose concentration without the sacrificing structural integrity ((Fig 3-left). This process included designing large and microscale corrugations for enabling variable refractive properties. In parallel, we developed a script for a material selection platform which enabled us to evaluate comparative scenarios of multi-objective integration (compressive strength, refractive index, thermal conductivity, etc.) (Fig 3-right). Subsequently, the research involved the calculation of Random Heterogeneous Materials (Microstructure and Macroscopic) and Electromagnetic Properties of Multiphase Dielectrics Modelling. The calculation of the effective reflectivity and normalized heating rate of the mixture enabled the definition of appropriate percentages. (Fig 4).

Our investigation concluded that the heating storage potential of the PMMA-sucrose mixture depends significantly in the concentration of sucrose. Our simulation results indicated that the best condition to achieve optical and thermal advantages for heat storage and effective reflectivity in façade applications is ~0.5 of sucrose concentration. In this zone, the normalized heating rate is of a 20% reduction with a decrease in light absorption to 60% in comparison to 83% in pure *PMMA*. The PMMA/sucrose mixture is currently being evaluated for structural, light and thermal optimization.

4.2. Active Multifunctional Matter

(A) Chemo-Opto Active Matter:

Case Study: *Solar Optics-based Active Panels (SOAP) for Greywater Reuse and Integrated Thermal (GRIT) Building Control* (M.P. Gutierrez, S. Hermanowicz, L.P. Lee- UC Berkeley).

Water, Light, & MicroOptics – In 1659, Isaac de Caus published "New Rare and rare Inventions of Waterworks". This compendium described his attempt to imitate the *Vocal Memmon* through a solar device (de Caus, 1959). Through the use of lenses on a wall de Caus focused sunlight to activate a water pump. Once concentrated the light was received by the water tanks and heated into water vapor to subsequently create air movement and sound. Optics was used to activate water thermally and create spatial performance. Dissimilar to traditional mechanical approaches to creating dynamic performance, de Caus designed activation through what would be defined centuries later as a solar passive use. De Caus system is a priceless precedent to the force of active systems triggered by passive design through the incorporation of optics.

Classical optics began with the fabrication of glass. The course of its development was influenced by critical contributions to determine the mathematical ratio between the angles of incidence and refraction, primarily through the efforts by Hariot, Kepler, Snell, Huygens, and Descartes in subsequent centuries (Bedini, 1963; Descartes, 1937; Lindeboom, 1974). The development of optics, however, took a radical turn in the last quarter of the twentieth century when diamond turning was incorporated in fabrication tools to generate "arbitrary" surface shapes. Advances were developed at unprecedented scales, comprising precision of fine mechanical parts of the order of 0.1 mm giving rise to a new field – microptics (Saleh et al, 1991). This frontier brought unforeseen advances in laser invention, low-loss optical fibres, and the introduction of semiconductor optical devices. Photonics involves the control of light photons in free space of matter while electronics encompasses the control of light flow in vacuum or matter. The two intersect since electrons often control the flow of photons and photons control the flow of electrons. Photonics has enabled unprecedented calibration of light transmission. Optical components such as lenses constitute some of the means that have revolutionized light transmission control capabilities. Despite photonics' potential for architectural applications where tunable light transmission control and concentration would be highly beneficial, the implementation of microlens remains unexplored (Gutierrez, 2013(b)). Similarly, advances in nanooptics, where the study of optical phenomena and technique is near or beyond the diffraction limit of light (Novotny and Hecht, 2006). This research explores the transformative potential of incorporating microptics for light concentration control through chemically and optically reactive microlenses for water regeneration and thermal generation enclosures.

The superior thermal comfort of water-based spatial heating derives essentially from lower radiant temperatures and higher energy efficiency due to smaller operating temperature differentials and lower energy consumption (transport). During the twentieth century we witnessed many attempts to use sunlight as means to heat water for spatial conditions. The Solar MIT House II in 1947 is a pioneering example of such attempts (Gutierrez, 2013(b)). In parallel, the use of sunlight for water disinfection was first published in 1877 (Malato, 2007). Almost a century later the engineering community began to take into serious consideration the benefits of solar energy for water disinfection. To any extents solar-based water disinfection is seen as a lowtech solution for treating water in developing regions. Solar disinfection is classified into two types: ultraviolet (UV) based or use of the full spectrum of light. While advances in UV based water disinfection has been accomplished in the recent decade the development of systems that use the full spectrum of light and its by-product (heating of the water) remain largely unexplored. This research explores the opportunity of concentrating sunlight synergistically for photocatalytic recycling of greywater and its use for thermal generation through the incorporation of microphotonics and titanium dioxide coating creating a chemo-opto active façade (Gutierrez and Lee, 2013).

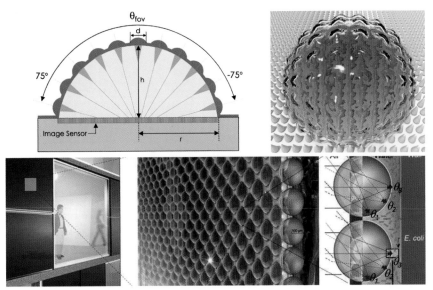

Figure 5: (clockwise from top-left) microlens diagram (Image by L.P.Lee); detailed rendering of microlens surface for SOAP; Render and cross-section of micro lens; Diagram showing SOAP panel at different scales; Integration of SOAP panel into building façade for passive heating (Images by author, LP.Lee and P. Suen) (Gutierrez and Lee, 2013).

The *SOAP* system proposes to reuse greywater as thermal energy in buildings in regions of water scarcity characterized by strong temperature (diurnal) swings. Up to date, we have concentrated in researching 3 systems. Here we present *SOAP Type A*, a solar optofluidic active panel that effectively concentrates solar energy to achieve photothermal energy storage and photocatalytic-based disinfection in greywater through a double-sided lens arrays coated with TiO_2 and nanoparticles (Figure 5). SOAP's lens radius and channel width has been optimized to maximize visible light concentration with independence

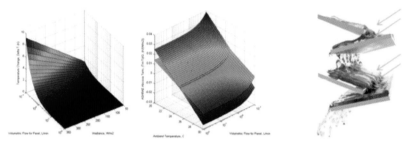

Figure 6 (image 12-13): (Left to Right) SOAP Panel Type B multiphysics simulation by V. Rao examining effects of volumetric flow rate and solar irradiance on temperature gain; Parameter sweep examining impact of ambient temperature and flow rate on ASHRAE 93 abscissa bulk term (standardized thermal efficiency equation); Rendered diagram of Type B 2.5cm-wide stepped plate concept (Image by P. Suen).

Figure 7: Close up of proof of concept experimental setup of Panel Type B by SOAP team (author, L.P.Lee, S. Hermanowicz, V. Rao, P. Hernandez, H. Kagey, D. Campbell, P. Suen, C. Irby) (Image by P. Hernandez).

to incident light wavelength and angle offering unprecedented potential for façade applications without the need of following the sun-path through mechatronics (Figure 6). An integral part of the research has been the development of multiple multiphysics platforms where the integration of both water regeneration and thermal generation is numerically tested across from the micro to the architectural scale. In this process multiphysics models as presented in Figure 7 (Top: superficial fluid velocity x cylinder spacing to define Reynolds number; bottom: irradiance, volumetric flow and temperature range of surface) have been iteratively developed in conjunction with characterization experiments. One of the most critical challenges of the computational processes in this study pertains to the complexity of creating integration paths for multi-objective criteria models that span from the nano-micro, mm-cm to m-regional scales implicated in this design. This challenge is further exacerbated when taken in consideration with other key design factors such as aesthetic, socioeconomic and cultural conditions.

B) Sensing and Actuation:

Case Study: *Self-Activated Building Envelope Regulation System* (SABERs) - NSF-CMMI- 2010-Award#1030027 (M.P. Gutierrez (P-I); L. Lee (co-PI) - UC Berkeley)

Light, Temperature, Humidity & Self-regulation- From primitive tents to high-performance textiles, architects have been fascinated by the role of flexible enclosures in the making of architecture (Drew 2008; Bechthold 2008; Semper, 1989) Nikolaus Laing presented in 1967 his revolutionary *breathing skin* at the International Pneumatics Colloquium in Stuttgart. His proposed membrane conceived air as a means to pump and deflate valves with the aim to control light, humidity and temperature (Laing, 1967). His revolutionary conception of an active membrane seems utterly timely more than fifty years later. The advances in material sensing and actuation endow us with the opportunity to revisit this

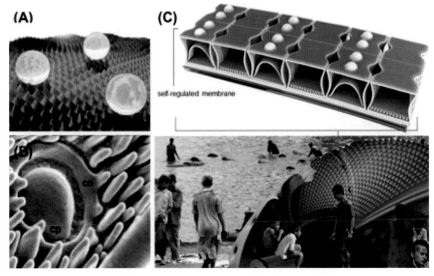

Figure 8: Biological inspirations from: (A) lotus plant system; (B) antenna branch of the silk moth (Keil, 1997); (C) biologically inspired Self-Activated Building Envelope Regulation (SABER) including optomechanical sensor/actuator network, smart external moisture-barrier layer, hygrothermal sensor/actuator network (and total integration on membrane of optomechanical sensor/actuator network), moisture barrier, hygrothermal sensor/actuator network, and micro venturi tubes.

concept not as a mechanistic model (pneumatic control), rather through material reactivity. This research addresses this challenge of producing a breathing membrane designed as an enclosure for deployable housing in tropical regions. Up to date several attempts have been made to produce integrated technologies to control humidity, light and temperature transmission through lightweight membranes. Yet, these technologies have been hindered by their low degree of sensitivity and the need to function through rather complicated mechanotronics and/or sensors that require heavy maintenance.

Smart building membranes are typically limited to one or two functions (e.g. structural resistance and light diffusion) lacking precise calibration and limited benefits for environmental control and resource efficiency. Building membranes must selectively control the transfer of humidity, light, air, and temperature while resisting weathering. Architectural membranes with self-actuation capabilities that are programmed for multi-optimization of resource use can be highly effective for sustainable indoor climate regulation and environmentally efficient. A critical limitation to accomplishing this aim pertains to the lack of capacity to program sensing and actuation materials for large scale applications. The primary obstacle for this key paradigm shift in sustainable building technology is the gap between lab manufacturing (nano and microscale) required for precise programming of reactions and large scale fabrication of construction materials.

|246

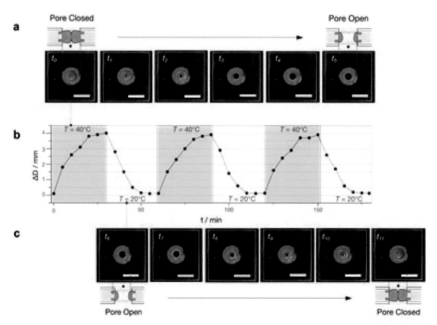

Figure 9: Characterization SABERs Phase 1, Simulation of time response, aperture and reversibility, by Y. Park (UC Berkeley)

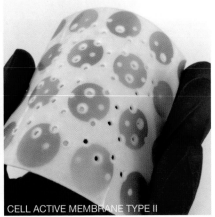

CELL ACTIVE MEMBRANE TYPE I   CELL ACTIVE MEMBRANE TYPE II

Figure 10: SABERs_M.P. Gutierrez, L.P. Lee, Assembly images of biopolymer and dual ETFE prototype, BIOMS and BioPoets team (B. Kim, P. Hernandez, C. Irby)

The calibration of interdependent adaptable functions to the range and time required in constructions requires multifunctional integration. For example an aperture for ventilation purposes needs to be programmed for a temperature shift of 5 degrees Celsius and in under approximately 10 minutes. However, if it rains that same pore must fully close in the minimum possible timeframe to prevent leakage unless if an inner liner can collect and re-conduct the water. Hence, multifunctional capabilities are directly tied to time precision which is not possible to be met by traditional large scale fabrications including advanced 3d printing.

Our research explores a self-activated optical and hygrothermal sensor and actuator onto a thin-film membrane made of material with programmed self-regulated capability. Inspired by insects' distinctive ability to control hygrothermal adaptability through their sensilla or hygroreceptors, we propose a self-activate optomechanical sensor and actuator that controls the closing and aperture of micropores (Steinbrecht, 1984; Altner, et al., 1977). The system integrates a polymeric microlens layer to photoactive polymers that contract as temperature rises. The photoactive contraction of the nanostructured hydrogels due to incident light via microlens array controls an integrated microvalve (external membrane) to increase the air intake. The skin composite is interconnected to an internal layer of biopolymeric desiccators that blocks moisture. The full membrane system facilitates climatic control (light and hygrothermal) for human comfort in portable housing units located in tropical regions without the need of non-renewable energy use.

SABERs addresses the opportunity of integrating multiple climatic factors to advance sensing and actuation technologies in construction grade membranes. Our initial research phase concentrated in a) designing a simple reversible actuator, thermally-

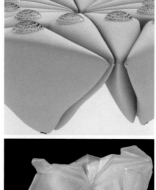

Figure 12: Top: SABERs_M.P. Gutierrez, L.P. Lee, Assembled prototype array of silicone Buckle wall, author and BIOMS team author and P. Hernandez (Gutierrez and Suen, 2013) (Currently exhibited at the Danish Center for Architecture); Bottom: Assembled silicone BUCKLE wall, BIOMS team (P. Hernandez, P.Suen, C. Irby - Self-actuated hygrothermal membranes, The Fifth Oslo Architectural Triennale, "Really sustainable", September-December 2013, Norwegian Centre for Design and Architecture).

Figure 13: SABERs_M.P. Gutierrez, L.P. Lee, Single silicone print for Buckle wall, author and BIOMS team author and P. Hernandez (Gutierrez and Suen, 2013); Array of 3D silicone-print SABERs prototype, author and P. Hernandez (Gutierrez and Suen, 2013)

and optically responsive actuators utilizing polymer composites; b) demonstrating thermal responsiveness of system based on specific morphology and material; c) lab fabrication and characterization of variable reactiveness and flexibility. By using radical polymerization and soft lithography we fabricated in Phase

1 a membrane with a programmed biopolymer supported Polydimethylsiloxane. This membrane demonstrated in cycling a macro pore 100% opening (diameter=1.75 mm/height=0.2 mm) at $T= 40^{\circ}$C and 0% closing at $T= 20^{\circ}$C ((Fig. 9). Full aperture was accomplished in 10 min. Our second iteration can be summarized in two types of geometric variations ranging from 12mm to 8mm (reactive biopolymer) with pores embedded between two laminations of laser-cut EFTE (Fig. 10). As a resultant we have a fully self-regulated membrane that responds in timely manner to hygrothermal and light calibrations.

As part, of the fabrication of SABERs we have developed a custom 3D printer *"Viscous 3D extruder"* (Disclosure BK-2014-065) that enables elastomeric printing using multiple

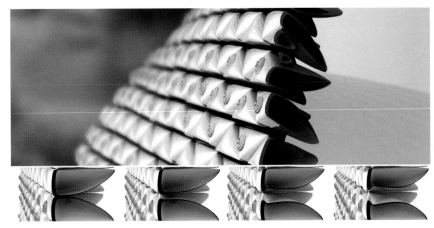

Figure 14: SABERs_M.P. Gutierrez, L.P. Lee, Simulation/ measurement microventuri tubes based on self-regulation to light, thermal, and humidity input, author and BIOMS team image by C. Irby

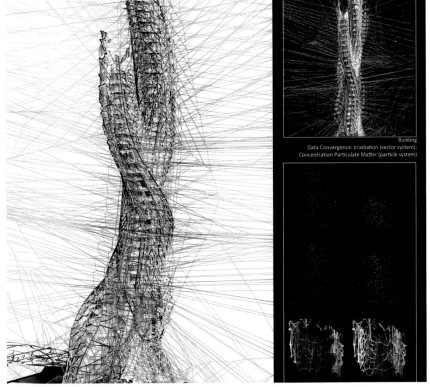

Figure 15: Detox Towers, Schematic diagram of parametric structural evaluation enclosure by author (M. P. Gutierrez, "Active Matter Matters", Frameworks, College of Environmental Design, p.1-2, April (2011))

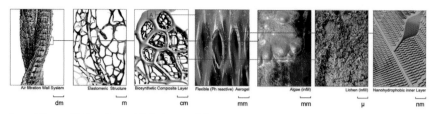

Figure 16 (image 26): Detox Towers_M.P.Gutierrez_2.tiff, Diagram of multi-scale approach to façade system by author (M. P. Gutierrez, "Active Matter Matters", Frameworks, College of Environmental Design, p.1-2, April (2011))

prototype syringes. Using a material already widely used in construction, the custom extruder was able to print geometries with a wide range of overhangs from 65.5° up to 116.5° through chemical curing without relying on heat, UV radiation, or support material (Fig. 12). Early estimates are demonstrating that this 3d printer technology opens new opportunities for low cost and materially efficient fabrication not only for construction applications but also for elastomeric applications in other fields such as biomedical industry (Fig. 13). Current research is focused in working through interfacing simulation platforms with data collected from material data of self-regulation (light, hygrothermal) (Fig. 14).

C) Live Matter Integration:

Case Study: *DetoxTower*- Live Matter Integration (M.P. Gutierrez, 2011, UC Berkeley). Finalist Evolo International Skyscraper Competition, 2011.

The incorporation of vegetation in architecture can be traced back to antiquity. The volition to use it as an active climate control system for cleaning air can also be traced from greenhouses to advances in the latter quarter if the twentieth century by research at NASA. In 1975, J. Wolverton was prototyping and researching at NASA the integration of plants for air and water detoxification (Wolverton and Wolverton, 1993; Wolverton, 1975) Yet, until recently the thought of live matter integrated into an active building system seemed either science fiction or simply absurd. Naturally, by now we are all too familiar with cases such as BIQ's algae façade in Germany and the potential of microoganisms and plants for environmental building systems (Lofgren, 2013). In 2011, Detox Tower, where proposed as a vision of a building typology with algae or lichen for active internal and external air detoxification and humidity control.

An initial analysis of multiple datasets of three categories of urban air pollutants (particulate matter, nitrous oxide and methane emissions) was used to determine the indexes and extreme locations of urban air toxicity. Evolo Skyscraper competition was used as a catalyst to generate a discussion around one of the most serious urban health issues and least explored field in sustainable architecture (Aiello, 2011). After early studies, we selected Tianjin in the year of 2050 as a testbed due to the extreme convergence of particulate matter, methane, and nitrous oxide emissions (Fig.15).

By embracing live matter vis-à-vis resisting it we can unfold unforeseen opportunities for air regeneration, humidity control and potentially energy generation. In addition to the climatic control component the proposal included a flexible floor system supported by a self-regulated structure of variable rigidity. The alternative real state for this proposal envisioned a system where inhabitants purchase a "sky-volume" lot equivalent to a typical ground share where owners can create their own layouts. The alternative inhabitation is imagined through an expansive/contractile structure that makes up a floor/wall system composite (elastomer/thermoplastic) (Fig.16). The regeneration system was envisioned through a self-regulated biosynthetic matter that combines algae or lichen (depending on the region) to a light and PH reactive aerogel (Fig.17 and 18).

Detox Tower pioneered into implementing live matter onto reactive synthetic matter so as to optimize control of microorganism growth and degradability. Organisms as lichen, fungus, bacteria have the possibility of not only reacting to environmental conditions but generating energy (thermal), light, and oxygen. A discussion on future architectural scenarios where live matter becomes a new material frontier was the fulcrum of this competition entry. It was an opportunity to launch current research at BIOMS on multiscale 3d printing of live and synthetic matter (Fig.19-21).

5. Conclusions

Radical advances in the ability for materials to self-generate and generate from the nanoscale to architecture depends largely in the continuation of

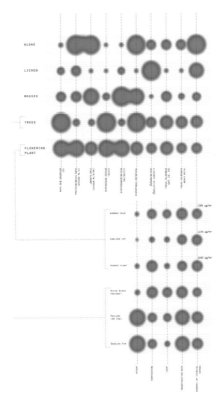

Figure 17: Detox Towers: Diagram of vegetation/detoxification/evapotranspiration properties by author

Figure 18: Detox Towers: Section of competition submission 2011 Evolo Skyscraper by author and BIOMS team (K. Han, P. Milusheva, C. Paz, J. Fainchney, B. Grieb) (Aiello, 2011).

Figure 19: Detox Towers: Section of presentation for 2011 Evolo Skyscraper by author and BIOMS team (K. Han, P. Milusheva, C. Paz, J. Fainchney, B. Grieb) (Aiello, 2011).

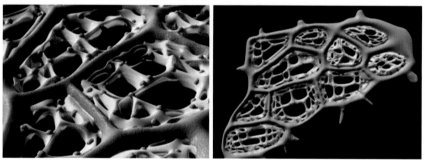

Figure 20: Detox Tower: Left: Algae/elastomeric membrane (rendering); Right: Algae/elastomeric 3d print model by author

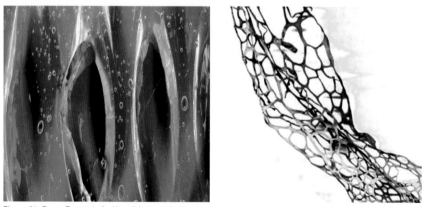

Figure 21: Detox Tower: Left: Algae/elastomeric membrane (3d print/cast); Right: bioinspiration for flexible structure (plant tissue dehydrated)

robust convergences of architecture, science and engineering. In this process advances in integrative fabrication and multiscale computation is critical (Malkawi and Augenbroe, 2004; Gutierrez, 2011(b)).

In upcoming decades, the research of smart systems is anticipated to advance in two areas: interfacing spaces and multifunctional, high-performance envelopes. For one part, we will witness a growth in the development of interactive spaces that emulate biological models through "neurological responses," applying high-cognition networks. In parallel, we will continue to pursue material innovation through building skins that can perform multiple and simultaneous operations through self-regulation and generation capabilities. More than a direct transfer from biotechnology, the next decades will continue strengthening convergences of architecture, engineering and biophysics. To streamline this frontier, architecture will experience major shifts in the development of three main areas: multi-objective simulation models that integrates research from the nano to the regional scale, multiscale digital fabrication for 3d printing materials with programmed responsiveness, and materials with biosynthetic integration from the molecular level to the architectural scale. Key advances can derive from these shifts. For instance, through a more robust synergy between the laboratory manufacturing and larger construction fabrication, architecture can eradicate unnecessary assemblages and joints required for complex building sensors and actuators (Gutierrez, 2008). Through these advances producing smart membranes that use bioinspiration for selectively resourcing energy, water, and materials will be progressively more attainable. Advances in complex cognition, adaptability, self-generation and regeneration, and phased material degradation will be met through this new frontier. By cross-pollinating the lab into the building scale and the building scale into the lab we can not only cement new ground in pluripotent matter, but transform the design agency of material invention.

253

REFERENCES

- Achilias, D.S.: 2007. Chemical recycling of poly (methyl methacrylate) by pyrolysis. Potential use of the liquid fraction as a raw material for the reproduction of the polymer, European Polymer Journal 43 (6) 2564–2575
- Aiello, Carlo (ed): 2011: "Detox Tower: Ecological Urbanism." EVOLO SKYSCRAPERS. eVolo: pp. 220-23.
- Aizenberg, Joanna, and Peter Fratzl: 2009. "Biological and biomimetic materials." Advanced Materials 21(4): 387-388;
- Altner, H., H. Sass, and I. Altner: 1977. "Relationship between structure and function of antennal chemo-, hygro-, and thermoreceptive sensilla in Periplaneta americana." Cell and tissue research 176(3): 389-405.
- Badarnah, Lidia, and Usama Kadri: 2014. "A methodology for the generation of biomimetic design concepts." Architectural Science Review ahead-of-print: 1-14)
- Bai, Hao, et al: 2012. "Functional fibers with unique wettability inspired by spider silks." Advanced Materials 24.20: 2786-2791
- Bauri, K., S. G. Roy, S. Pant, and P. De: 2013. "Controlled Synthesis of Amino Acid-Based pH-Responsive Chiral Polymers and Self-Assembly of Their Block Copolymers." Langmuir 29.8 (2013): 2764-2774
- Bar-Cohen, Yoseph: 2006. "Biomimetics—using nature to inspire human innovation." Bioinspiration & Biomimetics 1(1): P1.
- Bar-Cohen, Yoseph: 2011. Biomimetics: nature-based innovation. CRC press.
- Bassoli, Elena Andrea Gatto, Luca Iuliano, and Maria Grazia Violante: 2007. "3D printing technique applied to rapid casting." Rapid Prototyping Journal 13(3):148 – 155

- Bechthold, Martin: 2008. Innovative surface structures: technology and applications. Taylor & Francis Group.
- Bedini, S. A.: 1963. Seventeenth century Italian compound microscopes. Physics 5: 383–422.
- Brochu, Paul, and Qibing Pei: 2010. "Advances in dielectric elastomers for actuators and artificial muscles." Macromolecular Rapid Communications 31.1: 10-36.
- de Caus, Isaac: 1959. New and Rare Inventions of Waterworks. Moxon.
- Corr, S. A., Y.P. Rakovich, and Y.K. Gun'ko: 2008. "Multifunctional magnetic-fluorescent nanocomposites for biomedical applications." Nanoscale Research Letters 3: 87–104.
- Dear, Peter: 2008. The intelligibility of nature: How science makes sense of the world. University of Chicago Press.
- Descartes, René: 1998. Descartes: The world and other writings. Cambridge University Press.
- Descartes, R., J. Maire, and Maupertuis: 1637. Discours de la methode pour bien conduire sa raison, & chercher la verité dans les sciences: plus la dioptrique : les meteores : et la geometrie : qui sont des essais de cete methode. De l'imprimerie de Ian Maire
- Dong, Fuping, and Chang-Sik Ha: 2012 "Multifunctional materials based on polysilsesquioxanes." Macromolecular Research 20 (4): 335-343.
- Drew, Philip: 2008. New Tent Architecture. Thames & Hudson.
- Drisko, Glenna L., and Clément Sanchez: 2012. "Hybridization in Materials Science–Evolution, Current State, and Future Aspirations." European Journal of Inorganic Chemistry 2012.32: 5097-5105.
- Espinosa, Horacio D., et al: 2011. "Tablet-level origin of toughening in abalone shells and translation to synthetic composite materials." Nature communications 2: 173.
- Fernandez, John: 2012. Material Architecture. Routledge
- Fernández, R., J.A. Ramos, L. Espósito, A. Tercjak, and I. Mondragon: 2011. Reversible optical storage properties of nanostructured epoxy-based thermosets modified with azobenzene units. Macromolecules, 44(24), 9738-9746
- Fuentes-Alventosa, José Maria, et al: 2013. "Self-assembled nanostructured biohybrid coatings by an integrated 'sol–gel/intercalation' approach." RSC Advances 3(47): 25086-25096.
- Gaukroger, Stephen: 2006. The Emergence of a Scientific Culture: Science and the Shaping of Modernity 1210-1685. Oxford University Press.
- Gerber, David Jason, and Shih-Hsin Eve Lin: 2013. "Designing in complexity: Simulation, integration, and multidisciplinary design optimization for architecture." Simulation: 0037549713482027
- Gutierrez, Maria-Paz: 2008. "Material Bio-Intelligence": Proceedings of the 28th Annual Conference of the Association for Computer Aided Design in Architecture (ACADIA), University of Minnesota, College of Design, October 16 - 19, p.278-286
- Gutierrez, M.P.: 2011(a). "Matter, Sense, and Actuation: Self-Active Building Envelope Regulation systems (SABERs)", ACADIA 11: Integration through Computation, Catalog of the 31st Annual Conference of the Association for Computer Aided Design in Architecture (ACADIA), Banff (Alberta), 13-16: 114-120.
- Gutierrez, M.P.: 2011(b). "Innovative Puzzles", ACADIA 11: Integration through Computation, Proceedings of the 31st Annual Conference of the Association for Computer Aided Design in Architecture (ACADIA), Banff (Alberta), 13-16: 70-71.
- Gutierrez, M.P.: 2013(a). "Programming Selective Elasticity." Green Design, Materials and Manufacturing Processes. Helena Bartolo et al. (eds). Taylor & Francis: 525-530.
- Gutierrez, Maria-Paz: 2013(b). "Water and sunlight: regenerative hydronics." International Journal of Sustainable Building Technology and Urban Development 4.4: 260-273
- Gutierrez, Maria-Paz: Expected publication Issue 18(1) "Reorienting: Building Technology Innovation", Architectural Research Quarterly - Cambridge Journal
- Gutierrez, M.P.: Forthcoming 2016. Regeneration Wall. Routledge Press
- Gutierrez, Maria-Paz, and Luke P. Lee: 2013. "Multiscale design and integration of sustainable building functions." Science 341.6143: 247-248.
- Gutierrez, M.P. and P. Suen: 2013: "Self-Regulated Elasticity", Proceedings of the International conference on Adaptation and Movement in Architecture: p. 427-440. Canada
- Gutierrez, M.P. and T.I. Zohdi: 2013. "Effective Reflectivity and Heat Generation in Sucrose and PMMA Mixtures," Energy and Buildings, Volume 71, March 2014, Pages 95–103, http://dx.doi.org/10.1016/j.enbuild.2013.11.046).
- Harman, Peter Michael, ed.: 1985. Wranglers and physicists: studies on Cambridge physics in the nineteenth century. Manchester University Press.
- Harrison, Peter: 2001. "Curiosity, forbidden knowledge, and the reformation of natural philosophy in early modern England." Isis: 265-290
- Haglund, E., M.M. Seale-Goldsmith, and J.F. Leary: 2009: Design of multifunctional nanomedical systems. Annals of biomedical engineering 37: 2048–2063.
- Hesthaven, Jan S., and Tim Warburton: 2002."Nodal high-order methods on unstructured grids: I. Time-domain

solution of Maxwell's equations." Journal of Computational Physics 181(1): 186-221

- Hooke, R.: 1961. Micrographia: or, Some physiological descriptions of minute bodies made by magnifying glasses, with observations and inquiries thereupon. Dover Publications.
- Iwamoto, Lisa: 2013. Digital fabrications: architectural and material techniques. Princeton Architectural Press
- Keil, T.: 1997. Functional Morphology of Insect Mechanoreceptors. Microscopy Research and Technique 39, 506–531.
- Kellert, Stephen R., Judith Heerwagen, and Martin Mador: 2011. Biophilic design: the theory, science and practice of bringing buildings to life. John Wiley & Sons.
- Knippers, Jan, and Thomas Speck: 2012 "Design and construction principles in nature and architecture." Bioinspiration & Biomimetics 7(1): 015002.
- Laing, Nikolaus: 1967. "The Use of Solar and Sky Radiation for Air Conditioning of Pneumatic Structures," in IASS, Proceedings of the 1st International Colloquium on Pneumatic Structures, University of Stuttgart, Stuttgart, Germany: 11–12.
- Leatherbarrow, David: 2009. Architecture oriented otherwise. Chronicle Books.
- Lindeboom, G.A.: 1974. Boerhaave and Great Britain: three lectures on Boerhaave with particular reference to his relations with Great Britain. Vol. 7. Brill Archive.
- Liu, Kesong, and Lei Jiang: 2011. "Bio-inspired design of multiscale structures for function integration." Nano Today 6(2): 155-175
- Liu, S. et al.: 2010. "Multifunctional ZnO interfaces with hierarchical micro-and nanostructures: bio-inspiration from the compound eyes of butterflies." Applied Physics A 100: 57–61.
- Lofgren, Kristine: 2013. World's First Algae-Powered Building by Splitterwerk Architects Opens This Month in Germany. Inhabitat.
- Mainstone, Rowland J.: 1975. Developments in structural form. The MIT Press
- Malkawi, A. and G. Augenbroe (eds): 2007. Advanced Building Simulation. Routledge. pp. 1–5
- Mallakpour, S., and A. Zadehnazari: 2011. "Advances in synthetic optically active condensation polymers—a review." Express Polym Lett 5: 142-181.
- Martinelli, Luiz A., and Solange Filoso: 2008. "Expansion of sugarcane ethanol production in Brazil: environmental and social challenges." Ecological Applications 18.4: 885-898.
- Malato, Sixto, et al: 2007. "Photocatalytic decontamination and disinfection of water with solar collectors." Catalysis Today 122(1): 137-149.
- Maspoch, Daniel, Daniel Ruiz-Molina, and Jaume Veciana: 2007. "Old materials with new tricks: multifunctional open-framework materials." Chemical Society Reviews 36(5): 770-818.
- Mazzoleni, Ilaria: 2013. Architecture Follows Nature-Biomimetic Principles for Innovative Design. Vol. 2. CRC Press
- Meng, Harper, and Jinlian Hu: 2010. "A brief review of stimulus-active polymers responsive to thermal, light, magnetic, electric, and water/solvent stimuli." Journal of Intelligent Material Systems and Structures 21(9): 859-885.
- Meyer, Susan Sauve: 1992. "Aristotle, teleology, and reduction." The Philosophical Review: 791-825.
- Meyers, Marc André, et al: 2008. "Biological materials: structure and mechanical properties." Progress in Materials Science 53(1): 1-206.
- Monk, Peter: 2003. Finite element methods for Maxwell's equations. Oxford University Press.
- Nicole, Lionel, Laurence Rozes, and Clément Sanchez: 2010. "Integrative approaches to hybrid multifunctional materials: from multidisciplinary research to applied technologies." Advanced Materials 22(29): 3208-3214
- Novotny, L. and B. Hecht: 2006. Principles of Nano-optics. Cambridge University Press.
- Omenetto, Fiorenzo G., and David L. Kaplan: 2010. "New opportunities for an ancient material." Science 329(5991): 528-531
- Park, K. et al.: 2009. "New generation of multifunctional nanoparticles for cancer imaging and therapy." Advanced functional materials 19: 1553–1566.
- Pawlyn, Michael: 2011. Biomimicry in architecture. Riba Publishing.
- Perineau, Fabien, et al.: 2014 "Hybrid nanocomposites with tunable alignment of the magnetic nanorod filler." ACS applied materials & interfaces 6(3): 1583-1588.
- Pfammatter, U.: 2008. Building the Future: Building Technology and Cultural History from the Industrial Revolution Until Today. Prestel Pub, 180.
- Roth, Alfred and Hans Hildebrandt: 1927. Zwei Wohnhäuser Von Le Corbusier Und Pierre Jeanneret. Fr. Wedekind & Company, 5–7.
- Saleh, B.E.A., M.C. Teich, and B.E. Saleh: 1991. Fundamentals of Photonics, Vol. 22. Wiley, New York.
- Sanchez, Clement, et al: 2013. "Molecular engineering of functional inorganic and hybrid materials." Chemistry of Materials 26(1): 221-238.
- Schittich, C. , G. Staib, D. Balkow, M. Schuler, W. Sobek: 2007. Glass Construction Manual (Construction Manuals), 2nd revised and expanded ed. Birkhäuser, Architecture, Basel

- Schodek, Daniel L., Paulo Ferreira, and Michael F. Ashby: 2009. Nanomaterials, nanotechnologies and design: an introduction for engineers and architects. Butterworth-Heinemann.
- Semper, Gottfried: 1989. The four elements of architecture and other writings Cambridge, Cambridge University Press
- Steinbrecht, Rudolf Alexander: 1984. "Chemo-, hygro-, and thermoreceptors." Biology of the integument. Springer Berlin Heidelberg: 523-553.
- Vaezi, M., S. Chianrabutra, B. Mellor, and S. Yang: 2013. "Multiple material additive manufacturing–Part 1: a review." Virtual and Physical Prototyping, 8(1): 19-50.
- Vincent, Julian: 2009. "Biomimetic Patterns in Architectural Design." Architectural Design 79 (6): 74-81
- Vincent, Julian: 2012. Structural Biomaterials. Princeton University Press. Preface
- Weiland, Thomas: 1984. On the numerical solution of Maxwell's equations and applications in the field of accelerator physics. Deutsches Elektronen-Synchrotron (DESY). Hamburg (Germany, FR).
- Wilson, Stephen A., et al: 2007. "New materials for micro-scale sensors and actuators: An engineering review." Materials Science and Engineering: R: Reports 56.1: 1-129
- Wiseman, Howard Mark, Steve James Jones, and Andrew C. Doherty: 2007. "Steering, entanglement, nonlocality, and the Einstein-Podolsky-Rosen paradox." Physical review letters 98(14): 140-402.
- Wolverton, B. C., and John D. Wolverton: 1993."Plants and soil microorganisms: removal of formaldehyde, xylene, and ammonia from the indoor environment." Journal of the Mississippi Academy of Sciences 38(2): 11-15.
- Wolverton, B. C.: 1975. "Aquatic plants for removal of mevinphos from the aquatic environment."
- Xie, Zheng, Fu Wang, and Chun-yan Liu: 2012 "Organic–Inorganic Hybrid Functional Carbon Dot Gel Glasses." Advanced Materials 24(13): 1716-1721
- Yao, Hong-Bin, et al.: 2012 "A designed multiscale hierarchical assembly process to produce artificial nacre-like freestanding hybrid films with tunable optical properties." Journal of Materials Chemistry 22(26): 13005-13012.
- Yu, T. et al.: 2013 "Fabrication of all-in-one multifunctional phage liquid crystalline fibers." RSC Advances 3: 20437–20445.
- Yun, S. H. et al.: 2012: "Multifunctional silicon inspired by a wing of male Papilio ulysse." Applied Physics Letters 100(3): 033109
- Yunus, W., A. bin, A. Rahman: 1988. "Refractive index of solutions at high concentrations." Applied Optics 27(16) 3341–3343
- Zari, Maibritt Pedersen: 2010. "Biomimetic design for climate change adaptation and mitigation." Architectural Science Review 53(2): 172-183.

MARIA-PAZ GUTIERREZ is an architect and Assistant Professor of Architecture at the University of California, Berkeley. Her research focuses on integrated multifunctional building systems based on multiscale design. In 2008 she founded BIOMS, an interdisciplinary UC Berkeley research group that intersects architecture and microengineering to advance multifunctional optimization of building systems. Gutierrez interdisciplinary research is supported by organizations such as NSF, EPA and DOE. Her research has been published in prominent architectural and scientific journals including Science and ARQ Cambridge and in venues such as the Field Museum.

Gutierrez is recipient of numerous design and interdisciplinary awards such as the 2001 AIA Academic Medal, 2006 Best Interior Design (hospital), 2010 Blue Award first prize, and more recently 2011 Evolo International Competition Finalist. Her teaching innovation has been recognized by academia and industry through the 2011 Sarlo Distinguished Mentorship Award, 2011 Bentley Innovation Award and more recently the 2013 Odebrecht Sustainability Innovation Second Prize award (co-advisor). Gutierrez is recipient of the prestigious 2010 NSF-EFRI award (over 250 entries), is a 2011 Fulbright Nexus Scholar, and was recently appointed Senior Fellow of the Energy Climate Partnership of the Americas by US Dept. of State.

JENNY E. SABIN & PETER LLOYD JONES

ELASTICITY

& NETWORKS

—

DESIGN

COMPUTATION TOOLS

FOR ARCHITECTURE

& SCIENCE

Abstract

This article explores novel methodologies in computational design and for discovering new, formerly unseen relationships in dynamic biological systems. The text demonstrates how catalogs of visualization and simulation tools are used to discover new behaviors in geometry and matter. Project work from LabStudio and a co-taught graduate seminar titled Nonlinear Systems Biology and Design 2007-2010 (Graduate Dept of Architecture, PennDesign) form the basis for discussion and exploration. The paper highlights specific project work on the topic of cellular networking behavior through examples that examine the nature of nonlinearities, emergent properties and loosely coupled modules that are cardinal features of 'complexity'. Through the analysis of biological design problems in specialized 3D designer microenvironments, students were exposed to new modes of thinking about design ecology through an understanding of how dynamic and environmental feedback specifies structure, function and form. Specific physical (including 3D print and various digital fabrication outputs) and visual exercises (generative and algorithmic studies) will be explained to familiarize the reader with the topics in architectural and scientific terms.

Introduction

The ability to forgo disciplinary boundaries allows for unique views of similar issues, even at radically different physical & temporal scales. Whether scientists, architects, artists, engineers, musicians or mathematicians, we are all bound to deal with matter and its effects. Technology has afforded scientists and designers alike with an extraordinary ability to generate information, yet this has resulted in an ever-increasing inability to organize, visualize and model diverse datasets. As we become faced with petabyte datasets and beyond, it will become increasingly challenging to view and comprehend 4-D bio/medical data using existing means. While the end goals may differ in science and architecture, there is a driving necessity in both disciplines to spatialize, model and fabricate complex, emergent and self-organized non-linear systems. We ask "How can we intuit, see & understand complex wholes that are often indiscernible from their individual parts?"

Figure 1: Jones, Sabin, Lucia and Savig (left to right); Sabin+Jones Labstudio; Nonlinear Systems Biology and Design cluster, 2010 Smart Geometry Workshop at IAAC, Barcelona, Spain; SG2010 Working Prototypes.

The collaborations between architects, scientists, clinicians and engineers that LabStudio, 2006-2011, (a hybrid research unit exploring intersections at the forefront of design research & founded by Sabin and Jones in 2006 at UPenn) launched offer new venues for productive exchange in biology and design, while revealing powerful models for visualizing the complex and seemingly intangible.

Information gathers meaning when filtered through multiple modes of expression, and new models for visualization and interpretation will be essential to meet this need. Intuitive pattern recognition and alternative representations of complex datasets that can be seen, heard and even held (e.g. via rapid prototying), are essential. Using logic, sound design and intuition as guiding devices, relationships can be explored between the organizational properties of the biological design problem and captured datasets. In the production of relationships and correspondences, "tools" such as computer scripts are developed to orchestrate the movement between multiple modes of working. In fact, a rigorous understanding and analysis of these types of models will allow scientists and architects to retool and revaluate how to negotiate visualization and quantification within complex 3-D, biological phenomena. Translation will require all of our senses and intuitions, and this can only be achieved using unconventional approaches.

In support of the aforementioned concepts and models, this article provides specific examples of parallel design thinking between architectural research and cell biology that was garnered over 6 years of research and education within LabStudio, 2006 - 2011.

Specifically, this article explores one research track within LabStudio centered upon cellular networking behavior. Three case study examples are presented from student work. The paper concludes with one seminal project by LabStudio titled Branching Morphogenesis. The aim of this paper is to report upon one stream of research between architectural designer Jenny E Sabin and biologist Peter Lloyd Jones and to demonstrate to natural

Figure 2: Peter Lloyd Jones, Roland Snooks and Kyle Steinfeld at a final review for Nonlinear Systems Biology and Design, co-taught by Sabin & Jones, 2007 – 2010, Graduate Department of Architecture, School of Design, UPenn. Featured work by Misako Murata.

scientists and architects alike how high-risk, non-linear, design-driven philosophies and practices emanating from 3-D spatial biology and generative design in architecture can result in radical advances in both scientific and design research and applied architectural practice.

Background

The primary goal of the Jones Lab research group is to determine how the extracellular matrix (ECM), a cell-derived woven and globular protein network that envelopes or

259

contacts most cells within the body—an architectural textile of sorts—changes throughout development and disease, and how alterations in this 3D ECM environment feed back to control cell and tissue behavior at the level of the genome and beyond in real time.

Towards these goals, and in the context of the Sabin+Jones LabStudio collaboration, we began by studying the influence of different extracellular matrix components, such as laminin and type I collagen, on a number of nonlinear biological processes, including tumor formation, cell motility and networking behavior.

Ultimately, at the patho-physiological level, a major aim of our collaborative research is to derive new structural and functional information from each of these dynamic systems in an effort to diagnose, prognosticate and treat human disease.

Over the past three decades, it has been firmly established that 3D cell and tissue architecture, at the level of the ECM, exerts a dominant influence over the genetic makeup of a cell or individual. In this sense, the ECM represents a key phenotypic determinant of cells within tissues. In essence, much of the secret of life resides outside the cell within the extracellular matrix. Importantly, the ECM not only acts as a physical entity, which lends flexibility and physical support to cells within tissues, but it also behaves as an informational entity, an ongoing and historical document that records what transpires in and around a cell during the lifetime of an organism.

Clearly, these biological models are underscored at the cellular and molecular levels by complex non-linear responses to complex and dynamic scenarios. Thus, we posit that a rigorous understanding and analysis of these types of models will allow architects to retool and revaluate how we may negotiate topics such as nonlinear fabrication, feedback and performance in architecture. On the architectural side, rather than seeking direct translation of the science to architecture and vice versa, this research collaboration is about working through biological design problems that give rise to new modes of thinking and working in design and biomedicine.

On the design-studio side, our aim is to introduce biologists to digital and algorithmic architectural tools that may be used to reveal new complexities within the biological systems being studied. Additionally, by specifically examining dynamic cellular systems, our intent is to discover new ways of understanding, revealing and abstracting how these biological systems negotiate issues of auto- and artificial-fabrication. Here structure and material are inextricably linked. Cells and tissues not only produce their own underlying, self-produced fabric, but they modify and respond to this woven, felted or embellished environment. A digital code begets a physical code that informs the physical code and so on.

Networking

For the networking projects, we are investigating part-to-whole relationships during capillary formation by lung endothelial cells. At the biological level, coordinated cellular networking, a component of angiogenesis, is required to form the exquisite fractal network that emerges in the developing and mature lung to facilitate efficient gas exchange from birth onwards. Real-time imaging of endothelial cells cultured within a specialized extracellular matrix (ECM) microenvironment, designated the basement membrane, that either suppress or promote networking, formed the basis for these projects.

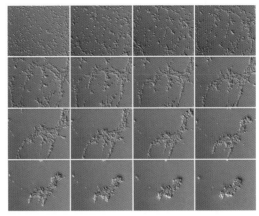

Figure 3: Real-time imaging of endothelial cells cultured within a specialized extracellular matrix (ECM) microenvironment, designated the basement membrane, that either suppress or promote networking, formed the basis for these projects. Courtesy of Jones Lab, University of Pennsylvania

The study and quantification of this vascular network allows for a greater understanding of how variable components give rise to structured networks in both biology and architecture.

Case Study 1: Scale Free Networks

By Joshua Freese, Jeffrey Nesbit, Shuni Feng

Sabin+Jones LabStudio

Rules and Logics of Scale-free Networks derived from the study of Angiogenesis

The angiogenic networking behavior of lung mesenchymal cells, designated RFL-6 or MFLM-4 cells, which have ability to transform into networking endothelial cells

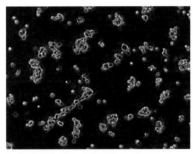

Figure 4: Networking without Prx-1. Courtesy of Jones Lab, University of Pennsylvania.

in response to basement membrane proteins, was evaluated in contrasting conditions: with or without Prx-1, a gene that enhances networking. When Prx-1 is absent, cells form clusters on basement membrane material. On the other hand, when Prx-1 is present, cells form branched networks on this matrix. The flow paths also influence these formations or topological geometries found within the underlying ECM. Thus, the roles played by Prx-1 (code) and the ECM (environment) are highly influential in creating these network morphologies by endothelial cells (components).

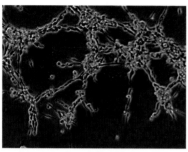

Figure 5: Networking without Prx-1. Courtesy of Jones Lab, University of Pennsylvania.

This collaboration between code, environment and component has to operate on a series of scales, which start with the single cells paring, grouping and clustering, and eventually reconfiguring the clusters into larger networks, which create the lung vasculature. By studying the relationship between these effectors, we can observe how inter-scalar relationships occur and move from the micro to the macro. Our research examines and explores a variety of organizational operations in biology and architecture by studying the scale-free networks that define order and relationships in global systems, including the internet and air travel. These network systems, like those in the biological model, rely on managing complexity by sharing simple organizing principles that govern behavior at all scales.

Scale-free networks, as opposed to random networks, represent complex systems in which some nodes have a tremendous number of connections to other nodes. The popular nodes are called "hubs". One characteristic of scale-free networks is that they are robust against accidental failures, yet are vulnerable to coordinated perturbations or attacks. A growing network with preferential attachment will become scale-free. Our objective is to understand the code as a switch that can amplify the generation of cellular structures in response to the environment, to study the relationships between component, code, environment, and the formations produced, and to understand networking behavior in a scale-free system.

262

The first phase of development included the establishment of a series of organizing principles derived from the biological models so that we could apply these logics to the computer model. The topics, which governed our operations, were connectivity and clustering. These terms imply a set of particular observed behaviors that are abstracted and controlled through the design and production of custom algorithms and digital tools. To understand connectivity, we first examined several principle modes for generating connectivity using criteria of proximity as an initial guide for establishing network connections. These inputs were based on neighborhood and community conditions as opposed to a hierarchical model. This scale-free approach, like the biological systems of study, gives rise to an organization that can add, shift, or translate its hubs and nodes over time and space without having fixed roles similar to top-down systems.

The next step entailed activating these connections through a web-like matrix, which could then pull and engage cells, thus converting a community of cells connected to a hub into a hub of cells. This hub could then attract other hub communities. This step exemplifies a basic concept of scale-free networking where behaviors and conditions remain the same as one navigates through various scales. Thus, the behavior of a node, hub, community, neighborhood, or region retains its governing principles through any relative scalar transition. This clustering effect defined which cells were hub cells, and which neighborhoods or communities could also become hubs at new scales. The definition of the hubs is significant because organization is established via their density and distribution such that an eventual assemblage of hub communities results. These hub communities exhibit formations similar to those observed in the angiogenesis phase.

A critical element in this project entailed the design and generation of a translational tool

263|

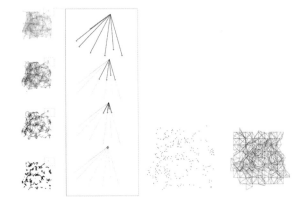

Figure 6: Cell to hub clustering establishing initial hub communities and neighborhoods. Image by Joshua Freese, Jeffrey Nesbit, Shuni Feng; Nonlinear Systems Biology and Design, Sabin & Jones, University of Pennsylvania, 2008.

Figure 7: A four-phased clustering model and the resultant mesh components produced. Image by Joshua Freese, Jeffrey Nesbit, Shuni Feng; Nonlinear Systems Biology and Design, Sabin & Jones, University of Pennsylvania, 2008.

for behavioral modeling, such that we weren't merely constructing mimetic or simulation models. This behavioral approach opened up new strategies for abstract component typologies, which also behaved within a scale-free system in response to their input cells (points), locations and behaviors. This pursuit of a component typology culminated in a method that could translate the relationship of hub communities and individual cells, and use them as inputs weighted by their community density. This in turn, defined a perimeter and interior geometry that provided more tangible means of studying, analyzing and iteratively testing the temporal progressions as the networks developed and clustered.

This process also established another scalar leap as hub communities network like the individual cells had in the previous scale/step. This is significant because as one moves

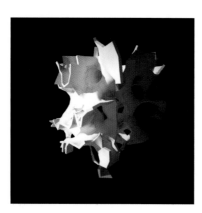

Figure 8: Secondary scale clustering and transitional mesh component results (below). Images by Joshua Freese, Jeffrey Nesbit, Shuni Feng; Nonlinear Systems Biology and Design, Sabin & Jones, University of Pennsylvania, 2008.

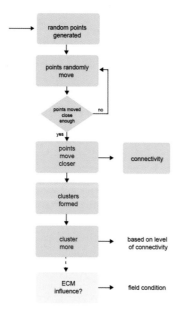

Figure 9: Schematic diagram of model development through conditional phases. Image by Joshua Freese, Jeffrey Nesbit, Shuni Feng; Nonlinear Systems Biology and Design, Sabin & Jones, University of Pennsylvania, 2008.

from the micro-scale to the macro-scale in these fractal like structures, a transitional method is necessary for shifting resolutions such that there are no disjunctions between all steps at all scales. Thus, the system exhibits cohesive and fluid transitions between scales where consistent behaviors of connectivity and clustering occur at all phases and scales.

Once a working model for connectivity and clustering was established within a random field environment, the next step included the integration of context. In the case of the biological model, context is defined as the extracellular matrix (ECM). This matrix establishes a base field for cellular movement and networking, which also has the capacity to influence and reform the ways in which the cells navigate, connect and cluster based upon the geometrical and directional properties of the matrix. This step is very relevant as it integrates and instrumentalizes the ability of cells to behave in different environmental conditions, again with and without the Prx-1 gene as a networking enhancer.

This last step includes the exploration of feedback relationships that are behavioral and anamorphic rather than static and fixed. We seek to produce a dynamic system that can be analyzed through the production of static temporal or phase based models, which may further inform and reform the dynamic model. The extracellular matrix could shift over time while the cells are connecting and clustering causing a perpetual catalytic feedback loop, which could generate infinite possibilities. The inclusion of the ECM doesn't alter the scale-free network towards a

265|

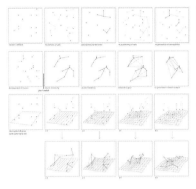 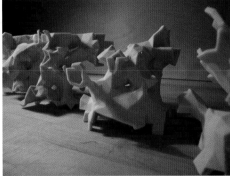

Figure 10: Diagram of potential variations of cellular formation given the deformation of an orthogonal or regular ECM and diagram of the scale-free networking process. Image by Joshua Freese, Jeffrey Nesbit, Shuni Feng; Nonlinear Systems Biology and Design, Sabin & Jones, University of Pennsylvania, 2008.

Figure 11: 3D printed mesh component family showing surface deformations based on networking density. Image by Joshua Freese, Jeffrey Nesbit, Shuni Feng; Nonlinear Systems Biology and Design, Sabin & Jones, University of Pennsylvania, 2008.

hierarchical model; rather it reinforces the scale-free network and becomes a component for maturing and evolving the cellular formations and their mesh outputs as part of the established system. The difficult task of establishing qualifications for defining what is a complete model is dependent upon at what scale and system we seek to apply these tools to. As previously stated, we don't seek to merely replicate or mimic the biological model; we are in pursuit of various inter-scalar applications ranging from the cellular to the architectural to the urban and eventually global.

As we discovered early on with scale-free networks, the same governing principles that define the network inside of a computer or mobile phone, also define the entire internet, telephone network and other systems like intercontinental air travel. This capacity for operations at any scale also points towards the significance of biological models in architecture. Certain aspects have to reform themselves at least in scalar terms, but the behavioral logic of how these systems, buildings and environments come together may rely on the same fundamental rules, elements and tools that together work to establish, develop and execute their production.

Through this behavioral and conditional modeling, we can establish and discover new relationships for designers to observe and build upon, not just in architectural terms but in many different professions and practices which also range from the micro to the macro in terms of phases, processes and products. These relationships and dependencies will inform both biology and architecture as we seek to cross-fertilize and inform new modes and methods for modeling, representing and solving conditions and problems that exist in various cases and at a myriad of scales.

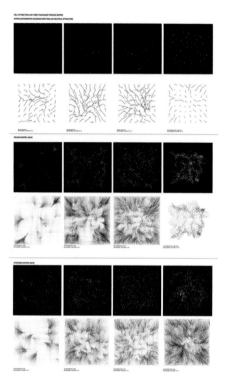

Figure 12: Cell attraction with force exchange through matrix. Matrix deformation diagram over time with multiple attractors. Images by Andrew Lucia and Christopher Lee; Nonlinear Systems Biology and Design, Sabin & Jones, University of Pennsylvania, 2007.

Case Study 2: Modeling Non-Linear Cellular Networking by Lung Endothelial Cells

By A.J. Chan, Kenta Fukunishi, Chris Lee, Jonathan Kowalkoski, Andrew Lucia

Sabin+Jones LabStudio

As was previously discussed, the main function of the lung is to allow for efficient gas exchange between the airways and blood vessels in post-natal life onwards. However, determining how networks of blood vessels (the lining of which is composed of interconnected endothelial cell (ECs) forming tubes) are generated and maintained during development represents a major challenge in contemporary lung biology. The aim of this project is to sequentially model the process of tube formation in vitro and in silico, and then to abstract this process into architecture. To approach this, we have studied the parameters that govern EC morphology in response to the underlying extracellular matrix (ECM), and how this alters cell-cell and cell-ECM interactions during networking. By comparing the behavior of human lung ECs cultured either on polystyrene (i.e. a non-networking branching environment) with those cultivated on reconstituted ECM (i.e. a condition that promotes network formation), we suggest that there are more than merely visible parameters governing the emergent structures and networks that eventually give rise to EC networks. Through our research, we have explored potential parameters that potentiate or prohibit networking behavior, including intercellular communication, environmental instigators, and cellular geometry.

Our initial investigations allowed us to consider the following questions: Given the environment, in this case the ECM, what makeup and density may allow for proper cell aggregation? Similarly, what are the forces that are at play in and amongst the cells and their environment? Certain behaviors are evident within the in vitro test systems that we investigated. By abstracting primitive parameters that govern these behaviors

|266

(cell-cell interactions, cellular geometry, and the influence of the surrounding ECM) simplified computer models were created. Studying these parameters within a parametric environment, allowed us to explore multiple configurations with dynamic variables, increasing the accuracy of our computer models, and continually defining, and redefining potential parameters. In addition, these investigations allowed us to reformulate in vitro models of EC networking that focused on the geometry and movement of the ECM during tube formation. Yet, given the conditions within the models, how can forces and relative densities be measured both within the simulation and the actual samples to determine accuracy?

If the models prove to be accurate, what conditions must be met within the models to achieve simulated networking? What are the non-visible variables (physical and chemical) that instigate aggregation and formation of ECs into blood vessels? What are the temporal/spatial elements at play? What role does the ECM play in proper vessel formation (i.e. in vivo vs. in vitro)? What role (if any) do forces generated by the cells within the ECM play in the establishment of proper vessel formation? Does this play a role beyond cell geometry or initial cell organization alone? What role does cell geometry play in angiogenesis? Above all, how can these novel studies lead to development of new rules of engagement in architecture at different time and length scales?

Summary: Given the models developed thus far, we are capable of measuring relative forces, rates of change amongst those forces, density of cells vs density of the ECM, angles of attractive forces, and rules of proximity. These factors can be adjusted to create stable or unstable networks thus far. However, at this stage we are unable to answer whether or not any of these simulated behaviors coincide with the actual test cases, or if they are merely visually corresponding scenarios. Answers to these questions will require additional in vitro experimentation.

Case Study 3:

By Kara Medow, Kirsten Shinnamon, Young-Suk Choi

Sabin+Jones LabStudio

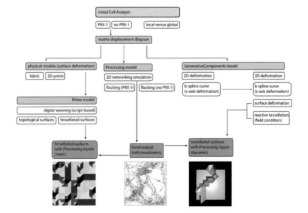

Figure 13: Feedback loop diagram showing algorithmic strategy for cell analysis and surface generation. Image by Kara Medow, Kirsten Shinnamon, Young-Suk Choi; Nonlinear Systems Biology and Design, Sabin & Jones, University of Pennsylvania, 2008.

Real-time imaging of endothelial cells cultured within specialized extracellular matrix microenvironments may either suppress or promote cell networking, i.e. angiogenesis. The relationship between cell-to-cell communications during the process of angiogenesis formed the basis of this project. Critical to our study was the impact of a gene designated PRX-1 on the process of angiogenesis. As was discussed previously, PRX-1 enhances endothelial cell networking on a specialized extracellular matrix called a basement membrane. At a functional level, expression of PRX-1 allows for the extension of cell "tips" on the basement membrane outwards towards other cells. In vivo, when PRX-1 is absent, blood vessels fail to form in the developing lung leading to demise at birth when the first breath is taken.

The ultimate aim of this project was to determine how PRX-1 facilitates networking between endothelial cells. An abstraction of those relationships would then fuel new investigations related to, but not exclusively about, cell networks. Resulting physical and digital investigations all centered about the notion that as cells network and converge in space, they distort the matrix they are plated on. This unique relationship between object, environment, and code laid the groundwork for the breadth of our studies, as all concurrent investigations took each of these three variables into account. The feedback between these variables played a vital role in our investigations; as variables changed in level or degree, so did the resulting outcome.

Primary analyses of cell cultures included studying two movies of cells exhibiting or not exhibiting networking behavior. From these movies, snapshots of cell behavior were extracted in order to extrapolate the rules by which cells behave under these distinct conditions. Through three concurrent digital investigations, we were able to study the local condition of cell to cell networking in distinct ways. Output from each of these studies ultimately created input for the other studies, so that the project itself exhibited a strong feedback loop condition. In all of the investigations, the basement membrane is abstracted and reduced to a surface condition that reacts to corresponding points or cells. The hyper local condition of cell-to-cell communication and the environment seemed inextricably linked, and through these studies we hoped to prove that connection.

Figure 14: 3D prints of surface deformation studies based on changes in networking density. Image courtesy of Sabin + Jones LabStudio.

Primary comparisons of these two different cultures of endothelial cells on basement membrane revealed that in the presence of PRX-1 cells at the periphery of overall clusters possessed a more elongated phenotype. In the cultures

269|

of cells plated in the absence of PRX-1, this elongated phenotype never occurred and the cells never seemed to reach any level of overall organization. In contrast, the cultures in the presence of PRX-1 seemed to form increasingly denser and more organized aggregations over time where these elongated cells appeared to be instrumental in facilitating the greater network of cells. Their length was perhaps a result of continuous interaction with the extracellular matrix as these longer cells were closer to the basement membrane due to their position at the edge of the cell clusters. At the local condition, these longer cells seemed to operate in particular directions in relationship to overall cell clusters: they trended towards being parallel or perpendicular to the existing aggregations of cells. As these cells networked and moved towards each other, they remained in contact with the matrix thus allowing for a distortion of the basement membrane.

The idea that points attached to a surface would distort that medium led to initial physical models where a flexible surface of canvas was distorted via the precise movement of a string or wire threaded through it. These physical models prompted the creation of a Generative Components model that utilized sets of B-spline curves organized in a field. These curves, reacting to points, or cells, would move between the top and bottom curve. As a surface was ultimately attached to sets of curves in the model, one or more points moving through the field would elicit an accurate distortion of those surfaces.

for length parameter 20

Figure 15: The notion of spline curves attached to a deformable surface led to the development of precise rule sets intended to create static deformed surfaces utilizing Rhino Script. Resulting output from the script creates a set of x- direction and y- direction curves that are woven together. Image by Kara Medow, Kirsten Shinnamon, Young-Suk Choi; Nonlinear Systems Biology and Design, Sabin & Jones, University of Pennsylvania, 2008..

This notion of spline curves attached to a deformable surface led to the development of precise rule sets intended to create static deformed surfaces utilizing Rhino Script. StringWeave2, written by Jenny E. Sabin & Raymond Kettner formerly of CabinStudio+, generates a series of digitally woven curves using binary inputs. In this script, sets of binary information acts as a digital on/off switch for the code, as 1 or 0 signifies an up or down movement of the curves. Resulting output from the script creates a set of x- direction and y- direction curves that are woven together. Initial tests utilized sets of x- and y-direction curves from randomly generated sets of binary data to create topological surface models from Patch, Surface from Curve Network, Sweep, and Surface from Edge Curves in Rhino. Ultimately, information was separated so that either the x- or the y- direction curves would serve as input to generate the surfaces. As well, the topological surface models were reduced to tessellated triangulated models (by ignoring the interpolated curve information and utilizing only the 1 or 0 up/down data) so that information could be more easily "read" from these increasingly complex surfaces.

To return to the notion of networking, it was necessary to infuse the information in our digital studies with some content related to cell-to-cell communication. Concurrent to the static Rhino surface model investigation, Processing models were developed in order to create data sets that simulated the difference between PRX-1 and non PRX-1 cell samples. Cohesion and alignment of points in a network determined the variables and parameters to create digitally scripted models of cells moving and flocking to ultimately cluster, which would imitate the condition of networking. Within the code, cohesion allowed cells to steer towards other local cells within a defined distance, while alignment allowed cells to navigate within a field of continuously moving and changing locations. The alignment parameter allowed the overall cell clusters to aggregate on a more global scale, due to the fact that the cohesion factor only happens on a hyper-local scale. The visualization of the raw data from the Processing movies indicated (in composite or frame by frame over time) the distinct behavioral difference between the varied cell cultures. The precise location of point to point movement in both the PRX-1 and non PRX-1 simulations in Processing were extracted as x,y,z coordinate sets so that the data could be imported back into the Generative Components and Rhino investigations.

In Generative Components, we input the point coordinates from the Processing simulations. The movement and convergence of the points as they change their x- and y- location allowed the surface to react in the z-direction. The final Generative Components models abandoned the B-spline condition for a triangulated tessellated representation so that ultimate visual comparisons could be drawn between the Generative Components and the Rhino surfaces, which used identical

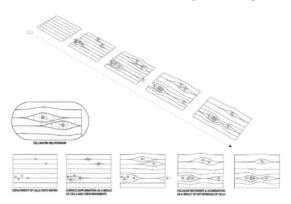

Figure 16: Cellular movement and aggregation as a result of networking of cells. Image by Kara Medow, Kirsten Shinnamon, Young-Suk Choi; Nonlinear Systems Biology and Design, Sabin & Jones, University of Pennsylvania, 2008.

Processing inputs. The reading of this surface condition, while literal, is an accurate representation of the convergence or non-convergence of cells over time.

The final Rhino models used the same point coordinates, separated out into frames so that the networking state of each set of cells could be analyzed as time progressed. As networks develop, connectivity between nodes increases. The point-to-point connections between discreet nodes in a network are, in effect, a binary condition: at any given point in time, each node is connected or is not connected to another node. Given varied length parameters, the cell points from the Processing studies were analyzed in order to determine network connectivity and thus, were able to generate sets of binary data that were directly related to the state of the network and its connections for that time frame.

This binary code created from point to point convergence information from the Processing data sets was fed back into the StringWeave2 script. The resulting x- and y-direction curves provided information to generate tessellated surfaces that then conveyed the increasing or decreasing degree of connectivity in both the PRX-1 and non PRX-1 simulations.

Ultimately, the resulting Processing, Generative Components and Rhino models have implications beyond the tooling and methodology used to construct these investigations. The tessellated surface models as well as the Processing data sets and their visual representations have potential for diagnostic tools for biologists in order to see simple

Figure 17: This installation materializes five slices in time that capture the force network exerted by interacting vascular cells upon their surrounding matrix scaffold. Time is manifested as five vertical, interconnected layers made from over 75,000 cable zip ties. Courtesy Sabin+Jones LabStudio.

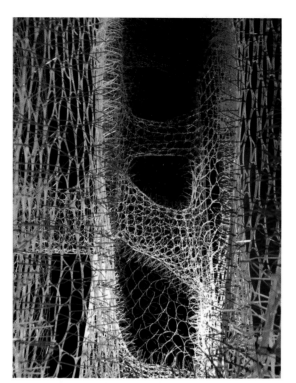

Figure 18: Gallery visitors are invited to walk around and in-between the layers of Branching Morphogenesis, and immerse themselves within an organic and newly created "Datascape". Dynamic cellular change is fused with the body and human occupation, all through the constraints of a ready-made. Courtesy Sabin+Jones LabStudio.

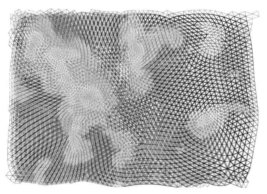

Figure 19: Construction mesh templates highlighting shifts in density within the simulated underlying extracellular matrix. Courtesy Sabin+Jones LabStudio.

part to whole relationships within a highly dense and complicated developing cellular network. As these models cull only the necessary information regarding one element of the communication between cells, these visualizations posses the capability of creating tools for early diagnosis of potentially dangerous medical conditions.

These investigations also capitalize on the visualization of information in a network through resulting surface conditions. The architectural potential for the use of these systems is vast: to be able to generate increasingly complex surfaces from the informational content of networks is a step beyond the notion of "building the diagram." The potential of these studies to move beyond the surficial and into the spatial dimension holds great possibilities for the process of creating new and different architectural typologies utilizing the ideas and data embedded in network conditions.

Case Study 4: Branching Morphogenesis

A project by Sabin+Jones LabStudio

Originally on view at the Design and Computation Gallery SIGGRAPH 2008 and subsequently at Ars Electronica, Linz, Austria, 2009-2010. Winning image of the AAAS NSF International Visualization Challenge, featured on the cover of Science, February 2009.

Design Team: Jenny E. Sabin & Andrew Lucia

Science Team: Peter Lloyd Jones & Jones Lab members.

Special thanks to Annette Fierro for critical commentary.

Production Team: Dwight Engel, Matthew Lake, Austin McInerny, Marta Moran, Misako Murata, Jones Lab members

Branching Morphogenesis is a scaled datascape that captures a creative process that encompasses intersections between design and science. 75,000 zip ties filter the force network exerted by cells at a micro-scale. At all stages of the filtering and scaling process, the network is adjusted by new constraints. The final artifact is a synthesis, a biosynthesis, for people to inhabit and experience.

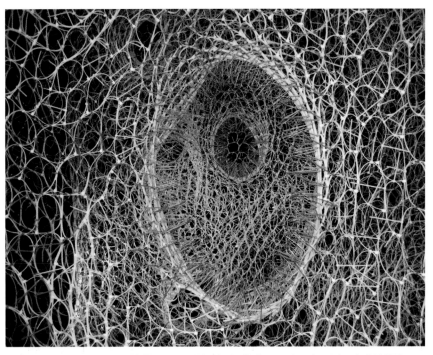

Figure 20: This image won the AAAS/NSF International Visualization Challenge and was featured on the 2-19-2010 cover of Science. Courtesy Sabin+Jones LabStudio.

Branching Morphogenesis explores fundamental processes in living systems and their potential application in architecture. The project investigates part-to-whole relationships revealed during the generation of branched structures formed in real-time by interacting lung endothelial cells placed within a 3D matrix environment. The installation materializes five slices in time that capture the force network exerted by interacting vascular cells upon their matrix environment. The time lapses manifest as five vertical, interconnected layers made from over 75,000 cable zip ties. Gallery visitors are invited to walk around and in-between the layers, and immerse themselves within a newly created datascape fusing dynamic cellular change with human occupation, all through the constraints of a ready-made.

The aim of this project is to sequentially model the networking process in vitro and in silico, and then to abstract this process into experimental architecture. To approach this, we have studied the parameters that govern branching morphology in response to the underlying extracellular matrix (ECM), and how this alters cell-cell and cell-ECM interactions during networking. We have explored potential parameters that prohibit networking behavior, including intercellular communication, environmental instigators, and cellular geometry. Models borrowed from architects--such as tensegrity structures and geodesic domes--have led to radical new insights into how living systems, including eukaryotic cells, tissues and whole organisms, are assembled and function, as well as to a new understanding of how the micro-ecology of cells influences the genome. Similarly, models borrowed from biology, particularly regarding self- organization and the emergence of complex, non-linear global systems from simple local rules of organization, have led to the discovery of new forms and structural organizations in architectural design. Through the investigation of controlled and uncontrolled cell tissue biological models, parallel models work to unfold the parametric logic of these biological and responsive systems revealing their deep interior logic. The result is a component-based surface architecture that abstracts and embeds both environment (context) with deeper interior programmed systems.

Conclusion

In the last decade, digital practices and the subsequent ability to explore iterative, systems-based and complex formal strategies have transformed architectural research and design. Concurrently, a post-genomic revolution in digital, systems-based thinking has occurred in the natural sciences. Given these overlapping philosophies and practices, a potential arises to reinvigorate (reinvent/discover) dialog between these separate fields with the prospect that a mutually beneficial hybrid field might emerge that is centered around design thinking. Certainly, the question 'What is Design Research?' is stirring pedagogical and infrastructural debate within architecture departments and schools: the concept of a research design laboratory replete with funded research and trans-disciplinary participants offers a challenging, yet fruitful addition to the design studio, both in terms of productive discovery, research and learning. Similarly, in the sciences, and despite mounting evidence to the contrary, data-driven or 'inductive' and/or intuitive advances in scientific knowledge, especially via collaborations with specialists in the arts and humanities, are still viewed as marginal or irrelevant. Our experience within LabStudio, however, clearly demonstrates that seemingly unrelated, open-ended, data-, systems- and technology-driven programs are not mere alternatives to the more traditional design studio or hypothesis-led research, but represent complementary, iterative and reciprocal approaches that benefit all participants. LabStudio is now viewed as a new paradigm for design thinking and has inspired other schools of architecture internationally to borrow and mimic the model that Sabin and Jones invented.

FOOTNOTES

1. "Research and Design," Sabin+Jones LabStudio, accessed July 2014, http://www.labstudio.org/research.html.

2. Jones, Peter Lloyd. "Context Messaging: Modeling Biological Form." Models 306090 11 (2008): 34-40.

3. Sabin, J. & Jones, P. "Nonlinear Systems Biology and Design: Surface Design" in Acadia 2008: Silicon + Skin, Biological Processes and Computation, ed. Kudless, A., Oct. 16-19, pp. 54-65, 2008.

4. Ihida-Stansbury, K., McKean D., Gebb, S., Martin J., Stevens, T., Nemenoff, R., Akeson, A., Vaughn J. and Jones, P.L. (2004). The paired-related homeobox gene Prx1 is required for pulmonary vascular development. Circ. Res. 94:1507-1514

5. Barabasi, Albert-Laszlo and Bonabeau, Eric. "Scale-Free Networks." Scientific American, May 2003: 60-69.

6. Ihida-Stansbury, K., McKean D., Gebb, S., Martin J., Stevens, T., Nemenoff, R., Akeson, A., Vaughn J. and Jones, P.L. (2004). The paired-related homeobox gene Prx1 is required for pulmonary vascular development. Circ. Res. 94:1507-1514

7. Sabin J, Lucia A, Jones PL (2009). Branching morphogenesis. Science. 327: 945 http://www.sciencemag.org/content/327/5968.cover-expansion (COVER FEATURE).

JENNY E. SABIN's work is at the forefront of a new direction for 21st century architectural practice — one that investigates the intersections of architecture and science, and applies insights and theories from biology and mathematics to the design of material structures. Sabin is Assistant Professor in the area of Design and Emerging Technologies in the Department of Architecture at Cornell University. She is principal of Jenny Sabin Studio, an experimental architectural design studio based in Philadelphia and Director of the Sabin Design Lab at Cornell AAP, a hybrid research and design unit with specialization in computational design, data visualization and digital fabrication. Sabin's clients and funders include companies and foundations such as Nike Inc., the National Science Foundation, the American Philosophical Society Museum, the Exploratorium and the Frac Centre. She is co-founder of LabStudio, a hybrid research and design network, together with Peter Lloyd Jones. Sabin holds degrees in ceramics and interdisciplinary visual art from the University of Washington and a master of architecture from the University of Pennsylvania where was awarded the AIA Henry Adams first prize medal and the Arthur Spayd Brooke gold medal for distinguished work in architectural design, 2005. Sabin was awarded a Pew Fellowship in the Arts 2010 and was named a USA Knight Fellow in Architecture, 1 of 50 artists and designers awarded nationally by US Artists. She was recently awarded the prestigious Architectural League Prize for Young Architects by the Architectural League of New York. She has exhibited nationally and internationally most recently at Nike Stadium NYC, the American Philosophical Society Museum and at Ars Electronic, Linz, Austria. Her work was recently exhibited in the internationally acclaimed 9th ArchiLab titled Naturalizing Architecture at FRAC Centre, Orleans, France. Sabin is the recipient of numerous grants, including NSF EFRI SEED, NSF EFRI ODISSEI, AIA Upjohn, Graham Foundation support and a CCA Biennial Faculty Project Award. Her work has been published extensively including in The Architectural Review, Azure, A+U, Mark Magazine, 306090, 10+1, ACM, American Journal of Pathology, Science, the New York Times, Wired Magazine and various exhibition catalogues and reviews. She co-authored Meander, Variegating Architecture with Ferda Kolatan.

PETER LLOYD JONES, when the Sabin+Jones LabStudio was launched; Peter Lloyd Jones was a tenured Associate Professor of Pathology and Laboratory Medicine at the University of Pennsylvania (Penn). He was also a lecturer in architecture and Director/Founder of the Penn-CMREF Center for Pulmonary Hypertension Cell Research at PennMedicine. Jones's work on the molecular and architectural control of lung development (including stem cell differentiation), pulmonary hypertension and breast cancer, has given rise to patents, and his research has been published and/or reported upon in more than 60 peer-reviewed journals and books including The New York Times, National Geographic, Nature and Science. Peter's teaching at the graduate level has included classes at Wharton, as well as at the Penn Schools of Engineering, Medicine & Design, notably with Jenny E. Sabin with whom he founded LabStudio, a hybrid research unit investigating intersections between architectural design and systems biology. In addition to co-developing a core curriculum graduate elective entitled "Non-Linear Systems Biology & Design", Jones also developed and taught a hands-on cell and molecular workshop for residents and fellows in Penn's Department of Pathology and Lab Medicine. Additional workshops have been taught both nationally and internationally, notably at the Smart Geometry Workshop in Barcelona. Work from his lab and LabStudio has been widely published and exhibited both here and abroad, receiving a number of honors and awards including the Upjohn Prize from the American Institute of Architects, and 1st prize in the 2010 National Science Foundation/American Association for the Advancement of Science International Visualization Challenge. Jones is the recipient of numerous grants and awards, including R-01 and PPG support from the NIH, AHA and the NSF, as well as the American Physiological Societies' Giles Filley Award for Excellence in Respiratory Medicine. Currently, he is living in Philadelphia and is co-authoring a monograph entitled "LabBook", and is preparing grants aimed at providing funding for his research into lung stem cell biology & novel therapeutic tools for the treatment and diagnosis of pulmonary arterial hypertension using tools developed in LabStudio.

DIGITAL DESIGN AS A MATERIAL PRACTICE

LEIRE ASENSIO VILLORIA AND DAVID MAH

As the design of the constructed environment is often regarded as a material practice, there has been some apprehension of how it may develop or transform with regard to the general adoption of digital media and computational tools within the design process.

The popular association between mathematical abstraction and computation often limits the capability for the design professions to recognize its resonances with actual material practices. This subsequently facilitates the general perception of a loss of material engagement and craft with their adoption in the design fields.

However, it has also been widely understood and most famously articulated by Robin Evans that the long established convention that assigns drawing as the authoritative notation system for coordinating the act of material assembly and construction has in fact already distanced designers from immediate contact with the artifacts and environments that they create.

While, the widespread integration of CAD, image manipulation and post production software may have flourished in the design professions, the persistence of these long standing design approaches are typically reinforced by this established engagement with digital media. These uses of computation for developing software that for all intents and purposes transpose existing analogue drafting practices to a graphical user interface typically reinforce traditional design processes and all its associated characteristics including the remoteness of the designer from immediate material action.

Through the development of a maturing series of alternative digital design approaches that more explicitly leverage computational processes, the abstraction and distance that designers have been accustomed to may be reconsidered through digital workflows that have a more immediate relationship between design, analysis, simulation, delivery and actualization. It is possible that this may allow for a return to a more explicitly material practice for design, overturning the concerns raised by amongst others: Richard Sennett of a loss of embodied knowledge or craft in the discipline vis a vis the adoption of digital tools.

The maturing engagement with digital media and computation in design practice has fruitfully generated multiple design approaches that occupy a wide spectrum of ambitions and motivations. This spans from the removal of the figure of the author through the use of data, simulation or stochastic processes as organizational devices to the digital arms race aimed at supporting more and more exotic design signatures. As a result it now becomes harder to address the engagement with digital media and computation in design as a singular practice and as a result; within this panoply, it is also possible to locate and position a design practice armed with a renewed engagement with material.

A productive approach to the deployment of computation in design for us has been to locate resonances and continuity with older practices that predate the recent "big bang" in digital design. One particular line of exploration that has provided a consistent point of reference is the study of what may be called "universal" material systems. These typically illustrate a partiality towards material strategies that allow for an open relationship to the circumscription or the framing of constructed artifacts and environments. This strategy reorients our conceptions away from the assumption that the constructed artifacts and environments we operate on be conceived as complete and whole.

For us the study and investigation into systems rather than the typical focus on singular artifacts is a fruitful area of consideration from which a number of more systematic design explorations may be derived. The fact that much of architectural and urban practice is already defined by the deployment of standard systems or is alternatively regulated through rules and codes riles a demand for designers of the built environment to actively reengage and adopt the role of open systems for the discipline. At one scale this operates in close proximity to the scope of product designers for constructive systems and on the other it requires the designer to translate a series of ambitions into codes that may be actualized and transformed by different agents over varying timescales.

This has urged us to take up computation within design processes that may be employed to address a range of scales. Far from the plaintive sentiment towards the assumed scale-less quality associated with digital design, it has allowed for the development of a design practice that engages and operates across scales,

(Re)fabricating Nervi by Sofia Koutsenko, Javier Martin Fuentes, Johannes Staudt, Juan Pablo Ugarte developed in Leire Asensio's (Re) Fabricating Tectonic Prototypes elective course at Harvard's GSD, Spring 2013

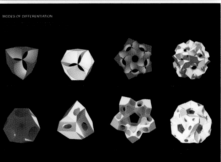

(Re)fabricating Fuller by Yun Fu, Chen Hao Lin, Ricardo Solar, Juan Yactayo developed in Leire Asensio's (Re) Fabricating Tectonic Prototypes elective course at Harvard's GSD, Spring 2013

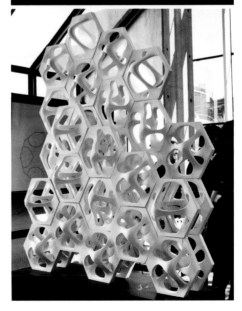

(Re)fabricating Hauer by Xin Lin, Olga Mesa.Lingli Tseng, Rachel Dickey developed in Leire Asensio's (Re) Fabricating Tectonic Prototypes elective course at Harvard's GSD, Spring 2014

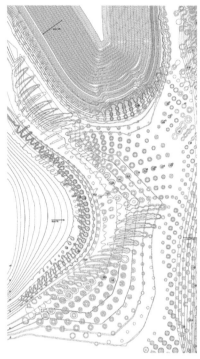

Landscape field overlaid with simulation of deposition and scour over time by Zi Gu and Jisoo Kim instructed by David Mah in the Fabricating Landforms Workshop at Harvard's GSD, Spring 2013

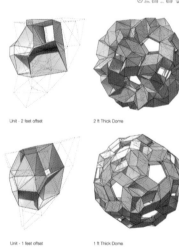

Unit - 2 feet offset   2 ft Thick Dome

Unit - 1 feet offset   1 ft Thick Dome

(Re)fabricating Fuller by Yun Fu, Chen Hao Lin, Ricardo Solar, Juan Yactayo developed in Leire Asensio's (Re) Fabricating Tectonic Prototypes elective course at Harvard's GSD, Spring 2013

addressing a wide scope of concerns within a varied yet consistent mode of operation. This consistency is something that deliberately echoes the growing awareness of a series of organizational processes that enable a number of recurring material arrangements that appear across a wide range of mediums and scales.

It offers a form of material practice that elaborates on the systematic definition of the iterative and/or recursive processes that give rise to various material formations. It also presents a model for material definition that may be more open ended, capable for growth as well as mutability, sharing many of the aspirations of an earlier theory of additive architecture proposed by Jorn Utzon.

In the following projects developed through our research as well as teaching, a series of widely diverging scales of operation are elaborated in order to offer a case for a consistent model of design practice that may leverage computation to address the material articulation of designs across diverse scales and scope. Through these projects, a number of possible approaches for engaging with digital tools in design as a material practice may be offered.

(Re)Fabricating Tectonic Prototypes

The following collection of projects developed within an elective course offered by Leire Asensio over a number of years at the Harvard GSD are framed by a general ambition to develop explorations in digital design, fabrication and parametric tools that is equally informed and enriched by historical precedent while still maintaining a speculative and novel outlook. As part of this reconsideration of existing models, the projects revisit older examples of designers who had been especially attentive to the development of patented and often prefabricated construction systems.

These precedents include the systemic designs of Jorn Utzon, Miguel Fisac, Buckminster Fuller, Pier Luigi Nervi, Felix Candela and Erwin Hauer. Through the course, these exemplars have been reconsidered in light of contemporary computational practices of design and production

Geometric description techniques as well as various models for simulating and describing material behavior developed for these precedent systems are studied and extended into digital associative and simulation models.

Integrating as many aspects of material design (from geometric design, to performance simulation to defining the modes of fabrication and assembly), the projects developed in the course extend the modern precedents into the more contemporary concerns for flexibility, adaptation and in parallel; material as well as performance specificity. While learning from the precedents, these projects also question the typically optimizing and standardizing impulses of the original designs and as a result focus more on the definition of techniques and workflows that allow for generating many different instantiations, rather than an optimal solution.

The re-evaluations of the precedents' performance are also drivers in the design process, allowing for the reconsideration of these prototypes relative to many other performance criteria beyond the originals concerns. From the transformation of Nervi's columns from cast in place construction to the development of flexible and reconfigurable yet still structural wooden tile units to the focus on diffuse lighting effects in the redefinition of the geodesic sphere, many of the projects locate new interest and potential for these earlier models to address multiple gradients of performance. The extension of these projects from mass producible or on site construction techniques to digitally fabricated systems are informed by the same yet more contemporary variations on the concepts of additive architecture.

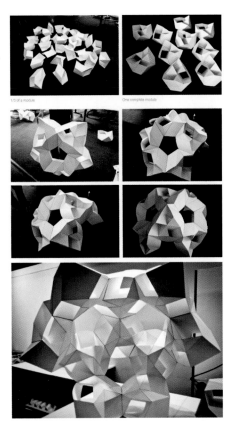

(Re)fabricating Fuller by Yun Fu, Chen Hao Lin, Ricardo Solar, Juan Yactayo developed in Leire Asensio's (Re) Fabricating Tectonic Prototypes elective course at Harvard's GSD, Spring 2013

Surface Deep

Surface Deep is a garden installed within the entry sequence for visitors to the Reford Gardens' Metis International Garden Festival in Quebec, Canada.

Revisiting the garden wall, an element that has been a consistent expressive element within the history of gardening, the entry wall is transformed to form a twisted ribbon-like surface with the help of associative design and modeling techniques. Its undulating form is a response to and gesture for a new entry sequence, framing the entry procession while also embedding an experimental moss garden within its surface.

The surface flips in function and association between a wall, a ground and a cover while creating multiple orientations and different microclimates for the moss garden. The surface's multiple orientations offers a number of different growing environments for the moss, from slopes exposed to sunlight to constantly shaded overhangs.

These microclimates informed the distribution of a number of moss species specific to each condition, where the first 11 units were made with Niphotrichum canescens (a sun-loving species), unit 12 is planted with Callicladium haldanianum while the other units remaining (13 to 22) were made with a mixture of Callicladium

haldanianum and other shade-loving, forest species such as Pleurozium schreberii, Ptilium crista-castrensis and others.

As the surface is defined through the aggregation and coordination of modular yet customizable units, the surface definition is intended to be transformable and potentially extendable. The relative simplicity of the units lends itself towards the possibility of their use as standard products that may be arranged to form a range of synthetic and reconfigurable microclimates.

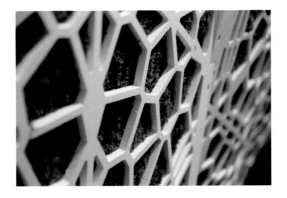

Surface Deep by asensio_mah installed at the Reford Gardens International Garden Festival, 2010 – 2014.)

Digital Media for Design

These projects, developed within an elective course offered by David Mah over a number of years at Harvard's GSD, engage with the potential of a range of emerging digital design techniques as a means to speculate on their potential application in generating novel material arrangements.

In the course this has ranged from Carl Koepcke and Marshall Prado's use of computational simulation to locate the form for pneumatic structures that they deployed as temporary substrates for constructing inhabitable ice landforms to Zheng Cui's leveraging of OOP (object oriented programming) to deploy

stochastic processes from which a material assembly emerges. These projects point towards a speculative impulse in computational design techniques and processes to locate novel material arrangements, potential performance or applications as well as breeding new design sensibilities.

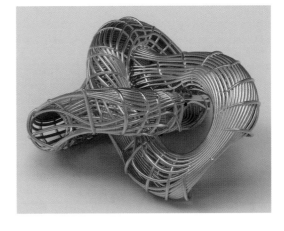

Trefoil Knot developed in David Mah's Digital Media For Design elective course at Harvard's GSD, Spring 2014

Landscape

The application of computational techniques in landscape design is typically associated with mapping and GIS (geographic information systems) with the rare application in actual material design. However,

283 |

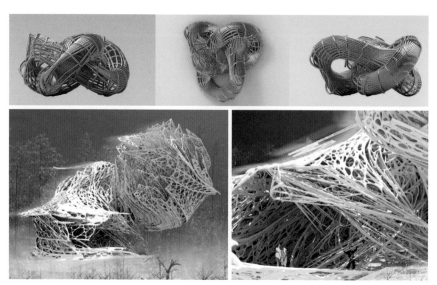

Trefoil Knot developed in David Mah's Digital Media For Design elective course at Harvard's GSD, Spring 2014) (Left) Synaesthetic Pavilion developed in David Mah's Digital Media For Design elective course at Harvard's GSD, Spring 2014) (Right) Synaesthetic Pavilion developed in David Mah's Digital Media For Design elective course at Harvard's GSD, Spring 2014)

the scales of material intervention through digital media are expanding as a result of an extension of the influence of computation in construction beyond the workshop through a number of tools that have the capacity to affect the organization of material at larger landscape scales. Large earth moving or ground keeping equipment linked to GPS or the deployment of robotic machinery, which are already practices in the agricultural and extractive industries, provide a scale of engagement typically not associated with the capacity for control associated with digital fabrication.

Paired with the capacity for material and fluid simulation as well as iterative and recursive processes this allows for landscape designers to systematically engage with the concepts of material transformation and change over time that have long been a central focus of the discipline. The projects illustrated here embed both material behavior (such as natural material angles of repose) as limits in their material design to the possibility of simulating the effect of deposition and scour over time (as in the work of Gu and Kim).

(Left) Pneumatic Ice Landform by Marshall Prado and Carl Koepcke developed in David Mah's Fabricating Grounds elective course at Harvard's GSD, Spring 2012) (Right) Pneumatic Ice Landform by Marshall Prado and Carl Koepcke developed in David Mah's Fabricating Grounds elective course at Harvard's GSD, Spring 2012)

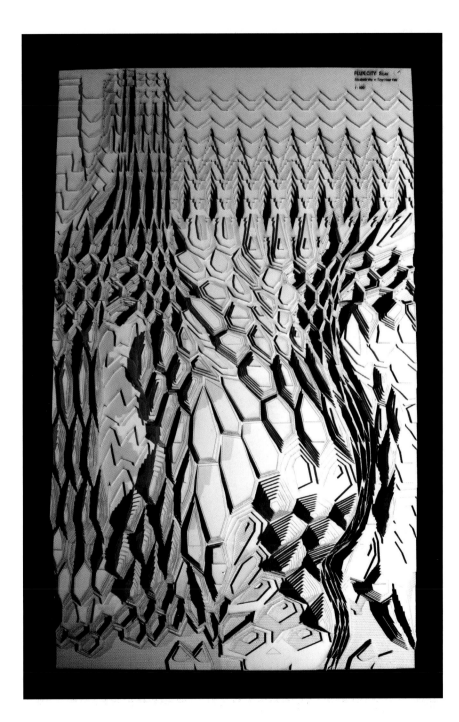

Landscape field
by Tzy Yeh and
Elizabeth Wu
instructed by
Leire Asensio in
the Fabricating
Landforms
Workshop at
Harvard's GSD,
Spring 2013)

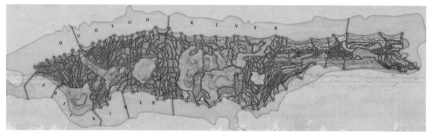

An Adapted
Manhattan Plan by
asensio_mah)

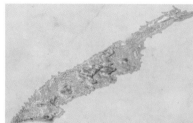

An Adapted
Manhattan aerial
view by asensio_
mah)

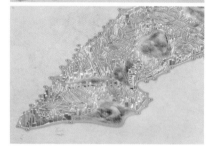

An Adapted
Manhattan Lower
Manhattan by
asensio_mah)

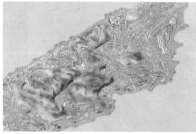

An Adapted
Manhattan Midtown
by asensio_mah)

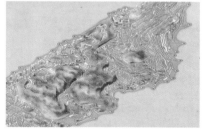

An Adapted
Manhattan Upper
Manhattan by
asensio_mah)

An Adapted Manhattan

The model of urbanization exemplified in Manhattan's 1811 Commissioner's grid resonates with a more general categorization of nineteenth century urban organizations that operate through a process of optimization and regulation. Typically associated with this category of urbanization is the synthesis of particular urban functions into replicable standards, producing a model for urbanization that enforces an assumed formal efficiency and archetype over the particularities of a territory.

Manhattan's urbanization could very well have taken a different approach, where a predecessor to the definitive 1811 plan, Mangin and Goerck's 1801 plan for Manhattan suggests a different sensibility towards urbanization. A sensibility that appropriates and studies existing or given conditions as the framework for its definition. Rather than an engineered exercise in optimization based on ideal efficiencies, Manhattan's urbanization may have evolved as a negotiation with and adaptation to the existing.

Through the analysis and reading of the site in its pre development state as recorded in the 1865 Viele map, the following series of speculative drawings and imagery riff off the hypothetical narrative of an alternative

Manhattan that emerges and evolves out of triggers both embedded and latent within the site. Topography as well as hydrological processes offer some of the initiating patterns that reorient the simplicity of the cadastral and infrastructural grid into a highly differentiated framework for urban growth.

The Commissioner's grid's relative neutrality and standardization offers a model for adaptability that benefits from redundancy as well as a rudimentary formalism that supports the easy replication and repurposing of city blocks. Our speculative adapted Manhattan, on the other hand, presents an intricate ecology that invites its colonizers to identify their respective niches within its elaborate network.

The formation of an infrastructural network is developed by adapting and reorienting the vectors of movement to negotiate its swelling geomorphology and to cultivate the island's surface hydrology. This reorients the development of the bundled infrastructural and cadastral grid from the actualization of a standard idealized functionality to the possibility of an organization that materializes from the function of adaptation. The resulting performance or functioning of this emergent organization as a plane for colonization no longer results from assumptions of linear relationships between form and its subsequent function but is a byproduct. It presents a conundrum in a number of parallel functional values that are often mistaken as mutually interdependent and interchangeable. The speculative re-imagination of an adapted Manhattan invites a split between these often bundled understandings of function.

LEIRE ASENSIO-VILLORIA is a registered architect and studied architecture at the ETSASS and she received her diploma in architecture (with honors) from the Architectural Association.

Asensio-Villoria is currently a lecturer at Harvard's Graduate School of Design. She was a design studioinstructor in graduate design school at Architectural Association and a Visiting Lecturer in Architecture at Cornell University's AAP.

In 2002, Asensio-Villoria, together with David Mah, founded asensio_mah, a multi-disciplinary design collaborative active in the design of architecture, landscape design and master planning. Asensio_mah have exhibited and lectured internationally. Casa Q, a new build residential commission recently completed in Spain, integrates digital fabrication techniques with traditional construction practices as well as landscape engineering and design.

DAVID MAH is an architect with parallel interests in landscape and urban design concerns. David Mah is currently a lecturer at Harvard's Graduate School of Design. Previous to Harvard, he has taught at Cornell University's departments of Architecture as well as City and Regional Planning and in the postgraduate design Landscape Urbanism program at the Architectural Association in London. David has been collaborating with Leire Asensio Villoria as asensio_mah since 2002.

NICK PUCKETT

IF MATERIAL IS THE NEW SOFTWARE, THEN HOW DO I WRITE IT?

—

ESTABLISHING AN OPEN SOURCE TOOL-CHAIN FOR RESPONSIVE MATERIAL DESIGN AND FABRICATION

NICK PUCKETT

The inextricable link between architecture and technology is famously expressed in Cedric Price's statement that "Technology is the answer, but what was the question?". The technology portion of the quote is what is typically given the attention, but it is also important to remember the vital role of the question. New technologies are still

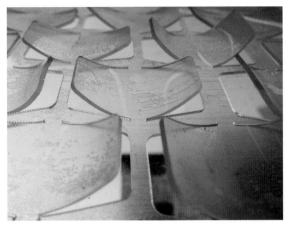

Figure 1: Investigation of the prototype as a responsive façade system.

an important driver of design, but the role that architects play in its development has drastically changed. Price's statement also could be seen as an assumption that technology is an external force rather than a byproduct of project and prototype development. As architects take an active role in the creation of the technology as well as the techtonics of the built environment the role of what that *question* might be has become an important driver of research. This integration of computational research into the architectural paradigm has created a new branch of architectural design that encompasses digital tool-making, robot wrangling, and ubiquitous computing. This trajectory began with the simple coopting of technologies from other disciplines and has become a full-blown outbreak of new architectural tools enabled by an ever-growing open source community of developers. These tools, much like architecture itself, have an intended purpose and an open-ended potential that is realized through use, reflection, and adaptation. The international community of open source designers and developers has formed an online ecology to create, test, and adapt new tools at a rapid pace. Working prototypes can be released into the wild almost instantly to a pool of motivated users who test and adapt the technologies within a variety of contexts. This paradigm began with digital tools for complex form-making and analysis, but more recently this field has focused on the role of computation and intelligence within the physical realm. The expansion of what is considered the domain of designers now includes digital fabrication, robotics, and responsive environments. As the domain of architecture expands further this issue of "what was the question?", becomes even more important. The realms previously seen as "beyond" the scope of architecture have been integrated through a process that begins by someone framing the question within an architectural language so that the wider community can participate in attempting to answer it. This democratization of technologies should be seen as a positive force, but as the line continually moves, the realms still beyond the reach of designers become more obscure. This process has now reached an interesting moment when many of the fields we have expanded toward,

Figure 2: A polymer sample created was laser cut to investigate the potential of manipulating the cured samples at a geometric level.

such as computer science, are moving towards the architectural domain in their research. Hardware development and 3d printing have brought focus back to the physical from the digital or cyber, and a great deal of scientific research is occurring on programming at the biological, nano, or chemical level. As this type of programming becomes more or temperature sensors to gather data, an electronic microcontroller for processing the data, and electric motors to actuate a response to the commonplace and accessible within the scientific community, claims that "Material is the new software" are now coming from the design community. Physical programming is not new to the architectural realm, as any structure can be understood as the "calculation" of the forces and matter that are connected, but physical material actively adapting to those conditions presents a new set of opportunities.

We are currently at a stage where the potential of responsive material can be seen, but their creation is beyond the scope of our current tools and knowledge base. Or to put it in Price's terms– we don't know the question, and without the question(s), the now massive architectural research and development community is stuck in the same situation that previously pervaded software and then hardware development. It now seems distant, but in the very near past designers relied on external "experts" to create and release the software tools they needed, design the sensing and actuating systems, and control

Figure 3: The test setup of the curing machine within the lab. A fume hood is needed for the curing process.

their robotic fabrication armies. Just as these domains were once seen as too difficult, it is now time to expand the design community's toolset to material programming. This expansion presents a fundamental shift in the given variables of computational design in its current state as it formally decouples computation and electricity, but it also presents a new range of potentials. What is at stake is creating a new relationship between the built environment and sources of energy by embedding intelligence into material.

Developments in low power computing and high capacity batteries have miniaturized and extended the range and mobility of computing, but material programming creates an altogether different set of possibilities. Take for example a responsive façade system that opens or closes based on current light levels and temperatures. In the electromechanical model the system would use a series of electronic light or temperature sensors to gather data, an electronic microcontroller for processing the data, and electric motors to actuate a response to the given conditions. In this model, the complexity and energy requirements of the system are exponentially scalar in relationship to the number of façade units. The more units you have, the more electricity it requires. This is problematic if the overall goal of such projects is to conserve electricity, as this methodology inherently requires electricity to save electricity. Programming at the material level collapses these discreet physical and electrical components into a chemical mechanism whereby the system utilizes embodied energy and local environmental conditions to sense and respond. This method creates a fully modular system where more units provide more granularity of response, not more electricity as each single unit is wholly autonomous. This method moves beyond notions of electricity and into energy by interfacing directly with a variety of sources including heat, light, or moisture rather than first converting these energy sources to electricity. This ability for designers to create behaviors at scales ranging from the microscopic to the urban presents a new domain for architects to work within, but the initial steps toward this goal need to be made.

Developing the Questions: Project BlackBox

It is no longer enough to talk in science fiction terms about how these new types of smart materials *could* affect design, so to return to Price, it might now be "Technology is the answer, but where do I start?" To begin the development of these questions this a class of smart materials known as shape-memory materials were investigated. Shape memory materials have the ability to dramatically alter their shape up to 400 percent in response to external stimuli. These stimuli are typically based on temperature, but can be programmed to other environmental factors as well.[1]

Figure 4: Chemicals used for the creation of shape-memory polymer. The ratio between the monomer and the cross-linker determine the response temperature of the material.

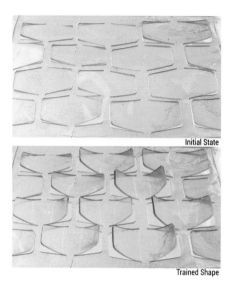

Initial State

Trained Shape

Figure 5: The polymer can move between its target and initial shapes in response to a programmed temperature.

Shape memory polymers (SMPs) are a class of this material that was first discovered in the 1980s, and like other polymers it can be molded or formed into surfaces.[2] The main variable for SMPs is the Glass Transistion, a value that determines the point at which the material changes states. In the case of temperature responsive materials, the Glass Transistion is the specific temperature at which the form can be molded to a temporary shape. Once the temporary shape is stored, if the material is heated beyond the glass transition again, it will deform itself back to its original state.[3] This key value of a shape memory material is the main factor in determining its behavior and is "programmed" into the material when it is created.

  SMPs have been created to respond to stimuli such as light, magnetism, or moisture in the same way, using a specified glass transition point within each stimulus.[4] The applied research in the field has seen SMPs used in projects ranging from medical applications such as smart drug delivery mechanisms, automotive actuators, and morphing aircraft wings.[5] There is a great deal of information available on these materials, and they are available from specialty suppliers, but this research seeks to open up the entire material formulation and creation process to those outside of material science. These research goals have taken shape as *Project BlackBox*. The aim of Project BlackBox is to bring the DIY and open source methodologies of software/hardware development to the realm of material science. The first step toward this goal involved two parallel strands of research

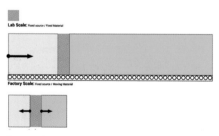

Lab Scale: Fixed source / Fixed Material

Factory Scale: Fixed source / Moving Material

Figure 6: Curing methods used at the existing laboratory and factory scales as well as the proposed prototype scale.

into the methods of creating shape memory polymer. One strand was a hands-on in depth look at how polymer is produced within a material science laboratory, and the second looked more generally at how polymer was created in a variety of scales and contexts. The latter revealed that production within this field occurs at 2 very distinct scales: the material science laboratory and the material factory. The material science

Figure 7: Filling a three-part mold with polymer solution.
Figure 8: Removing the cured polymer sample from the mold.

lab is focused on developing new materials via small samples and the factories are focused on producing those materials at a very large scale. Typically the labs develop materials without any specific function in mind, and this distinct separation opens up the potential for a third scale in the overall scope: the material prototype. The goal for the material prototype scale is to design and create materials within the lab setting, but to produce sheets that can be used in real-world test applications rather than small samples.

Since the material science lab is the focus for where this scale of work can be created, an in-depth study was done of the methods and tools used to create polymer within this setting. At its most basic level this process is achieved within four stages. Firstly, the 3 ingredients of the polymer: a monomer, a cross-linker, and a catalyst are mixed together at a given ratio. This ratio between the monomer and the cross-linker is what determines the Glass Transition (in this case temperature) of the SMP. The catalyst is determined by a basic percentage of the overall amount of the monomer/cross-linker mixture. It is fundamentally a one variable system and by adjusting this ratio of the mixture the response temperature of the materials can be programmed anywhere in the range of -30C to 70C.[6] The mixture is then poured into a three-part mold typically comprised of 2 sheets of glass, a Teflon spacer, and a series of clips to hold the mold together. The mold is then placed within a high intensity UV curing machine that cures the mixture to a

solid sheet. The shape of this sheet determines the original shape that the polymer will return to once it has been deformed. Once the mold is remove from the curing machine it is taken apart and the material is washed to remove any uncured solution. Overall, it is a process similar to creating UV cured resins, but the energy required for curing is much higher.

Figure 9: Ultra-violet light emitting diodes

This process is very straightforward within the confines of the Material Science Laboratory, but it is also limited by the nature of the lab's typical work of producing material samples. After studying this process it became clear that the primary hindrance to creating larger material prototypes within the lab was the size of the curing machine. This very specialized piece of equipment was produced to perform the very specific task within the typical functions of the lab. Larger sizes of material are not needed within this process, so the machines do not currently exist to produce them. In response, this phase of work focused on creating a curing machine based on readily available parts that could create larger sheets, but occupy a small footprint within the confines of the lab setup. The idea was to shift away from seeing the curing process as a machine that is purchased and examine the base functionalities needed to perform the task. It was determined that there are two basic factors that enable the curing process: the wavelength of the UV light (nm) and the energy intensity of the light ($mWcm^2$). Depending on the base materials used, the polymer is cured by applying a specific wavelength of UV light and achieving the minimum energy requirements as dictated by the base chemicals to create the chemical reaction. Using these parameters as a guide, UV leds were sourced that matched the given characteristics required.

Given the high cost of these leds, it was not possible to create a fixed grid large enough to create a usable sheet of material. The solution was to mount the curing lamps onto a linear actuator that would pass over the material in a fashion similar to a document scanner. The initial test of the curing system utilized the all of the other existing protocols of material creation (mixing, mold, etc) and substituted itself for the existing curing

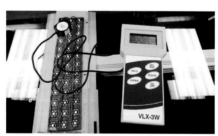

Figure 10: Testing the wavelength and energy output of the curing leds.

Figure 11: First test of the polymer curing machine

equipment. This test yielded a small sample of polymer and confirmed the viability of the DIY curing system. At this stage a first series of experiments were carried out with the material on the methods of manipulating the material after the curing process.

These experiments uncovered that the SMPs could be laser cut or etched using standard equipment, which opens up another line of research in the realm of pattern and geometric response. Overall, the focus of this first curing prototype was to establish the basic viability of creating a DIY system and determining the parameters involved at each stage. Though these first samples were not much larger than what was possible with the existing lab equipment, the

295|

DIY curing machine was created from widely available components at a cost of less than $1/10^{th}$ of the commercially available version.

The lower cost created a very different relationship to the machine, as it was no longer using a very expensive instrument that should be carefully operated. Instead it became a device that could be

Figure 12: A moldless forming system was developed to allow greater levels of experimentation within the chemical mixtures.

hacked, altered, and experimented upon with a much greater degree of abandon. This new working method led to the second phase of the work, which focused on using the newly created curing machine as a testbed for experimentation within the polymer creation process. Other portions of the creation process were also investigated, and specifically, the forming stage also seemed ripe for innovation as the needs of the material produced were changed. First a new type of mold was created to deal with the problem of releasing a larger piece of material from the mold. Also, greater volumes of the liquid polymer mixture required more secure sealing of the mold. After a series of these experiments with the new molding system it became apparent that an entirely different approach was needed. Rather than created a glass mold that rested on another sheet of glass within the machine a new method was developed that cured the polymer directly on the glass bed of the machine. Though the overall form of the polymer created from this method was less controlled, it allowed for a previously unavailable potential of mixing multiple mixtures within a single sheet.

In this way, the mixtures were created to match the multiple transition temperatures and were then poured onto the surface and then cured into a single sheet. This process was tested within the Beyond Mechanics research cluster at Smart Geometry, which allowed other designers to experiment with the methods. These series of tests created a previously unseen result: bistable shape-memory polymer. Unlike typical SMP the bistable polymer was pretensioned to curl as a base shape, but would release the tension at the preprogrammed

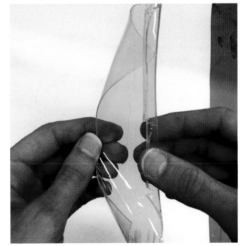

Figure 13: Bistable shape memory polymer created from moldless curing method.

glass transition temperature. This type of behavior creates the basis for a temperature driven actuator by removing the need to program the temporary shape. The first small breakthrough was made possible simply by interfacing the process to a group of designers and signals the potential of this work as it becomes more mainstream.

Asking the Questions

Though the curing process was the first case study within Project BlackBox, the overall goal of establishing an open source toolchain remains larger. When examined holistically, the areas of research needed to establish the toolchain fall under four distinct categories: Material acquisition, Polymer formulation/ mixing, curing, and material post-production. The initial research can be understood as a general audit of the process, and each of these stages has distinct issues to be overcome. Establishing the questions to be solved allows for future work to be done within each sub area.

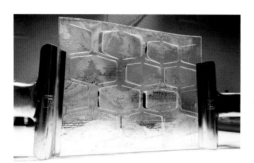

Figure 14: A secondary test to develop responsive perforation patterns within the polymer sheets

Material Acquisition

Currently the raw materials needed to create these materials are limited in availability to labs/universities as they are relatively toxic. Suppliers must establish that customers are part of an approved organization before they will sell the material. Many Universities currently have well-established relationships with these suppliers through other departments, so there is a distinct pathway to obtaining them.

Formulation / Mixing

Beyond the basic lab equipment needs of a gram scale, the difficulty in this stage of the process is based around the need for all work with the chemicals to be performed within a fume hood. The materials are toxic and cannot be used within an open environment.

Curing

The curing process is limited by the availability of the uv leds and the need for fume extraction during the process. When the solution is cured an off-gas is produced that must be filtered. Similar to the issues with formulation and mixing, the need for fume extraction or collection is the greatest challenge in the overall process.

The most important finding of this stage of the research was that the idea to bring the realm of material programming to designers seems remarkably possible. The skills and toolsets that are needed for this work- custom fabrication systems, electronic actuation/

sensing, and material simulation are currently being developed within the design community and it would only be a small move to focus them into this new area. Much like the development of robotic fabrication techniques, University research labs have a key role to play in the initial stages of this work as they have access to the materials and equipment needed for the development process. Future stages should allow for this infrastructure to be bypassed, but currently it is a vital part of the production methods. If architectural design is to play a role in shaping these highly relevant technologies of the future it is vital that it takes an active role in its development. Otherwise we will once again be relegated to a role where we might know that technology is the answer, but we can't do anything about it.

FOOTNOTES

1. Ji F, Zhu Y, Hu J, Liu Y, Yeung L, Ye G. Smart polymer fibers with shape memory effect. Smart Mater Struct 2006;15:1547–54.
2. Behl M, Lendlein A. Shape-memory polymers. Mater Today 2007;10:20–8.
3. Lendlein A, Langer R. Biodegradable, elastic shape-memory polymers for potential biomedical applications. Science 2002;296:1673–6.
4. Yang B, Huang WM, Li C, Li L. Effects of moisture on the thermomechanical properties of a polyurethane shape memory
polymer. Polymer 2006;47:1348–56.
5. Yin WL, Fu T, Liu JC, Leng JS. Structural shape sensing for variable camber wing using FBG sensors. In: SPIE international
conference on smart structures/NDE, San Diego, USA, Proceedings of the SPIE 7292 2009,72921H:1-10, 8–12 March, 2009.
6. Kim BK, Lee SY, Lee JS, Baek SH, Choi YJ, Lee JO, et al. Polyurethane ionomers having shape memory effects. Polyme 1998;39:2803–8.

NICK PUCKETT is the founding director of AltN Research+Design, a design practice focused on creating dynamic links between software, robotics, biological agents, chemical engineering, and material behavior that generate new potentials for the design of intelligent environments. The work of AltN Research has been exhibited in venues including the The FRAC Centre, Venice Architecture Biennale, International Biennial of Contemporary Art of Seville, and the Art Institute of Chicago. The work has also been published in the books including Fabricate: Making Digital Architecture, Hyperlinks, and Inside Smart Geometry. Nick is currently an Assistant Professor in the Digital Futures Initiative at OCAD University and has previously taught within departments of architecture, design, chemical and electrical engineering, and computer science. He is also the co-director of the ANThill research lab, which has developed collaborative projects with partners including Autodesk Research to Marina Abramovic.

MATIAS DEL CAMPO

AUTONOMOUS

TECTONICS

II

„The machine has no feelings, it feels no fear and no hope ... it operates according to the pure logic of probability. For this reason I assert that the robot perceives more accurately than man. „ -----------------------MAX FRISCH, Homo Faber: A Report

The Postdigital Shift – a preface

Computational tools have become a standard in the discipline of architecture, in that extent we can think of a saturation of the field with computational tools. From early design stages, to visualization to the execution of building designs, every aspect of the industry is dominated by the use of computers and software. Insofar computational tools do not form the exception but have become today´s standard, the rule, the norm. The consequence is not necessarily the omnipresence of sophisticated applications, on the contrary the predominant method relies on the translation of conventional, pre-digital, design methods such as the drafting of plans and sections and visualization of preconceived ideas. This can be described as computerized methods in contrast to the opposite end of the spectrum which relies on computational ideas1. These will be the field of inquiry for this paper. Considering the ubiquitous presence of digital tools in the discipline, we can consider our current stage as the dawn of the Postdigital Age the initial fascination with the opportunities inherent in computational tools has evaporated, instead we enter a phase of maturation, of virtuosity and of exploration into alternative design methods relying on computational ecologies consisting of code and computer controlled machinery. The thesis of this paper proclaims a shift away from architecture design paradigms discussing issues of visualization and simulation towards an exploration of in situ matter management, historically a core competence of architecture, within the frame of computer controlled machines.

The rise of 3D printing along with all the opportunities inherent in computer controlled fabrication (Laser Cutting, CNC Milling, Robotics etc.) serve as an indicator for an era of individualized fabrication which has been described by commentators as the Third Industrial Revolution3. Aspects such as machine learning, robot-human cooperation4 and cognitive machines5 are expanding and transforming the entire ecology of production, morphing from economies of scale to economies of agglomeration6. For the discipline of architecture to be part of this massive shift, it is of paramount importance to understand how the Postdigital Age will change the game in terms of architectural production and design, as well as how it produces a novel culture at large. A culture which brokers the realities (and uncertainties) of programming, coding and alternative material systems.

To address the before mentioned paradigmatic shift, from visualization and simulatio to real-time matter management the paper will rely on two examples based on robotic fabrication, both are emergent deposition modeling systems which rely on sets of simple rules to generate highly intricate spatial conditions. The first example is a result, the second example a speculation. The catalogue of terms to describe the results of this explorations include vocabulary such as index, indexicality, emergence and autonomous behavior.

Figure 1: construction of first prototype model at the FabLab of Taubman College, University of Michigan

Robotic construction, autonomous tectonics, thermo formations

The emergent modeling techniques, examined in this paper, were first explored in Autonomous Tectonics, a paper published by the authors at the proceedings of the Design Modeling Symposium Berlin9 2013.

Autonomous Tectonics is based on explorations into emergent robotic fabrication methods and basic research on autonomous material formations. These primary explorations were conducted at Taubman College, University of Michigan (fig.1) in fall 2012 and RPI, the Rensselaer Polytechnic Institute, NY (Fig.2) in fall 2013. This two-pronged approach allowed to explore aggregations of matter, based on rule sets on the one side, and specific material behavior on the other. These included the programming of procedures to infuse a robotic setup with the possibility to, independently, make decisions about material deposition based on criteria defined as a result of the information perceived by the robotic setup10. The information processed by the robot included the building perimeter

Figure 2: explorations in material behaviour based on variations in material and thermoformic properties, RPI, New York, Photo © Jessica Collier 2013

and the scanned result of the initial material deposition. Following this initial tests the focus shifted from the programming, and algorithmic aspect of the investigation to the performative qualities inherent in alternative material systems (Fig.3). Performative in this realm of thinking is not intended primarily as a noun describing utilitarian qualities but as an index of qualities encompassing primeraly intensive properties such as firmness, plasticity, malleability, elasticity, refractiveness, density, anisotropy, translucency and transparency. The technique applied in order to create a spatial formation can be described as emergent modeling. To generate a clear picture of the intention of the paper it is necessary to clarify the criteria that form a technique such as emergent modeling.

Definition of Emergence

There is no common definition of the term emergence, as its application in various fields demands the adaptation of the concept to the respective discipline. Areas of inquiry that make expansive use of aspects of emergence include Biology, Economy, System Theory, Psychology and Art. Biology can be considered a result of the emergent properties of the laws of chemistry11, neurobiological behavior can be described as an emergent condition thus rendering it a field of interest for Psychology and free market theories understand economical ecologies as an emergent condition12. The term itself was coined by the

Victorian philosopher George Henry Lewes, who described the phenomenon as being the result of either a sum or a difference of co-operant forces; their sum, when their directions are the same – their difference, when their directions are contrary. Further, every resultant is clearly traceable in its components, because these are homogeneous and commensurable. It is otherwise with emergents, when, instead of adding measurable motion to measurable motion, or things of one kind to other individuals of their kind, there is a co-operation of things of unlike kinds. The emergent is unlike its components insofar as these are incommensurable, and it cannot be reduced to their sum or their difference.13

In the case of Autonomous Tectonics we will rely on a Biological model, as the observed behaviors and properties clearly indicate a proximity to biological systems. As an instance we can compare it to the observation that in

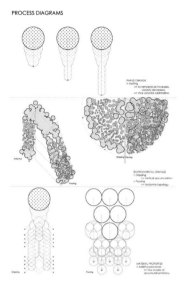

PROCESS DIAGRAMS

Figure 3: Rules defined to observe the emergent behavior of material agglomerations.
© RPI, Matthew Hickey 2013

Biology Emergence is defined by causation and effects as well as their iterative properties. These behavior results in synergetic properties that are described as the underlying cause of evolution itself14. However, it is important to understand that rules, or laws per se do not possess any causal efficacy, meaning they are void of the ability to generate any output whatsoever. In nature those rule based systems are utilized primarily to describe consistent relationships. Agents of causality need to be specified separately15. Specifically if we are discussing a computationally controlled output system we need to address the issue of weak and strong emergence. Weak emergence is a type of emergence in which the emergent property is amenable to computer simulation. This is opposed to the older notion of strong emergence in which the emergent property cannot be simulated by a computer16. Emergent Modeling proposes an alternative mode of thinking in terms of weak or strong emergence in the process of material organization (deposition) Albeit being a computational process the emergent properties of the result are not simulated by any software, rather a trajectory is taken in which the agents of causality, (the applied rules) are the agents of an emergent mode of material aggregation (Fig.4). Similar to a wasp depositing pulp following an instinctual behavior in order to build a nest (Fig.5), the robot does not know the resulting form - the same is the case with the programmer behind the code, penned to provide the machine with a flow of information, in order to change the motion of the robot, and the deposition of material. The elegance of this solution does not unfold itself in respective, preconceived, morphological result, but in the elegance of the underlying set of processes. This can be described as emergent modeling technique.

Figure 4: Emergent properties in a prototype model. Photo © RPI Jessica Collier 2013
Figure 5: A wasp building a nest. Innate behavior as forming agent. Photo © Sanjay Acharya 200

The suspicious index and aspects of indexicality

One result of the initial exploration of emergent modeling is the distinctive discoursive push towards a debate about index and indexicality in architectural production. In order to be able to elaborate on the topic, a clarification is necessary to define the main differences between the terms index and indexical. Both have the same root, the Latin indico17, meaning to show, mark, point out, recommend advice or to indicate, but also to discover and to spy. Index18 is used in a multitude of meanings that range as far as from the realms of mathematics, expressing the raise of a suffix indicating the power, to economics, as a single number calculated from an array of prices or of quantities; to programming where it indicates an integer or other keys defining the location of data within an array, vector or database table, to an alphabetical listing of items and their location, such as terms and names in a book. In a robotic environment we can read the g code as an index of numerical information, a list of operations, which controls the position of the robot within a three-dimensional Cartesian grid. This index however can be read as a list, encompassing the range of possible motions the robot can execute in the process of making.

Indexicality on the other hand, has a different set of meanings. Whereas the index clearly points to an existing set, or list, of operands (objects, rules, numbers, names, materials, ideas, terms) Indexicality operates within the realm of the trace, the artefact, the imprint and ways to read this within the manifested material condition.

Alternatives to architectural alphabets, lists and indices

Index in architecture is defined by two conditions. On the one side the aspects established by the frame defined by the designer. This can be defined by the conventions of architectural representation such as plan and section, as well as by any other model wither this be physical or digital. A predefined set of rules defining the spatial configuration of matter to subdivide (undermine) an object. Following conventions of architectural planning means also simultaneously the application of a specific sequence in terms of time: the holy trinity of architectural production: designing-planning-building. This notion is questioned and interrogated by a notion that proposes the integration of all processes into one: the autonomous behavior of cognitive machines19 integrate aspects of programmed behavior and autonomous decision making to achieve properties of emergence in the built object.

The aspects of index in architecture can encompass a wide array of meanings. Aspects can vary from index trough the design process (the definition of form is per se an index) to a wide range of aspects such as programmatic needs, material restrictions, construction methods, building codes, laws and of course the designer's sensibility. Whereas aspects such as program and materiality can be formulated as belonging to the realm of extensive conditions, aspects of sensibility are included within the realm of intensive notations. The question remains, should these aspects be described within a Deleuzian paradigm, or can they be described as part of a speculative reality, where there would be discrete differentiations between the two states? Are those two states, intensity and extensity in a continuous network condition? Or can they be described as individual objects (Harman, Heidegger) in constant negotiation? The common ground for this line of explanation is the idea that index, as a list, is present in architectural production on a multitude of levels. Every instance that can be assigned a position within a list can be considered a condition of index behavior. The number of Windows, columns, bricks, arches, rooms, corners, square-meters, stairs and rails.

Indexing or Indexicality however relies on activities, on operations within the realm of the trace, the artefact, the imprint and ways to read this within the manifested material condition. In architectural ecologies this would describe indexing of the ground by the building, the indexing of building processes, such as concrete casting, brick stacking. The indexing of materiality through its transformations (clay to bricks, indexing of matter trough chemical transformation in the firing process) Indexing can be described as a process which involves the imprint of an event into a constant spatial condition. In conclusion it can be stated that also the processes in action in Autonomous Tectonic systems are not void of indexicality. In this extent it does not refer to any physical form giving scaffolding, such as formwork leaving an imprint, for example the grain of the wood planks in concrete, but the motion of the robot being an event which creates an imprint in the resulting physical object. The indexical imprint of the negotiation between activity (the robot arm) and materiality (the extruded matter). To reference Peter Eisenman. The Rebstock park project can be interpreted as the result of an event, the imprint of the fold onto the urban grid. It creates an indexing of a geometrical condition onto the urban texture20.

The void of index (but not of indexicality, as we learnt) within the design realm opens new opportunities for the design agents, which are not based on rational and decisions, or sensibility, but on information provided by the emergent behavior of an autonomous construction process. As an initial statement it is important to clarify that the robot does not do anything without first being programmed, in any way, to perform a specific task.

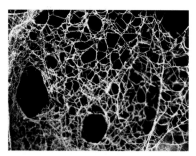

Figure 6: Spider web as result of innate behavior,
Photo © Dominicus Johannes Bergsma 2013

In this instant the task is defined by a coded set of commands that defines deposition and motion, based on information input, and an envelope of construction. As an instance from nature we can use the behavioral patterns of spiders building a web. A spider has a program in order to fulfill the task to build a web. It is not a learned process, but part of its instinctive behavior (Fig. 6). It certainly can be stated that the spider does not design the web, the web emerges out of the process of its construction. Innate behavior21 as an agent of autonomous tectonics. A consequence, and logic step, within the discussed discourse is the debate of aspects of intentionality, of design intention within the discussed methodology. It can be stated that the main points of discussion would encompass a conversation from Formwille to design intention as abstract machine, however this paper does not cover this topic.

Conclusion, speculation and projection

There are three main aspect in terms of the discursive approach covered by this paper. Aspects of Emergence, Aspects of Index and aspects of Indexicality. This elements, and all their definitions, form the explanatory model for Emergent Modeling and Autonomous Tectonics. The main step forward in this ecology of thinking is the critical interrogation of aspects of preconceived form, as well as the prevailing methods of planning in architecture at large. This paper proposes the opportunity to abandon well explored paths in order to explore the potentialities within alternative modes of architectural production, in which (controlled) uncertainty22 becomes an inherent quality and vagueness an integral part of a novel sensibility. The results so far, from both courses, at Taubman college, University of Michigan as well as from the course at RPI, New York can be considered small scale proof of concept models, which allow for further speculation. One of those branches of thought touches on the problem of scalability of the process. There are two main schools of thought regarding this problem. On the one side, the idea that the resulting model from the process can be considered as scaled model of the actual size architectural environment. This would mean that the technique is merely used as device to generate scaled models of a real situation. (Which in fact would ask again for an undermining of the object in order to achieve a construct-able scale) The alternative mode of thinking would regard the process as being the one to one scale. Meaning that designing turns into construction ad hoc. The first prototypes of the concept were built with a large industrial robot, in contrast to this idea the use of swarms of robots would be able to translate the process into an actual 1:1 scale process. This school of thinking is based on the knowledge gained through the initial research in Autonomous Tectonics. Aspects such as Index, Indexicality and Emergence remain the same. The main shift is from the large scale machine, from the big robot arm, that fulfills all the tasks at once, to a swarm intelligence capable of creating similar results, but on a larger scale utilizing smaller machines. The main lineage of thought is to use a redundant system of building agents in order to achieve constructions on site, instead of in the workshop. Once more the example of the wasp and the nest can be stressed, as it is not about the amount of paper pulp one wasp can carry to build the nest, but about the multitude of agents executing a repetitive task to create a highly intricate result, the wasp nest. Several of the elements necessary for such an ecology of construction can be found in the cognitive abilities and precision motoric of contemporary drones such as quadro-copters, hexapods et al.

Figure 7: Drones building a bridge in an Alpine Canyon.
© Matias del Campo 2014

This Swarm Tectonics form the next batch of explorations into alternative design methods in a Postdigital Age. The setup for the next explorations would abandon the industrial robot in favor of drones, hexacopters, which would allow to deposit material (Fig.6). The fabrication workshop has to be abandoned in favor of field experiments with machines controlled by agents of causality and innate behavior. The prediction is that the resulting constructions behave borderline natural, erasing the line between organic and synthetic ecologies.

FOOTNOTES

1. Whilst the former needs computers, as a mean of translating a preconceived idea into digital files to achieve a result, the later does not, as it relies on various forms of computation including but not limited to Analogue Computation and Material Computation.

2. Marjan Colletti, Digital Poetics', Ashgate 2013, Surrey UK, P. 17-18: "Historically, there has been a strong rationalist epistemological approach to digital theory, technology and culture that emphasized processes.....Despite their different biases, both the epistemological theoretical system and my phenomenological/poetic theoretical system attempt to extend digitally into a postvirtual, and postdigital material context of innovative fabrication, extensive applicability and sustainable use."

3. Paul Markillie, The Third Industrial Revolution, The Economist, April 2012, P.46-52

4. David Bourne, My Boss the Robot, Scientific America, Volume 308, Nr.5, New York, May 2013,P.39-41

5. Autonomous Tectonics, Matias del Campo et al, Procedures of the Design Modeling Symposium Berlin 2013, P.58-67

6. Manuel de Landa, Computer and the War Machine, presented at NetAccess, Vienna, Austria 1996

7. Graham Harman, The Quadruple Object, Zero Books, Winchester USA, 2011, P.7-20

8. Albeit Neil Leach being the author who coined the term Swarm Tectonics in his essay Swarm Tectonics a Manifesto for Emergent Architecture (Archis, Nov. 2002) the authors of this paper would like to propose an alternative use of the terminology, precisely describing the properties of collaborative robots on the construction site.

9. Autonomous Tectonics, Matias del Campo et al, Procedures of the Design Modeling Symposium Berlin 2013, P.58-67

10. Robotic system is composed of a Kuka KR100 HA L90 arm, K-1500-3 linear axis, BAK Extruder 6007CS, Canon EOS 600D as optical sensor.

12. Peter A. Corning, The Re-Emergence of Emergence: A Venerable Concept in Search of a Theory, Complexity 7, Lichfield Park, Arizona,2000, P.18-30

12. Jeffrey Goldstein, Emergence as a Construct: History and Issues, Emergence, Lichfield Park, Arizona, 1999, P.49-72

13. G. H. Lewes, Problems of Life and Mind (First Series), London 1875, P.78-92

14. Peter A. Corning, The Re-Emergence of Emergence: A Venerable Concept in Search of a Theory, Complexity 7, Lichfield Park, Arizona,2000, P.18-30

15. Peter A. Corning, The Re-Emergence of Emergence: A Venerable Concept in Search of a Theory, Complexity 7, Lichfield Park, Arizona,2000, P.18-30

16. Mark A Bedau, Weak Emergence, Philosophical Perspectives: Mind, Causation, and World, Vol. 11, Wiley-Blackwell, Hoboken, NJ, 1997 P. 375-399

17. http://www.latin-dictionary.net/definition/23397/indico-indicere-indixi-indictus retrieved 03.20.2014

18. http://en.wikipedia.org/wiki/Index retrieved from Wikipedia, 03.20.2014

19. Cognitive machines in the extent of this conversation are defined as machines with the ability to sense aspects of their environment. This does not imply intelligence, but the possibility of responsiveness and autonomous behavior.

20. See Peter Eisenman, Rebstock Park Project.

21. Konrad Lorenz, Die Rückseite des Spiegels, Versuch einer Naturgeschichte menschlichen Erkennens, Piper & Co Verlag, München 1973, S. 47-54: Instinct or Innate behavior ist he inherent inclination of a living organism towards a particular complex behavior. The simplest example of an instinctive behavior is a fixed action pattern, in which a very short to medium length sequence of actions, without variation, are carried out in response to a clearly defined stimulus.

22. See also the works of Francois Roche

IMAGES CREDITS
Figure 2: explorations in material behaviour based on variations in material and thermoformic properties, RPI, New York, Photo © Jessica Collier 2013
Figure 3: Rules defined to observe the emergent behavior of material agglomerations. © RPI, Matthew Hickey 2013
Figure 4: Emergent properties in a prototype model. Photo © RPI Jessica Collier 2013
Figure 5: A wasp building a nest. Innate behavior as forming agent. Photo © Sanjay Acharya 2008
Figure 6: Spider web as result of innate behavior, Photo © Dominicus Johannes Bergsma 2013
Figure 7: Drones building a bridge in an Alpine Canyon. © Matias del Campo 2014

MATIAS DEL CAMPO studied architecture at the University of Applied Arts Vienna, Austria, where he graduated with distinction. Together with Sandra Manninger he founded the Architecture Office SPAN in 2003. Apart from his role as founder and principal of SPAN, his academic qualifications include an appointment as visiting Professor at the DIA, Dessau Institute of Architecture (Dessau, Germany), the ESARQ, Universitat Internacional de Catalunya, in Barcelona, Spain, a lecturer position at the University of Pennsylvania, UPenn, USA. In fall 2013 he was appointed as Associate Professor of Architecture at Taubman College, University of Michigan. In 2008 and 2010 he served as curator for the ABB, Architecture Biennale Beijing. His main projects include: The Austrian pavilion at Shanghai EXPO 2010; The Microblur project, commissioned by Microsoft Austria and The Austrian Winery Boom, exhibition design for ACF, New York, commissioned by the Architecture Center Vienna. In 2012 the work of SPAN was on show at the Venice Architecture Biennale. In 2013 the work of Matias del Campo and Sandra Manninger was on display at the 9th Archilab Exhibition of the FRAC Center in Orleans France, Naturalising Architecture. His work is part of the permanent collection of FRAC Orleans, the MAK in Vienna and the Albertina, Vienna.

CREATIVE ARCHITECTURE MACHINES

JASON KELLY JOHNSON
CCA & FUTURE CITIES LAB, SAN FRANCISCO

Since the late 1990's architects and designers have typically used commercial CAD software to feed CAM programs to feed CNC machines. These "computer-aided" processes and "numerically-controlled" machines are most often used to increase efficiency and make the prototyping and fabrication processes more routine, faster and cheaper. In architecture and design schools around the world students are increasingly being taught to use standard suites of software and industrial hardware technologies such as laser cutters, robotic mills and 3d printers as ways to precisely model and fabricate the formal and geometric aspects of their designs. Yet these fabrication technologies and machines are rarely interrogated in and of themselves, nor are they explored or hacked in a critical or creative fashion. Why is it that architects and designers are most often taught to be mere users of technology rather than innovators or hackers? Why are the core creative tools of these professions designed by systems engineers? What creative potential exists at the heart of these machines, where bits intermix with atoms, where digital code meets material logic?

The architecture studio and work illustrating this essay sought to engage these questions through an exploration of design and fabrication processes that were novel and untested. Through the production of experimental and speculative fabrication machines the studio endeavored to contribute to a wider debate within architecture about the role architects might play in an emerging world where the lines between the digital and the physical are rapidly blurred, and where architects might become critical and creative builders of both software, hardware and the machines of design, iteration and production. A parallel ambition of the studio was to explore the efficacy of digital processes and their potential to contribute to a wider conversation about architecture, technology and culture.

(Figure 1A, B,C,D) Creative Architecture Machines from the students of the Johnson and Shiloh studio, CCA, 2014

(Figure 2A, B) Creative Architecture Machines from the students of the Johnson and Shiloh studio, CCA, 2014

Architects have always been tasked with creating sets of drawings and documents that guide the construction process including structures, materials, methods and more. Traditionally architects have created representations and codes that are handed off to a contractor, who then employs various trades to fabricate and construct a building or a landscape using whatever means they could. The Creative Architecture Machines studio questioned these traditions and explored what would happen if design and construction processes began to converge. How would the profession of Architecture need to shift as this convergence takes place? Instead of deploying hundreds of workers to complete a building, what if architects were tasked with designing and deploying intelligent and creative robotic machines?

Studio participants explored these ideas through the iterative prototyping of working technologies. In Phase 01 of the semester students created two-dimensional robotic "drawing machines" that responded to indeterminate inputs (sun, wind, sound, etc.) from their environment to create novel drawings, paintings, drippings, etchings, compositions in light and pixels. In Phase 02 students created four-dimensional (X, Y, Z plus time) machines for the production of a radical new class of architecture constructed insitu out of indigenous materials. During this phase students created scaled fabrication machines that approximate full-scale processes at an architectural scale. Students worked back and forth between processes of design, prototyping, playing, hacking, coding, learning and feedback.

The work of the studio was situated at the intersection of architecture, robotics engineering and DIY hacker culture. We explored how allied design fields, such as those inventing new robotic devices, military systems, prosthetic engineering, high-

(Figure 3A, B) Creative Architecture Machines from the students of the Johnson and Shiloh studio, CCA, 2014

(Figure 4A, B) Creative Architecture Machines from the students of the Johnson and Shiloh studio, CCA, 2014

tech clothing, furniture, lighting, automobiles, and more, are latent with new material, spatial and ecological possibilities. The studio was be extremely "hands-on" and asked students to work iteratively and inventively through modes of digital and analog modeling, simulation, fabrication and performance testing. Structured technical workshops covered the use of micro-controllers (Arduino) and a variety of sensors, actuators and other integrated electronic media, as well as modes of parametric modeling (including Grasshopper and Firefly) and rapid prototyping. Everything produced during the studio (including code, fabrication files, and assembly files) were released "open-source" on the Instructables project sharing website (www.instructables.com).

(Figure 5, 6) Creative Architecture Machines from the students of the Johnson and Shiloh studio, CCA, 2014

FOOTNOTES

Creative Architecture Machines is a one semester architecture vertical options studio at the CCA (California College of the Arts) in San Francisco. More information can be found at: http://digitalcraft.cca.edu.

The work illustrating this essay was produced in Fall 2014 in a studio co-taught by Assistant Professor of Architecture Jason Kelly Johnson and mechanical engineer Adjunct Professor Michael Shiloh. Student participants included (in alphabetical order): Ibrahim Al Gwaiz, Matthew Boeddiker, Megan Freeman, Taylor Fulton, Yuliya Grebyonkina, Timothy Henshaw-Plath, Swetha Kopuri, Jeffrey Maeshiro, Mary Rixey, Abelino Robles, Max Sanchez, Mary Sek, Darshini Shah, Cassondra Stevens, Ryan Uy, Jia Wu.

IMAGE CREDITS

All images courtesy of Jason Kelly Johnson

JASON KELLY JOHNSON is a founding design partner of Future Cities Lab, an experimental design and research office based in San Francisco, California. Working in collaboration with his partner Nataly Gattegno, Jason has produced a range of award-winning projects exploring the intersections of design with advanced fabrication technologies, robotics, responsive building systems and public space. Future Cities Lab is at the forefront of exploring how advanced technologies, social media and the internet of things will profoundly affect how we live, work, communicate and play in the future. Their approach to design and making, which has been described as "high performance craft", is also deeply experiential, interactive and materially rich. Future Cities Lab is an interdisciplinary studio employing an adventurous team of designers, architects, technologists, digital craftspeople, urban ecologists and more. Jason is also an Assistant Professor at CCA San Francisco where he co-coordinates the Digital Craft Lab. Jason has also recently collaborated with Andy Payne on the FIREFLY for Grasshopper toolbar. Firefly offers a set of comprehensive software tools dedicated to bridging the gap between Grasshopper the Arduino micro-controller and other input/output devices. It allows near real-time data flow between the digital and physical worlds.

ORKAN TELHAN

DESIGNING WITHIN

—

A SPATIAL THEORY

FOR DESIGNING

BIOLOGIES INSIDE

THE LIVING

Synthetic biology, a field emerging at the intersection of life sciences, biotechnologies, and computational design, is driving research towards a new type of architecture that is practiced at the molecular domain. The field is developing tools and research methods for working with living matter to design novel biological, chemical and computational functions that can be shaped by spatial and computational design.

Today it is possible to design cell-like vesicles for encapsulating new types of living, semi-living, or biological hardware to build new materials, medicine, or biological circuits (Telhan 2012). Such vesicles—commonly known as artificial cells, protocells, or chemical cells (chells)—can function inside living organisms or in external fluidic environments where they deliver chemical, biological, or computational instructions. While the potential of such encapsulations are still being researched, they increasingly find applications in drug delivery—where they are used to transport a biochemical payload to a location inside the body—or for releasing chemicals on the surface of the body such as cosmetic masks or foams.

Based on emerging methods on vesicle-based design, this paper offers a systematic framework to compartmentalize liquid media and build encapsulations, assemblies or structures within the interiority of a living body. The framework specifically focuses on the role of architectural design for living environments where biological and chemical functionalities can be designed and regulated with spatial methods. Being rooted in a different interpretations of structure, spatiality, and computational design, it approaches vesicle-based design at three stages: 1) the design of the basic units of the living out of lipid vesicles called liposomes (Units) 2) how different vesicles can be arranged and assembled for different functionalities and biological behavior (Logic), and 3) the design of the biological contexts where vesicle-based artifacts perform their objectives (Context) within a fluidic environment.

The paper will feature a number of examples for the vesicle-based design framework and discuss the practice of space making—as encapsulation of living matter—that would not only serve for scientific outcomes, but also claim aesthetic, symbolic, and cultural affordances. Here the liquid environment that lies within the living is suggested as a new design space whose private interiority can shift into public domain for hosting new architectures.

A Unit of Spatial Design: Liposome

Liposomes are artificially created spherical vesicles that that are made of lipid molecules. These molecules align and form semi-permeable membranes that can physically and chemically separate an interior space from its outside in liquid media and allow selective exchange between the two environments. Known as the fluid mosaic model, the structure of the membranes are usually made of two layers of natural lipid molecules which consist of a hydrophilic head and a hydrophobic tail. Lipid molecules in the membranes can have different head groups (Singer and Nicolson 1972). They can be positively- or negatively- charged, be non-ionic (non-charged) or zwitterionic (hybrid or neutral)—including both charges. Different head groups allow the membranes to exhibit different electrostatic properties and therefore influence the interactions between different liposomes so that they can attach, repel, or fuse with each other. Due to having both hydrophilic and hydrophobic parts in their composition, the bilayer lipids enclose onto themselves and form spherical cavities when introduced to aqueous environments. During this auto-encapsulation process, other molecules in the environment can be trapped inside. Once formed, various compounds, proteins and ions can flow in and out through the membrane's environment due to the internal and external osmotic pressure difference between the liposome and its environment or the charge difference between the molecules and the membrane. Units can also be loaded after they are formed with ingredients using micro-injection techniques.

Liposome sizes can vary from tens of nanometers to tens of micrometers. They can be produced with a number of methods such as reverse evaporation or sonication and filtered to be made fixed size or as vesicles with identical properties.

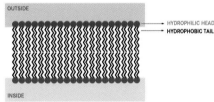

Figure 1: The fluid mosaic model of the structure of liposomes.

Based on their molecular composition, liposome membranes exhibit different phases and change their form depending on their transition temperatures. They stay in rigid form between lower temperatures and their phase temperature and turn into gel form in warmer temperatures. The integrity of liposome membranes can be disrupted with external stimuli—such as changing the PH-level, introducing charged molecules, or applying acoustic pressure from the environment.

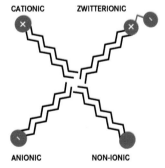

Figure 2: Liposome head groups

The ability to control the size, physical shape, payload, membrane polarity, coating, and durability has made liposomes a very attractive research area since their discovery in 1960s. They have found industrial applications in cosmetics, food and cleaning industries, and pharmacology, in which they are

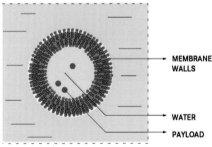

Figure 3: Enclosed bilayers form liposome

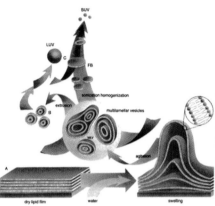
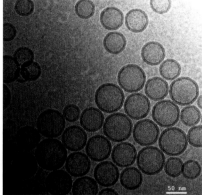

Figure 4: Preparation of Liposomes (Fig 4. image from Vanniasinghe et al. 2008)
Figure 5: Cationic Liposomes (Fig 5. image taken from Battersby et al. 1998)

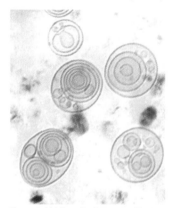

Figure 6: Multilamellar liposomes (Fig 6. image taken from http://www.dr-baumann-turkiye.com)

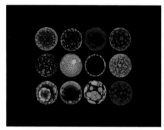

Figure 7: Giant unilamellar and multilamellar vesicles (liposomes) imaged by Dr. Jorge Bernardino de la Serna (Fig 7. image taken from (http://www.nikonsmallworld.com/gallery/search/all/liposome/2

used as carriers for drug delivery or compartments that can host alternative chemical reactions.

Smaldon and co-workers also theorized a liposome-based logic, in which liposomes can become the units for information processing circuits for various types of computation (Smaldon et al. 2010).

A Spatial Context for Living Media

Microfluidic systems are a general name given for single or multi-layer circuits that are built to move around picoliter or microliter amounts of liquids within capillary channels.

They are made of biocompatible transparent materials such as glass, quartz, Polydimethylsiloxane (PDMS), Poly(methyl methacrylate) PMMA or other kinds of thermoplasts, where different geometries are etched or molded using photolithography techniques.

Microfluidic systems are usually equipped with digitally controlled pumps, valves, reservoirs, heating and cooling elements, which can precisely control the flow, mixing, circulation, and storage of multiple liquid streams at different temperatures.

315|

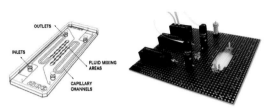

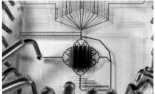

Figure 8: ample Microfluidic chip design from Dolomite Co.
Figure 9: Micfrofluidic workbench with integrated pumping and automated valves from Labsmith Co.
Figure 10: Multi-channel and multi-layer mIcrofluidic chip design from Albert Folch Laboratory.

Among their many uses for conducting biochemical experiments, it has also been demonstrated that such systems can be built as bioreactors for growing and monitoring microorganisms and cell-cultures (Balagaddé et al. 2005) (Pasirayi et al. 2011), used as PCR machines for synthesizing genes (Kong 2008), function like biochips to design proteins (Buxboim et al. 2007), and become interfaces that can separate liquid mixtures—such as milk or blood—into their constituents (Grenvall et al. 2009) (Yang et al. 2005).

Prakash and Gershenfeld demonstrated that it is possible to do computation within liquid circuits by implementing a bubble-based Boolean logic that relies on the precise timing and placement of bubbles within capillary junctions (Prakash & Gershenfeld 2007).

The use of liposomes has been investigated in numerous spatial contexts. While most emphasis is on their *in vitro* use—in which vesicles freely move about within an animal or human body—microfluidics are extensively used during the precise manufacturing of liposomes (Tan et al. 2004). Inside the capillary environment, it is easier to control their transportation, structuring, and interaction with each other. Microfluidics also provide spatial contexts where chemical, biological, physical, electromechanical and computational design principles can be combined with each other.

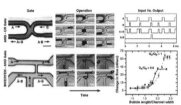

Figure 11: Bubble logic (Prakash & Gershenfeld 2007).

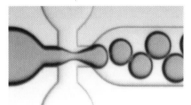

Figure 12: Dolomite Microfluidic chip with X-junction

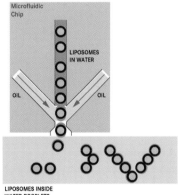

LIPOSOMES INSIDE WATER DROPLETS DISPENSED INTO OIL

Figure 13: In theory, bubble generators with a moving head can disperse different droplet geometries and spatially group them in continuous media.

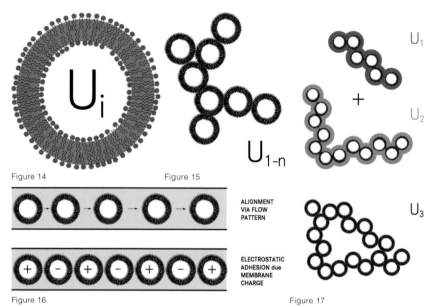

Figure 14   Figure 15

ALIGNMENT
VIA FLOW
PATTERN

ELECTROSTATIC
ADHESION due
MEMBRANE
CHARGE

Figure 16   Figure 17

Liposomes can be encapsulated within liquid droplets using microfluidic droplet generators that have X, Y or T type capillary junctions.

Once captured inside water droplets liposomes can be moved around using different flow strategies. They can be treated both in static and moving design contexts. A liposome vesicle inside a droplet is both a discrete, addressable, and movable unit within the design space, and also an individual element that can be equipped with chemical or biological agency that can determine its own interaction with other units.

Theory of Liposome-based Design

IDENTITY: A self-enclosing liposome can be identified as a unit.

It can be visually marked by staining its membrane with a dye or incorporating a light-emitting biochemical agent such as the green fluorescing proteins as its payload. Magnetic particles or radioactive dyes also offer non-visible tracing options if their use does not interfere with the objectives of the application.

ASSEMBLY: Different liposome units can be grouped together within capillary tubes. Groupings can be non-adhesive and based on accumulation in compartments or alignment caused by flow and circulation conditions when units are forced to float and follow each other in the direction of the flow.

By interleaving vesicles made of membranes with cationic (+) and anionic (-) lipid head groups one after the other, liposomes can be made to adhere to each other electrostatically and form "string-like" structures.

Once they became identifiable, discreet units can still be traced optically or through sensing devices that track their markings.

Different groupings can be assembled into larger structures and become new units. By pumping free floating structures back into the capillaries, units can be reconfigured into different organizations.

TYPES OF UNITS: Liposomes can be characterized into different types of units based on their physical characteristics, contents, and how the units can be used to represent other phenomena.

Biological/Chemical Units: Liposomes are foremost created for encapsulating content and carrying that content to a different location where the ingredients can be part of a reaction. They can also be used as the site where reactions and chemical or biological events such as *in vitro* DNA replication or protein synthesis can take place.

Informational Units: Like bits that represent information by sequential ordering of states (e.g., 101011), liposome streams can be lined up to represent digital information. By loading the vesicles with a traceable marker (e.g., optical dye, electrical charge, magnetic particles, etc.), it is possible differentiate between visible/non-visible, negative/positive states as the liposomes flow through capillary channels.

Geometric Units: By utilizing different membrane adhesion methods

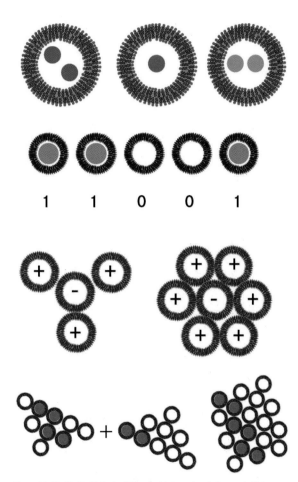

Figure 18, 19, 20, 21: Biological/Chemical, Informational, Geometric Units.

liposomes can form geometrically meaningful formations. They can be lined up to string structures or more advanced constellations. Multiple units can form primitive geometries that can also be grouped to create complex shapes.

Liposomes can exhibit multiple typologies at the same time. They can be assembled into traceable

geometries which can be represented with symbols or numbers. By adding unit groups to each other, one can also create higher level abstractions and compose more complex organizations. Units can not only change features over time (e.g., change color) due to their internal reactions or by incorporating other liposomes, but also change their type. A chemical unit can switch to an information-carrying unit over time, or from application to application.

The polymorphic nature of the units can be utilized during different assembly operations. For example, visual operations can have chemical consequences; biological operations can be visualized by different optical compositions; and strings of liposomes can be composed like machine- or human-readable words and form text-like assemblies as they are prepared for biological or chemical processes.

INTERACTION: The interaction between different types of liposomes is extensively studied and four types of interaction have been commonly reported (Paleos et al. 2011) (Stano & Luisi 2009).

While adhesion can be used for combinatorial structuring of the units (by maintaining their identity), with fusion, incorporation, and division it is possible to design structures with irreversible transformations, which can extend the use of liposomes beyond

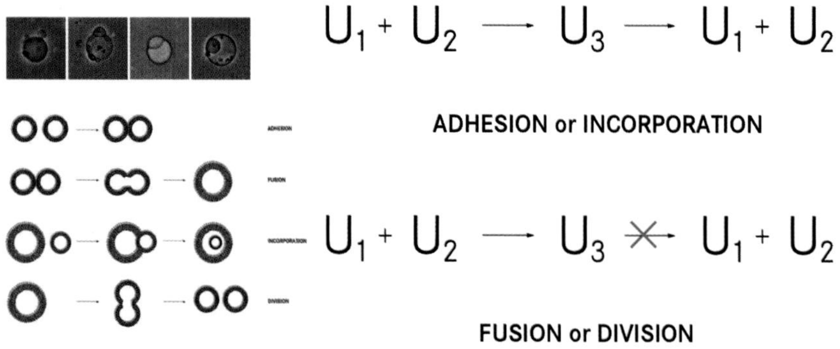

$$U_1 + U_2 \longrightarrow U_3 \longrightarrow U_1 + U_2$$

ADHESION or INCORPORATION

$$U_1 + U_2 \longrightarrow U_3 \not\longrightarrow U_1 + U_2$$

FUSION or DIVISION

Figure 22,23: Image from Paleos et al. (2011)

combinatorial applications.

The interactions among the liposomes are primarily due to their membrane chemistry. However fusion and adhesion operations can be modulated with changes in temperature,

Figure 24, 25: Based on Paleos et al. (2011), Stano (2009), and Stano & Luisi (2012)

PH levels, by incorporating extrinsic molecules such as Ca^{+2} to the membranes (Bailey & Cullis 1997) or by applying external forces such as high-intensity sound waves or magnetism. For example, magnetite cationic liposomes are often used for interacting with DNA molecules that are negatively charged (Shinkai & Ito 2004). They can be used not only to guide vesicle-to-vesicle interaction, but also to pass different ingredients to the membranes in controlled ways.

Once liposomes arrive to a certain size they can divide into smaller and more stable units. Thus, growth and self-division have been among the most attractive features of liposomes. These features have motivated researchers to build simplified, proof-of-principle cell-models that can mimic single cell organisms (Luisi & Stano 2011).

Designing with Vesicles

While the research with artificial vesicles are at its infancy, they already began to shape the language of contemporary architecture, mainly in the works of Rachel Armstrong and Philip Beesley. While Armstrong's work aspires to use protocells to design "metabolic" materials which, for example, would allow buildings to respond to the changes in their environment, and participate in more sustainable architectural practices, Beesley explores the potential of using them to generate

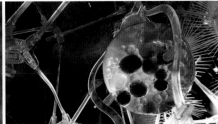

Figure 26: Microfluidic droplet generation using X-juction chip obtained from Biorad (Bio-rad.com). Source: Telhan
Figure 27: Dye-in-oil droplet formation in emulsion using a -junction chip (6-image sequence)

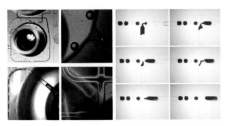

Figure 28: Water-in-oil continuous droplet formation using a T-junction chip (2-image sequence)
Source: Telhan

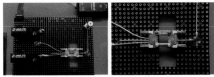

Figure 29, 30: Programmatical droplet formation using liquid syringe pumps at a prototyping workbench. Pumps, control interface, and workbench obtained from Labsmith, the microfluidic chip is from Dolomite). Source: TelhanSource: Telhan

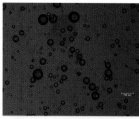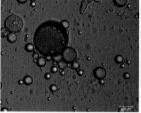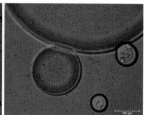

Figure 31,32, 33: Liposomes. Source: Telhan

Figure 34: Adhesion and incorporation experiments with liposomes. Source: Telhan

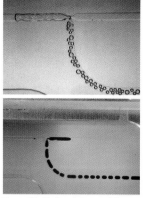

Figure 35, 36: Droplet assemblies can carry liposomes and help them merge their contents Source: Telhan

Figure 37: Two droplets merging and combining contents. Source: Telhan

energy in immersive installations (Spiller and Armstrong 2011). While these protocell-based design propositions offer applications based on the interaction between the cells, they do not necessarily address the potential of using vesicles organized in different assemblies or architectures.

When liposomes are designed within a microfluidic manipulation framework, they especially offer novel ways to think about addressability, encapsulation, compartmentalization, transportation and differentiation for designing new applications.

Droplets provide a form of articulation to the otherwise continuous space of liquids. They partition the aqueous design space into different geometries and make it quantifiable, addressable, and controllable by different applications of rational design. They can provide both a static, grid-like partitioning and also a moving space, in which liquid streams can carry units that join, split or fuse with each other and interact with each other in different speeds.

Liposomes-in-droplet formations combine the features of the liquid typology, its animated character—such as flow or circulation—with biochemical capabilities. As liposomes can encapsulate different types of living and non-living agents, they can be utilized to assemble new forms of biological artifacts that can partially exhibit life-like behaviors. Liposome formations can incorporate parts of living elements and host reactions that produce chemical compounds.

Liposomes with different membrane properties can be assembled in bead like formations, which then can be

|32C

used to form assemblies that can have different biochemical, chemical, visual, geometric, and informative functions.

Droplets with different contents and placing them next to each other such that as the droplets merge they can share content and start new reactions (Figure 6).

Liposome assemblies, can be used to bring together a desired set of molecules to create novel colors and smells, or designed to carry basic biological components such as DNA, RNA, Ribosomes, to be able to synthesize proteins and enzymes with biological properties.

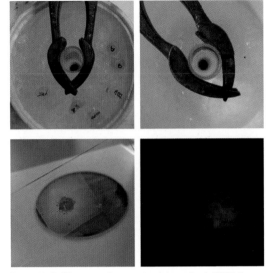

Figure 38: Cell-free green florescent protein synthesis (GFP) done inside liposomes Source: Telhan

Lipid-based constructs can also carry charges that would allow them to precisely assembled and mobilized using magnetic beads. Thus vesicles with various payloads—such as genes, bacteria, and energy molecules—can be brought together for building structures where the shape, volume or the assembly order of the molecules can determine biochemical functions.

The representational and physical meanings of liposome units introduce a different way of thinking about abstraction in design. If one uses a semiotic context, linear liposome constructs—or 'words'— can follow different rules of assembly (syntax), where their interaction would have visual (e.g., color), geometric (both visual and structural), chemical, biological, informational or computational meanings (semantics). Here, the physical function of the units (themselves) and what they may

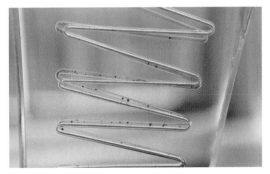

Figure 39: Vesicles used to juxtapose chemical compounds for designing smell with specific characteristics. Designs are featured in a fluidic environment (Source: Telhan)

mean in relation to each other (their mapped meaning, or what they can stand for beside their physical function) provide a different way to compose design interactions. Thus a biological arrangement can have visual meaning; a visual arrangement can have different chemical consequences; a biological event can be recorded as digital information and so on.

Designing Within

Microfluidic channels not only add additional articulation and control over the liquid design space but also provide computational control and automation for liposome-based design. The ability to control the confinement of newly created biological constructs— both physically and chemically—makes them quite important in their role of managing the containment and confinement of biological design in relation to everyday products. As microfluidic channels can be designed with different soft and hard materials, they can interface liposome-based designs with different forms of products such as medical or food packaging, liquid bottle containers and so forth.

On the other hand, while this biochemical design space offer a rich potential to think of containment and confinement conditions, the particular affordances of the static or flowing liquid environment, the temperature, humidity and lighting conditions require a major shift in thinking about the aesthetic and the symbolic functions of the design created inside a living body.

While vesicle assemblies may not be directly visible inside a living system, they can still have observable outcomes once they appear outside the body. Color or smell change, for example, can indicate the presence of biochemical products when vesicles can be manifested on teeth, skin, sweat or human manure.

However, for assemblies, constructs, and biological artifacts that are designed to remain inside the body, the experience of the symbolic, aesthetic and cultural meaning cannot rely on visibility or the senseability of the design from outside. *In vitro* designs may only be observed directly or indirectly with their somatic and psychological influences on the body. The timing of the release of food, its fermentation or the precise control of the interaction between food assemblies in the mouth or stomach, for example, can be the basis of new culinary experiences in molecular gastronomy.

The stomach, a space that is inhabited by billions of bacteria since the earliest moments of our lives, can be redesigned as a synthetic ecology that can spatially juxtapose selected organisms and control their interaction through vesicular activities. More invasive designs can also feature vesicle assemblies that can transform the microbial landscape of the gut flora. By providing external genetic material into the environment, vesicles can transform bacteria and allow them to synthesize a range of molecules from insulin, serotonin to Vitamin C in response to food allergies, dietary or medical needs. Vesicular structures can time the duration of biochemical synthesis as vesicular interactions catalyze or inhibit each other at different time scales. Similar to circadian rhythms, they can create alternative rhythms in the body; source chemicals at times favored by different personal or social needs. Stomachs can be designed not only to meet spatial preferences—get reduced in size for weight loss—but also made to respond to temporal choices. Slow or fast processing of the food, for example, can be aligned with meditative practices, fasting or diets.

The space that lies within the human body is obviously not limited to the stomach or the guts. From blood vessels to tissues or inside the individual cells there is a vast amount of liquid space that renders itself designable at the molecular domain. Yet, in the history of design, the ways to design the space within a living body is still very undertheorized—almost not articulated—compared to the vast literature available on the design and experience of architecture that lies outside the boundaries of our corporeality (Sloterdijk 2011). However, as synthetic biology advances in its tools and methodologies, and include spatial design methods from contemporary design, integrative design practices can demonstrate significant potential in expanding the theory and practice of design from inert to living matter. Spatial design methods that span across life sciences, engineering, and architecture will inevitably diversify the both the commercial and speculative products of design and increase their chances to respond the emerging needs and wants of our times.

FOOTNOTES

1. Bailey, A L, and P R Cullis. 1997. "Membrane Fusion with Cationic Liposomes: Effects of Target Membrane Lipid Composition." Biochemistry 36 (7) (February 18): 1628–1634. doi:10.1021/bi961173x.

2. Balagaddé, Frederick K., Lingchong You, Carl L. Hansen, Frances H. Arnold, and Stephen R. Quake. 2005. "Long-Term Monitoring of Bacteria Undergoing Programmed Population Control in a Microchemostat." Science 309 (5731) (July 1): 137–140. doi:10.1126/science.1109173.

3. Buxboim, Amnon, Shirley S. Daube, and Roy Bar-Ziv. 2008. "Synthetic Gene Brushes: a Structure–function Relationship." Molecular Systems Biology 4 (1) (April 15). doi:10.1038/msb.2008.20. http://www.nature.com.libproxy.mit.edu/msb/journal/v4/n1/full/msb200820.html.

4. Grenvall, Carl, Per Augustsson, Jacob Riis Folkenberg, and Thomas Laurell. 2009. "Harmonic Microchip Acoustophoresis: A Route to Online Raw Milk Sample Precondition in Protein and Lipid Content Quality Control." Analytical Chemistry 81 (15) (August 1): 6195–6200. doi:10.1021/ac900723q.

5. Kong, David Sun. 2008. "Microfluidic Gene Synthesis". Thesis, Massachusetts Institute of Technology. http://dspace.mit.edu/handle/1721.1/45755.

6. Paleos, Constantinos M., Dimitris Tsiourvas, and Zili Sideratou. 2011. "Interaction of Vesicles: Adhesion, Fusion and Multicompartment Systems Formation." ChemBioChem 12 (4): 510–521. doi:10.1002/cbic.201000614.

7. Pasirayi, Godfrey, Vincent Auger, Simon M. Scott, Pattanathu K.S.M. Rahman, Meez Islam, Liam O'Hare, and Zulfiqur Ali. 2011. "Microfluidic Bioreactors for Cell Culturing: A Review." Micro and Nanosystemse 3 (2) (July 1): 137–160. doi:10.2174/1876402911103020137.

8. Prakash, Manu, and Neil Gershenfeld. 2007. "Microfluidic Bubble Logic." Science 315 (5813) (February 9): 832–835. doi:10.1126/science.1136907.

9. Shinkai, Masashige, and Akira Ito. 2004. "Functional Magnetic Particles for Medical Application." Advances in Biochemical Engineering/biotechnology 91: 191–220.

10. Sloterdijk, Peter. 2011. Bubbles: Spheres Volume I: Microspherology. Los Angeles: Semiotext.

11. Smaldon, James, Francisco J. Romero-Campero, Francisco Fernández Trillo, Marian Gheorghe, Cameron Alexander, and Natalio Krasnogor. 2010. "A Computational Study of Liposome Logic: Towards Cellular Computing from the Bottom up." Systems and Synthetic Biology 4 (3): 157–79. doi:10.1007/s11693-010-9060-5.

12. Stano, Pasquale, and Pier Luigi Luisi. 2010. "Reactions in Liposomes." In Molecular Encapsulation, edited by Udo H. Brinker and Jean-Luc Mieusset, 455–491. John Wiley & Sons, Ltd. http://onlinelibrary.wiley.com/doi/10.1002/9780470664872.ch17/summary.

13. Stano, Pasquale, Paolo Carrara, Yutetsu Kuruma, Tereza Pereira de Souza, and Pier Luigi Luisi. 2011. "Compartmentalized Reactions as a Case of Soft-matter Biotechnology: Synthesis of Proteins and Nucleic Acids Inside Lipid Vesicles." Journal of Materials Chemistry 21 (47) (November 22): 18887–18902. doi:10.1039/C1JM12298C.

14. Stano, P., and P. L. Luisi. 2011. "On the Construction of Minimal Cell Models in Synthetic Biology and Origins of Life Studies." Design and Analysis of Bio-molecular Circuits: 337.

15. Spiller, Neill, and Rachel Armstrong, ed. 2011. Protocell Architecture: Architectural Design. 1st ed. Wiley.

16. Tan, Yung-Chieh, Jeffrey S. Fisher, Alan I. Lee, Vittorio Cristini, and Abraham Phillip Lee. 2004. "Design of Microfluidic Channel Geometries for the Control of Droplet Volume, Chemical Concentration, and Sorting." Lab on a Chip 4 (4): 292. doi:10.1039/b403280m.

17. Telhan, Orkan, Discursive Methods in Synthetic Biological Design in the proceedings of Design Research Society Conference (DRS 2012), Bangkok, Thailand, 2012.

18. Yang, Sung, Akif Undar, and Jeffrey D Zahn. 2005. "Blood Plasma Separation in Microfluidic Channels Using Flow Rate Control." ASAIO Journal (American Society for Artificial Internal Organs: 1992) 51 (5) (October): 585–590.

19. Orkan Telhan is interdisciplinary artist, designer and researcher whose investigations focus on the design of interrogative objects, interfaces, and media, engaging with critical issues in social, cultural, and environmental responsibility.

IMAGES CREDITS

Figure 4: Preparation of Liposomes (Fig 4. image from Vanniasinghe et al. 2008)

Figure 5: Cationic Liposomes (Fig 5. image taken from Battersby et al. 1998)

Figure 6: Multilamellar liposomes (Fig 6. image taken from http://www.dr-baumann-turkiye.com)

Figure 7: Giant unilamellar and multilamellar vesicles (liposomes) imaged by Dr. Jorge Bernardino de la Serna (Fig 7. image taken from (http://www.nikonsmallworld.com/gallery/search/all/liposome/2)

Figure 11: Bubble logic (Prakash & Gershenfeld 2007).

Figure 22, 23: Image from Paleos et al. (2011)

Figure 24, 25: Based on Paleos et al. (2011), Stano (2009), and Stano & Luisi (2012)

Figure 26: Microfluidic droplet generation using X-juction chip obtained from Biorad (Bio-rad.com). Source: Telhan

Figure 27: Dye-in-oil droplet formation in emulsion using a -junction chip (6-image sequence).

Figure 28: Water-in-oil continuous droplet formation using a T-junction chip (2-image sequence) Source: Telhan

Figure 29, 30: Programmatic droplet formation using liquid syringe pumps at a prototyping workbench. Pumps, control interface, and workbench obtained from Labsmith, the microfluidic chip is from Dolomite). Source: Telhan

Figure 31, 32, 33: Liposomes.Source: Telhan

Figure 34: Adhesion and incorporation experiments with liposomes. Source: Telha

Figure 35, 36: Droplet assemblies can carry liposomes and help them merge their contents Source: Telhan

Figure 37: Two droplets merging and combining contents. Source: Telhan

Figure 38: Cell-free green florescent protein synthesis (GFP) done inside liposomes Source: Telhan

Figure 39: Vesicles used to juxtapose chemical compounds for designing smell with specific characteristics. Designs are featured in a fluidic environment Source: Telhan

ORKAN TELHAN is Assistant Professor of Fine Arts - Emerging Design Practices at University of Pennsylvania, School of Design. He holds a PhD in Design and Computation from MIT's Department of Architecture. He was part of the Sociable Media Group at the MIT Media Laboratory and the Mobile Experience Lab at the MIT Design Laboratory. He studied media arts at the State University of New York at Buffalo and theories of media and representation, visual studies and graphic design at Bilkent University, Ankara.

Telhan's individual and collaborative work has been exhibited in venues including the 13th Istanbul Biennial, 1st Istanbul Design Biennial, Ars Electronica, ISEA, LABoral, Archilab, Architectural Association, Architectural League/ NYC, MIT Museum and the New Museum of Contemporary Art, NYC.

BEYOND PROTOTYPING

JENNY WU, OYLER WU COLLABORATIVE

(Figure 1)
Necklace One
Diagram

Additive manufacturing1, more commonly known as 3D printing, is a process invented by 3D Systems in the 1980s2. A 3D printer, translating information from a digital CAD model, first deposits layers of powdered material onto a print bed then uses a laser to heat and solidify the material. A three-dimensional object is then formed through the build-up of solidified layers of material. During the 1990s, significant advances in 3D printing technology were made with the invention of the Stereolithographic Apparatus Machines (SLA). At that time, 3D printing was primarily used for prototyping in specialized manufacturing and making advancements in bioengineering for medical technology. However, in the 1990s, high prices and specialized handling made it difficult for 3D printing to enter the mass market. In 2006, the first Selective Laser Sintering (SLS) machine was introduced; this development opened up greater possibilities in printing objects with complex geometry. This technology eliminated the need for an internal support structure, which had been necessary to create any voided cavity inside the printed object when using the SLA printing process. This advantage also significantly simplified the post production procedure. Since the advent of SLS machines, many critical improvements in the 3D printing technology have coincided, which has prompted many industries to integrate it into the production of finished products rather than using 3D printing for prototyping alone.

Of the advancements in 3D printing technology, there are a few that have had a deep impact upon the extensive growth of the industry into areas previously unimagined. The biggest improvement in 3D printing is the larger bed size (up to 5 feet in width on SLA machines); this advancement allows for the printing furniture sized objects. Most recently, robotic 3D printing machines are attempting to print objects as large as a building3.

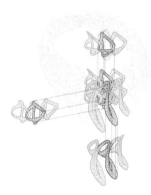

(Figure 2)
Necklace Two
Diagram

Secondly, Direct Metal Laser Sintering (DMLS) and Selective Laser Melting (SLM) have made metal printing possible with resolution high enough to achieve complex geometry. Finally, the price of 3D printers has dropped significantly in the past 4 years: machines that were once $30,000 can now be bought for $1,0004. Even without owning a machine, amateurs and design professional can now use 3D printing service bureaus and marketplaces, such as Shapeways and Cubify, to print high quality finished products at an affordable price. All of this progress has propelled 3D printing both technologically as well as in its widespread popularity. Now, nearly every industry is scrambling to find ways of incorporating 3D printing, either to aid the process of mass production or to print actual finished products. For these reasons, when we set out to design a line of jewelry and accessories this past year, it seemed most logical and appropriate to use 3D printing as the primary production method.

A 2013 article in The Economist insightfully noted, "3D printing is not competing with conventional manufacturing, but is hybridising with it."5 This attitude seems fitting when considering how 3D printing can redefine the design and manufacture of a product. Innovation in design can only occur by developing an intimate understanding of the technology and its technical characteristics. At the very basic level, it is important to understand what the technology does well and what it does differently than a conventional manufacturing process. In our 2010 essay, "Cumulative Processes and Intimate Understandings," we noted that architecture has always been a field at its best when the synthesis of a variety of ideas and issues is of paramount concern. The ability of architecture to bundle and process material, program, structural, and mechanical issues (just to name a few) while maintaining and relating artistic and poetic intentions has been a defining character trait. In contrast to more traditional notions of expertise gained through focused and specific research, architects have an obligation toward synthesis.6 Our approach to jewelry design is no different than our approach to architecture in the sense that it is essentially about synthesis. By synthesizing a range of issues from technical to artistic and testing them through a relentless iterative process, we are closer to developing a set of qualities in the design of this jewelry line that will ultimately make the pieces distinctive.

(Figure 3)
Necklace One
Photo One

(Figure 4)
Necklace One
Photo Two

The Design

Stria, the first necklace in the collection, takes advantage of the SLS printing process and its primary advantage over the SLA process. Instead of having support structure that has to be removed manually after printing, the support structure in SLS printing process is a bed of loose, unsintered powder that can be brushed off easily leaving only the final printed object7. This means that very fine internal cavities can be designed into the object without the risk of being filled up by support structure that is hard to remove. The design of Stria exploits this advancement by weaving a set of intricate, interlocking elements into a chain. This chain of various modules can be printed as a whole, rather than producing individual components separately that are then assembled afterwards. The interlocking quality is achieved by designing each element with air cavity around it. Once the print is completed, each element is released from the support powder produced during the printing and is free to move within the chain. This rather simple idea allows us to create interconnected components that would otherwise be very costly and time consuming to make and assemble in a traditional jewelry making process. We are also able to apply the intricate, line-based geometry from our architectural work and extend it into the design of the jewelry.

(Figure 5)
Necklace One
Photo Thre

In Tangens, the second necklace in the collection, we were interested in designing a piece that has similar geometric qualities as Stria but behaves differently when worn on the body. The design incorporates the chain-like quality of Stria in one portion of the necklace and then add more structure and volume to the piece. Unlike Stria, Tangens holds its overall form when it is worn. The design of Tangens can be broken down into three tiers, each tier consists of self-similar modules. The lowest tier is a row of modules that is completely connected, not chained. This forms the shape of the overall necklace. Each "petal-like" module of the first tier lies perpendicular to the body, rather than flat on the body. The play between what is solid and void gives the piece its volumetric reading. The middle tier is a set of chained modules that is tethered between the fixed lower tiered modules and the loose upper tiered modules. This means that while there is some movement in the module, the tier still maintains its overall form even under tension. The upper tiered modules are connected only at the lower portion of the module allowing for most movement at the top of the necklace. This is designed to contour and move with the movement of the neck so that the piece is comfortable when worn. This tiered modular design strategy enhances the spatial and three-dimensional quality of the necklace, but still allows for some movement in its design.

So far, the pieces have been described from the more technical and functional aspects of the design, both in its mechanical details and to its relationship to the body. It is important, at this point, to also describe how 3D printing can contribute to the qualitative aspects of the necklaces, specifically in terms of their geometry and patterning. As described earlier, the necklaces are composed of a set of modular elements. Since the necklaces are printed as a whole rather than one module at a time, there is no need to make identical modules for the ease of manufacturing. We are able to incorporate a gradient quality into the design, whether it is in the sizing or the shaping of each element. For example, in Tangens, each module is self-similar in terms of its form and shape but each one is scaled in size and rotated incrementally to give a subtle difference from the front to the back of the necklace. This type of scaling works well with the contour of a person's lower neck and shoulder. The incremental rotation of each module reveals the totality of the "petal-like" geometry in one seamless gesture. 3D printing makes these subtle but critical design moves easily achievable without any added complication in terms of manufacturing. Another important quality of the necklaces that capitalizes on the 3D printing technology is the range of thickness and profile shapes that can be incorporated into each element of the module. No two elements have the same cross section. Each element changes thickness and profiles fluidly, from a simple circle to a complex volume with sharp edges and smooth transitions. This is all made possible because 3D printing breaks down any geometry, simple or complex, into layers of pixilation. The critical difference to the time and cost of realizing each 3D printed design is in the amount of material that is necessary to build the final product. This approach is conceptually different than taking a stock material and tooling it to shape.

Moving forward

The design of both necklaces fundamentally stems from the idea that a small piece of jewelry can make a statement on the body. The heart of the design is in the weaving together of many fine elements to create something that appears volumetric and bold from afar, but intricate and refined when close up. It also aspires to be more than a piece of jewelry but may be conceived as a type of a garment (i.e. a collar, scarf, etc). This type of hybrid reading of both form and use is part of the opportunity for design innovation moving forward. Coupling this with new designs catered towards printing in metals as well as elastic polymer will further push the design of the jewelry towards hybridized products, like a necklace/scarf or bracelet/glove combinations. The speed of advancement in 3D technology is opening possibilities for manufacturing products that are already on the market in new ways for

(Figure 7)
Necklace Two
Photo One

many industries. As designers, we should look beyond the obvious and seek opportunities that will yield new, meaningful results. With this attitude, we are one step closer to designing something that not only works with the technology but uses the technology in new and unexpected applications.

REFERENCES
- Excell, Jon. "The rise of additive manufacturing," The Engineer, (May 24, 2010).
- "The Journey of a Lifetime," www.3dsystems.com/30-years-innovation.
- Jeffrey, Colin. "Team of 3D-printing 'Minibuilder' robots print large-scale structures on site," Gizmag.com, (June 18, 2014).
- Manyika, et.al., "Disruptive technologies: Advances that will transform life, business, and the global economy," McKinsey Global Institute, (May 2013).
- "3D printing: 3D printing scales up". The Economist. September 7, 2013.
- Dwayne Oyler and Jenny Wu, "Cumulative Processes and Intimate Understandings," in Gail Peter Borden, ed., Matter: Material Processes in Architectural Production (New York, NY: Routledge, 2012), 279-291.
- 7. "How Selective Laser Sintering Works". THRE3D.com

FOOTNOTES
1. Excell, Jon. "The rise of additive manufacturing," The Engineer, (May 24, 2010).
2. "The Journey of a Lifetime," www.3dsystems.com/30-years-innovation.
3. Jeffrey, Colin. "Team of 3D-printing 'Minibuilder' robots print large-scale structures on site," Gizmag.com, (June 18, 2014).
4. Manyika, et.al., "Disruptive technologies: Advances that will transform life, business, and the global economy," McKinsey Global Institute, (May 2013).
5. "3D printing: 3D printing scales up". The Economist. September 7, 2013.
6. Dwayne Oyler and Jenny Wu, "Cumulative Processes and Intimate Understandings," in Gail Peter Borden, ed., Matter: Material Processes in Architectural Production (New York, NY: Routledge, 2012), 279-291.
7. "How Selective Laser Sintering Works". THRE3D.com.

IMAGES CREDITS
Design Team: Jenny Wu, Dwayne Oyler, Huy Le, Sanjay Sukie, Zack Matthews, James Choe
Photography: Christian K. Coleman
3D Printing: Shapeways, Materialise

JENNY WU is a partner at the Los Angeles based architecture and design office, Oyler Wu Collaborative, which she started in 2004 with Dwayne Oyler. The office has been published globally and is recognized for its experimentation in design and fabrication. Their work straddles between two scales, small scale, experimental installations and large scale iconic building projects in Asia and US. She started LACE, a line of 3D printed jewelry and accessories, which she plans to launch in the Fall of 2014. The office has won numerous design awards, including the 2013 Design Vanguard Award from Architectural Record, 2013 Emerging Talent Award from AIA California Council, 2012 Presidential Honor Award for Emerging Practice from AIA LA, Taiwan's ADA Award for Emerging Architect, and 2011 Emerging Voices Award from the Architectural League in New York. They published the book, Pendulum Plane, in 2009, and are working on their latest publication, Trilogy, which will be coming out Fall of 2014. Jenny received her Bachelor of Arts from Columbia University and Masters of Architecture from Harvard Graduate School of Design.

Their recent projects include the Cube, the winning entry pavilion for the Beijing Biennale, Stormcloud, a pavilion for Sci-Arc 40th anniversary event, Taipei Sales Center, a 5 story commercial building , as well as a 16 story residential tower in Taipei, Taiwan. She is currently a design faculty at the Southern California Institute of Architecture (Sci-Arc), and has lectured extensively in the US, Europe and Asia.

KATHY VELIKOV AND GEOFFREY THÜN

TOWARDS

AN ARCHITECTURE

OF

CYBER-PHYSICAL

SYSTEMS

"As a result of these cybernetic, sub-theoretical developments, many architects *wanted* to design systems but, on the whole, they were expected to design buildings…there is a sense in which the brief given to an architect has widened during the last decades."

–   Gordon Pask

"we inhabit a kind of informational weather"

–   Michel Serres

Our work operates within what Fritjof Capra has termed the *ecological paradigm*. (Capra, 1994) This can be summarized as an approach and sensibility towards the broader schema-patterns, connections, relations and co-evolutions between things and - particularly of interest to us - between buildings, inhabitants and environments. Although our design research engages both the macro-urban scale of regional systems, and the micro-material scale of responsive building envelopes, it is the latter on which we will focus in the following pages. As a means to address the questions posed to authors contributing to this volume, we situate our recent work within the intellectual history of ideas developed by pioneers in cybernetic theory from the middle of the last century, and frame the works within three computational paradigms; summarized as systems thinking, prototyping, and embodying information, that we believe, defines an architecture of cyber-physical systems.

Relational Topologies

In his article "The Architectural Relevance of Cybernetics," published in the September 1969 issue of *Architectural Design*, Gordon Pask proposed that cybernetic theory was precipitating a new design paradigm for architecture – one that would implicate *both* the objects of design, and the design process itself, as systems operating adaptively with their environment. The term cybernetics was coined by mathematician Norbert Wiener, whose early work focused on the study of stochastic and nonlinear processes, and who, during the Second World War, led the development of the Anti Aircraft Predictor; one of the first servomechanisms that would not only operate through feedbacks (from locational data to the stability of the aircraft), but would also *learn* the behavior of the specific pilot operating it, and would adapt accordingly. (Galison, 1994) Wiener quickly saw beyond the instrumentality of the operational functions of this device, to a model for beginning to understand individual perception and physiological feedback systems - the circuit as a model of the brain – publishing the first edition of *Cybernetics: Or Control and Communication in the Animal and the Machine* in 1948. After the war, cybernetics emerged as a transdisciplinary field wherein computation moved beyond the functional tasks of calculation, and became the basis for understanding adaptive, interactive and evolutionary processes in societal and biological systems. Computation was not understood merely as a *tool*, but as a *model* for system and process-based design thinking and practices.

It is, however, worth returning to Pask's article, in order to mine deeper some of the propositions that he developed regarding design practice. Pask argued that once architecture is conceived to operate meaningfully within an extended and temporal context, it becomes a system, and not merely an object. Christopher Alexander had earlier framed the term *system* within an architectural context, by focusing on the process by which architecture is continually and concurrently defined by its interaction with culture and environment (Alexander, 1964). This expanded the notion of architecture and form as a dynamic entity, which encapsulates activity as well as physicality. Pask extended this idea of systems beyond physical and material, to human and communicative systems as well: "It follows that a building cannot be viewed simply in isolation. It is only meaningful as a human environment. It perpetually interacts with its inhabitants, on the one hand serving them and on the other controlling their behavior." (Pask, 1969: 494) Pask conceived of this interaction between buildings and inhabitants as a mutual form of dialogue; one that would be enabled by embedding both evolutionary principles and mechanisms within the design itself (be they computer controlled sensing technologies, adaptive apparatuses, as were conceived for the *Fun Palace* on which Pask collaborated with Cedric Price, or urban schemas designed to evolve as an ecology over time). If systems thinking is fundamentally relational, computation can be understood as the descriptive and conceptual language of these relations – topologically, algorithmically and temporally.

One of the most interesting aspects of Pask's argument comes at the end of the article, where he speculated on how cybernetics was not only relevant in terms of the designed system and its interaction with inhabitants and environments, but also constitutive of a paradigm shift in terms of the design process itself, refiguring the relationship between the designer and design. Pask proposed a new conception of the designer as a "controller *of* control" systems, qualifying that "'controller' is no longer the authoritarian apparatus which this purely technical name commonly brings to mind. In contrast, the controller is an odd mixture of catalyst, crutch, memory and arbiter." (Pask, 1969: 496) Some forty-five years later, this proposition resonates still, as the anxiety around the role of the designer within a computational context is a recurring topic of academic discourse, especially when evolutionary design processes are on the table. Pask's proposition implicates a new sense of agency on the part of the designer, placing the act of design within the highest order of the system hierarchy, being simultaneously purposed and reflexive.

From Object to System

Once architecture was conceived of as a system as opposed to an object, the architectural brief, as Pask asserted, indeed grows wider, and, we would argue, deeper. At one time, in the words of Le Corbusier, architecture was described as the "masterly, correct and

333

magnificent play of masses brought together in light." Systems thinking turns our attention far more intently to the processes of formation, production and operation of these masses and surfaces, which, within this new paradigm, are increasingly understood as thickly layered material assemblies, defined not only by their multi-faceted characteristics and behaviors, but also by their processes of formation, production and manufacture. They are not just *in* light, they can shape and control it, harvest its latent energy, producing a cascading set of relationships beyond those delivered by their environmental effects alone. The term *material system* posits a perspective that necessitates both the study and execution of material formation in simultaneity with the measure of contextually responsive behavior; where form is defined as performing and responsive, its nature emerges via a material's behavior in relation to a specific and specialized environment. (Menges 2008) If we build upon this idea to explicitly account for embedded sensing, actuation, energetic distribution and control mechanisms conceived of as an integrated dimension of the material proposition, then we are discussing the potentials of an architecture of *cyber-physical systems.*

There are multiple ways in which this computational paradigm of systems thinking can play out within contemporary design practice. In our work, we focus on the design of architectural elements conceived of as deep surface assemblies that develop material and cognitive dialogue between built form, humans and the environment via experimentation with prototypes for responsive envelopes that engage the soft matters of architecture, such as energy, light, thermal gradients, air quality, acoustics and information. (Velikov et al., 2012) Although projects described in the following paragraphs – *North House, The Stratus Project, Resonant Chamber* and *PneuSystems* – all deploy computational design, simulation, fabrication, sensing and controls, that is the least paradigmatic aspect of their conception and actuality. Systems thinking not only leverages the embedded intelligence within materials and geometries to interact with environmental forces, but also embeds capacities for augmented intelligence and decision-making within these architectural elements themselves, engaging in active exchange and co-evolution with the dynamic contexts of environment and human participation.

|334

Projects and Propositions

North House is an 800sf proof of concept prototypical prefabricated solar powered home designed for near-northern climates (42°-55° latitude) that aims to advance approaches to responsive envelope design and challenge conventional assumptions regarding the design of domestic typologies with highly glazed surface areas through the pairing of hybrid integrated active and passive envelope systems with interactive controls. In combining these technologies, the *North House* prototype delivers a net energy-producing dwelling that sponsors new relationships between inhabitants, their surrounding environment, building systems and energy infrastructures. Central to this effort was an ambition to shift the associations of 'home' and the domicile towards a locus for active engagement with the world through a dwelling interface in which we learn and produce interactions with the broader environment while simultaneously minimizing the legible presence of these systems to prioritize the materialization of their effects. While the design of the *North House* incorporates a broad suite of sustainable design strategies such as creative use of smaller living spaces, on-site food production, greywater processing and mass customization techniques, here we will focus on innovations that incorporate feedback and response between the building, the inhabitant, and the environment. *North House* proposes a whole building system that "learns" to perform more efficiently precisely because the inhabitant, who is part of the system, learns to occupy and dwell more intelligently, a conscious participant within broader contextual systems.

Unique to the project, the design research team developed the Distributed Responsive System of Skins (DReSS), a composite assembly to manage passive thermal gains, natural daylight penetration and distributed renewable energy production by responding to climatic conditions, diurnal cycles, and real time dynamic feedback. (Thun et al. 2012) The DReSS is comprised of active exterior shading, high-performance glazing, building integrated photovoltaics (BIPVs), and interior surfaces imbued with additional thermal storage capacity through the incorporation of phase-change materials. In consort, these elements constitute a hybrid approach to active and passive environmental response, delivering a net annual energy surplus while radically refiguring current practices regarding the extent of transparent glazing systems for building design in the near-north. When tied to the grid, the home is rendered part of a distributed network of renewable energy production, the inhabitant, now a participant in an extended energy production and distribution economy.

The physical components of the DReSS are paired with a Custom Home Automation System (CHAS) that registers exterior and interior conditions and manages systemic operation, prioritizing the reduction of energy demand load consumption through the activation of various components of the system. Operating in partnership with CHAS, the team developed the Adaptive Living Interface System (ALIS) to directly engage occupants through a new form of gradient and feedback-based controls. ALIS applies approaches borrowed from ubiquitous computing, and advancements in digital personal interfaces, to provide dynamic feedback to users regarding the performance of the home. The interface provides the inhabitant with simple, intuitive controls, monitoring performance while providing meaningful feedback at cascading degrees of numeric detail on the resource consumption impacts of their behavior. ALIS also includes building integrated ambient environmental cues regarding energy and water use status, as well as social network-based motivational tools that connect inhabitants with a broader community of like-minded home-owners. This enables inhabitants to share performance data, experiences with building system technologies, and assists in producing new constituencies of net energy positive residents. (Velikov et. al 2013)

In aggregate, this set of responsive building technologies (DReSS, CHAS, and ALIS) render apprehensible one's immediate physical relationship to the climate, energy and landscape. At the same time they are intended to support the transformation of behavior toward more sustainable patterns of living and building use habits through actively producing a domestic ecology of responsive building systems and engaged human participants.

The Stratus Project develops a model for a kinetic, sensing and environment-responsive interior envelope system that aims to attune our attention to the air-based environment and to the physical conditions that produce and mediate it. A thick suspended textile senses movement, proximity, temperature, humidity, CO_2 and airborne VOC pollutant levels, and reacts according to individuated occupancy triggers and processing algorithms to modify comfort conditions. On the underside of the soffit surface are located the "breathing cells." These are individually servo-actuated cells forming a translucent, light-diffusing skin, opening like gills to allow for localized thermal conditioning, air supply and extraction. Beneath this thickened stratum, personalized and social atmospheres defined by light and air are produced in response to environmental and occupancy variables.

The structural foundation of *Stratus* is a suspended tensegrity weave, providing deformational flexibility, while also supporting a woven meshwork of sensors, actuators, lights, fans, servos, and light diffusing fabric panels impregnated with phase-change coatings to enhance thermal performance. Light-based communication informs occupants of air conditions, operating as a communicative interface. Specifically, when carbon dioxide or other pollutant levels increase, a set of extraction fans activates, and blue LED lights turn on alerting the breather of the reduced air quality. The social politics of the air thereby becomes presenced; not only are inhabitants concerned with the escalation of indoor air contaminates, becoming aware of their participation as active agents in producing these atmospheres, with each exhalation from their lungs.

The system is designed to also physically displace in response to occupation. Sensor-based stepper motors modify the volume of conditioned space by raising the textile as large groups undertaking active inhabitations gather, and lowering for low intensity intimate occupations. This envelope is thus physically and operationally programmed to produce flexible architectural interiors where both activities and uses co-define microclimate conditions and spatial volumes.

Resonant Chamber is an interior envelope system designed to transform the acoustic environment through dynamic spatial, material and electro-acoustic modification. The project aims to develop a soundsphere able to adjust its properties relative to changing sonic conditions, dynamically and in real-time altering the acoustic properties of a space as well as the patterns and relationships between human agents active therein.

Resonant Chamber is designed as a multi-functional adaptive surface, transformable through the geometric properties of rigid origami into predictable spatial configurations through its surface properties of developability and flat fold-ability. This allows for both gross deformation to dynamically alter aural volume, and localized variability of the ratios of acoustically reflective and absorptive surfaces exposed. The constructed prototype uses a tessellated origami pattern first developed by Ron Resch, which deploys two sizes of triangular cells. This was developed into a system where, through computational software, different origami folding patterns can be generated and customized in terms of their scale and material properties to suit a variety of spaces, potential aural volumes and uses.

Three types of performative composite panels were developed within a material and geometric framework: reflective, absorptive and sound generating. The sound generating panels have DML exciters embedded within their composition, rendering the surficial panels as electro-acoustic speakers. Synchronized actuation of the surface geometry allows for early and late acoustic energy control. Early acoustic energy, occurring shortly after the direct sound at both a listener and performer location, is controlled by automated adjustment of the surface height, location and curvature. Late acoustic energy - that is, diffusion and reverberation - is controlled by adjustment of the absorptive material exposure and location. Frequency and acoustic pressure sensors process audio input to trigger physical or electro-acoustic responses. Occupancy and gesture sensors trigger transformations of the surface relative to location, number and activity of participants. While *Resonant Chamber* can produce an acoustic environment that may be tuned for audio performance-based optimization, it is also conceived of as an architecturally scaled instrument and dynamic aural environment that not only facilitates performance, but itself begins to perform; an interactive soundsphere, a new auditory envelope, tunable and playable through both direct and indirect means. (Thun et al. 2012)

PneuSystems examines the performative, formal and aesthetic potentials for cellular pneumatic membrane-based aggregate assemblies towards deep, lightweight and adaptive architectural skins, shaped and controlled through the material agency of air. Air or liquid held captive by a membrane in tension is one of the basic structural principles of living organisms; from the microscopic scale of packed cellular pneumatics as found in living cells and bone structures to composite pneumatic formations such as caterpillars or the Venus Flytrap, where motion is produced through variations in turgor. Abstraction of these biological examples into architecturally-scaled systems opens a broad territory of speculation for novel envelopes comprised of variable geometries of pneu arrays that form cellular surface assemblies within which individual components may perform specific tasks, such as variable thermoregulation and aperture control.

The geometric system of units that constitute this prototype are derived from studies of topological interlocking principles (elements of a special shape that are kept in place by kinematic constraints imposed through the shape and mutual arrangement of the elements) combined with geometries of stacking, braiding, weaving, and knitting that are deconstructed to be comprised of individual cells. This allows the assembly to behave much more like a textile than foam or packed bubble structures. In parallel, we are developing a physical vocabulary of forms non-directional pneumatic motion, informed by soft robotics, that can be integrated within the aggregate arrays to achieve specific changes either within the field of the system (e.g. an aperture) or as an actuator within the system (e.g. to introduce a force that alters other cell relations). This produces a deep surface that allows for apertures or actuators to be operated at various points within the array without adversely affecting other zones in the skin. All units within a given topological family can be aggregated across the array at a regular interval and interchanged according to situation-specific, demand-based parameters mapped onto the surface (curvature, stiffness, porosity, R value, etc). (Velikov et al, 2014)

This body of work in cyber-physical systems research anticipates a model that favors flexibility and firmness, extensibility over finitudes. We advocate for an architecture whose main virtue lies not in Vitruvian "firmitas" but in its ability to be *in-firm*; to not resist change, but to embrace change as its ally. Through this work, we aim to develop architectural constructs that simultaneously support instrumentality and affinity, performativity and affect, explicit and implicit knowledge, technological optimism and the uncanny.

From Representation to Prototype

It is a well-known adage that architects do not make buildings, they make representations of buildings. The practice of architecture has, since the Renaissance, operated through conventions of abstraction communicated through the various modalities of representation. In all cases, one of the most important aspects of architectural representations is scale, and its proportional relationship to the architectural object. It has also long been recognized that architectural representations play not only a translational role relative to an anticipated reality of some kind (reproductive, reductive, pragmatic, relational), but are also realities in their own right, and subject to their own laws.
A significant, and much discussed paradigm shift that has accompanied computational design has been (perhaps somewhat ironically) an increased focus on the production of *physical* artifacts as an essential activity of the design process. This ranges from digitally crafted objects, now able to be fabricated by robotic manufacturing equipment much more easily accessible to designers, to the miniaturization of intelligent technologies facilitate interaction with almost any object or surface possible, to the increasing tendency for designers to develop their own full-scale prototypes and models as means of experimenting with, demonstrating, testing and evaluating novel structural and material systems for architecture. (Sheil, 2012) While this "experimental turn" within the discipline shares certain affinities with science, this should not be understood as a form of pragmatism, or as architectural design simply taking on the mantle of engineering and product design. Instead, we understand this as a new territory of permanent innovation,

forging novel relationships between craft and knowledge-making, or, in the words of philosopher Avital Ronell, between "*techné* and *epistémé*". (Ronnell, 2011)

Within this turn, the status of the model is undergoing a radical shift. Models are no longer presumed to be scaled representations or abstractions, but are now the *thing itself*, manifest at 1:1 scale. We are also witnessing an expansion of the conceptual vocabulary around the word model; designers have begun to interchangeably use the terms model and prototype, as well as the even more "scientistic" term, testbed. These new models operate less and less as abstractions, instructions or descriptions conceived of in relation to something outside of themselves, but become instead active *things*, simultaneously real and idealized, forging their own instable and manifold relationships between themselves, their environments and humans. (Johnson and Gattegno, 2010) The *map* has now collapsed into the *territory*. (Vollen and Clifford 2010) In part, this prioritization of the prototype is also predicated on the practical exigencies of cyber-physical systems: performance-based characteristics such as material behavior, gravity, thermal performance, airflow, acoustics and associated human interactions constitute qualities and effects that necessitate empirical and experiential investigation at full scale.

We identify two significant disciplinary implications of the emergence of the full-scale model as a central practice and object of design research. First, is in relation to systems thinking: as the conception of architecture shifts from object to system, then design may take on intensive investigations that result not in complete building designs in the traditional sense, but rather in the design of architectural components and elements. The full-scale models developed for the *Stratus Project*, *Resonant Chamber* and *PneuSystems*, were all installed and presented within a gallery exhibition context, and were conceived of as prototype-based demonstrations, or perhaps swatches, of more extensive, building integrated responsive envelope systems. Although *North House* was developed as a fully integrated demonstration home, the DReSS, CHAS and ALIS were conceived of as a system that could be portable and scalable to other building applications and environmental contexts.

Second, is that the material behavior of the physical model is advanced in tightly coupled interrelation with its computational counterpart, and that the feedbacks between the two form an iterative design process wherein computational simulations are developed, continually informed and verified by material research and conversely, material behaviors are more systematically and creatively understood through methods of computational analysis. (Menges 2008, Ahlquist and Menges 2013) Here, the computational paradigm shifts from the operation of the system to the integral method of its exploration, yet operating once again through communicative feedbacks between digital and physical realms.

In the *PneuSystems* project, combinatory approaches for computational simulation, design and energy performance of pneumatic structures were developed as part of the design research process. In the prediction of the final inflated form of pneumatic cells, we utilize a combination of animation and customizable physics engine-based software. In order to verify the computational models, single cells are also physically prototyped, inflated, and 3-D scanned. The scanned prototype is compared to the digital model, and feedback from resulting variations is utilized to refine the definition parameters so that it may more closely simulate the final form of the inflated cells. (Velikov et al, 2014) In order to anticipate the thermal performance of the arrays, we developed a dual approach utilizing CFD modeling to simulate convective air movement within individual cells comprising the assembly over time, running both transient (time-based) and steady-state simulations to understand heat transfer across the aggregate assembly. Temperature measurements from a physical test installation are used to assess simulation results and refine their methods. In *Resonant Chamber*, specific materials combined with a series of geometric and scalar variations were tested in a laboratory environment for subjective acoustic impressions, sensitivity and frequency response. The results that yielded the smoothest curve through the dB range across the third octave frequency were fed back into the computational geometric evaluation of particular origami patterns and their potential spatial deformations as an aggregate system in order to address multiple spatial and acoustic performance criteria. The final decision to use a tessellated origami pattern based on a 457mm triangle, constructed of bamboo plywood and a laminated PEPP composite, in combination with the MAG-063 DML exciter was a result of this combinatory feedback between digital and physical testing. (Thun et al, 2012) In the *North House*, active occupation of the testbed is enabling an ongoing re-evaluation of systemic performance, component replacement, and refinements to the operational system algorithms and interface design.

Informational Atmospherics

Consider a house, and a street, for example. The house has six storeys and an air of stability around it. One might almost see it as the epitome of immovability, with its concrete and its stark, cold and rigid outlines. Now,
a critical analysis would doubtless destroy the appearance of solidity of this house, stripping it, as it were, of its concrete slabs and its thin non-load-bearing walls, which are really glorified screens, and uncovering a very different picture. In the light of this imaginary analysis, our house would emerge - permeated from every direction by streams of energy which run in and out of it by every imaginable route: water, gas, electricity, telephone lines, radio and television signals, and so on. Its image of immobility would then be replaced by an image of complex mobilities, a nexus of in and out conduits. By depicting this convergence of waves and currents, this new image, much more accurately than any drawing or photograph, would at the same time disclose the fact that this "immovable

property" is actually a two-faceted machine analogous to an active body: at once a machine calling for massive energy supplies, and an information-based machine with low energy requirements. The occupants of the house perceive, receive and manipulate the energies which the house itself consumes on a massive scale.

Henri Lefebvre, The Production of Space, 1968

Although Henri Lefevre is a philosopher seldom associated with computational design practice, the above quote perhaps encapsulates best the paradigm of the material embodiment of ambient information and energy. This notion of the expanded and networked boundary has of course been elaborated on more fully by William J. Mitchell in his seminal *Me++*. (Mitchell, 2003) As computing becomes increasingly pervasive throughout our built environment, the contemporary urban dweller exists within in a milieu characterized by an excess of data, constantly connected and exposed to digital information flows, living in a continuous cloud of ambient information. (McCollough, 2012) Since these data oceans can be registered, collected and communicated via the ubiquity of electronic devices, architecture becomes not only a part of these systems of energy and information, but also an apparatus that actively manages, controls and communicates these flows, and it is precisely the active recognition of, and engagement with the potentials of this new cyber-physical reality that will characterize near-future architectural production.

Perhaps most imperative is the flow of energy through our built environment, and the contemporary agenda to reduce its use and the atmospheric impacts of its production. In the *North House*, the integrated photovoltaic and solar thermal systems generated a net surplus of energy, and the dynamic exterior shades coupled with the (passive) performance of the building envelope assembly (DReSS) managed by the CHAS, optimized energy usage while maintaining interior comfort. However, an essential aspect of the design was the ALIS. ALIS is more than just a smart home control application; although it does include both a web and smartphone interface, its focus is on developing an *information ecosystem* integrated within the design of the home itself through a variety of data-rich and haptic ambient interfaces that provide meaningful feedback to inhabitants, mapped physically and temporally on their daily use of the home. (Velikov et al 2013)

This paradigm may be more specifically described as a shift away from information being presented or delivered to inhabitants, to information playing a central role in the structuring of space, spatial experience and spatial practices. The *Stratus Project* experiments with this notion most directly. The physical envelope is no longer just a wrapper or surface, but itself operates as an interface through which individuals might develop more sensible and cognitive relationships between their own actions, the spaces, and broader atmospheric domains they inhabit. On one hand this new envelope becomes a thick, sensing dermis, providing perceivable and sentient modification and response relative to breathers and their air-based medium. At the same time, it is fragile, soft and malleable, causing the breather to become almost painfully aware of the thickness of the air and the work required to condition it and make it possible for us to inhale. In this way, the *Stratus* envelope both supports inhabitation and offers a platform for communication, interaction, and environmental negotiation.

Back to the Future

In the attempt to reflect upon and summon a description of 'new paradigms' in computation with respect to design, it has been useful to return to Gordon Pask's "The Architectural Relevance of Cybernetics" as a seminal manifesto that anticipated the nature of current transformations within both the scope of architectural design and its related processes. In the era of 'the internet of things', there can be no doubt that architects will be ever more consciously designing cyber-physical systems, and that the interrelationships between matter, environment, control logics, information and human participants will constitute simultaneously both the ecosystem that is being designed, and in which design praxis is undertaken. We are thinking through and working upon and within systems. Advanced file to fabrication techniques will not simply change the nature of descriptive practice, construction protocols and material administration, but will, along with simulation and predictive digital design tools mobilize the act of 'prototyping the model' as the primary act of design in the production of cyber-physical systems. In this context, Pask's evocation of the designer as a catalyzing arbiter of systems rings true, and yet, beyond simply synthesizing complexity and working across systems, the fundamental task of design must be radically rethought from the Vitruvian imperatives that have dominated the architectural landscape through its modern and post-modern periods. We are no longer able to conceive of the mere layering of advanced technologies within stable material constructs as architecture's response to the digital turn. An architecture of cyber-physical systems will be one of embodied information. The resulting work will be situated within extended networked systems of infrastructure and exchange, be developed though iterative prototypes and testbeds, will be adaptive in response shifting environmental contexts, co-evolving dynamically over time in dialog with human participation.

|342

Acknowledgements

We are grateful to the numerous individuals that have been integral in the development of these projects and to the agencies that have provided support. For full team and funding lists, please refer to the cited works, or to www.rvtr.com/research.

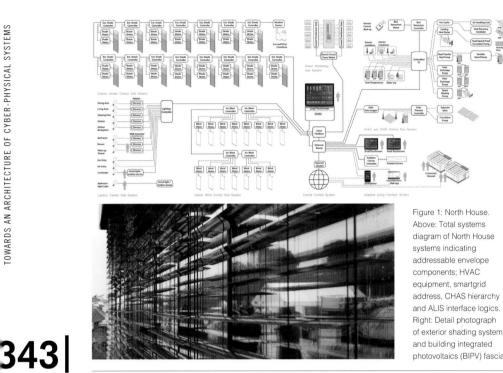

Figure 1: North House. Above: Total systems diagram of North House systems indicating addressable envelope components; HVAC equipment, smartgrid address, CHAS hierarchy and ALIS interface logics. Right: Detail photograph of exterior shading system and building integrated photovoltaics (BIPV) fascia.

343|

Figure 2: The Stratus Project. Clockwise from top right: Breathing cells opening and blue indicator lights engaged in a context of escalated carbon dioxide concentration in the air; The envelope as a surface of sensible encounter; Installed prototype, underside with breathing cells open; Prototype tensegrity weave integrated with distributed air circulation, lighting, sensing, actuation, and control technologies.

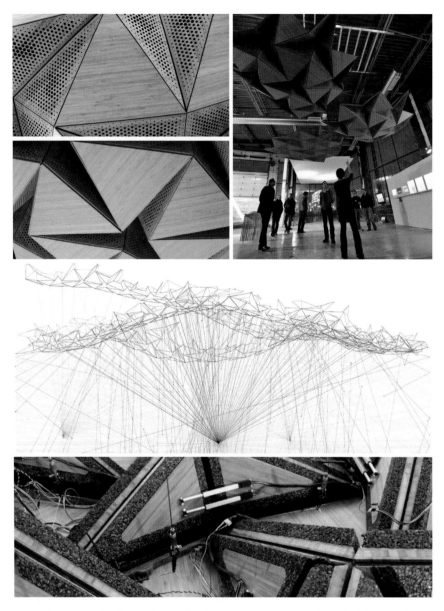

Figure 3: Resonant Chamber. Clockwise from top right: Resonant Chamber surface detail comprised of acoustically reflective (solid) absorptive (perforate) and electro-acoustic (hollow) panels distributed within the rigid origami pattern; Gallery installation of 9-cell 'cloud' prototypes in various stages of actuation; Top surface of composite panels with PEPP panel inserts and linear actuators controlling local surface deformation; Ray-tracing analysis of dynamic system performance in multiple positions, with centralized point source and resultant hybrid absorptive/reflective first and second order reflections.

KATHY VELIKOV AND GEOFFREY THÜN

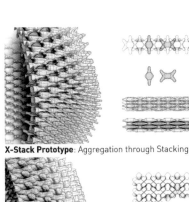 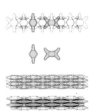  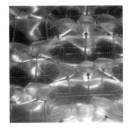

X-Stack Prototype: Aggregation through Stacking

 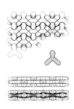  

Y-Stack Prototype: Aggregation through Stacking

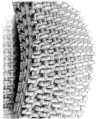 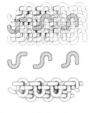  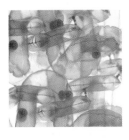

S-Weave Prototype: Aggregation through Weaving

   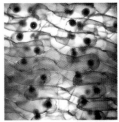

X-Weave Prototype: Aggregation through Braiding / Knitting

 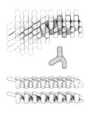  

λ-Weave Prototype: Aggregation through Weaving

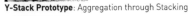

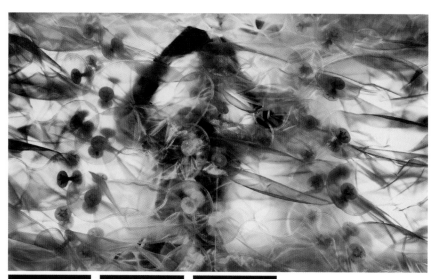

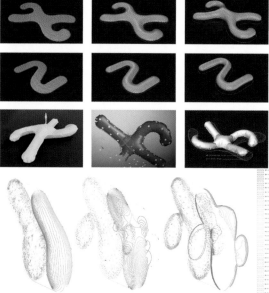

Figure 4: PneuSystems. Opposite: Computational and physical prototype explorations of stack, weave, braid and knit topologies translated into various interlocking multi-cellular pneu arrays. Above, clockwise from left: Installation of prototype X-Weave array; Comparative framework of 3D laser scanned figures in comparison with simulation volumes and overlay imaging to inform parametric code in subsequent systemic simulations; Results from simplified CFD simulation models demonstrating: (l) internal convection of a single pneu cell, (c) internal convection of multiple layered pneu cells not thermally coupled, and (r) of multiple layered pneu cells thermally coupled, with a temperature of 0°C applied to the outside boundary surfaces, and a temperature of 30°C applied to the inside boundary surfaces.

FOOTNOTES_CITATIONS

- Ahlquist, Sean, and Achim Menges (2013) "Frameworks For Computational Design of Textile Micro-Architectures and Material Behavior in Forming Complex Force-Active Structures" ACADIA 13: Adaptive Architecture (Proceedings of the 33rd Annual Conference of the Association for Computer Aided Design in Architecture): 281-292.

- Alexander, Christopher. (1968) "Systems Generating Systems," Architectural Design, December, 7/6: 90-91.
- Capra, Fritjof (1994) "Systems theory and the New Paradigm," in Carolyn Merchant ed. Key Concepts in Critical Theory: Ecology. Amherst, N.Y.:Humanity Books: 334-341.
- Connor, Stephen. (2010) The Matter of Air. London: Reaktion.
- Galison, Peter. (1994) "The Ontology of the Enemy: Norbert Wiener and the Cybernetic Vision," Critical Inquiry, Vol. 21, No. 1: 228-266
- Johnson, Jason and Nataly Gattegno (2010) "Live Models" in Flip Your Field, Proceedings of the ACSA 2010 Regional Conference: 171-176.
- Menges, Achim. (2008) "Integral Formation and Materialisation: Computational Form and Material Gestalt," in B. Kolarevic and K. Klinger eds. Manufacturing Material Effects: Rethinking Design and Making in Architecture. Routledge: New York: 195–210.
- McCullough, Malcolm (2013) Ambient Commons. Cambridge and London: MIT Press.
- Mitchell, William J. (2003). Me++: the cyborg self and the networked city. Cambridge, Mass.: MIT Press.
- Pask, Gordon. (1969) "The Architectural Relevance of Cybernetics." Architectural Design, September 1969: 494–496
- Ronell, Avital. (2004) The test drive. Urbana, Ill.: University of Illinois Press.
- Sheil, Bob, ed. (2012) Manufacturing the Bespoke: Making and Prototyping Architecture. UK: Wiley.
- Thün, Geoffrey and Kathy Velikov. (2012) "North House: climate responsive envelope and control systems," in F. Trubiano ed. Design and Construction of High Performance Homes. London: Routledge: 265-282
- Thün, Geoffrey, Kathy Velikov, Lisa Sauvé, Wes McGee (2012) "Design Ecologies for Responsive Environments: Resonant Chamber, an Acoustically Performative System," in ACADIA 12: Synthetic Digital Ecologies (Proceedings of the 32nd Annual Conference of the Association for Computer Aided Design in Architecture): 373-382
- Velikov, Kathy, Geoffrey Thün, Mary O'Malley (2014b) "PneuSystems: cellular pneumatic envelope assemblies," ACADIA 14: Design Agency (Proceedings of the 34rd Annual Conference of the Association for Computer Aided Design in Architecture). forthcoming
- Velikov, Kathy, Lyn Bartram, Geoffrey Thün, Lauren Barhydt, Johnny Rodgers and Robert Woodbury, (2013) "Empowering the Inhabitant: Communication technologies, responsive interfaces and living in sustainable buildings," in R. Henn and A. Hoffman eds. Constructing Green: The Social Structures of Sustainability, eds. (Cambridge: MIT Press): 171-195
- Velikov, Kathy, Geoffrey Thün and Colin Ripley (2012) "Thick Air," Journal of Architectural Education (JAE) 65: 2: 69-97
- Vollen, Jason Oliver and Dale Clifford. (2012) "Porous Boundaries," in M. Meredith and G. P. Borden eds. Matter, Material Processes in Architectural Production. London: Routledge: 155-169

IMAGES CREDITS
Kathy Velikov and Geoffrey Thün

KATHY VELIKOV is Assistant Professor of Architecture at the Taubman College of Architecture and Urban Planning at the University of Michigan. She is a licensed architect and founding partner in the research-based architectural practice RVTR: a platform for exploration and experimentation in the agency of architecture and urban design within the context of dynamic ecological systems, infrastructures, materially and technologically mediated environments, and emerging social organizations.

GEOFFREY THÜN is Associate Dean of Research and Associate Professor of Architecture at the Taubman College of Architecture and Urban Planning at the University of Michigan. He is founding partner in the research-based architectural practice RVTR: a platform for exploration and experimentation in the agency of architecture and urban design within the context of dynamic ecological systems, infrastructures, materially and technologically mediated environments, and emerging social organizations.

ALEXANDER ROBINSON

OWENS LAKE RAPID LANDSCAPE PROTOTYPING MACHINE REVERSE-ENGINEERING DESIGN AGENCY FOR LANDSCAPE INFRASTRUCTURES

ALEXANDER ROBINSON

349|

"Certain forms of knowledge and control requires a narrowing of vision. The great advantage of such tunnel vision is that it brings into sharp focus certain limited aspects of an otherwise far more complex and unwieldy reality. This very simplification, in turn, makes the phenomenon at the center of the field of vision more legible and hence more susceptible to careful measurement and calculation. Combined with similar observations, an overall, aggregate, synoptic view of selective reality is achieved, making possible a high degree of schematic knowledge, control and manipulation."

– James C. Scott, Seeing Like A State[1]

While not always well recognized, agency is deeply intertwined with our ability to identify and extract measurements and world parameters that enable an effective synoptic level of control. While acknowledging the necessity of this practice, the political scientist James C. Scott identified that this methodology and subsequent power has led to powerful disaffections and dystopic conditions. The hazards of employing a inevitably narrowed vision of the world required for administrative management, one that crops out far more of a phenomenon than it contains, are compounded by how we build to feed these measurements, structuring a world that maximizes select parameters and neglecting a world "outside of the brackets".[2] However, with the powerfully transformative advances in computational power should there not be the promise to measure better and more and administer more richly textured schematics?

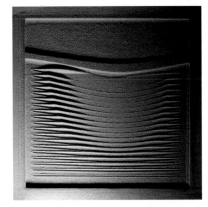

Figure1: Sand model, moat and row, graduated effects // By following simple robotic arm tool paths the machine manipulates sediment into berms for reducing wind velocity on the lake. The forms take their cues from the curvature of the road, mirroring a synaesthetic experience of driving

Yet, while we are witnesses to a seemingly un-abating revolution in measurement and data distribution the effect has been to fortify the hegemony of what can be well measured (and well predicted) while not substantially correcting a missing breadth of measurements. Even if we concede that the measurements of the previously unmeasurable, including a few qualitative aspects critical to fully valuing landscape architecture, has markedly improved, the data remains fuzzy and incomplete compared to the increased synoptic understanding and representation of physical or economic phenomenon.[3] And though there is an interesting and disruptive democratization of sensor technology,[4] the potential for dystopic design remains alarming.[5] Furthermore, as tools of design advance computationally, sometimes becoming overtly opaque, specific or complex, the unmeasured and difficult to measure (such as qualitative values) risks becoming further marginalized and unrecognized. That that is well measured, sometimes the byproduct of interest by other professions, gains an unquestioned, if somewhat arbitrary leveraged authority within landscape architectural (and architecture) design.

Figure2: toolpaths and sand... perspective ... process of building up landscape // Landscapes, such as islands to support vegetation above the highly saline water table, are constructed through the algorithm produced robotic toolpaths, here seen projected before and after their application.

Figure3: projection matrix... whole series of projection types and analysis types // Following the the sedimentary manipulation the landscape is scanned and a custom software system illuminates the form with topographic and experiential analysis.

Such a cautionary assessment does not sub sequentially promote a Luddite approach to the technologies, many of which represent some of the most promising opportunities for design innovation and advancement. These technological innovations are rapidly building agency and becoming embedded within all levels of practice in ways that mostly should not or at least largely cannot be reversed. However, how they are appropriately embedded with or checked by what cannot be quantitively measured – what may be best qualitatively assessed by individuals – is unresolved. Yet, within the professional scopes of most Landscape Architecture or Architecture practice, this crisis remains in the future. It is within the practice of the landscape infrastructures, an attractive territory for landscape architecture and one traditionally directed by Civil Engineers, that this crisis is currently pressing.

Wile within contemporary landscape design practice there is a incessant drum beat for advancing measurable performances, there remains a fundamental foundation in the qualitative. Digital tools and computational power increasingly inform and condition design practice, but metric performance analysis and logistical computations are still relatively nascent. The former primarily operates outside actual design processes as a means to speak to power. By seeking to adopt these methodologies to analyze past projects the profession aspires to place itself within the orbit of metric-based funding paradigms.[6] Even with great universal interest in advancing measurable instrumentality in design practice, landscape projects engage this in inconsistently and are less innovative than they are given lip service for.

Figure4: close up on islands and projection seqquence... // The approach is promiscuous with its rendering of the landscapes; switching between simple lit form, dust control surface treatments, and experiential analysis (viewshed).

Running largely opposite to this paradigm, though representing an unconfessed aspiration of some landscape architects, Civil Engineering design practice is rooted and gains agency in its demonstrable performance assessments of function and value. With the parallel rapid advancements of data and simulations, at times paired with design re-combination tools and massive scales of production, some parts of the profession has become a model for an effective design science, though one that through its unconsciously radical adherence to instrumental interventions often has many other unconsidered and unmeasured spatial consequences.

Thus while the morphology and topology of these interventions relate well to other qualitative opportunities, such as aesthetic or open space systems, there are many

examples where the methodologies failed to leverage even close-at-hand opportunities for increased public benefit.[7] Civil Engineers have often recognized this failure and seek to rectify it, but the means for collaboration with qualitative designers can be stymied by the increasingly tightening ball of engineering methodological complexity and are therefore often additive or compensatory rather than integral adjustments. Such a methodological separation and approach has advantages that should not be disregarded, but the approach can be faulted. Placing these other values as a compensatory appliqué retreats from what is likely a much greater potential for design within civil engineering.

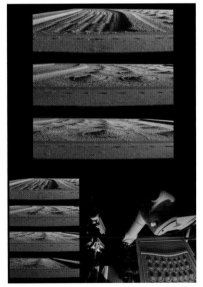

Figure5: islands side view... side photo documentation ... shows robot with camera // The documentation process of each sand model with the robotic arm reproduces parallax viewing of the lake by car.

The work presented in these pages, developed by my Landscape Morphologies Lab, addresses this often weak integration of traditionally qualitative design considerations in the topologies of civil engineering design for landscape infrastructures. Capitulating to the powerful agency of the civil engineering tooling, it seeks to selectively reverse-engineer instrumental methodologies and retool them to allow performance aligned explorations of other values.

With measured performance and engineering topologies the anchor, the typical landscape architecture design paradigm is reversed – qualitative features must conform to civil engineering paradigms and architecture must re-group to building the weakened agency of the qualitative within a strongly fortified quantitive or demonstrable performance territory. The work insinuates that the agency of civil engineering design, even with its blind spots (endemic to any profession!) and likely over entrenchment, owns its position by the pragmatic virtues of its methodology – one that will continue to define design arenas, particularly in large scales of production. In this context landscape architecture must not only provide compensations or dressings for any qualitative short-coming, but should find ways to advance other values deeper within the design process of civil engineering.

The Owens Lake Dust Control project represents a civil engineering project at a scale of production where the established agency of a maximally efficient approach to design seems well justified. The primary mandated function of the infrastructure is to control dust control on half of a 108 square mile lake. The mostly dry lake, in the arid and scenic Owens valley, must be mitigated for dangerously microscopic dust caused by the diversion of water out of the lake's watershed to feed the city of Los Angeles. While the operations and resource expenditures exceed local municipalities and have real consequences at the scale of a megalopolis, dictating an adherence to greatest resource efficiency, the scale of such a highly visible, iconic, and historic landscape feature also invites an expectation to address multiple values. Even so, given the marginality of the locale and city-state juggernaut that is Los Angeles, considerations of the latter would likely have been largely disregarded as luxurious except for legal provisions enforced by California's Public Trust Doctrine.

A powerful David to the Goliath that is the city of Los Angeles, the Public Trust Doctrine requires the dust control project's manager, the Los Angeles Department of Water and Power (LADWP), to not only control dust, but also provide a variety of public trust values that would be appropriate to a lake, dry or not. When the LADWP first proposed to use shallow flooding of water to control dust, which they largely saw as a low-capital rapid means to meet the fast encroaching (and often exceeded) deadlines for dust control, it was accepted by the state authority as a straightforward means to provide provide public trust values by making the dry lake, more lake-like. While effective for meeting initial air quality benchmarks, the LADWP didn't anticipate the extent that re-placing water on the lake would revive dormant ecologies, regional interest, and hope for what long been a regionally deleteriously void.[8]

The utilization of water to meet dust control and public trust requirements represents a neatly integral approach, but it is largely untenable for a water utility. While for the time being, the LADWP will not back-track all their "lake" re-making, finding satisfying alternatives is difficult. The LADWP has found it challenging to adapt their resource efficient designs to the assessments of public trust. After a failure to find acceptance for a water-less dust control method called "Moat and Row", recent negotiations conceded low public-trust value gravel beds in exchange for compensatory design embellishments in other areas, maintaining a more comfortable silo-ed approach to design rather than try to embed these values into the resource efficient dust control landscapes that now define the lakebed.

Figure 6: timelapse overlay of robot doing documentation... //Timelapse of the arm automated documentation process. An operator manipulates lighting and controls the camera remotely.

LML's Owens Lake Rapid Landscape Prototyping Machine was developed as a means towards a more integral design of the lake's dust control infrastructure. The project proposes to create a methodological common ground, a gesture towards professional inclusion, that helps develop qualitatively and quantitively acceptable designs and stimulate a reconsideration of the strategy and tooling currently being employed for the design on the lake. The system itself does not claim authority in providing final design suggestions with absolute quantitive results, but represents an extrapolation of the current design conditions and a prototype for an improved design environment. Rigor and improved design exploration is facilitated by means of a representationally enriched, but computationally powerful, set of custom tools. At the center of the toolset is a physical sand model manipulated with a 6-axis robotic arm, augmented by digital projection, and assessed by the combination of a 3D laser scanner and a custom software suite.

As a medium for design sand modeling represents a powerful layering of topologies, material behaviors, and representation power. Paired with the precision of contemporary robotic technology, laser scanning, and projection, the medium can outstrip, but not entirely depart from the fundamental behaviors and familiar associations with beach sculptures or Japanese sand gardens. From the perspectives of landscape design the strength of many scaled physical modeling techniques, lies with its ability to combine realtime scaled material performances with a robust and rich representation to designers and stakeholders.

Whereas traditional physical models provide spatial computational power for complex on-going environmental processes, such as hydraulic or wind performance, the sand modeling in this project models the process of human intervention: a topological construction

Figure 7: all the tools laid out... // The system employs a set of custom end arm tools.

process. Through engagement with a set of simple end-arm tools attached to the robotic arm, driven by algorithmic tool-paths, the medium simulates the sedimentary assembly of landscape. While the physical engagement with the medium, a robotic tool and dry sand, is idealized compared to the actual messy material choreography of common earth moving equipment and their characteristically duller results, the sedimentary analogy is fundamental by its processes of manipulation, subtraction, and addition that engage with endless sedimentary computations of aggregate repose and balanced cut/fill. Furthermore, even without the custom surface treatment and performance software, the measurement of tool paths and assessment of earth displacement can be translated to roughly analogous and metricized cost calculations.

The approach creates an analogous composite of value oriented design pressures born out of the complex of design, material, and production. By limiting the construction of new forms to "manipulation", the simulated and idealized rake of a tractor back-hoe, rather than finish surface making with subtraction (as would be easily rendered by a regular CNC mill or a suction tool with sand), the designer must immediately develop effective balanced cut/fill choreographies of material manipulation specific to each design. Form is therefore explicitly linked to efficiencies of material manipulation, naturally producing a rigor that is aligned with value rather than directly with form. It concedes a level of finished formal control by anchoring itself to an exploration of material construction process rather than visual or programmatic preferences, but nonetheless presents a rich representational base with which to explore other values. This exploration is facilitated by the effortless computational power and capacity of sand and its ability to be re-formed and re-used rapidly and without any additional material expenditure.

A critical component of this paradigm of design, of developing additional values within the integral design of highly instrumental landscapes, is that design has to adapt to operating within efficiencies and thus scale itself to connect qualitative thresholds with quantitative or logistical based ones. The sand modeling system and associated analysis tools provide an instrumental basis with rich qualitative assessment potential, but in order to cultivate this linkage a custom experiential software and surface design adjustment system aids in the exploration of qualitative thresholds. The value-making of this system becomes quickly apparent on the extremely dry lake-bed where visual perception regularly encounters its own limits and graduated effects. The software enhances the sand forms with morphologically-based adjustable surface treatments (and assessments of their cost)

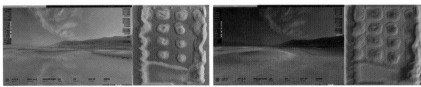

Figure 8: screenshot of software flooded // The custom software systems allows users to apply and adjust critically important surface treatments to the topographic landscapes as well as engage in a set of analysis tools. This scheme is using a thin layer of water to control dust.
Figure 9: with vegetation and night sky // Users can select a time of day to find the optimal moment for the experience of their calibrated landscape.

355|

and real-time perceptual analysis tools that begin to assess traditionally qualitative effects within a quantitative framework.

Scaling perception and experience and thus the extent of related public trust values can enable a new kind of value-making and suggest that the integral design of large infrastructures for qualitative eccentricities can be adjusted within measures of effectiveness. While the qualitative content and impact cannot be empirically assessed, perceptual analysis tools, based on Tadahiko Higuchi's seminal Visual and Spatial Structure Of Landscapes,[9] offer a means to measure the spatial extent of qualitative impacts, whatever their content may be, and speaks to the levers of metric agency. Engineers on the project have appreciated that these tools can help scale the qualitative interventions and their ability to create public trust values, relative to their physical perception on the valuing subjects.

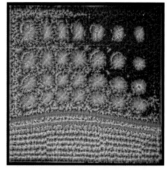

Figure 10: slope lines ... from above ... islands // Slope analysis visualization reveals a fractal drainage network.

In addition to providing perceptual analysis and surface treatments, the software system also functions to disrupt the favored views of instrumental design. The seamless introduction of simulated 1st person experience and realtime plan-o-metric representations of view shed does more than measure allow qualitative assessments and measurements of experience. The representations of these views engage an agent corporality that is often missing from instrumental design. While one outcome of this neglect might produce a "technological sublime",[10] the introduction of this view and the easy association any corporal being has with it could even improve or make more efficient this effect, if not induce other more commonly appropriate values.

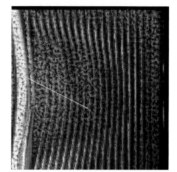

Figure 11: slope lines ... from above ... islands // Slope analysis on the re-designed "moat and row" wind-slowing berms.

This inherently accessible experiential simulation system, conflated with a variety of analysis, both perceptual and material and resource performance, can also further disrupt the agency embedded in centralized engineering entities. The game-like interface provides easy access to expertise and allows stakeholders to become agents of informed design and explore and judge within the presented design solution space. The public outreach system developed in this project, an interactive landscape "player", entices users with a familiar joystick and eventually engages them with design controls that allow them test thresholds between the design of public trust values and resources.

In this way and others the system presents a set of dialectics: tool paths and sand, perceptual analysis and resource efficiency, 1st person and plan-o-metric, resource use and experience, to excite a deeper engagement that can span inevitable gaps in explicit simulation and measurement, while remaining true to the levers of agency and instrumentality. With this complex and rich set of representations and engagements the system draws out the somewhat mythical ability of individual designers to cultivate solutions for complex integral designs, even when checked by challenging logistics, scales, and instrumentalities.

FOOTNOTES
1. Scott, James C. Seeing Like a State: How Certain Schemes to Improve the Human Condition Have Failed. New Haven: Yale UP, 1998. Print.
2. Scott, James C. Seeing Like a State: How Certain Schemes to Improve the Human Condition Have Failed. New Haven: Yale UP, 1998. Print. p20.
3. Slavin, Kevin. "How Algorithms Shape Our World." TED Global. Scotland, Edinburgh. 2011. TED. Web. 4 July 2014.
4. "Public Lab." : A DIY Environmental Science Community. Public Lab, n.d. Web. 10 July 2014.
5. McAdams, Lewis. "FoLAR ARBOR Comments." Letter to Josephine R. Axt, Ph.D. 18 Nov. 2013. MS. N.p.
6. Deutsch, Barbara. "Landscape Performance: Tools to Estimate Benefits and Promote Sustainable Landscape Solutions." Landscape Architecture and Urban Planning Spring 2012 Lecture Series. Texas A&M, College Station, TX. 2 Feb. 2012. YouTube. Web. 4 July 2014.
7. Los Angeles River is a poster-child for this kind of failure (though it was hardly recognized as such at the time of construction).
8. Chrisholm, Graham. "For the Birds." Boom: A Journal of California 3.3 (2013): n. pag. Web.
9. Higuchi, Tadahiko. The Visual and Spatial Structure of Landscapes. Cambridge, MA: MIT, 1983. Print.
10. Nye, David E. American Technological Sublime. Cambridge, MA: MIT, 1994. Print.

GENERAL CREDITS
• Designer/Principal Researcher/Etc: Alexander Robinson
• Andrew Atwood was an initial collaborator on this project (work not shown).
• Research Team: Nicholas Berger, Alex Dahm, Jianjun Li, Brendan Kempf, Kate Hajash, Steve Moody, Feng Wang, Yan Hou.

All images courtesy of Alexander Robinson and the Landscape Morphologies Lab

ALEXANDER ROBINSON is an assistant professor in the University of Southern California School of Architecture Landscape Architecture program, principal of the studio oOR Landscape + Urbanism and director of the Landscape Morphologies Lab. His research and practice explores the growing role of performance within landscape practice, both in terms of core landscape systems and landscape design within infrastructural territories. Robinson is the co-author of Living Systems: Innovative Materials and Technologies for Landscape Architecture (Birkhauser, 2007), a treatise on advanced material practices in landscape architecture. With his Landscape Morphologies Lab he continues this research into landscape infrastructures and other performance systems by developing innovative tools and methodologies to engage their design. Recent work includes a rapid landscape prototyping machine for the Owens Lake and hydraulic modeling for the Los Angeles River. He has worked for Mia Lehrer & Associates, SWA Group and StoSS Landscape Urbanism on a range of projects, including the Los Angeles River Revitalization Master Plan. Robinson is a graduate of Swarthmore College and received a MLA from the Harvard Graduate School of Design.

SYNTHETIC MUDSCAPES

BRADLEY CANTRELL

Embedded within the sands and silts of shifting coastal surfaces, multiscalar relationships between urban cores and their outskirts render vibrant cultural landscapes. Incorporating gradients of population, industry, investment, and regulation, the stretch of shore between Houston, Texas and Mobile, Alabama presents one of the most vulnerable megaregions throughout the entirety of the United States. Within this urban-economic expanse, the tri-city delta landscape between New Orleans, Baton Rouge, and Houma-Thibodeaux has evolved to maintain significant cultural and industrial value; the central wetland of Louisiana is embedded within an expansive web of resources. Synthetic mudscapes speculates on the potential of alternatives where human occupation effectively strengthens

(Figure 1) Tri City Delta Urbanism

environmental resilience in the face of sea level rise, subsidence, coastal erosion, and increased storm frequency.

In order to defend infrastructure, economy, and settlement within the region, it is essential to re-establish a rapidly disappearing landscape by constructing new land to alleviate increasing risk. Links between urban environments and economic drivers have constrained the dynamic deltaic soils for generations, now threatening to undermine the ecological fitness of the entire region. In order to found a resilient, layered mitigation strategy, three distinct land building practices provide an arc of transforming systems to fortify spectrums of inhabitation. Within the Isle de Jean Charles Crescent, dredge material and drill cutting debris are deposited nearby continually deepened transportation lanes and expanding oil fields; high diversity and concentrated seeding is dispersed to sustain land growth in material repositories. Expanding from an outlet in the Mississippi River Levee System, the Myrtle Grove Diversion releases sediment and sifted landfill material transported from the river basin is deposited to accelerate natural land building processes. Combining treated sewage for wetland fertilization as well as

(Figure 2) Socioeconomic Gulf Coast Megaregion

wave attenuation arrays in nearby open waters, the lake Ponchartrain Enclosure evolves as a constructed topography, incorporating strategic infill of repurposed waste from nearby urban areas. Each of these strategies reintroduce fluctuation and adaptive management in order to form the foundations of protective, fertile fabrics.

Static methods of measuring, controlling, and valuing land fail within a territory that is constantly in flux; amongst the mudscape, a finite element grid establishes a framework for constant methods of measurement in a continually transforming environment. Changes and developments in urban ecosystems are continually registered and the system projects viability and success of reconstructive design processes; the density of the mesh communicates variations in the landscape through a limited fidelity. This virtualized ecosystem becomes the fidelity upon which decision making occurs, the virtual model begins to construct a new landscape form. The edges, vertices, and shapes that define mathematical bounds are the current limits to which curatorial, maintenance, and physical alterations are implemented. The mesh renders a "pixelated" image of a complex ecosystem, rendering itself in ever higher fidelity throughout time as new methods of simulation, recording, and data acquisition are developed. This methodology relies on two facts, the delta landscape is infinitely complex and prediction has a limited temporal scope.

Sensing, monitoring, and recording within the region is tied to both local acquisition and global sources. Within the delta a myriad of sensing paradigms are employed to extract data from scientific explorations that are focused on specific niches of ecological activity. This local data is tied with generalized local climate, hydrological, and physical data at finer increments of fidelity. Each of these data points is orchestrated to adhere to time intervals to create an ever increasing

(Figure 3) Isle de Jean Charles Crescent

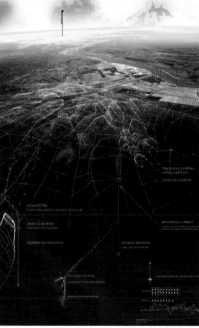

(Figure 4) Myrtle Grove Diversion

realtime view of deltaic conditions. Most of these methods of sensing exist in the delta through multiple agencies and for varying scientific and economic purposes, the shift would be to assimilate these data points into an open and accessible realtime database.

(Figure 5) Lake Ponchartrain Enclosure

The methods of prediction through simulation that are employed exist on a gradient of micro and macro temporal scales. The micro scale provides predictive tools at the minute, hour, day, and year timescales depending on the processes being evaluated. The macro scale accesses processes that exist across decade, millennial, and may span geologic epochs. It is understood that prediction at this scale is not possible but instead relies on past trends and historic precedent. The micro temporal scale is then tuned based on an ever changing image of the macro temporal scale, for example this might push for the curation of algae ecologies that have 30 day life cycles affecting local water oxygenation but contribute to a reduction in carbon effecting a fuzzy future view of increasing global temperatures within a century long time span. The simulation of the gulf then becomes tied to a local decisions aligned with planetary conditions and can respond as a logical unit within competing models that are slowly tied together as global computation increases.

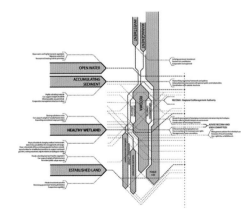

(Figure 6) Urban Ecosystem Regional CoManagement

The acquisition of ecosystem data and modes of simulation allow for interplays between information and design decisions; deposition and integration strategies are based on continually monitored ecosystem vitality at the scale of inhabitation.

The information acquired in satellite locations provides the capacity for energetic cartographies to become embedded with layers of relevant information; data becomes a tactic for understanding relationships between scales in time and the landscape. Challenging the rigidity of urban margins, Synthetic mudscapes incorporates considerate data assimilation to promote the integration of design and implementation practices; a resilient, urban, coastal ecosystem arises from interwoven cultural and regulatory relationships.

Bradley Cantrell

Jeff Carney

Matt Seibert

Elizabeth Anne Williams

THE COASTAL SUSTAINABILITY STUDIO is a transdisciplinary research and design operation at Louisiana State University. The workshop is a collaborative effort incorporating multiple departments, including architects, landscape architects, urban planners, civil engineers, and coastal scientists. The studio addresses issues stemming from coastal erosion and wetland disintegration, running projects in emergent futures and grounded in present realities. Currently supervised by architect Jeff Carney, the organization develops a portfolio of work that engages informed research alongside industrial objectives. Incorporating computation and data visualization, Director of the Robert Reich School of Landscape Architecture, Brad Cantrell, informs the development of project imagery and conceptual frameworks within the studio. Elizabeth Anne Williams is a visiting research fellow and a systems strategist, employing design methodologies for projects proposed at various scales. Matt Seibert explores discernable landscape phenomenologies through imageries of these cross-disciplinary collaborations. This project also included Ben Hartman, Gyan Basyal, Clay Tucker, Katrina Durbak, Patrick Michaels, Emily Powell, Silvia Cox, and Ian Miller.

BRADLEY CANTRELL is a landscape architect and scholar whose work focuses on the role of computation and media in environmental and ecological design. Professor Cantrell received his BSLA from the University of Kentucky and his MLA from the Harvard Graduate School of Design. He has held academic appointments at the Harvard Graduate School of Design, The Rhode Island School of Design, and the Louisiana State University Robert Reich School of Landscape Architecture where he led the school as graduate coordinator and director. Cantrell's work has been presented and published in a range of peer reviewed venues internationally including ACADIA, CELA, EDRA, ASAH, and ARCC.

Cantrell's research and teaching focuses on digital film, simulation, and modeling techniques to represent landscape form, process, and phenomenology. His work in digital representation ranges from improving the workflow of digital media in the design process, to providing a methodology for deconstructing landscape through compositing and film editing techniques. Cantrell is the co-author of two books that focus on digital representation techniques specific to the profession of landscape architecture: Digital Drawing for Landscape Architecture and Modeling the Environment.

Addressing the synthesis of computation and ecology, Cantrell develops and designs devices and infrastructures that create complex interrelationships between maintenance, evolved processes, and environmental response. This approach specifically addresses the interface between old modes of representation and direct connections to ecological processes. In collaboration with co-author Justine Holzman, Cantrell is currently developing a manuscript to be published by Routledge in the Fall of 2015 entitled,Responsive Landscapes. Responsive Landscapes highlights a range of case studies in architecture, landscape architecture, computer science, and art that employ responsive technologies as mediators of landscape processes.

TOM BESSAI

IDEAL MODELS VS HYBRID MODELS: FEEDBACK FROM PHYSICAL AND DIGITAL PROCESS ARTIFACTS IN ARCHITECTURAL DESIGN

363|

The increased reliance on computation methods within architectural design and production is part of a shift in emphasis in the discipline from abstract frameworks, often based in critique or affirmation of previous regimes and ideas, towards material frameworks, where-in substances and artifacts are organized and manipulated according to their evolving properties- not into meaningful finite arrangements, but rather as responsive or inter-connected formations. Architectural design and design development methodologies must be

(Figure 1) Hybrid Structure, Sarah Ward, Golnaz Karimi, Adaptive Architecture Studio, Carleton University, Winter 2014

adapted to take advantage of this shift toward material frameworks. This survey posits an ideal working model as a frame of reference for a series of hybrid design explorations. The hybrid models each in their own way build design clarity through an iterative but open-ended process that includes material testing, computation and prototyping. By managing imprecise feedback amongst a range of digital and physical process artifacts, genuine architectural development is achieved.

In a recent paper entitled *Integrative Design Computation*, Achim Menges argues for the integration of computation and fabrication techniques within a design process that is very attentive to material performance. Menges argues for:

"a computational design approach that synthesizes performance-oriented form generation and physical processes of materialization. Here, the design space is defined and constrained by material behavior, fabrication and production. This understanding of design computation as a calibration between the virtual processes of generating form and the physical becoming of material systems, should not be conceived as limiting the designer, but rather as enabling the exploration of unknown points in the search space defined by the material itself."[1]

IDEAL WORKING MODEL: DIFFERENTIATED TENSILE WOOD-LAMINATE MORPHOLOGIES

A research-based design project that is exemplary of this thinking is an Independent Diploma project from the Institute for Computational Design (ICD), Stuttgart by Bum Suk Ko, 2012, entitled, *Differentiated Tensile Wood-Laminate Morphologies*.[2] Under the supervision of Achim Menges and Sean Ahlquist, this project was executed to the highest standard of both computational precision and material craft.

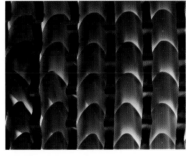

(Figure 2) Differentiated Wood-Laminate Morphologies, BS Ko, ICD, 2012- Prototype

The work is exemplary of an ideal empirical method and traces basic steps common to many of the research projects being conducted at ICD.

Hypothesis

A computation model can deliver accurate prediction of the behavior of material assembly. In this case, the computation model is a spring-based simulation; the material system is one comprised of wood laminates developed to resist tension forces.

Material Selection and Testing

Material performance is gauged through physical testing leading to the development of metrics for input into the computational model.

Iterative Design Process

The computation model is deployed to generate and govern physical prototype development. Feedback from digital fabrication methods is factored into the manufacturing process and, as possible, into the evolving computation model.

Comparative Geometry

Physical artifacts and assemblies are carefully scanned and registered as digital models across the full spectrum of their behavioral capacity. Comparison between the characteristics of the computation model and the physical prototype are made. If the two models are comparable, then it can be concluded that the computational model is predictive.

The empirical underpinnings of this research work is very sound. The development of reliable predictive computation methods is essential for engineering and material research. But, such a strict methodological formula is difficult to apply to architectural design, in particular to real-world building situations, where contingencies and unknowns share the design space with certainties.

HYBRID WORKING MODEL: BUNDLED BENDING-ACTIVE COMPONENT SYSTEM

(Figure 3) Concept model, closed-loop bending-active pavilion structure

The following research project was undertaken as the capstone to the Master of Science in Material Systems Degree at the University of Michigan Taubman College, 2013. Working under Sean Ahlquist, I engaged in the methodology outlined above, this time applied to the bundling of bending-active structures. The research proceeded along the determined course, but then migrated to accommodate feedback that was outside of the initial set of controls.[3]

Hypothesis

Bundling of bending-active structural elements will augment structural versatility and capacity leading to a broader range of design potentials for bending-active structures.

Material Selection and Testing

Metrics and limits are developed for GFRP rods in bending both individually and in bundled configurations for input to a computational model alongside observation of characteristics of bundling. Exploration of connection strategies to achieve bundling is carried out.

Iterative Design Process

A controlled bundling exploration is carried out on 1:1 closed-loop physical test figures using different bundled combinations. Note that a spring-based computation model for accurate estimation of bundled structures has yet to be developed.

Based upon close observation of the physical test models, an innovation is introduced whereby individual bundled members are spread apart from each-other across the non-optimized

365|

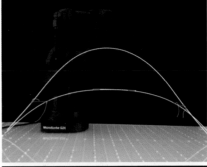
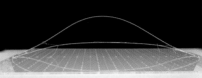
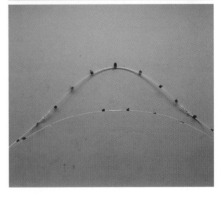

(Figure 4, 5, 6) Closed-loop bending model- physical prototypes

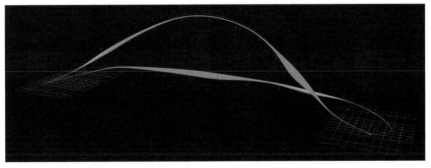

(Figure 7) Computation model, grasshopper: optimization of sectional dimension based upon bending radius

(Figure 8) Comparative physical prototypes of closed-loop structure: pure bundled below; trussed/bundled hybrid above

(Figure 9) Pavilion prototype model, 1:20

(Figure 10) Partial mock-up at half of full scale

curving segments of the closed-loop figure. The development of local struts or trusses allows spanning strength over straight segments of the figure without compromising bundled capacity over optimal radii sections of the figure as per the material tests.

This observation has led to the development of an algorithm to determine overall cross-sectional diameter for trussed spanning elements at curvature radii less than the optimal bending-active range of radii based upon the material tests.

Comparative Solutions: Pure Bundling Vs Bundle/Truss Hybrid

Specific comparison is made through a series of iterative physical models of the test shape. The pure bundled configuration is compared with the graduated truss configuration. While the future development of a predictive computation model is more likely for the pure bundled system than for the truss-based hybrid system, the advantages of the latter to architectural space-making and structural efficiency are undeniable.

Prototype Pavilion

Further investigation through an architectural project development process is carried out to further explore the hybrid conditions proposed. Prototype models at successive scales lead to a 1:2 mock-up that begins to challenge the components of the design system in new ways requiring larger diameter GFRP rods and polycarbonate connectors.

The bending-active project recognizes the architectural design development potential of a hybrid process that accepts imprecise feedback and a loose relationships between digital form-finding and physical mock-ups. With the goal of further exploring hybrid methods, I conducted a winter 2014 graduate level architecture studio at the Azrieli School of Architecture, Carleton University that was designed to leverage both material systems investigations and generative computation within the context of an iterative architectural design process.[4] Below are excerpts from the studio syllabus.

ADAPTIVE ARCHITECTURE STUDIO: DIGITAL CRAFT AND MATERIALISM

In the studio students engage in an iterative design process explored through computational and physical modeling and prototyping. 'Material Systems' research and production in architecture constitutes the principal frame of reference for the studio and for the creation of structures capable of deployment, adaptation and responsiveness to users and environments. The following five topics constitute the investigative context of the studio:

1. Expanding the Discipline of Architecture- Technology

The Techno-cultural utopian explorations from the 1960s by Archigram and Cedric Price, in particular

Instant City and the Fun Palace, represent a central historical antecedent to the methods and ideas if the studio. Although these projects were unable to be realized due to lack of technical knowledge or engineering capacity, their ambition of adaptability and temporality as well as the anticipation of cybernetic 'smart-systems' set them well outside of the boundaries of the discipline as it was understood by most of their peers.

2. Matter and Material Systems in Sciences and Engineering; Architecture

The gradual alignment through the 1990s to the present of the ambitions of architectural culture with the disciplines of the sciences, mathematics and engineering on the topic of material formations and coded or evolutionary processes. The principles put forward by Michelle Addinton and others on an architecture that leverages advanced material systems in the creation of responsive local environments in lieu of global or generic spaces and building systems.

3. Performance Criteria- Engineering vs. Architecture; Behavior

Discussions of 'performance' vs. 'behavior' in engineering and architecture in the context of material systems. In engineering, specific performance criteria can usually be identified- metrics for strength, thermal performance, bending etc. Within the discipline of architecture, the necessity for a broader and often less immediately empirical spectrum of goals or requirements must be considered. These begin to establish themselves as behavioral criteria or even as programs for the studio work: atmospheric, sensory, responsive to users and to climate, adaptive, demountable, re-configurable, deployable. All become valuable but possibly competing criteria for project development. With this constellation of objectives, there exists the possibility and even advantage for redundancy amongst the systems at play. Reference to complex systems in nature is useful in understanding these behaviors while respecting the distinction between organic or natural systems themselves and engineered systems.

4. Form-finding through Material Engagement and Testing; Observation

This important topic is framed upon the broad body of empirical research into the performance of natural materials conducted by and under the supervision of Frei Otto in Germany over the 1970s until the 1990s. Otto's 'IL ' numbered publications and his material testing methods as conducted at the Institute of Lightweight Structures will be referenced in the studio. Material testing is closely aligned to the design process in the studio and will inform the project work in a direct way.

5. Digital Craft; Materialism

Computational methods are becoming increasingly accessible to architects and students of architecture. In the context of material studies, architectural assemblies and their 'performance'/ 'behavior' as discussed above. Students must consider the role of digital modeling and digital simulation methods and their parallel to physical material testing and exploration all within the framework of form-finding and design. The two central questions being asked of these techniques within an iterative design process are:

a/ Can and do digital simulations accurately reflect real material tolerances and performance; what is the advantage of digital simulation over physical simulation/ testing?

b/ Given the close relationship that is evolving between digital simulation/modeling and physical production/ fabrication, what are the tolerances- both as limits and as potentials- that machine fabrication/ physical production feed back into design.

(Figure 11) 1:20 Prototype Model, Deployable Pneumatic/Pleated Hybrid Structure, Sarah Ward, Golnaz Karimi

Working within this framework, students are encouraged to develop design and design development methods leveraging both computation models and physical mock-ups.

Initial research into materials and material systems performance is carefully directed towards an architectural goal- a pavilion structure for the gathering of athletes at the Pan Am games to be held in Toronto in 2015.

Two projects are documented below.

HYBRID WORKING MODEL 2: PLEATED PNEUMATIC STRUCTURES

This project was by Sarah Ward and Golnaz Karimi. Their research began with an exploration of pneumatic structures and took the form of a hybrid project with the introduction of complimentary folding/pleating strategies. The deployable pavilion design that was developed began with material research in pneumatics. Computation and reverse engineering strategies were central to the early development of the project. Design development was heavily influences by the behavior of and feedback from scale models, prototypes and mock-ups at incrementally larger scales approaching 1:1.

The following description is based on the students' project statements and summarizes the key methods and stages to their research and design development on the project.

Pneumatics Research and Testing

Pneumatic technology was initially developed from hot air balloons and the implementation of temporary nylon structures in military operations during the Second World War. It proliferated in the fields of architecture and engineering in the 1960s and 1970s with the works of Frei Otto, Buckminster Fuller and others. One strategy from this era was to combine pneumatics and compartmentalization producing self-structuring 3-dimensional shells from the inflated compartments. From the works developed during this period of innovation arose various contemporary examples that hybridize pneumatic technology with additional systems for greater interactivity. The 'Orbit' installation, by Tomas Saraceno, 2013[5] is an example- a project that enables the suspension of inflated spheres via the tension of netting and cables attached to fixed points. When attempting to produce a pneumatic system, the student research began with an analysis of known materials and systems such as balloons and netting.

(Figure 12) Initial pneumatic tests using netting to control the inflation of segmented balloons

(Figure 13) Initial pneumatic compartment studies

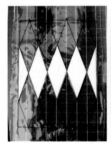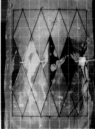

(Figure 14) Polyethylene patterned compartments sealed with a heat sealer

They quickly graduated to sealed air compartments composed of materials such as vinyl, polyethylene and Mylar. Methods used to create these seals were glue, tape, laser cutting and heating using a heat gun and heat sealer.

The system that was deemed most successful was polyethylene sealed with a heat sealer as it created a strong seal that resisted a significant amount of air pressure. When accommodating a larger scale the heat sealer can be adapted to a larger size or an adaptable system such as a sealing head attached to a CNC machine or robotic arm.

(Figure 15) Folding and pleating form studies with laser cut museum board and tie-back elements

After various tests regarding the organization of the sealing lines and the pneumatic pillows that they create, three main systems emerged as most efficient: a global system, where all pillows are inflated, a linear system, and a diagonal system. Each system provides different means of inflation as well as different levels of air pressure.

Hybrid System Development

Through the development of more particular patterning arrangements in the pneumatic studies, it was recognized that regular repeating pneumatic modules were consistent with the logic of folded structures, and that the latter could be animated and controlled by pneumatics. Pleated assemblies derived from regular origami folds allowed the system to expand and collapse seamlessly. Various installations and pavilions that utilize such systems at an inhabitable scale were researched. One example is the 'Cardboard Banquet' project, 2009 by architecture students at Cambridge University- a pavilion constructed entirely out of folded cardboard that is collapsible[6], providing insight into materiality and joinery. Material research and physical testing were conducted with scale models and prototypes to develop an understanding of the relationship between 2-dimensional scoring and folding and the system's three-dimensionality and deploy-ability. Experimentation was done with various paper thicknesses and laser cutting settings as well as with the scale of the folds.

The folded system was explored digitally for its capacity to deploy and be transformed. Physical models were digitized and instances in the folded geometry were recorded in Rhino. Photogrammetry was also used. A hand scanner and mesh creation software were engaged to build 3D meshes from physical models to further examine more complex forms. In order to examine the hinging movement and displacement of the folded forms, a parametric model using Rhino Grasshopper and Kangaroo was also developed.

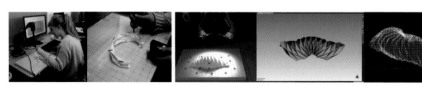

(Left)(Figure 16) Digitizer used to measure physical models
(Right)(Figure 17)Photogrammetry, Geomagic Studio 3D; export mesh to Autocad

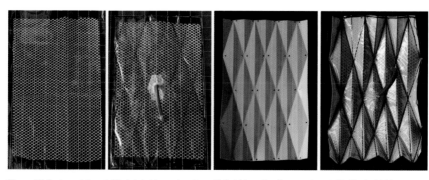

(Figure 18) Scale prototype 1:20 of global layered system of inflatable cells: all compartments fill with air; initial introduction of folded substrate

While no single simulation, parametric model or scanned set provided complete knowledge of the emerging architectural system being developed, the combination provided a strong substrate of both documentary and predictive information that was central to project development.

371|

The combination of the pneumatic and the folded elements were exhaustively studied in prototype models. Many of the innovations in the project directly emerged from the process of solving this synthetic relationship through physical prototypes at increments in scale.

Pavilion Prototype

The site for the temporary pavilions for the 2015 Pan Am Games is the 'International Centre'- a median area between the high security athletes' village and the general public. The area accommodates meetings, ceremonies and downtime for the athletics. The hybrid

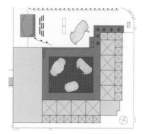

(Figure19A) Site Plan, Pan-Am Games Athletes' Village; 20b: perspectival view of pavilion

(Figure 19B)

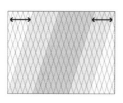
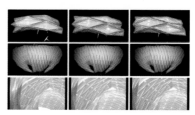

(Left)(Figure 20) Pneumatic Cell lay-out unfolding diagram; plan and elevation views; blue cells are inflatable
(Right)(Figure 21) Stills from process videos that demonstrate pneumatic action in the prototype assembly and pavilion mock-ups

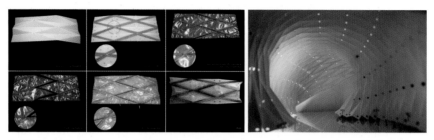

(Left)(Figure 22) Developed pneumatic hybrid pavilion assembly prototype, 1:4 scale, layers of assembly shown
(Right)(Figure 23) Interior View of pavilion showing transmission of light through translucent wall assembly

pneumatic/ pleated pavilions act as adaptable tents that can house various activities from vendors, intimate meetings or group interaction.

The inflatable cell groupings are coordinated into specific patterns on the exterior face of the pavilions and control expansion, contraction and deployment. The combination of tensioning cables, pneumatic pillows, and grounding pegs creates dynamic modifiable forms. The folded plates themselves are revealed to the interior. The entire assembly is both light weight and allows the transmission of light.

Corrugated cellular plastic sheets were selected for rigid portion of the pleated hybrid system. They are both weather-resistant and light weight and are able to accommodate the bending action of the folded plate system. They are translucent for light penetration, as well as easy to score for bending seams. These sheets are available in limited sheet dimensions. Therefore, a means of joining multiple pieces together was crucial. The insertion of dowels within the corrugations formed a structural bond between distinct panels to create a complete system. The dowels along with the pneumatic polyethylene system produce a strong hybrid composite able to bend, deflect and inflate.

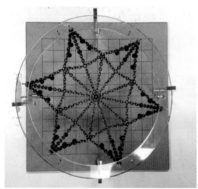

(Figure 24A, B) Hanging Chain Model; Kangaroo Studies with Triangular and Quad Meshes

HYBRID WORKING MODEL 3: STRUCTURAL VAULT WITH PATTERNED SURFACE

This research was undertaken in the context of the Azrieli studio by Tim Lobsinger. His ambition for the project was to explore structural form-finding as well as surface-based pattern making via generative computation methods. Several precedents were discussed in depth that began to bookend the solution space of the research. On one hand, the elegant dome of the Louvre Abu Dhabi project by Jean Nouvel proposes a regular and rational structural rhythm around which a discreet layered cladding system is deployed[7]. The structural system does not participate in the expression or behavior with respect to light and shadow of the dome. On the other, the Shellstar pavilion by Andrew Kudless, Matsys was closely studied for the combined constructive and expressive nature of the form-found structure, neatly detailed to leverage each tessellation in the overall composition[8].

Form-finding

Initial material explorations delivered a hanging chain model, while computational form-finding was conducted in Grasshopper/ Kangaroo. In both the models, careful attention was given to tessellation and support. Coarser quad figuration was seen as potentially compatible with infill panels.

Alongside these form studies, an analytical framework was established with the use of structural design software to explore axial load paths, vault deformation and other loading characteristics.

Pattern Generation

(Figure 25A, B) 2D parametric and scripted pattern studies including reaction diffusion system

Recursive scripts were explored to generate differentiated dot patterns and line patterns for cladding. While the pattern development was conducted independently of the structural form-finding, the myriad issues of its deployment were intensively explored in the context of the emerging structural and formal characteristics. The cladding patterns could be set locally or globally at distinct scales. The important question being posed was, to what extent would it fuse itself with the structural members? The richness of the project as a research exercise and its success as an architectural design was and is intimately tied to this discussion of hybridization of two systems. The design criteria for the performance or behavior of this synthesis remain open for debate.

Prototype Pavilion: Combination of Systems

Amid much discussion and experimentation, a direction emerged for the conflation of two systems. A vaulting iteration was selected for its symmetry and stability. It would act

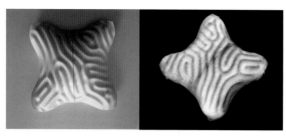

(Figure 26) Plan view and x-ray view, 3D print of monolithic geometry

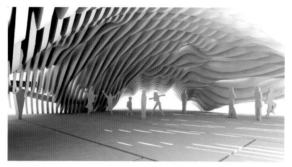

(Figure27) Visualization of pavilion developed with contoured iso-curves as structural beams

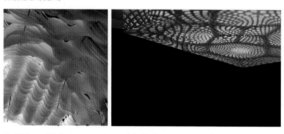

(Left)(Figure28) Prototype scale model with fine contouring of the base geometry to create an ephemeral light filter (Right)(Figure 29)Lightbox: scale model prototype

as a canvas for the global application of a pattern based upon a reaction diffusion system. The latter delivers complex path formations that are formally distinctive, but that resist load bearing. With the pattern mapped to the host surface, a height-mapping script was developed that impregnates the surface with the pattern. Contouring along the iso-curves of the host surface delivers an exciting structural logic that begins to address fabrication issues and constructability.

Fabrication logistics for the creation of scale models and prototypes offered important feedback to the design at different scales. The monolithic 3D printed artifact reveals the potential of the combined system to deliver exciting lighting and shadow characteristics, but resists development at a large scale. Contouring along iso-curves begins to engage structural capacity and light transmission. This was explored in both model and visualization producing a range of compelling possibilities.

CONCLUSIONS ON DESIGN DEVELOPMENT AND IMPRECISE FEEDBACK: BUILDING UPON MATERIAL FRAMEWORKS IN PRACTICE

This paper has argued that the onset of advanced computational and digital simulation techniques must be carefully considered and harnessed for the pursuit of material frameworks in architectural design. Specifically, it is by the iterative management of imprecise feedback amongst the suite of often imperfect digital and physical processes and artifacts available, that architectural development is achieved. These processes and artifacts include material testing, computational simulation and prototyping through digital fabrication.

It is this synthesis and careful cross-referencing of distinct and related research and assembly regimes that will contribute value to design and project development from conception to construction. I will briefly describe these combined methods at play over the course of two related commissions by Denegri Bessai Studio to shed light on issues and potentials in this regard.

(Figure 30) Delaware Lightbox: final Installation, Denegri Bessia Studio

375|

The first project, the *Lightbox* is a feature element within a residential renovation project in Toronto described thus in the project literature of the studio:

"This feature element combines pattern and light to animate the ceiling plane over the kitchen and eating area at the rear of the house. It is a smooth translucent acrylic light-box that measures approximately eight feet by seven feet in its plan dimension filling the majority of the full width of the kitchen. Its structure is concealed within the dominant geometry of the surface pattern. The pattern emanates and sub-divides from the four central halogen spots in the space and diffuses their light. The lightbox produces a range of natural and artificial ambient lighting effects in the space over the course of the day and night. Moderate down- light produces a diffuse glow in the space, while full halogen lighting produces high relief projected patterning on the adjacent walls and counters. In the absence of artificial light, the box picks up daylight through surface reflection. The box volume extends the ceiling plane downward at a gentle angle, concealing a step-down in the section of the space."[9]

The design and research focus for this project was upon pure effect- the delivery of complex patterned shadow and light characteristics to the space. A range of subdivision strategies were created and tested through combined computational

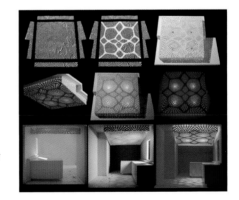

(Figure 31) Lightbox testing: transparency/light transmission, layering, color and shadow

(Figure 32) Lightbox assembly and installation requiring steel structural armature for span; stability

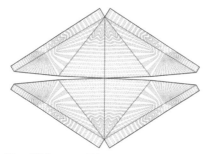

(Figure 33) Queensway Lightbox: diagram of subdivision and folding lines

(Figure 34) 1:24 model studies- ceilings element only; spatial studies showing the relationship to new millwork elements below

models and physical scale models, and the most dynamic pattern was carried forward. Testing was conducted to evaluate and explore layering, color distribution, levels of transparency and reflection, and shadow distribution. Compatibility with CNC machining techniques and material/machine dimensions were projected and tested at 1:1.

Based on this range of imprecise indicators, the project was moved into construction. Structural support, connection details and construction sequence were not woven into the research framework of the project. Had further simulation been conducted in these areas, several necessary elements of the final constructed project would have been more carefully folded into the design solution.

A follow-up commission for a feature ceiling element in a large retail space on the Queensway in Toronto allowed the studio to expand the material system research beyond the consideration of pure effect alone and widen the testing space to include structural and assembly characteristics. A subdivision strategy was quickly developed with the benefit of the iterations derived for the earlier project. While the original lightbox presented a principal planar face with two nested hierarchies of subdivision, in the Queensway project the global pattern was actuated along folding lines.

Through early physical models, folded spatial/structural compositions were studied. These models provided excellent feedback on the overall planometric and sectional dimensions of the feature in the space, and its registration with related design elements including prismatic triangular merchandise displays.

In the design development phase of the project, very precise digital modeling was

(Figure 35) Detail from digital model showing developed folding geometry, perforation pattern and structural system

required to design the layering of non-structural facing elements upon the folded support frames. Structural simulation was used to minimize the extent and weight of the steel frames and test the effect of patterning/ perforation on strength and rigidity.

377|

Further physical prototypes were created to verify geometry, material attributes and ambient effects.

A partial 1:1 mock-up in steel and acrylic was created in collaboration with the fabricator in order to test general assembly requirements and connection details as well as to explore the folded seams at the range of local angles that were derived.

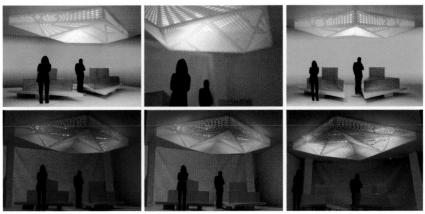

(Figure 36) 1:8 model study with developed folding geometry, perforation pattern and structural system; color variation tests

(Figure 37) 1:1 partial mock-up

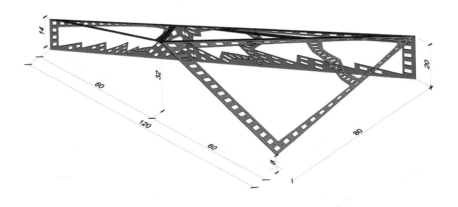

(Figure 38A) Structural frame assembly diagram

|378

Finally, fabrication tolerances were input into the digital model in order to produce workable digital templates for manufacture at reasonable cost.

No individual physical or digital model/simulation was sufficient to carry the project from concept design through to fabrication and construction. Rather, imprecise feedback amongst the various digital and physical artifacts have shaped and guided the project.

This principle of project-based exploration and the building of design knowledge iteratively via imprecise feedback from both digital and physical models will continue to demonstrate its importance as we move forward in the contemporary context of architectural design, fabrication and construction. It encourages richness in the overlap of behaviors and characteristics that any single model might not account for.

(Left)(Figure 38B) finished steel elements on site

(Right)(Figure 39) Queensway Avenue construction site- ceiling prepped for steel frame installation

FOOTNOTES

1. Integrative Design Computation, Achim Menges, 2011 In: Proceedings of the 31th Conference of the Association For Computer Aided Design In Architecture (ACADIA), edited by Branko Kolarevic

2. Differentiated Tensile Wood-Laminate Morphologies- Independent Diploma Project, Institute for Computational Design, Stuttgart University, Bum Suk Ko, 2012

3. Bending-active Structures Capstone Project, Taubman College of Architecture, University of Michigan, Tom Bessai, 2013 http://www.academia.edu/7407739/ACADIA_2013_Adaptive_Architecture

4. ARC 5106 Graduate Studio: Adaptive Architecture, Carleton University Azrieli School of Architecture and Urbanism, Tom Bessai, 2014

5. 'In Orbit' Installation, Dusseldorf, Tomas Saraceno, 2013, www.tomassaraceno.com

6. Cardboard Banquet Installation, Cambridge University, Pleatfarm, 2009. www.pleatfarm.com

7. Louvre Abu Dhabi Project, Saadiyat Island, UAE, Jean Nouvel Architectes, 2007-2014. en.wikipedia.org/wiki/Louvre_Abu_Dhabi

8. Shellstar Pavilion, Hong Kong, Andrew Kudless, Matsys, 2012.

9. Delaware Avenue Project Description, Denegri Bessai Studio, 2013, www.denegribessaistudio.com/delaware/

ACKNOWLEDGEMENTS

- Differentiated Tensile Wood-Laminate Morphologies is an Independent Diploma project from the Institute for Computational Design (ICD), Stuttgart University by Bum Suk Ko, 2012. The work was conducted under the supervision of Professors Achim Menges and Sean Ahlquist.
- Bundled Bending-active Component Systems is a research project undertaken as part of the Master of Science in Material Systems Degree at the University of Michigan Taubman College of Architecture and Urban Planning by Tom Bessai, 2013. The principal advisors to the project were Assistant Professors Sean Ahlquist and Kathy Velikov, and Associate Professor Geoffrey Thun.
- The Adaptive Architecture Studio: Digital Craft and Materialism, was a graduate level studio run at the Carleton University Azrieli School of Architecture and Urbanism in the winter 2014 semester as part of ARC 5106 taught by Assistant Professor and Azrieli 2014 Scholar-in-residence, Tom Bessai. The ARC 5106 coordinating instructor was Assistant Professor Inerbir Singh Riar.
- Pleated Pneumatic Structures, by Sarah Ward and Golnaz Karimi, and Structural Vault with Patterned Surface, by Tim Lobsinger are research projects conducted as part of the graduate level Adaptive Architecture Studio: Digital Craft and Materialism, Azrieli School of Architecture and Urbanism under advisor Tom Bessai, winter 2014.
- The Delaware Lightbox and Queensway Interior are projects of Denegri Bessai Studio Architecture |DBS Fabrication.
- Delaware Lightbox, 2012-2013
- Project team: Tom Bessai, Maria Denegri, Dave Reeves, Omri Menache, Dave Freedman, Alex Warwick, Andre PaesAlmeida
- Queensway Interior, 2014
- Project team: Tom Bessai, Maria Denegri, Duncan Sabiston, Andre PaesAlmeida
- Construction: DeMan Construction Ltd.

WORKS CITED

- Achim Menges. 2011. "Integrative Design Computation". In: Proceedings of the 31th Conference of the Association

For Computer Aided Design In Architecture (ACADIA), edited by Branko Kolarevic, 72-81, Calgary.

- Tomas Saraceno. 2013. "In Orbit" Installation, K21 Ständehaus, Düsseldorf, www.tomassaraceno.com.
- Pleatfarmer. 2009. "Cardboard Banquet" Installation, Cambridge University, UK, www.pleatfarm.com.
- Jean Nouvel. 2007-2014. "Louvre Abu Dhabi" Project, Saadiyat Island, UAE en.wikipedia.org/wiki/Louvre_Abu_Dhabi
- Andrew Kudless, Matsys. 2012. "Shellstar Pavilion" Installation, Wan Chai, Hong Kong
- matsysdesign.com/2013/02/27/shellstar-pavilion/

IMAGE CREDITS

Figure1: Golnaz Karimi and Sarah Ward, Carleton University, 2014
Figure 2: Bum Suk Ko, Institute for Computational Design, Stuttgart University, 2012
Figure 3, 4, 5, 6, 7, 8, 9: Tom Bessai, University of Michigan, 2013
Figure 10: Bennett Scorcia, University of Michigan, 2013
Figure 11: Golnaz Karimi and Sarah Ward, Carleton University, 2014
Figure 12, 13, 14, 15, 16, 17, 18, 19, 20, 21, 22, 23: Golnaz Karimi and Sarah Ward, Carleton University, 2014
Figure 24, 25, 26, 27, 28: Tim Lobsinger, Carleton University, 2014
Figure 29: Andre Paes Almeida, Denegri Bessai Studio, 2014
Figure 30: Alan Hamilton, Alan Hamilton Photography, 2012
Figure 31: Andre Paes Almeida, Denegri Bessai Studio, 2014
Figure 32,33: Tom Bessai, Denegri Bessai Studio, 2012
Figure 34: Andre Paes Almeida, Denegri Bessai Studio, 2014
Figure 35: Tom Bessai, Denegri Bessai Studio, 2014
Figure 36, 37: Andre Paes Almeida, Denegri Bessai Studio, 2014
Figure 38A: Duncan Sabiston, Denegri Bessai Studio, 2014
Figure 38B, 39: Scott Norsworthy, Scott Norsworthy Photography, 2014

TOM BESSAI is a registered architect and founding partner with Maria Denegri of the Toronto-based architecture firm Denegri Bessai Studio. Projects from the studio have been published nationally and internationally. He has recently established DBS Fabrication- a satellite research and production workshop that augments the computing, design and prototyping facilities of the practice. He is an Assistant Professor at the J.H. Daniels Faculty of Architecture at the University of Toronto. He holds a Master of Architecture from UCLA and is completing a Master of Science from the University of Michigan's Taubman College with a specialization in Design and Material Systems. His research and teaching explore computation and fabrication strategies for adaptive architecture. His recent work on force-active assemblies was presented at ACADIA 2013.

Tom Bessai BA, BArch, MArch, OAA, MRAIC
Principal, Denegri Bessai Studio Architecture
Principal, DBS Fabrication
1088 Bathurst Street, Toronto ON. Canada M5R 3G9
tel: 416 538 1088 | cel: 647 839 2339
www.denegribessaistudio.com | www.dbsfab.com | tom@denegribessaistudio.com
Assistant Professor
John H. Daniels Faculty of Architecture, Landscape, and Design
University of Toronto
230 College Street, Toronto ON. Canada M5T 1R2
www.daniels.utoronto.ca | tom.bessai@daniels.utoronto.ca

VOLVO PURE TENSION PAVILION NEW PRECEDENT FOR ALTERNATIVE ENERGY AND PERSONAL MOBILITY

ALVIN HUANG / SYNTHESIS DESIGN + ARCHITECTURE

(Figure 1) Pure
Tension Pavilion
at Urban Stories
Event, Milan, Italy

(Left)(Figure 2)
Pavilion assembly
diagram
(Right)(Figure 3)
Frame optimization
diagram

(Left)(Figure 4)
Solar incidence
analysis diagram
(Right)(Figure
5)Fabrication
process images

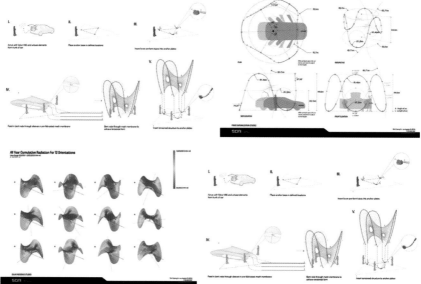

382

FROM COMPETITION WIN TO GROUND-BREAKING STRUCTURE IN 4 MONTHS

Named one of Time Magazine's Top 25 Inventions of 2013
2013 AIA|LA Next LA Design Award

Pure Tension, the high-tech, portable solar-powered tensile membrane structure designed by Los Angeles-based Synthesis Design + Architecture, is the culmination of months of design refinement, research, and engineering after the firm won Volvo's "Switch to Pure Volvo" competition, organized by international architecture magazine THE PLAN this past summer.

(Figure 6) Detail of PV panels embedded in pavilion mesh skin

The pavilion, commissioned by Volvo Car Italia for the new Volvo V60 plug-in hybrid electric car, not only charges the car but also flat-packs to fit in the trunk and assembles in less than one hour. It is an experimental structure that, similar to a concept car, is a working prototype that speculates on the future of personal mobility and alternative energy sources while also exploring digital design methodologies and innovative structural solutions.

For Pure Tension, digital design technologies were harnessed not only to create an iconic piece of original design but also a vision for the future of transportation.

SDA won the international competition by fulfilling Volvo's wishes for a portable, yet iconic structure to showcase the V60 on a press trip through Italy. However, SDA strategically added two key elements to the design that made it stand out: one was the lightweight fabric and aluminum structure that could be collapsed into the trunk of the vehicle and deployed by two people with ease, the second element was a photovoltaic skin that charges the vehicle, essentially the first-of-its-kind portable charging station for a hybrid car.

LOCAL DESIGN/GLOBAL PROCESS

"We wanted to challenge the notion of solar power as something that is an additive piece of engineering infrastructure," says Synthesis founder and principal, Alvin Huang. "The solar panels became a design feature and design driver, rather than something applied after the fact. The goal was to balance utility with beauty," he adds.

The pavilion is the result of a global effort with design and engineering being carried out

(Figure 7) Pure
Tension Pavilion in
Palm Springs, USA

in Los Angeles by SDA with Buro Happold Engineers, fabrication being done by Chicago based Fabric Images, solar panels being sourced from Ascent Solar of Texas.

The completed pavilion was then shipped to Italy to embark on a 9 month, multi-city promotional tour starting with the launch event hosted by Volvo in Milan. The next stop for the pavilion was the EcoMondo Trade Fair of Sustainable Material & Energy in November 2013. The tour ended at The Plan Magazine's annual Perspective event in Venice in the summer of 2014, coinciding with the Venice Biennale.

DESIGN, FABRICATION, AND DEPLOYMENT

SDA derived the original design geometry through a conceptual form-finding process known as dynamic mesh relaxation. The mesh topology produced by SDA was then further developed by Buro Happold, who provided an engineered form-finding process that takes into account material properties to rationalize the contours. Engineering revealed that the SDA form-finding process was within 90-95% accurate with a maximum deviation of about 2 inches. The continuous tensioned skin of pavilion is articulated by three hierarchies of geometric pattern that collectively define the geometry and produce a visually engaging moiré effect.

The pavilion is an expression of the tensioned equilibrium between its elastic membrane skin and rigid perimeter frame. The perimeter frame of the structure is defined by 24 CNC bent aluminum pipes with swaged slip fit connections, while the skin is materialized as a pair of vinyl encapsulated polyester mesh membranes with a zippered seam and spandex sleeves that wrap the frame. The entire pavilion collapses neatly into two 65"x15" x15" 'B-cases' and weighs 150lbs in total and can be assembled and taken down in just under an hour by a team of two to three people.

(Figure 8) Pure Tension Pavilion at EcoMondo Fair, Rimini, Italy

252 lightweight flexible photovoltaic panels are embedded within an applied graphic pattern of vinyl tiles along the mesh. The PV pattern is the result of intensive solar incidence analysis on the structure that found the average annual solar incidence of the skin for 360 degrees of orientation and mapped PV locations to the areas of greatest average annual solar incidence. Additionally a MPPT (Maximum Power Point Tracking) controller is utilized to sample the output of the cells, and selectively disable those that are not collecting enough energy, thereby ensuring that the pavilion is receiving as much charge as possible. The pavilion can recharge a fully depleted car in about 12 hours in optimum sun conditions.

The target goal to achieve the minimum power required to charge the car was 300 watts of power. The current skin is testing at about 450 watts of power on optimum sun conditions. The wiring of the PV panels is integrated into the seams of the fabric and feed a portable battery system which in turn charges the Volvo V60. Current estimates have the pavilion recharging a fully depleted car battery in about 12 hours. Technical requirements for the charging of the V60 were developed in collaboration with the Volvo Design Center in Camarillo, CA and solar consultant FTL Solar in New Jersey.

Design Team: Alvin Huang, Filipa Valente, Chia-ching Yang, Behnaz Farahi, Yueming Zhou
Structural Engineering: Buro Happold Los Angeles (Greg Otto, Stephen Lewis, Ron Elad)
Fabrication: Fabric Images, Chicago
Custom Photovoltaic panels: Ascent Solar, Texas
Solar Consultant: FTL Solar, New Jersey
Client: Volvo Italy
Competition Organizer: The Plan Magazine (Italy)
Opening date: October 9, 2013
Program: Rapidly depoloyable pavilion to showcase the Volvo V60
Area: 36 sqm 0
Materials: vinyl encapsulated polyester mesh membrane, photovoltaic panels, CNC-bent aluminum pipe

SYNTHESIS is an emerging contemporary design practice with over 20 years of collective professional experience in the fields of architecture, infrastructure, interiors, installations, exhibitions, furniture, and product design. Founded in 2011, our work has already begun to achieve international recognition for its design excellence. Our diverse team of multidisciplinary design professionals includes registered architects, architectural designers and computational specialists educated, trained, and raised in the USA, UK, Denmark, Portugal, and Taiwan. This diverse cultural and disciplinary background has supported our expanding portfolio of international projects in the USA, UK, Russia, Thailand, and China.

Originally founded in London January 2011 by Alvin Huang, Synthesis Design + Architecture is a forward thinking international design firm exploring design at the intersection of Performance, Technology and Craft. Following an appointment as Assistant Professor of Architecture at the University of Southern California, Alvin subsequently relocated the office to Los Angeles. The design trajectory and ethos of the office is rooted in balancing both the experimental and the visionary with the practical and the pragmatic to achieve the extraordinary.

ALVIN HUANG is the Founder and Design Principal of Synthesis. He is an award-winning architect, designer, and educator specializing in the integrated application of material performance, emergent design technologies and digital fabrication in contemporary architectural practice. His wide ranging international experience includes significant projects of all scales ranging from hi-rise towers and mixed-use developments to bespoke furnishings.

Prior to forming SYNTHESIS, he gained significant professional experience working with Amanda Levete Architects, Future Systems, Zaha Hadid Architects, and AECOM.

Alvin received a Master of Architecture and Urbanism from the Architectural Association Design Research Laboratory (2004) in London and a Bachelor of Architecture from the University of Southern California (1998) in Los Angeles. His work has been widely published and exhbited and has gained international recognition, including being selected to represent the UK at the Beijing Biennale in 2008. In 2009 he was awarded a D&AD Award for Environmental Design.

Alvin is currently a Tenure-track Professor at the USC School of Architecture in Los Angeles. He has also taught design studios at the Architectural Association (London), Tsinghua University (Beijing) and Chelsea College of Art (London). He has been an invited critic and guest lecturer at various institutions in the UK, US, Germany, Spain, Israel, Switzerland and China.

DAVID JASON GERBER

PARAMETRIC

TENDENCIES

AND

DESIGN AGENCIES

The combination of design computing paradigms, the parametric and the generative are discussed through examples of the two becoming more and more coupled and intertwined. The essay presents, through a personal evolution and experimental progression, results that include both top down design decision making with all of the idiosyncrasies of aesthetics, signature and style and the intricacy and complexity brought into the work by bottom up generative recursion and correlation. In other words the essay focuses on how simple correlation can be and is coupled with the more naturally complex. The research and position of the author is in part predicated on the affect of a number of technological trends. These trends are a purposeful way to address the question or declaration of a paradigm, one where the author is reticent to do so for two reasons, one there is a plurality at work and two once declared the paradigm itself is perhaps already obsolete. These trends include exponential increase in access to computing power and therefore to more design relevant forms of agency. Here the notion of agency is a purposeful inclusion of critical practice and the architectural project but also of the more specific use of artificial intelligence techniques in a design setting, that of multi-agent systems. So while Design Agencies have evolved from explicit and then through parametric design it is argued that they are inextricably linked via the cumulative of these trends in design computation. At its most fundamental, parametric design has enabled for architecture a profound ability to design explore the options of a design logic, and

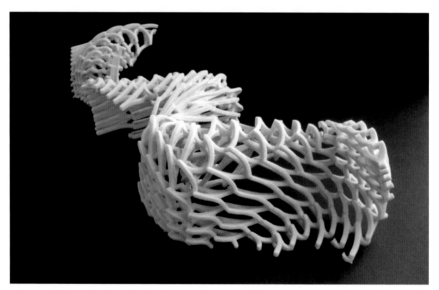

Figure 1: A parametric design and prototyping project illustrating topological continuity with a high degree of geometric variation. The 3D printed model is of non-uniform elements that illustrate the intricate capabilities of parametric design while maintaining constructability. The models were design explored, prototyped and tested in the CATIA environment in on of Dr. Gerber's design research seminars, Dr. David Jason Gerber with Rachel Brown.

389|

secondly to control a projects' performances more accurately including fabrication, costs, and environmental objectives to name a few. Parametric design has enabled both the building to improve but perhaps even more importantly the process of design to become more efficient, more correlated across the myriad of goals and is producing more intricate and articulated work.

Parametric Tendencies inclusive of geometric design, form finding and optimization, now coupled with Design Agencies of multi-agent systems lead to a productive feedback system - a human-machine design dialogue- that yields design results intricate in beauty and delight, fluid in morphology and often more performative across an ever increasing set of design requirements, qualitatively and quantitatively. The ability to bring to our work both design exploration in emergent and pre-defined methods has been brought about through the trends we subsequently describe but as well through the conceptual drive to build the complex, the articulated, the intricate and at the same time performative tectonically, socially, economically and environmentally.

In contemporary design practices parametric design allows for rapid design variation and simple evaluation but when combined with design agency incorporating dynamic behavioral data becomes possible and productive. We have brought to our work a combination of the Cyber Physical Social which can be understood through notions of access to data from the physical world, live feedback and expansive inclusion of human behavior, opinion and preference from the social world, informing our cyber design i.e. digital design and simulations and then our built results again physical. As previously cautioned, in relation to predictions or the declaring of paradigms of the digital future, there are trends that are clear and fundamental to our contemporary design discourse and proliferation of techniques, and products. It is really a set of trends that we credit for the exponential speciation of design technology, tools, techniques, theories and critical projects that are much more productively and exquisitely meeting the challenges of this evolving cyber physical social design setting. These technology trends include; one, with the infinite computing paradigm we can continue to expect the cost of calculation to decrease over time. In other words we will be able to much more robustly design explore ever more complex or complicated design solution spaces. This notion of design exploration is a critical and intrinsic concept as design is an iterative and synthetic process always in need of improvement. Secondly, what this leads to is most succinctly an understanding that the cost of complexity will continue its downward curve, 3D printing and its exponential spread is obvious evidence as well as the ability to model ever more intricate designs through millions of polygons, NURBS, and parametric or algorithmic trees and graphs. What is meant by the use of the term complexity includes, cyber based design modeling and simulation but as well, analogue material or physical tectonics, implying the building of the complicated is becoming ever more facilitated by access to computing. Therefore analyzing and fabricating the bespoke is no longer the grand challenge, rather, infusing the bespoke with meaning, content and synthetic –artificial and human- intelligence is. A third trend is the integration of live data, real time feedback and the inclusion of behavior in our design process, models, and simulations. These behaviors are multi-scalar and multi-disciplinary as they relate to design. Designers can now access the social networks –the crowd and the cloud- and include realistic behaviors of our systems and societies. Designers can now model biomimicry and the science of material systems much more fluidly and seamlessly. These real time data streams, behavioral models and the network effect will continue to have a greater influence upon architecture, urbanism, and design in general. The social aspects of preference and habits, the "likes and dislikes" will become increasingly made valuable and influential, as well the incorporation of human behavior in near real time increasingly more productive, predictive and therefore useful in the design setting. From these technological trends in concert with those who engage in critical design practice where self reflection and the production of design is in and of itself a trend, we predict a path towards an increase in the informing of form for the cyber physical social where parametric tendencies persist and where design agencies of all kinds can be incorporated into design and architecture.

It is via a continual curiosity in my own work and critical practice, at the intersection of design and computation, that there is much research to pursue when it comes to the uniqueness of the nexus of the design problem and the unambiguous of computation. Much of my thinking must credit the work of Alexander (Alexander 1968), Negroponte (1969), Mitchell (1990), Frazer (1995), Burry (2011) Schumacher (2012) Terzidis (2003) to name a select few; Alexander for his delineation of the design problem as a system of generating systems and introduction of object oriented thinking to design problem decomposition; Negroponte for his vision and distinction of the human machine interface and the defining of the computerized versus computational; Mitchell for his clarity in introducing the parametric design process; Burry for his influence and foundational re-engagement into mathematics as tantamount for computational designers; Terzidis for his elevating of the conversation around algorithmic design process; and finally Schumacher who has, though with much criticism and fanfare, been a leading thinker in the field of design and computation. Schumacher I would argue in the context of his espousing of parametricism has equally never lost sight of architectures' most important responsibility, to deliver buildings that delight, communicate and touch their constituents.

In order to develop beyond purely parametric design and the inherent limitations of the logical determinism it requires and to critically incorporate computer science, social science, and engineering beyond the cursory attempt, we must also ensure creativity be carefully left un-bounded and un-constrained in a design setting. In essence it is this fine line, a tight rope of sorts, between scientific methods for maintaining rigor in discovery and that of more open ended design research methods for form finding and design exploration so engrained in the critical project. For design one primary objective

Figure 2: A Design Agency experiment illustrating structural "Nests" form found through the combination of parametric design surfaces, and performance driven multi-agent systems.

391|

is to develop both the unbounded creativity and rigorous mathematical, logical and robust models, insofar as control, craft, and ideation are seen as linked and tantamount for the critical architectural project. Design ingenuity needs to be fostered by both the un-abashed and unconstrained as well as by the technical rigor which now design can more accessibly harness given the technological trends and now abundant parametric and algorithmic design capabilities. As a not so aside, this leads to an important distinction and clarity of the definitions of the parametric versus the algorithmic so often misunderstood and misappropriated in contemporary architectural discourse. In its' most basic the parametric in design terms is a means for modeling with relations and associative geometry, in its truest form deterministic and not easily made into a recursive and therefore emergent design exploration as found in agent based approaches. Design agencies or more specifically multi-agent systems are of interest for their ability to be generative, providing results that are cognitively impossible to foresee or predict yet still providing design solutions within a predefined behavior setting, rule base and complexly coupled set of objectives. In both cases however one critical aspect remains for designers, both require skill, expertise, and ingenuity in the structuring of design problems and the ordering of relationships whether linearly or recursively. In the context of hybridizing the parametric with the generative agent based approaches, there are thankfully affordances in design technology such as; user centric graphical programming environments; shareable extensible, programming languages and libraries; the infinite computing paradigm providing design with rapid visualization and evaluation; all of which placates the now and immediacy expected of the current generation of designers.

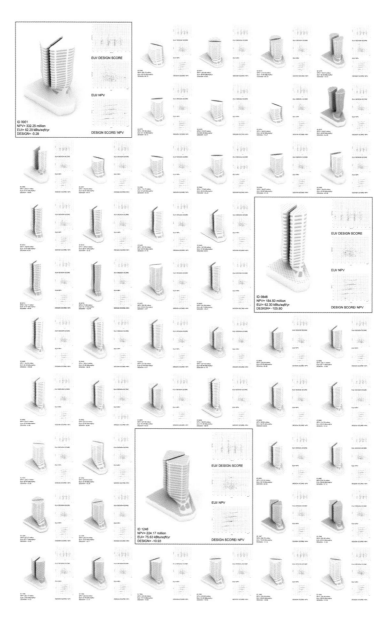

Figure 3: This "Design Optioneering" illustration presents a subset of the solution space generated through the combination of a complexly curved parametric model, the factoring of parameters into design genes, then the use of a Genetic Algorithm to pareto optimize multiple design objectives. This sub-set presents a novel design interface where geometry, empiricism and automation are presented to the designer, enabling improved design decision making through informed form and feedback.

Parametric Arborescence

Presented by a colleague is the neologism of "arborescence" used to describe the structuring of parametric design and project organizational trees. It has remained of personal interest in that "arborescence" does suggest the necessity for logic and abstraction in developing parametric designs. In ruminating on the etymology it convey a sense for implicitly intelligent structure and order yet one that can deliver highly differentiated and heterogeneous outcomes, that of aesthetic quality of intricacy and tectonics. While again there is an acknowledgement of the difference between the parametric and the generative, what is important in both classes of design computing as it relates to arborescence is a rigor in the establishment of genotypical structures, orders, and systems that in both classes generate design solution spaces of phenotypical variety and intricacy. In declaring this axiom of arborescence a re-emphasis needs to be made about the distinction of computerization and computation. Computerization can most readily be understood through thinking about tasks that are automated, explicitly defined and then counted by a computer. In opposition to or more productively on top of computerized automation is the classification of computation, where as Negroponte suggests a man machine interface is where a design dialogue is fostered. Akin to biological models whether at the molecular or systems levels, computational design is understood best through the use of algorithmic processes. Even before we discuss the recursive and heuristics we would be smart to again define design exploration, an acknowledgement that the design problem is not often reducible to a single equation and solution but one that requires a recursive search and reflection; a feedback loop of tool, model and designer. Design is in itself a problem solving class, generally understood in design studies and ontology circles as a problem with which there are more often than not, not a simple well-defined solution, or one "optimal" solution but rather a solution space and even more complexly a problem definition space. What this suggests is that there is a need for exploring the options, a need for iteration informed by parametric and design agencies. Now iteration can occur at multiple levels of details, scales, and in multiple parallel feedback loops. So fundamentally, design exploration is a generative process and now one that is greatly enhanced by advances and access of computation of both the parametric and design agency.

While there is consternation over the use of the term parametric or now parametricism, having worked on and written some of the earliest projcts and research on the topic (Gerber 2007), I choose to support the use of the term both in its' broadest sense but also in its' true definition (Gerber 2009). In the pure definition it is correct to understand associative parametric modeling as a tool kit that requires a deterministic a priori definition of relationships -driving and driven- as stated previously. In its most broad it is purported as a means to theorize the importance of difference, correlation and communication of contemporary architecture. Both have their place and value. Here we are intentionally more inclusive of both classifications for modeling design and for

Figure 4: The image is of a selection of the 3D printed and empirically scored design solution as shown at the TED 2012: full Spectrum Conference and traveling exhibition. The research and exhibit of the work speaks to a future for design decision making hybridized with physical, virtual and quantified design media.

exploring and for how arborescence is understood as the design expertise that ties these two lineages of parametric design and design agency together.

Evolutionary Biases

Inherent in the development of digital models, simulations and of real world data centric design workflows is the problem that much of what is on the screen or in the computer remains in the computer; our current version of the label "paper architect." Fortuitously these boundary conditions along with others between the material computation and social computation are being broken down through a hybrid approach where parametric models and multi-agent systems and digital manufacturing are being conflated and synchronized to the real world. As a means to illustrate the conflation of the parametric with design agencies a series of projects are shown all of which are works that incorporate parametric tendencies with design agencies. Upon reflection of the evolution of my critical project as well as in relation to the essays curated into the this book, there is clearly a personal bias towards the biological and evolutionary. On one hand there is the literal aspects of the work that include the biological –our use of evolutionary models and the genetic algorithms for example- and on the other there is a lens through which I see my critical project and many others through taxonomies, and as genotypes, phenotypes, and finally as highly complex and interactive ordered and self ordering systems.

An on going research has been on developing the integration of parametric models and evolutionary algorithms to experiment and validate exhaustive solution spaces enabled by

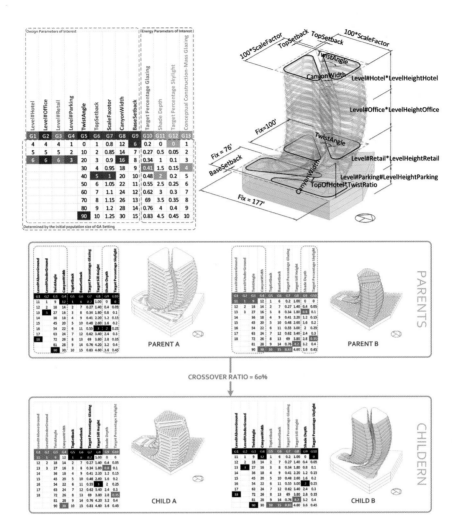

Figure 5: The image illustrates a detailed view and then set of steps taken for form finding the optimal design solutions through a multidisciplinary design optimization technology developed by Dr. Gerber called the H.D.S. Beagle. The work conveys for each design phenotype the parameter coupling, factoring to design genes, GA and the simultaneous quantifications from which a designer continues to design explore in a combined parametric and agent based algorithmic approach.

cloud computing for multi-disciplinary design optimization problems. To be clear, the use of the term optimization is easy to misconstrue or even reject in a design context. So here it is understood as a means to breed performance of all kinds, into designs which evolve higher objective scores in competition with other objective scores providing designers with both a geometric visualization and an analytical and quantified ranking across

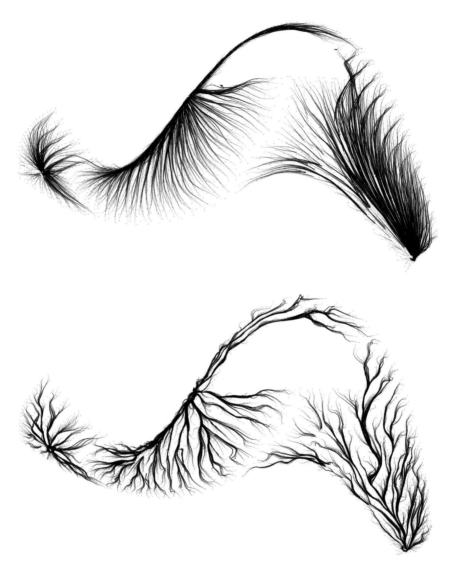

Figure 6: A Design Agency experiment illustrating the combination of parametric modeling, form finding techniques and the recursive re-informing of the surface topology through a multi agent based scripting technique. The results yield surface patterning and classification and represent a synthesis of both parametric and generative design approaches. The top is exclusive of stygmergy where as the bottom pattern emerges out of a global and local negotiation of the agents reacting to surface energies and local attractions for improving tectonic efficiencies.

Figure 7: A Design Agency experimental project driven by an interest in a highly intricate structural "weave" form found through the combination of parametric design surfaces, and performance driven multi-agent systems

these multiple domains; often using a pareto front. The work necessitates both the use of the parametric model as well as the use of generative programming techniques and in particular the genetic algorithm. My system "The Beagle", named after Darwin's ship, provides designers with rapid parametric variation and simultaneous analysis of complex parameter design problems with varying degrees of coupling and geometric complexity. The inherent complexity produced is beyond human cognition and requires and provides further argument for the increase in use of cloud computing for design integration. It must also be admitted, while I can generate a near infinite set of designs, this is not a solution for the designer as it is intractable in terms of evaluation and choice. Therefore the Beagle finds a set of better or improved –"optimized"- designs for designers to explore through computer designer interaction and automated iteration. The work speaks to the trends quite literally in that it harnesses infinite computing, it includes real world complexity and correlation, and promotes the behavior of complex social dynamics into the design. Requisite is the expertise of a designer to construct rigorous models of both the parametric and generative structure of the design space, and in some sense both an understanding of the evolutionary and generative lexicon as well as that of parametric tree structures, again arborescence.

Exploiting Agencies

The inclusion of multi-agent systems into the iterative loop of design is another one of our team's research thrusts, and one that is still arguably experimental. The knowledge we had hoped to impart is that of the design agencies potential for creating intricacy, performance and design quality that cannot be wholly foreseen, nor top down drawn and design explored. We do not claim to be original in this by any means, though some of the work in process is quite unique in the research and development and application of computer science, social science, and technological hybridization when applied to architectural design. It is only through the application of a generative multi-agent system that we can visualize and formalize geometrically the complex interaction of multiple behavior systems and design objectives. The experiments begin the associative parametric modeling of design scenarios to enable a solution space and deign exploration approach. The work integrates the use of form finding through dynamics engines to design explore the affects of physical and system behaviors. A next step is the introduction of probabilistically informed multi-agent systems to generate a reactive feedback and set of visualizations and then digitally manufactured prototypes of performance directed patterning and architectural forms. This is achieved through the use of multiple mathematical approaches from AI research and multiple scripts to explore the recursive and reciprocal affects of multi-agent systems across the surface where feedback and recursion foster more intelligently intricate, self-ordered and rigorous architectural results. What the research demonstrates is the productive coupling of parametric modeling with generative modeling and simulation. In geometric and project terms, as more than just graphics, the work begins to measurably prove the benefits of both the top down and bottom up approaches to design in combination. While the projects have a signature driven starting point, an overall massing and or patterning of modules into shells for example, they are in fact being re-informed by form finding techniques as well as swarm like and other self organizing behaviors intrinsic to the surface geometries, performance objectives and material tectonics.

Parametric Tendencies and Design Agencies

As instigation for the future, what is becoming rapidly accessible is the productive hybridization of both parametric and emergent or generative design agency techniques. The productivity is argued for in terms of supporting both a top down decision making which incorporates the importance of design aesthetics and style and starting order – one kind of arborescence- along with the intricacy and complexity brought into the work by generative recursion and correlation -a second kind of arborescence- that of design agency. In other words simple correlation can be coupled with the behaviorally complex further harnessing the technological trends that make accessible real world complexity. To reiterate, design is becoming more able and gaining more access to computing power and to more intelligent forms of agency; to model, design, simulate, design explore ideas and solutions which are in part driven and in part self organized as a systems of systems generating systems. It is the concept of arborescence, again an intentional neologism that highlights the importance of design structure, order, adaptability and self organized intelligence literally found in the natural system of the tree but more broadly and analogously necessary to control the possibilities of the combined parametric and generative multi-agent systems. In other words geometric design, form finding and optimization, coupled with multi-agent systems lead to a productive feedback system - a

The rendering above is of the One North Masterplan by Zaha Hadid Architects in 2002. It was the first parametric urbanism project and shows the capability for fluid urban morphology and continuos differentiation within the filed. The image below illustrates a combined parametric and generative urbanism where the mixed method leads to a bottom up and top down form finding of a regenerative urban fertility. The image is courtesy of Zaha Hadid Architects and David Gerber with Rodrigo Shiordia (2014).

human-machine explorative design dialogue- that most importantly yields design results intricate in beauty and delight, and fluid in morphology more appropriate for the dynamics of our cyber physical social contemporary design paradigm. It is in the context of the critical project of architecture, where the acts of modeling, making and finding meaning is an important recursion where we can really see Parametric Tendencies and Design Agencies' influence on the architecture of the present and future; a present and future, where behavior – design, social, material, digitally simply and complexly coupled- are correlated and articulated.

FOOTNOTES
- Christopher Alexander, Architectural Design, Systems Generating Systems, Architectural Design, December issue no 7/6 John Wiley & Sons Ltd (London) 1968 pp 90-1
- Nicholas Negroponte, "Towards a Humanism through Machines', Architectural Design, September issue no 7/6 John Wiley & Sons Ltd (London) 1969 pp 511-12
- William J Mitchell, "The Logic of Architecture" MIT Press, Cambridge mass 1990.
- Mark Burry, Architecture and Practical Design Computation, John Wiley and Sons Ltd 2011
- Patrik Schumacher, Parametricism: A New Global Style for Architecture and Urban Design, Org. English first published in : AD Architectural Design - Digital Cities, Vol 79, No 4, July/August 2009
- Frazer, Frazer J.H., An Evolutionary Architecture, Architectural Association, London, 1995
- Kostas Terzidis, Algorithmic Form, Expressive Form, Spon Press - taylor and francis Group 2003, pp 65-73 Taylor & Francis, 2006
- David Gerber, "The Parametric Affect: Computation, Innovation and Models for Design Exploration in Contemporary Architectural Practice",. Design and Technology Report Series, No 2008-2, Harvard Design School, Cambridge MA (100+pages). ISBN 978-1-934510-02-5., (2009)
- David Gerber, "Parametric Practices: Models for Design Exploration in Architecture" D.Des. diss., Harvard University (2007).
- David Gerber, Lin, S., Senel Solmaz, A., "Designing-In Performance in Early Stage Design through Parameterization, Automation, and Evolutionary Algorithms." In CAADRIA 2012 Proceedings. Chennai, India, April 25-28, 2012.

IMAGES CREDITS

DAVID JASON GERBER

DR. DAVID JASON GERBER is an Assistant Professor of Architecture at the University of Southern California and was awarded a courtesy joint appointment as Professor of Civil and Environmental Engineering in the Sonny Astani Department of Civil and Environmental Engineering in the Viterbi School of Engineering at USC. He has held executive and board positions for design technology start-up and mature companies. From 2008 to 2010 Dr. Gerber was a Vice President at Gehry Technologies Inc., a global innovator in Building Information Modeling and building industry technology consulting. Dr. Gerber has worked as an architect in the US, Europe and Asia, for the Steinberg Group, Moshe Safdie, Gehry Technologies, and as a project architect for Zaha Hadid Architects. While working for Zaha Hadid Architects, Dr. Gerber worked on a number of the built projects including the contemporary art museum in Cincinnati, and a number of un-built projects. He then was project architect and project manager for the One North masterplan in Singapore.

Dr. Gerber has been awarded research fellowships at MIT's Media Lab, as well as numerous teaching and research fellowships at Harvard University Graduate School of Design and as a Harvard University Frederick Sheldon Fellow. He was full time faculty at the Southern California Institute of Architecture (SCI Arc) from 2006-2009, a technical tutor at the Architectural Association's Design Research Laboratory in London, and held lecturer positions at UCLA's AUD, Stanford University, Innsbruck University, the EPFL Switzerland, Tec de Monterrey Mexico, and Tsinghua University China.

At USC he instructs students in design research seminars and design studios emphasizing design computation as a means of design exploration and realization. Included in Dr. Gerber's teaching roles is the chairing and advising of numerous PhD students in architecture and engineering. Dr. Gerber leads a multidisciplinary research lab team focused on innovating at the intersection of design with computation and technology. His work has been exhibited as part of TED 2012 Global Gallery and is funded by the National Science Foundation and numerous Industry partners. Publications of his design work and research have been included in "Young Blood," AD (2001); "Corporate Fields," AA Publications (2005); and in Interactive Cities, Hyx Publications (2006). Portions of his PhD work was published by Harvard University Graduate School of Design The Parametric Affect: Computation, Innovation and Models for Design Exploration in Contemporary Architectural Practice (2009). He has published over 30 widely cited research appears in conference proceedings and journals including Design Studies, Automation in Construction, International Journal of Architecture and Computing, Simulation, Computing in Civil Engineering, Energy and Buildings, and IT in Construction. Dr. Gerber is a guest editor for the Journals of Simulation and the International Journal of Architecture and Computing.

David Gerber received his undergraduate architectural education at the University of California Berkeley (Bachelor of Arts in Architecture, 1996). He completed his first professional degree at the Design Research Laboratory of the Architectural Association in London (Master of Architecture, 2000), his post professional research degree (Master of Design Studies, 2003) and his PhD (Doctor of Design, June 2007) at the Harvard University Graduate School of Design.